DATE DUE

MAY 0 4 '98			
MAY 2 6 '0			
'00			

Congressional
Women

CONGRESSIONAL WOMEN

Their Recruitment, Integration, and Behavior

Second Edition, Revised and Updated

Irwin N. Gertzog

Westport, Connecticut
London

12

Library of Congress Cataloging-in-Publication Data

Gertzog, Irwin N.
    Congressional women : their recruitment, integration, and
behavior/ Irwin N. Gertzog.—2nd ed.
        p. cm.
    Includes bibliographic references and index.
    ISBN 0–275–94740–8 (alk. paper).—ISBN 0–275–94741–6 (pbk.).
    1. Women legislators—United States—History—20th century.
    2. United States. Congress. House—History—20th century.
    I. Title.
    JK1319.G47 1995
    328.73′073′082—dc20   94–42817

British Library Cataloguing in Publication Data is available.

Library of Congress Catalog Card Number: 94–42817
ISBN: 0–275–94740–8
        0–275–94741–6 (pbk.)

First published in 1995

Praeger Publishers, 88 Post Road West, Westport, CT 06881
An imprint of Greenwood Publishing Group, Inc.

Printed in the United States of America

(∞)™

The paper used in this book complies with the
Permanent Paper Standard issued by the National
Information Standards Organization (Z39.48–1984).

10 9 8 7 6 5 4 3 2 1

Contents

Tables

Preface

A casual statement uttered in 1976 by a now-forgotten source who claimed the women elected to Congress in the 1970s were very different from those who preceded them provided the initial spark that led to this study. Contemporary congresswomen, according to this observer, brought more political experience with them to Washington than did earlier female Representatives. They also possessed a richer range of professional skills in such specialties as law, communications, and management—vocations whose routines readily lend themselves to lawmaking and representational pursuits. One consequence of this change, said the analyst, is that women serving today are more effective legislators than those elected to Congress from 1917 through, roughly, the 1950s.

These observations seemed reasonable enough, but they were unaccompanied by empirical evidence. Although a specialist in Congress, I was unaware of changing background characteristics of the few women who had been elected to Congress, and I could not call to mind significant changes that had come about either in the workings of Congress or in the nature of public policy which could be attributed to the arrival in Washington of a new type of female lawmaker. Consequently, I decided to test the soundness of some of these generalizations.

I gathered information about the families, vocations, and political experiences of all women who had served in the House of Representatives from 1917—when the first woman took her seat in Congress—through the mid-1970s, and placed each into one of three time periods, 1917 to 1940, 1941 to 1964, and 1965 to 1976, depending upon the year she was first elected to the House. I then compared the combined background characteristics of the women falling within each of the three time periods. Figures were compiled determining, among other things, the proportion of women in each category who might have relied on family connections to secure election to the

House, who could have exploited substantial wealth for the same purpose, and who, before coming to Congress, had secured a law degree or successfully contested a race for another public office. Inferences drawn from the comparison did, indeed, suggest women with experiences different from their predecessors were being elected to the House, and the fruits of the project were eventually published in "Changing Patterns of Female Recruitment to the U.S. House of Representatives," *Legislative Studies Quarterly*, vol. IV, August 1979.

Information collected for this study confirmed what was widely known—many of the women elected to the House succeeded husbands who had died in office. But it also persuaded me to reject the popular view that widows of House members are *regularly* nominated to succeed spouses who die in office. In fact, relatively few congressional widows followed their husbands into the House. Moreover, the factors contributing to their selection were not the same for all. Widows chosen from Southern districts tended to be tapped for different reasons than those nominated from districts outside the South, although there were several exceptions within each region. These findings were published in "The Matrimonial Connection: The Nomination of Congressmen's Widows for the House of Representatives," *The Journal of Politics*, vol. 42, August, 1980.

But even while the study of widows was in its earliest stages, my interest in congresswomen became an absorbing one—primarily because they were becoming far more active and visible than they had ever been. In 1977, female lawmakers formed the Congresswomen's Caucus and national media began to give these women more attention. As a result, I expanded the scope of the inquiry so that I might compare not only recruitment patterns, but the behavior of contemporary congresswomen with that of their predecessors. I soon realized, however, that changes in behavioral regularities could not be fully understood unless I also explored shifts in the ways male and female House members interacted with one another and in the extent to which the former were prepared to accept the latter into what everyone believed was a male preserve. By the end of 1977, an undertaking once limited to the recruitment of congresswomen had been expanded into a more comprehensive examination of their entire congressional experience over time.

I went to Washington in December 1977 and spent three months in the Library of Congress trying to squeeze out evidence about the congressional activities and treatment of women who had served in the House before World War II. An additional three months on Capitol Hill were devoted to asking male and female Representatives serving in the 95th Congress about the experiences of contemporary congresswomen. Thirteen of the eighteen congresswomen and eleven of the twenty-five congressmen to whom I had written agreed to meet with me and, with few exceptions, the interviews were unusually rewarding. (The semistructured questionnaire appears in

Appendix C.) In addition, thirty-six legislative, administrative, and press aides of House members, most of whom worked for congresswomen, were queried about the experiences and behavior of female Representatives. Many were asked to elaborate on observations other informants had offered. Responses from all of these interviews were relied upon while writing Chapters 4, 5, and 6, and some informed the analysis in other chapters as well.

During subsequent visits to Washington in 1979 and 1981, thirty additional interviews were conducted, four with Representatives, the remainder with staff assistants. Questions raised followed no set pattern, inasmuch as respondents were chosen because of specific information they could provide. Many of the questions dealt with the workings and future of the Congresswomen's Caucus, a group later transformed into the Congressional Caucus for Women's Issues, and these responses provide much of the basis for Chapters 10 and 11.

Congressional Women: Their Recruitment, Treatment and Behavior was published in 1984, and at the time, I believed I had said as much as I was likely to say about congresswomen. The election of 1992 changed all of that. The dramatic increase in the number of new women elected that year, the circumstances leading to their success, and the promise of a significant change in the identity of the U.S. House of Representatives because of their presence in it were good reasons to impose a contemporary perspective on *Congressional Women.*

In May 1993 I began six weeks of interviews with members of the 103rd Congress. Seventeen of the twenty-four first-term women, sixteen of the twenty-three women holdovers, and twelve congressmen were kind enough to meet with me. Questions posed to them were drawn from the questionnaire in Appendix C. I also talked with twelve staff personnel, most of whom were working for congresswomen. Information and ideas from these conversations were supplemented by the customary documentary sources, cited throughout, to bring the earlier volume up-to-date. While the word *Treatment* in the earlier version's subtitle seemed appropriate at the time, it was changed to *Integration* for the present volume. Interview responses indicated that a good deal of change had taken place in the ways that congresswomen and congressmen interact and that, while women are by no means fully integrated into the House, they have come a long way in that connection. Moreover, the term *Treatment* appears to place congresswomen in the position of passively accepting whatever fate male House members are prepared to impose on them. This may have been largely true at one time (see Chapter 4), but it has certainly not been the case in recent years. For these reasons, the subtitle now reads *Their Recruitment, Integration, and Behavior.*

I am deeply grateful to the more than seventy Representatives and the scores of staff aides who patiently answered my questions and who were willing to speak candidly about the matters I raised with them. Their frank replies were encouraged by my promise to keep their identities confidential when referring to the observations and insights they volunteered. My debt to them is difficult to overstate, however. Among those who gave generously of their time and observations during the summer of 1993 are: Ross Brown, Chris Burnham, Angela Campbell, Azar Kattan, Eddie Patterson, Lesley Primmer, Howard Wolfson, and Elizabeth Linaberger.

But these Representatives and staff personnel were not the only ones assisting me on this project, and I welcome this opportunity publicly to offer my thanks to all others who helped. Several congressmen permitted me to use their offices as places to hang my hat and catch my breath during visits to Capitol Hill, and their hospitality is deeply appreciated. In 1978, 1979, and 1981, Congressman Stephen Solarz, his staff, and his wife, Nina, were gracious hosts, as were Congressmen Marc Lincoln Marks and Tom Ridge. My debt to Congressman Lionel Van Deerlin and his wife, Mary Jo, is enormous. Our professional association and friendship began in 1963 and, until he left the House in 1981, no trip to Washington was complete without a visit to his office. I am grateful, as well, to Mr. Van Deerlin's staff for their interest, support, and friendship over the years. Especially helpful were Alan Ciamporcero, Shirley Dave, Cindy Holson, Mona Knight, John McLaren, Sieg Smith, Carole Staszewski, and Dan Yager.

In 1993, Congressman Ridge once again allowed me to work out of his office and without the help of his aides, I would have been unable to interview as many sources as I did. My thanks go to Mark Campbell, Lauren Cotter, Leslie Fitting, Joel Frushone, David Hixon, Marla Skinner, Stephen Suroviec, Mary Whalen, David Williams, Rob Zimmer, Charles Zogby, Jason Zoto, and especially to Tim O'Brien. While living in Washington in 1978, I was fortunate to be able to count on the hospitality and companionship of many friends, including Anne and Larry Pearl, and David and the late Renee Unger. Portions of the manuscript were written in the solitude and quiet of summer retreats, and for the use of their homes I thank Beverly and Charles Edwards, and Barbara and Mark Kronman.

Manuscript chapters were read, analyzed, and discussed by colleagues whose judgments were unusually valuable. I profited especially from the information and criticism provided by Stanley Bach, Frances Butler, Jean Dexheimer, Pat Gilmartin-Zena, Jackie Litt, Burdette Loomis, Susan Roe, Lauren Sloan, and Joan Hulse Thompson. Comments by Rita Mae Kelly and Ruth Mandel were extremely helpful, and, like many others who study women in politics, I found the information provided by the Center for the American Woman and Politics indispensable. Efforts to find details about the lives of congresswomen were facilitated by librarians in Washington and Meadville, and my special thanks for this assistance go to Marjorie Hopkins and Laurie Tynan of the Meadville Public Library, and to Reference Librarians Cynthia Burton, Don Vrabel, Jane Westenfeld, and Dorothy

Jeanne Smith of the Pelletier Library at Allegheny College. Miss Smith was painstaking in preparing the index for this volume, as well as for the 1984 edition. The skills and good judgment exercised by Carolyn Dougan, Lou Hanners, Gail Kralj, and Mary Lee McQuiston while typing drafts of the 1984 manuscript are deeply appreciated. Aggie Sakanich exhibited the same care and skill when preparing the revised manuscript.

Gathering the data for this work was a long and tedious process, and I am grateful to the many Allegheny College students whose research papers and Capitol Hill internships were so fruitful. They include Dan Auriti, Susan Devor, Kathy Dorr, Kathy Eck, Tracy Erway, Joanne Forbes, Lisa Freeman, Amy Goldsmith, Karen Harvey, Cindy LeVine, Kelly McBride, Clair Miller, Carol Morrissey, Barbara Patterson, Lisa Pepicelli, Matthew Peterson, Janet Pfieffer, Jennifer Rastro, Barbara Ross, Cynthia Saydah, Susan Scott, Nancy Seamans, Michele Simard, Michael Slotsky, June Swanson, Susan Swigart, Donna Tatro, Kevin Wegryn, and Sally Wissel. The present volume could not have been completed as quickly as it was without the research assistance of Kristin Kapsiak, Valerie Knowles, Laura McGarry, and Jennifer McPeak. Nakul Lele was meticulous in preparing camera-ready copies of the Tables.

My gratitude extends to the Allegheny administration and my colleagues in the Political Science Department, as well. The moral and financial support provided by the college underscored its belief that an excellent teaching institution can retain its quality only if it encourages scholarship. The liberal reprinting policies of *The Legislative Studies Quarterly* and *The Journal of Politics*, permitting its authors to republish material originally appearing between their covers, is also appreciated.

My greatest debt is to my wife, Alice, who encouraged me to undertake this project and who commented constructively upon the manuscript as it was being written. To her this book is affectionately dedicated.

Part I

Introduction

1

Exploring a Small Universe

The 1992 congressional election was a milestone for women aspiring to national office. Twenty-three incumbent congresswomen running for re-election and twenty-four women seeking a House seat for the first time were successful. Together they constituted by far the largest aggregation of women ever to serve together in the U.S. House of Representatives, and they brought to 142 the total number ever elected to that body.[1]

This outcome was historic, but it did not go far enough for many who believe too few women hold public office. Since 1789, almost 10,000 men have served in the House. The first woman, Jeannette Rankin, was elected in 1916. It took sixty-six years for as many as one hundred women to be elected, and twelve more before they became as much as 10 percent of the House membership.[2] These small increments over the years once prompted then Michigan Congresswoman Martha Griffiths to ask the Legislative Reference Service (now the Congressional Research Service) to calculate how long it would be before women became a House majority if they maintained the pace kept since Jeannette Rankin was elected. An analyst responded, presumably with a straight face, that it would require 432 years (Lamson 1968, p. 87). It is no wonder then, that scholars' interest in congresswomen has, until recently, been sparse.[3]

During the 1980s, the number of women running for the House grew substantially, and by the early 1990s these higher numbers produced more optimistic forecasts from Congress watchers. A larger number of women were contesting open House seats (Burrell 1992, p. 502), and many believed it would not be long before the rate of increase among women in the House would begin to approximate growth in the proportion of women in state legislatures—a rise of about one percentage point every two years.[4]

The 1992 election provided some justification for these expectations. Studies published after the election offered useful insights into why a breakthrough occurred when it did. These analyses conclude that the political success of women at the state and local levels during the 1970s and 1980s produced a sizable pool of highly qualified potential candidates for the House; that these women were well positioned all over the country to seek nominations for open seats—ninety-one of which were created in 1992 because of redistricting, retirements linked to scandal, and retirements motivated by campaign finance law (Wilcox 1994, p. 3); that many (especially Democrats) were able to secure nominations in districts where their party enjoyed a registration advantage (Chaney and Sinclair 1994, p. 136); that these women received encouragement and a fair share of funds from party committees (Biersack and Herrnson 1994, p. 172); that they were beneficiaries of extraordinary financial contributions from women's Political Action Committees, assistance especially useful in securing party nominations (Nelson 1994, p. 182); and that they were running in a year when women were seen as better able than men to govern (Chaney and Sinclair 1994, p. 127).

Central to these developments is the emergence in the United States of women who are *strategic politicians*—experienced, highly motivated, career public servants who carefully calculate the personal and political benefits of running for higher office, assess the probability of their winning, and determine the personal and political costs of defeat before deciding to risk the positions they hold to secure a more valued office. They are politicians who have the "incentive and opportunity to cultivate other politically active and influential people and to put them under some obligation" (Jacobson 1992, p. 47). Chaney and Sinclair explain their behavior in the 1991–92 election cycle in this way:

Acting as we would expect strategic politicians to behave, a large number of these well-prepared women ran for their party's nomination in a year that promised an unusually high probability of success. Democratic women in particular ran in districts favorable to their party. . . . To a large extent they won because they were good [experienced] candidates who took advantage of their opportunities—in a favorable year and a favorable district. (1994, p. 136)

Responses to questions posed during interviews with seventeen of the twenty-four first term women elected in 1992 support this observation.[5] Almost all explained their decisions in terms of boundaries produced by their state's redistricting process, the political appeal of the competitors they were likely to face in primary and general election, relative to their own strengths, and/or their chances of raising sufficient funds to run an effective campaign. Most noted general policy goals they hoped to realize as well, and the word "change" came up often. On the other hand, fallout from such events as the Supreme Court's 1989 Webster decision on abortion, the "Tailhook" convention, the Clarence Thomas confirmation hearings at which Anita Hill testified, and the House Bank and Post Office scandals were mentioned by only three first-term congresswomen as factors influencing their decisions to run. Two of the three had never held public office.

Women strategic politicians have been around since the end of World War II, and their numbers have grown steadily, especially after the women's movement got underway. Their ubiquity by the late 1980s and early 1990s made the term "Year of the Woman," invoked on at least three earlier occasions, shopworn and stale when applied to 1992. True, as an election year "tag," it called attention to women's intensified political activities. It also built excitement among observers and activists, and helped the media frame and simplify a complex story. But, notwithstanding the appeal of catchy phrases, the so-called "Year of the Woman" was only one important act in a far grander scenario of political change. Moreover, its attachment to a single year minimized unjustifiably the successful political efforts women had been making routinely over time.

Repetitive use of the term by media reporters and commentators was also potentially damaging to the women's movement, inasmuch as it invited the kind of attention that wanes immediately after one election season when, by implication, politics-as-usual returns. Naming a special year for women in politics was a quintessentially American coinage—encapsulating and packaging a process of significant social and political change into one year's product. The entrepreneur's 1992 commodity was "political woman." If she did not sell, or sold in limited quantities, no investment would be made to promote her again. Thus, the phrase implied "political woman as fad," good for one year's sales, then discounted and discarded.[6]

The full account of women in congressional politics is an engrossing and profound story about democracy in transition and women's empowerment. The 1992 election results represent an important chapter in that story, but they are only a part of an ongoing saga whose full significance can be understood by studying the events leading up to it and those that followed, matters addressed later in this book. A series of encounters and decisions occurring after the election illustrates the far-reaching social and political shifts described and analyzed in the chapters below. These developments taken collectively signal the changing identity of the House of Representatives.[7]

Item: When the spouses of new House members convened for a two-day orientation session on Capitol Hill, a dozen husbands of first-term congresswomen attended. During the afternoon of the first day, the men met alone with the husbands of veteran Congresswomen Nita Lowey and Connie Morella—who acknowledged, only partly in jest, that Dennis Thatcher, husband of former British Prime Minister Margaret Thatcher, was their role model. This was the first orientation session ever conducted for husbands of House members, and they were briefed on the responsibilities and problems they would encounter as spouses of congresswomen. They were advised never to forget that their wives, not they, were the lawmakers; that their spouses' "schedulers" should be consulted before they make social and other engagements at which the congresswoman is expected to be present; that good relationships with their wives' office staff was essential; and that constituents approaching them to express or solicit points of view should be referred to their wives. One discussion leader noted, "Because, as men, you will be perceived by many as the dominant member of the family, people will approach you to support legislation or vote in a certain way. It is tempting to assume you know what your wife will do. But don't try. You haven't been elected to anything." When one spouse stated he planned to serve as his wife's Administrative Assistant, he was told it would be a mistake for any congressional spouse to be so integrally involved in his wife's career.

Item: Early in January, just after new members were sworn in, a first-term California congresswoman and her husband hosted a brunch for all new California members—six other women, thirteen men—and their spouses. Although not all attended, most did. They were greeted at the door by a host who had never met most of his guests and he had to be told by each couple as they arrived which of the two was the House member.

Item: After Hillary Clinton met with women Senators on Capitol Hill to discuss health issues, the *Washington Post* story reporting the event appeared in its "Lifestyle" section. First-termer Karen Shepherd of Utah wrote a letter to the newspaper admonishing it for ignoring the substance of the women's discussion "in favor of gossip overheard in the hall and a description of Clinton's clothing." Her letter concluded: "Come on. This is 1993, not 1950."

Item: For the first time ever, Republican leaders tapped a woman, Washington state's Jennifer Dunn, to represent her class of first-termers on the party's Committee on Committees. For the first time ever, Democratic newcomers named a woman, North Carolina's Eva Clayton, president of their class. And Florida's Tillie Fowler and Shepherd were named co-chairs of their respective party's newly created Freshmen Reform Task Forces. When a white, first-year congressman said, "Cheez, what do you have to do to get anywhere in this [Democratic] Caucus, be a woman or a minority?" he was told, "For 200 years that was *not* the way to do it."

Item: When one day a senior congressman looked in vain for a place to sit in the members' cloak room, he surveyed a scene filled with brightly clad women colleagues and with annoyance declared in a stage whisper "the women have taken over this place."

Item: House leaders ordered swinging doors to be placed at the entrance to a men's restroom situated just off the House floor. For years this facility had been used by congressmen to answer calls of nature, usually while the

House was in session. "All of this with a wide open door that allowed anyone walking down the hall to catch a glimpse of Members using the bathroom" (*Roll Call*, Jan. 11, 1993). The presence of twenty-eight women in the 102nd Congress was apparently insufficient reason to install doors. Forty-seven in the 103rd must have constituted enough of a critical mass to force congressmen to recognize they share the House with women.

Item: A first-year Representative described in an interview how she established rapport with other new congresswomen:

Soon after we met we discovered that we used the same pollster, even though we were from opposite ends of the continent. We began to compare our experience with him—does he return your phone calls promptly, is his advice sound, would you go to him again, would you recommend him to others and we realized we were talking about our pollster the way we used to talk about our gynecologist.

This last episode, like most of the others, almost certainly *would not* have taken place in the 1960s, or even later. But it almost certainly *could not* have occurred in 1993 if the groundwork had not been prepared by women activists and strategic politicians who promoted feminist causes in the years preceding the so-called "Year of the Woman."

GOALS OF THE BOOK

The goals of this book are to examine selected factors contributing to the recruitment of congresswomen, to describe the rate at which these women have been integrated into the House, and to trace the patterns of behavior that, over time, have marked their House performance. Furthermore, the linkages among these elements—recruitment, integration, and behavior—and their implications will be explored. Few studies of such linkages are extant.[8] This is true not only in the case of women lawmakers, but with respect to women and men legislators generally. As one analyst remarked, "If students of legislative recruitment and legislative careers are to progress beyond providing 'interesting' descriptive material, they must do a better job of demonstrating how recruitment matters." They must look at the connections between legislative recruitment and careers, on the one hand, and legislative behavior, on the other. They have the additional obligation of examining how these connections affect the legislature's ability to "build or reinforce governmental legitimacy" (Matthews 1985, p. 18).

The pages that follow attempt to heed Matthews' admonition. They begin by discussing change in the backgrounds and experiences successive congresswomen brought with them to Washington. When these backgrounds are analyzed, we find that the structure of political opportunity has expanded for women and that they have begun to emerge from more politically relevant callings than they once did. Apparently, contemporary politicians, opinion leaders, and voters have been giving less weight than their predecessors to such characteristics as family connections and wealth when choosing congresswomen and more to achievements bespeaking familiarity with tasks House members are expected to perform. Moreover, the domestic responsibilities women normally undertake as wives, mothers, housekeepers, and helpmeets are not the deterrents to service in Congress they once were. The importance of these findings is difficult to overestimate. They mean that a socioeconomic component of our population once systematically denied access to national office has increasingly gained seats in the House and that the political recruitment process in the United States has become more penetrable.

When we elect to Congress citizens who are part of groups whose entry into that body was once improbable, we increase the likelihood that perspectives and beliefs shared by many group members will be reflected in government decisions. That is, a recruitment process which links the society and the polity more intimately is apt to produce political institutions more sensitive to changing public values and goals and, in the long run, to fashion a more orderly, stable political system. But these ends cannot be realized unless the beneficiaries of a more democratic recruitment process are accepted as equals by other public officials and unless they are able to create and capitalize on occasions for shaping public policy. For these reasons, this study looks into how congresswomen have interacted with congressmen, and the opportunities these women have had to gain access to the chamber's informal communication's networks, to its decision-making centers, and to its leadership positions.

As we shall see, recent congresswomen have been integrated into legislative life more fully than were their predecessors. Top leadership positions continue to be reserved for men, but virtually all informal groups and standing committees have opened their doors to congresswomen. It seems clear, as well, that the polity has been more sensitive to social needs felt directly by women because congresswomen have established a professional rapport with congressmen; because they have developed and articulated distinctive policy orientations which past House members, women as well as men, tended to ignore; and because they organized their resources so as to improve the chances their voices will be heard. These achievements were facilitated by formation of a Caucus whose principal focus is on how national laws and their implementation affect women.

Contemporary congresswomen have also formed coalitions with a new cohort of congressmen, House members who are sensitive to the same social currents nourishing the legislative objectives of the women with whom they are allied. Thus, emerging policy changes have been a product of a more democratic political recruitment process, fuller integration of women into the workings of the House, and the election of a new generation of men and women who have promoted a national agenda embracing economic and social goals which until recently remained unaddressed.

These developments have been accompanied by changing gender and legislative role orientations among House members. Consequently, an additional aim of this study, an objective related to establishing links between recruitment and behavior, is to explore changes in the way Representatives identify themselves as women and men and as lawmakers. The final chapter of this book attempts to trace changes in House members' legislative and gender role orientations and the factors contributing to "role de-differentiation." The term refers to a process by which standard items of behavior associated with a well-established role are abandoned. The process also occurs when items once found exclusively in the components of one role become part of another role's repertoire (Lipman-Blumen 1973). The principal premise of "role de-differentiation" is that established behavioral patterns associated with specified roles, whether they be gender or legislative in nature, are not immutable. Changes in the socialization process, in the social structure, and in social imperatives contribute to role de-differentiation.

An argument will be made in Chapter 12 that gender and legislative role orientations of women and men in the House have undergone incremental, palpable change, a change which is ongoing and whose ultimate reconfigurations are still unclear.[9] The argument begins by noting that congresswomen have traditionally been perceived as fulfilling two often contradictory roles. One role is ascribed to them and has to do with their gender. The other is linked to their tasks as lawmakers and is defined by what that occupation implies. Stereotypically, the latter mandates a rational, assertive, confident, and independent public demeanor. The former typically called for an intuitive, ameliorative, tentative, and dependent private orientation, including a propensity to please (Janeway 1971, p. 114). Whereas the qualities, orientations, and goals men are expected to possess as "males" are the very same attributes valued in lawmakers, congresswomen have had to try to balance competing roles as women and legislators. Because the qualities assigned to each are not easily reconciled in a public arena, and because women in the House have had to battle conscious and unconscious sexism, they have adopted a variety of strategies to cope with the dilemma, as is made clear in Chapter 12. These strategies rely on both the resources they capitalized upon to gain a seat in the House and the gender-related policy goals they harbor. They have had the effect of altering gender and legislative role orientations.

Most congresswomen who succeeded their husbands or depended upon other ascribed characteristics to secure election to the House resolved the dilemma by emphasizing their "womanliness," giving little attention to legislative responsibilities. These women were later replaced by congresswomen who had served in public office before they came to Washington, who had built a career in politics, and who were generally perceived by congressmen as professional lawmakers. But many of the latter saw their gender as a potential political liability, and they avoided identification with what were generally considered to be "women's issues." They believed too close association with such issues would subvert their reputation as serious, valuable legislators who were more interested in the international security and economic vitality of the country than in what were seen as the parochial and, ultimately, illegitimate concerns of women as a "special interest." This second group of women was commonly found in the House during the late 1940s, the 1950s, and the 1960s.

They have been replaced in recent years by congresswomen who possess extensive political experience, who have become better integrated into the committee, leadership, and informal group structures in the House, and who have come to be accepted as equals by a new generation of congress- men whose perspectives on lawmaking are less constrained by the tradi- tional gender role orientations held by their predecessors. Furthermore, these women Representatives have had no compunctions about placing women's issues at the top of their agendas. They often see themselves as representing American womanhood, and they are intent on promoting equality among men and women. In Chapter 12, typologies of gender and legislative role orientations are applied to each of the three groups in an effort to describe and analyze changes in the predispositions of House members.

ORGANIZATION OF THE BOOK

Parts II through V of this book portray congressional women within a micropolitical, as well as within a macropolitical, frame of reference. The recruitment, integration, and behavior patterns reflecting their collective careers are accompanied by accounts of their personal experiences. Accord- ingly, the next eleven chapters highlight individual as well as collective experiences defining women's congressional identities. Almost all include descriptive references to selected congresswomen within the context of the general discussion. Some whose performances are described are Jeannette Rankin, Mae Nolan, Ruth Hanna McCormick, Margaret Chase Smith, Clare Boothe Luce, Helen Gahagan Douglas, Leonor Sullivan, Edith Green, Martha Griffiths, Julia Butler Hansen, Margaret Heckler, Shirley Chisholm, Bella Abzug, Marjorie Holt, Elizabeth Holtzman, Barbara Jordan, Patricia Schroeder, Lindy Boggs, Millicent Fenwick, Marilyn Lloyd, Gladys Spell- man, Barbara Mikulski, Barbara Kennelly, Olympia Snowe, and Maxine Waters.

Chapter 2 examines the frequency and conditions under which women have replaced their husbands in the House after these men died. This "matrimonial connection" occurs in other Western democracies, but not nearly as often as it does in the United States. In fact, it seems to happen with such frequency that speculation about the availability of a spouse almost always surfaces when a married congressman dies—sometimes before the poor man's body is cold. The fact is, however, that relatively few spouses have received the nomination to succeed their husbands and fewer still have been elected. The chapter defines the factors contributing to the selection of some widows and the rejection of others, and explores the importance of regional variations in explaining both the election of congressional widows and the length and quality of their careers. It also examines future use of the matrimonial connection.

Chapter 3 traces the background characteristics of all 142 women who have served in the House and draws inferences from aggregate information about the factors contributing to their elections. Family connections and/or wealth were virtually indispensable to would-be congresswomen before World War II. Being the daughter of William Jennings Bryan, three-time Democratic nominee for President, could do nothing but help House aspirant Ruth Bryan Owen, and the stunning wealth of Republican Ruth Baker Pratt and Democrat Caroline O'Day surely strengthened their candidacies.

Since the mid-1940s, family connections and wealth have given way to advantages deriving from legal training and political experience. Moreover, congresswomen elected since the mid-1960s are less inhibited by marital and domestic responsibilities, qualities which promise longer House careers, as well as the potential for influence that only House seniority offers. Harvard Law School graduates Patricia Schroeder and Elizabeth Holtzman were blessed with neither political families nor large sums of money when trying to convince voters of their worthiness. State legislators Shirley Chisholm and Barbara Jordan, city councilwomen Barbara Mikulski and Mary Rose Oakar, and county officials Gladys Spellman and Barbara Boxer also lacked these endowments. Wealth and family connections are still important, but most contemporary congresswomen exploited other resources on their way to Washington, and an increasing number (Schroeder, Boxer, and Marge Roukema, for example) have coupled political careers with those domestic obligations accompanying marriage and school-age children.

While the interaction between men and women in state legislatures has received some notice, almost nothing has been written about their relationships in Congress. Chapters 4, 5, and 6 seek to remedy that deficiency. Women serving in the House fifty years ago were hardly noticed and, when they were, congressmen smothered them with gallantry and condescension. Contemporary congressmen, on the other hand, are inclined to behave differently, in spite of the fact that, along with virtually all congresswomen, they acknowledge that the House continues to be a "male institution."[10] Moreover, today's congresswomen are not prepared to suffer the conscious and flagrant chauvinism their predecessors witnessed in silence. Instead, these women employ a variety of tactics to make clear discriminatory behavior is unacceptable.

Congresswomen are now members of virtually all informal House groups. Their membership in "class" groups organized by aggregations of Democratic and Republican first termers is, of course, automatic. But they have joined, among many other caucuses, such respected groups as the Conservative Opportunity Society and the Mainstream Democratic Forum, as well. In addition, women have recently been admitted to influential informal groups once closed to them, notably the Chowder and Marching Society. Their one-time exclusion from such structured groups and from unstructured cliques—Sam Rayburn's Board of Education, for example— doubtless contributed to their limited influence and an inability to obtain important party positions. Entree to the first and the virtual disappearance of the second portend the selection of women to top leadership positions. Chapter 6 makes clear congresswomen have had to be content with secondary leadership roles until now, but may be on the verge of a breakthrough.

Changes in congresswomen's substantive interests are explored in Chapters 7 and 8. They have expanded their range of concerns, maintaining a specialization in matters thought to be within the competence of members of their gender—education, welfare, children, for example—but also mastering domains more typically defined as men's—defense policy, business and banking regulation, and taxation, for example. At the same time, they have obtained appointments to the House's most prestigious committees with greater frequency, filling vacancies on the Ways and Means and Rules committees, and acquiring seats on the Budget Committee soon after it was created in the mid-1970s. Partly because of the proliferation of subcommittees, congresswomen have managed to keep pace with congressmen in securing leadership positions on these policy-shaping panels.

The attention all House members, men as well as women, have given to "women's issues" has undergone important changes over the years. Modest proposals to help women that were advanced before World War II have been replaced by more sweeping measures calculated to address modern women's diverse needs. Whereas the earlier bills were fashioned to reinforce women's traditional roles, contemporary legislative proposals are designed either to secure greater equity for women or to affirm their worth after decades of deprivation suffered in a society whose values and goals have been defined largely by men. Accompanying changes in the emphases given to women's issues have been changes in congresswomen's representational role orientations. Almost all who serve in the House today support at least some portion of what is commonly defined as the feminist agenda.

The increasingly feminist orientation of congresswomen is both a cause and an effect of the formation in 1977 of the Congresswomen's Caucus. One of the curious features of the group's development was the delay in its appearance. Women's caucuses in a few state legislatures and in local political and quasi-political settings had been operating for several years before a comparable organization was established in Congress. The crucial parts played by Leonor Sullivan and Bella Abzug in inhibiting its formation have never been fully explored. They are discussed in Chapter 9.

Once under way the Caucus provided the support and momentum for hundreds of legislative proposals. The creative energies of Elizabeth Holtzman, Margaret Heckler, and Shirley Chisholm, among others, fueled the Caucus engine. Chapter 10 describes how its members sought not only to leave their imprint on the legislative agenda, but to influence those who interpret and implement policy in the executive branch, as well. The organization's survival in the 1980s required a fundamental alteration in its composition and character, a transformation explained in the chapter's conclusion. Chapter 11 describes Caucus efforts to promote its members' agenda in the face of hostile Reagan-Bush administrations and a divided Congress. It also discusses the legislative consequences of having forty-seven women Representatives in the 103rd Congress, and analyzes the personal and institutional uses of the Caucus.

Changes in the resources, skills and interests of congresswomen have had an impact on their integration into House activities and on the contributions they have been able to make to that body's decisions. Contemporary congresswomen are being accepted as equals by congressmen, not least because of the legislative talents they bring with them and the gender role orientations held by the more liberated men currently being sent to Washington. Thus, the House has undergone subtle changes, just as the experiences and frames of reference of its members have changed. Chapter 12 sums up these developments and describes gender and legislative role orientations adopted by congresswomen over time. It also explores the future of women in the House, a future inextricably linked to their numbers and to the positions they secure within the committee and leadership hierarchies. Although the House continues to be perceived as a male institution, its character will be a much less gendered one by the start of the twenty-first century.

NOTES

1. Mary E. P. Farrington, a nonvoting delegate representing the territory of Hawaii from 1953 to 1957, and Eleanor Holmes Norton, elected first in 1990 as a non-voting delegate from the District of Columbia, are not counted among the 142 women. They have been excluded because non-voting delegates have neither the status nor the legal standing of House members elected from one of the states. Jeannette Rankin, Chase Going Woodhouse, and Patsy Mink were elected for nonconsecutive terms, but each is counted only once. In the analysis of recruitment patterns in Chapters 2 and 3, however, each of their nominations as nonincumbents is treated separately. The principal sources used to identify women Representatives are Chamberlin (1973); "Women in Congress, 1917–1976," published by the U.S. Congress' Joint Committee on Arrangements for the Commemoration of the Bicentennial, 1976;

Schwemle (1982); U.S. House, Office of the Historian, *Women in Congress, 1917–1990*; and the periodic "Fact Sheets" and "News and Notes" distributed by the Center for the American Woman and Politics. Women in the Senate are not a part of this study, unless, as in the case of Margaret Chase Smith, Barbara Mikulski and Barbara Boxer, they first served in the House. Senate women were excluded because of their small number to date (twenty-one), the infrequency with which they served one term or more (ten served fewer than six years), and the infrequency with which they were initially elected (ten were appointed to office). For a list of the first 142 women elected to the House, see Appendix A.

2. The more precise figure is 10.8 percent.

3. For many years, the two most-cited volumes on women in Congress were Chamberlin (1973) and Engelbarts (1974). The first is an unintegrated collection of biographies. Its goal is to highlight the positive contributions each woman made while in office, and it often exaggerates the value of these contributions. The background data are useful nonetheless. The second offers biographical information about each congresswoman and cites sources in which additional material may be found. Chamberlin provides little analysis, Engelbarts none at all.

4. Until 1992, the increase of women in the U.S. House of Representatives was about one percentage point every decade. The 1992 election brought the House to one-half the proportion of women holding seats in state legislatures, which is about twenty percent (Center for the American Woman and Politics, "Fact Sheet," January 1993).

5. The interviews were conducted in Washington by the author in May and June, 1993. The seventeen first-term women were part of a larger group of respondents which included thirty-five congresswomen and twelve congressmen. The questionnaire employed appears in Appendix C.

6. Much of the material in the preceding two paragraphs is taken from Irwin N. Gertzog and Ruth B. Mandel, "'Year of the Woman': A Note of Caution," in Center for the American Woman and Politics, "News and Notes," Fall 1992.

7. Except were indicated, information about the events and decisions cited in the *Items* below were derived from the interviews referred to in footnote 5.

8. Works dealing with the recruitment of congresswomen include Amundsen (1971); Andersen and Thorson (1984); Benze and Declerq (1985); Bernstein (1986); Bullock and Heys (1972); Burrell (1985, 1988, and 1992); Cook, et al. (1994); Darcy, et al. (1987); Deber (1982); Ferraro (1979); Lamson (1968); Lee (1977); Lynn (1975); Mandel (1981); Rule (1981); Tolchin and Tolchin (1974); Van Hightower (1977); Werner (1966); and Witt, et al. (1994). Among the few studies touching specifically on women's integration into the House are Dreifus (1972); Gehlen (1969); Tolchin and Tolchin (1974); and Werner (1966). Studies of congresswomen's priorities and behavior include Abzug (1972); Dodson (1991); Gehlen (1969); Norris (1986); and Welch (1985).

9. Lipman-Blumen (1973) suggests role change takes place in four stages. In the beginning stage, role behavior is "undifferentiated." In the second stage it becomes "differentiated," with stage two followed by "role de-differentiation" and, finally, "role reconfiguration." Chapter 12 provides a fuller discussion of each of these stages.

10. The terms "female" and "male" are employed throughout this volume as synonyms for "women" and "men." Their use is not meant to imply biological determinism. Definitions of a "male institution" are provided in Chapter 4.

Part II

Recruitment

2

The Matrimonial Connection

Mae Ella Hunt was a quiet, intense young woman. She was devoted to her Irish Catholic parents who had settled in San Francisco when they arrived in the United States from County Mayo, and deeply committed to her neighborhood and church. She attended St. Vincent's Convent and later enrolled in Ayres Business School. Mae was a diligent student and when she completed the business program, she found a job as a stenographer with the Wells Fargo Express Company.

It was during her employment with Wells Fargo that she met John Ignatius Nolan, and soon the politically active, muscular iron-molder and the small, slender brown-haired office worker were married. The year was 1913. Just months before, John had been elected to the House of Representatives on Teddy Roosevelt's Bull Moose ticket. The couple left California and spent their honeymoon aboard a steamer bound for Washington, D.C., via the Panama Canal. John took the oath of office soon after they arrived, and he began a career dedicated to the needs of people who worked with their hands. The San Francisco lawmaker was regularly reelected, and became chairman of the House Committee on Labor. He also became one of the most respected members of Congress, a reputation that made the loss all the more painful when he died in 1922, at the age of forty-nine, days after his fifth reelection to the House.

After the mourning period, business, labor, and civic leaders met in Nolan's district to decide how to fill the vacancy and agreed, in the end, to ask Mae to run to succeed her husband in a special election. She accepted the offer, won the contest, completed the remainder of her husband's term in the 67th Congress, and served the entire period for which he had been reelected in 1922. But Mae was unhappy with political life in Washington, and, before the 68th Congress finished its work, she announced that she would not seek another term. "Politics," she said, "is entirely too masculine to have any attraction for feminine responsibilities." She longed to return permanently to California, where she and her ten-year-old daughter, Corliss, could have a "normal home life" (quoted in Chamberlin 1973, p. 50).

Mae Nolan did not make a significant legislative contribution during her short stay in the House. But she merits recognition, nevertheless, for beginning a sometime Washington ritual. She inaugurated the practice by which a congressman's widow succeeds her husband when he dies in office.

The matrimonial connection is not a phenomenon peculiar to the United States, although its incidence in Congress has been greater than that exhibited in other Western democracies. The British House of Commons comes closest to the U.S. House in this regard, although wives of MPs occasionally replace their spouses for reasons other than death. The first woman to serve in Parliament was Lady Nancy Astor, who succeeded her husband Waldorf when her father-in-law passed away and left a vacancy in the House of Lords that Waldorf was obliged to fill.[1]

Some observers find little wrong with use of the "connection," maintaining that, on the contrary, it has notable advantages. One British political commentator refers to the practice as "male equivalence," and argues that a woman who replaces her husband under these circumstances is better able than a stranger to pursue the policy goals he had already charted. Moreover, because she knows the constituents and they know her, she is more likely to provide a brand of representation district residents find suitable (Currell 1974, pp. 58–59). And few would cavil at the variation on the matrimonial connection adopted by widows of World War II resistance leaders in France immediately after hostilities ended. Their springboard to the National Assembly was the wartime underground activities of their husbands rather than prior legislative service. Resistance widows made up the bulk of the six percent of the Assembly that was female at the time, a figure which declined markedly in the post-war years and which has only recently been approximated (Currell 1974, p. 170; Rhoodie 1989, p. 202).

American students of the practice have not been as charitable, perhaps because it is more regularly employed on this side of the Atlantic, but also because, for a time, it seemed as if all women serving in the House were widows of former Representatives. In the twelve Congresses from 1916 to 1940, fifty-four percent of all women members had succeeded their husbands.[2] One-time Democratic party activist Emily Newell Blair believed that suffragists would have approved of the practice, and she responded to its critics by asserting:

Inheritance of a man's political assets by a woman is a great step forward. Why in our day a woman did not even inherit her own money or her own child, let alone the opportunities and the responsibilities that she and her husband had built up together. (Blair 1925, p. 516)

The sarcasm of a political scientist who took a different view is more characteristic of feminist reaction. She suggested that one cause of this "sentimental nepotism" resided in the belief that any woman who survives the refractory and willful personalities of the men we usually send to Washington deserves her constituents' approbation. The widow's mandate may also be a form of a sentimental tribute, "of the kind we offer when we subscribe to a memorial window: something to please the family" (Comstock 1926, p. 384).

The practice continues to generate comment, even though the number of widows benefitting from it has declined in recent years and in spite of the fact that an increasing proportion of women elected to the House have pursued a different path to Washington. But much less is known about the "connection" than is warranted by professional and popular curiosity.[3] Questions about its incidence, the circumstances under which it is employed, and the future of the matrimonial connection need to be addressed more fully than they have been.

THE INCIDENCE OF WIDOWS' SUCCESSION

When a married congressman dies in office, speculation about his successor often touches on the availability of his wife. Mention of the spouse is partly based upon what many believe is the high frequency with which wives have replaced congressmen-husbands. This belief is understandable, after all, because women have been named to succeed their husbands in Congress on more than a handful of occasions, and, even when they were denied the opportunity, it was often not for lack of trying. Between 1983 and 1992, for example, twenty-three Representatives died in office, fourteen of whom could have realistically been replaced by a female spouse. Four wives were nominated to succeed husbands and the names of three others were mentioned publicly as possible successors.[4]

But recent instances of widow's succession, actual or proposed, should not obscure the fact that the great majority of Representatives' widows have *not* succeeded their husbands. During the period from 1916, when the first woman was elected to the House, through the 1992 election, 404 Representatives died in office. Among this number, 114 could not have been replaced by wives because they were bachelors or widowers, or because the timing and circumstances of their deaths made succession by a spouse unlikely if not impossible.[5] This leaves a total of 290 women who could have conceivably filled House vacancies created by the death of a spouse. Of these, only forty-five were nominated to run for the office, about one in seven.[6]

Inflated perceptions about the incidence of widow's succession are probably the result of three factors. One is the extraordinarily large proportion of widows who, once nominated, were indeed victorious in the general election. A second is the lengthy period many congressmen's widows have served in the House, relative to the average tenure of other congresswomen. A third factor is the productive legislative performance turned in by a handful of unusually visible widows—women whose celebrity status has led many to believe congressmen's spouses are regularly chosen to replace them.

The success rate of women nominated to follow their husbands into the House has been high. Thirty-eight of forty-five won the general election contests for which they were nominated. Of course, some of these women had only token opposition, and a few had none at all, but a good many were challenged by skillful, well-financed adversaries.[7] The figures in Table 2.1 help highlight the remarkable success rate congressmen's widows experienced over the years. Since 1916, these women won eighty-four percent of the elections they contested. Nonincumbent women House candidates who were not Representatives' widows were successful only 14 percent of the time. However, a comparison between the two groups is not entirely appropriate because an unusually large proportion of widows ran in special rather than biennial November elections, and they competed in districts were their names were well known and where their parties (and their husbands) had prevailed in the last House election. When acquiring their perceptions of widow's success, however, most observers are unconcerned with such distinctions. They know that women nominated to succeed their congressmen-husbands face unusually appealing odds, and they do not have to make too great an inferential leap to conclude that more widows secured their parties' nominations than has, in fact, been the case.

The average number of House terms served by those who capitalized on the matrimonial connection, compared with the number recorded by other congresswomen, also contributes to the illusion that widows have been frequent successors to their husbands. Between 1917 and 1940, the average for each group of women was about the same, two and one-half terms. But between 1941 and 1964, women who succeeded their husbands spent an average of five and one-half terms in the House compared with three and one-half terms for other congresswomen. The difference has narrowed in recent years, but from 1965 to 1994, the former continued to record a longer average tenure, four and one-half to three and-three-fourths terms. Thus, the fact that wives who replaced their husbands have stayed in Congress longer than other women may have given some the impression that more of them run for House seats. This perception, in turn, feeds public expectation and media speculation about who a deceased Representative's successor could (or should) be.

Table 2.1
Noncumbent Widows and Nonwidows* Nominated and Elected to the House, 1916–1993

	Years (Congresses) and Status							
	1916-1940 (65th-76th)		1941-1964 (77th-88th)		1965-1993 (89th-103rd)		1916-1993 (65th-103rd)	
	Widows	Nonwidows	Widows	Nonwidows	Widows	Nonwidows	Widows	Nonwidows
Number nominated	15	69	17	130	13	491	45	690
Number elected	14	11	14	21	10	66	38	98
Percent elected	93	16	82	16	77	13	84	14

*Nonwidows contesting special elections are omitted.
Sources: Congressional Quarterly, Inc. (1985); Gertzog and Simard (1981); and Congressional Quarterly Weekly Report election results, 1986-1993

Finally, the matrimonial connection is probably perceived as more common than it is because several widows who had long and distinguished careers acknowledged their initial dependence on it. Margaret Chase Smith, for example, had no compunctions about articulating the importance of her spousal role. She said: "I am a product of nepotism—a living symbol of nepotism—for I would not be in the Senate today had I not been a $3,000-a-year secretary to my late husband when he was in the House" (Lewis 1972, p. 299). Leonor Sullivan's views about her own election to Congress were the same.

I won on the strength of John's name and reputation. John Sullivan had a program I wanted to carry out. He believed in good government and that you had to fight to get it. In time I hope to build a reputation of my own. Then I can run as Leonor Sullivan. (*Washington Star*, September 3, 1967)

Both Smith and Sullivan did, indeed, establish reputations of their own, the former mainly through her contributions to national defense policy, the latter primarily as a champion of consumer rights. Others, such as Edith Nourse Rogers and Frances Payne Bolton, also acquired celebrity status. Their legislative accomplishments, coupled with House longevity, contributed to the belief that widows are nominated to succeed their husbands with a regularity that cannot be supported by the facts.

Whatever the popular conception, the incidence of widow's succession has not been reflected uniformly throughout the country. Party leaders, activists, and voters in the South have been more apt to nominate spouses than have their counterparts elsewhere. One of every four deaths of Southern congressmen has been followed by the nomination of their wives. Use of the matrimonial connection in the other three regions is considerably less frequent, as is made clear in Table 2.2.

This regional variation is important, for it reveals not one but two explanations for selection of a spouse to succeed her husband in Congress. One accounts for a preponderant percentage of the cases in the South, the other for most of the instances of widow's succession outside the South. Put another way, widows have followed two different pathways to their party's nomination, with each route partly a product of the regional political culture that defines the role of women in public life.

TWO EXPLANATIONS FOR THE CONNECTION

Just why some women were nominated to succeed their husbands and most others were not is a question that has not received systematic analysis, although several writers have offered possible explanations. Some have suggested, for example, that widows whose husbands had enjoyed considerable seniority and influence in the House were nominated to succeed their spouses because the latter's formidable reputations were expected to bene-

Table 2.2
Regional Use of the Matrimonial Connection, 1916–1993

Region*	Number of married congressmen who died	Number of widows nominated to fill vacancies	Percent of vacancies for which widows were nominated
South	78	21	27
Northeast	94	11	12
Midwest	77	9	12
West	41	4	10
Total	290	45	15

*The distribution of states among regions is as follows: South includes Alabama, Arkansas, Florida, Georgia, Kentucky, Louisiana, Mississippi, North Carolina, South Carolina, Tennessee, Texas, and Virginia; Northeast includes Connecticut, Delaware, Maine, Maryland, Massachusetts, New Hampshire, New Jersey, New York, Pennsylvania, Rhode Island, Vermont, and West Virginia; Midwest includes Illinois, Indiana, Iowa, Kansas, Michigan, Minnesota, Missouri, Nebraska, North Dakota, Ohio, South Dakota, and Wisconsin; West includes Alaska, Arizona, California, Colorado, Hawaii, Idaho, Montana, Nevada, New Mexico, Oklahoma, Oregon, Utah, Washington, and Wyoming.

Sources: *Congressional Record, 1916-1993; Congressional Quarterly Weekly Reports, 1955-1993;* Schwemle *1982.*

fit their widows' standing with the voters and with their former colleagues (Amundsen 1971; Gruberg 1968; Tolchin and Tolchin 1974). When a congressman serves his district for many years and acquires power in the process, he is more likely than a House newcomer to leave his mark on the district—in the form of post offices, better roads, larger military installations, and more federal money—and thereby make his spouse a better-known, more appealing candidate.

The degree of party competition within a district may also affect the incidence of widows' nominations. Party leaders are said to be more likely to support congressional widows when their party dominates elections within the district than when it sometimes loses House contests, and when factional disputes within the dominant party are more threatening to party hegemony than the candidate nominated by the opposition (if, indeed, an opponent is even nominated).

To test these hypotheses, the seniority, leadership, and district characteristics of congressmen whose wives succeeded them were compared with these same characteristics possessed by congressmen whose wives were not nominated to succeed them when they died in office. At first blush, these variables seem to explain little about the matrimonial connection. Among the 290 wives who could have conceivably succeeded their husbands, the percentage of those who did differs little from the percentage who did not when level of seniority, leadership status, and magnitude of previous election victories are held constant. Only after Southern and non-southern districts are treated separately do the three variables help uncover serviceable explanations for widows' succession.

When this regional distinction is made, the findings show almost one-third of deceased Southern House members whose wives were nominated to succeed them had served eight terms or more. The comparable figure for widows nominated in districts outside the South is 8 percent. Similarly, more than four in ten of the Southern members whose deaths were followed by their widows' nominations had held formal party leadership positions, compared with 16 percent of non-Southern congressmen whose spouses were nominated to succeed them. And 29 percent of the group of Southern members had run in safe rather than competitive districts. Only 11 percent of their non-Southern counterparts had been similarly "safe."[8]

These findings support the claim that there is not one but two paths along which congressional widows have traveled to obtain House nominations. Many whose husbands represented Southern districts seemed to have had their nominations affected significantly by the seniority or leadership roles of their spouses, or by the degree of competitiveness reflected in district elections. Among the twenty-one widows from the South, nineteen followed spouses who served eight terms or more, or held a party leadership position, or were elected from a safe district. The two women whose husbands could be described in none of these ways, Elizabeth Pool and Sheila Smith, lost either the special election or the next regularly scheduled general election following their nominations. Widows' nominations outside the South, on the other hand, seem to have been unrelated either to the length of service or House status of the Representatives who died. Furthermore, these men were just as likely to have contested elections in competitive districts as they were to have run in safe districts. (See Appendix B for a list of all widows nominated between 1916 and 1994 and identification of their spouse's seniority, leadership, and district characteristics.)

If the nomination of widows outside the South cannot be accounted for in terms of the characteristics of their husbands' service or districts, how, then, might it be explained? Some answers to this question emerge when five additional distinctions are made between Southern and non-Southern women who were named to succeed their husbands. First, fewer than one-half (48%) of the former faced serious opposition in either the primary or general elections, whereas almost all of the widows outside the South (96%) had to deal with a primary or general election challenge. (See Appendix B.)

A second important distinction between Southern and non-Southern widows is that, among the former, few received the party's nomination for a second term, while most of the latter were selected for at least one additional term. Two-thirds of the congresswomen who succeeded husbands whose districts lay outside the South were renominated at least once. By contrast, only 18 percent of the widows from the South were awarded their parties' nominations after completing an initial term.

Third, before the 1992 election, Southern widows who thought about running again after their initial success may have been discouraged by the fact that so few women who were not wives of former congressmen had represented Southern constituencies. Among the eighty-one female Representatives who served from 1917 to 1992 and did not succeed their husbands, only seven were from the South.[9] Consequently Southern widows who may have desired longer tenure in the House had few role models upon which to hinge their aspirations. Congressional widows outside the South had many such models. The importance of learning from the behavior of others is highlighted by Fowler (1993, p. 88) who observes:

Individuals learn about their own ambitions and discover how to pursue them through experience: by winning elections for other offices; by comparing themselves with the men and women who have sought the post of senator or representative before them; by hearing the praise and criticism of political activists and party leaders.

A fourth distinction between Southern and non-Southern widows is in their average ages when first elected to office. Age is of concern to men as well as to women who compete for elective office. But it is normally important to voters and party leaders only when a candidate is perceived as being either too young or too old for public office. Age may also limit the length of time a candidate serves once elected, and it is relevant to the present discussion because of the considerable difference in the mean age of widows nominated to succeed husbands in each of the two regions. The average age of widows nominated outside the South is forty-nine years, a figure markedly lower than the fifty-three year average of widows nominated in the South. Only three of the widows outside the South (13%) were over sixty at the time of their first nomination. On the other hand, eight of the twenty-one Southern women were at least sixty years of age (40%). (See Appendix B.)

The fifth difference between widows falling in each regional grouping has to do with the extent to which members of each played a part in the political lives of their husbands. Information about some of these relationships is fragmentary, but it would appear that a smaller proportion of Southern than non-southern widows were an integral part of their spouses' political careers. Among the thirty-eight women about whom evidence is available, seventeen were elected to southern districts, twenty-one to non-southern districts. (See Appendix B.) Six of the former, but none of the latter, played little or no role in their husbands' Washington and district activities.[10]

The degree to which a wife is familiar with the political affairs of her spouse is among the most important factors affecting the matrimonial connection. If a widow is awarded a complimentary nomination, one which sends her to Washington to complete only the remainder of a spouse's term, her understanding of the people, places, and things that were important to him is of little consequence. But if a woman is looking beyond the current term, close friendships with activists upon whom her husband relied, and an understanding of the problems salient to the district become necessary, even if not sufficient, conditions for nomination and renomination. She is in a position to capitalize on the contacts and financial support that aided her husband and to speak and act in ways which do not violate fundamental constituency values. A wife who knows little about her husband's work and who has no rapport with his political and financial supporters is far less likely to be able to aggregate the resources needed to succeed him for more that the unexpired portion of his term.

The close ties between Margaret Chase Smith and her husband Clyde is a case in point. An associate of the former congresswoman described the relationship in this way:

Margaret was an active wife, in fact, Clyde Smith's top staff member. . . . They campaigned as a team, Clyde was the candidate, Margaret the manager. She drove the car and she maintained a current blackbook of maps of all the routes in the district with the names of key people and their residences and offices along the routes. In Washington she handled the correspondence, which was the backbone of the operation keeping the political fences mended back in Maine. Many times she typed until midnight or later. (Lewis 1972, p. 65)

A contemporary congresswoman who was similarly well connected when her husband died is Lindy Boggs, a woman reputed to have been as much a part of husband Hale's political life as any wife could be. Perhaps so intimate a political relationship was required to persuade Louisiana's Democratic leaders to ignore tradition and support a congressional widow beyond the expiration of her husband's term.

Sala Burton's extensive political activity paralleled the development of her husband's career and doubtless facilitated her own election to the House after his death in 1983. The new congresswoman had been a co-founder of the influential California Democratic Council, President of the San Francisco Democratic Women's Forum, a member of the California Democratic Central Committee, and President of the Democratic Wives of the House and Senate. For many in the Burtons' Bay area district and in Washington, her succession seemed only natural.

The experience of Peggy Begich, widow of Congressman Nick Begich, was very different. Her husband was in the same plane carrying Hale Boggs when it was lost during the 1972 campaign. Mrs. Begich had not been active in her husband's political career, however, spending much of her time bringing up their six children. When she announced an interest in running for the vacant seat, Democratic leaders in Alaska were astonished. Most withheld their support and a party convention denied her the nomination. Said one party leader who was sympathetic to her newfound aspirations: "The response to her candidacy was not good. But how could it have been good? The party people had no feeling for her; they just didn't know her. They could not relate to her as part of Nick."[11]

Georgia voters had similar difficulties accepting Kathryn McDonald as the legitimate heir to her husband after he was killed in the crash of a Korean Air Lines passenger jet in 1983. She received the highest vote count, 31 percent, in the primary, but lost badly in the runoff election. Her loss surprised few because she was virtually unknown in the district and her opponent had considerable support from the Democratic party organization. Kathryn McDonald had spent much of her adult life in California and had moved to Virginia after marriage to the Congressman. She had spent little time in his conservative Georgia district, except after launching her own campaign, and the voters simply could not relate to her in the way they had identified with her husband.

Finally, there is the case of Katharine Byron of Maryland, wife of Congressman William Byron, who succeeded her husband after he was killed in a 1941 plane crash. Following a hard-fought special election campaign, featuring visits to the district by celebrities of both parties, she managed to win by little more than 1,000 votes. Byron had worked closely with her husband as a confidante and aide, and, once in the House, she established good rapport with Democratic leaders. She filed for reelection in 1942, but was unacceptable to some district Democratic leaders, notably Montgomery County Chairman E. Brooke Lee. The county leader had supported her nomination for the special election with the understanding that she would not seek reelection, and he eventually forced her out of the race.[12]

These examples make plain, first of all, that not all Southern widows fit the pattern described here, with Boggs an important exception to it. Complete immersion in her husband's career and her unusual political skills probably explain much of the aberration. The success achieved by Smith and Burton and Begich's failure, on the other hand, suggest that, outside the South, widows normally must demonstrate political virtuosity—acquired in most cases while serving their spouses' professional needs—if their battles to secure nominations are to be fruitful. Kathryn McDonald's experience makes clear that absence of strong ties to district residents is a significant obstacle to widows' succession. And Katharine Byron's experience indicates, first, that Southern widows are not the only ones muscled out of a reelection attempt; and second, that a close working relationship with a spouse may be necessary for triggering the matrimonial connection, but it is not a sufficient condition for perpetuating it.

The lessons to be drawn from this evidence are clear. Widows' succession cannot be treated adequately in unidimensional terms. The factors contributing to the recruitment of widows were not the same for all. Selection of Southern women to fill spouses' seats has been influenced by the venerable status of the men who died and the safeness of the seats their husbands had vacated. Most wives chosen were those whose spouses had served long enough and well enough to have left a demonstrable legacy in their districts, a legacy upon which wives could capitalize while ambitious males in the district vied for long-term control of the seat through established nomination processes. Widows selected in districts outside the South, on the other hand, were usually required initially to confront serious primary or general election opposition. They were also expected to secure renomination and, unlike their Southern counterparts, they could look to a number of successful female House members in their region—women who had not succeeded husbands—as models by which to define their own political identities. Furthermore, these women were younger than Southern widows and they were also more likely to have been an integral part of their husbands' political careers.

It seems fair to conclude that, with a few exceptions, the selection of widows in Southern districts had less to do with the personal or political identities of these women and more to do with their husbands' reputations and the nature of their districts. Their nominations seem to have served as a part of a holding action until a real (i.e., male) successor emerged from the interstices of more orderly, more deliberate internal party conflict.

Widows outside the South, on the other hand, were chosen under considerably different circumstances. Most were selected close to their prime of life—a time when they could do more than simply serve out the remaining months of their husbands' terms. They were, as a group, more politically vigorous than their Southern counterparts, more likely to have been active in their husbands' careers, and young enough to look forward to careers of their own. Thus the qualities of their own candidacies, more than the characteristics of their husbands or of their districts, seem to have contributed to their receiving the nomination.

WIDOWS' SUCCESSION AND POLITICAL RECRUITMENT

There is another perspective within which to interpret these findings. When discussing recruitment to local office, Prewitt (1970) considers the population as comprising four politically involved groups. He calls these groups the "dominant social stratum," another name for which is "eligibles"; the "politically active stratum"; "recruits and apprentices"; and "candidates." According to the dynamics of this hierarchy, "political activists" emerge out of a pool of "eligibles"; "recruits and apprentices" come out of the ranks of "activists." "Candidates," in turn, are selected from "recruits and apprentices."

The first group, the eligibles, is made up of social and economic community elites. They constitute the pool from which potential leaders are likely to be drawn, and they possess the economic and social resources that allow them to contribute materially to the political process. Political activists, the second group, are a part of the dominant social stratum. They differ from the rest of the eligibles in that they evidence more interest in politics. They work for and probably know public office holders, and they participate in activities carried out by political parties and politically relevant community groups, often dominating these organizations.

Recruits and apprentices are those political activists who harbor aspirations for public office and who are in the process of developing legitimate claims to such office. They engage in activities that permit them to survive the legal and political screening processes putative candidates must pass. Many are able to demonstrate their worthiness as political candidates by successfully raising money, mobilizing voters, supporting candidates, and fulfilling other campaign-related tasks. The fourth group, candidates, are ambitious recruits and apprentices who persuade members of the other three strata they are worthy of appearing on the ballot and who contest races for public office (Prewitt, 1970, pp. 9–12).

This recruitment pattern is not followed in all cases, however. An eligible need not necessarily become an activist or a recruit in order to secure nomination to office. According to Prewitt, some people who are neither may be inducted directly into the political arena, usually by political parties, but by interest groups and friends, as well, and by the emergence of politically charged events. Entry into electoral politics, in short, need not be a product of a long-standing interest in public life. Indeed, a person may not evidence serious aspirations for office until he or she actually secures a major party nomination and is elected (Prewitt 1970, p. 59). Although Prewitt confines his analysis to local recruitment patterns, his conceptual framework can be applied to patterns observed beyond the community level.

Over the years, virtually all congressional spouses, including the scores who never dreamed of running for office, possessed the characteristics that qualified them as "eligibles." If they did not have them before marriage, they acquired them afterwards, when they were part of the lives of men destined for a seat in the most prestigious legislative body in the land. Having committed themselves to roles as wives of aspiring public officials, they were unlikely to engage in self-promoting activities normally pursued by ambitious political activists and apprentices. Of course, many performed politically relevant chores to help their husbands' careers, but it is difficult to imagine more than a few doing so in a way which anticipated a candidacy of their own.[13]

When their husbands died suddenly, a great majority had neither the political skills nor the ambition sufficient to justify a race for Congress. Most had no reason to adopt patterns of behavior followed by Prewitt's "eligibles," who became "activists" and "recruits" before advancing to candidacy. Even if they decided to seek a House seat, opportunities to succeed their husbands were threatened by the ambitions of other candidates, almost always male, whose compelling claims to the nomination were based upon experience in public office, established political connections, abundant financial resources, and the support of opinion leaders. Many of these men had been waiting for the incumbent to retire or commit a serious blunder so that they could advance their own candidacies for Congress. Some, in fact, were prepared to run against him at the first opportunity. Death gave them an unanticipated head start, and they became the principal adversaries to congressmen's widows who aspired to replace their husbands. It was this point in the widows' recruitment process that regional differences helped determine which of the two routes to the House widows would employ.

In the South, widows who did secure their party's nomination were expected to hold office only for the remainder of their husband's terms. Those who seriously considered replacing spouses over the long term were almost always discouraged from running, usually by the men who had been waiting in the wings for the seat to become available. These women simply could not compete with resource-rich, ambitious males in a region disdainful of political women. In the meantime, an election system fashioned to accommodate the needs of established party leaders was permitted to work its will. Districts that were mostly one-party Democratic witnessed a primary election followed by a run-off primary. The process normally produced a consensus choice, a person already well known to constituents and almost certain to reflect the basic values of district leaders and voters. These steps were taken while the Southern widow acted as a caretaker of her husband's seat. To have conferred the vacancy on someone else might have given that person too big an edge in the battle for long-term control of the seat.

The real choice then, was selected through political machinery that had been legitimated by long use and which made authentic widow's succession unlikely. As Prewitt points out, entree to candidacy in the political recruitment process is influenced significantly by established legal arrangements and by the prevailing political culture. Of course most male leaders in the region found all female candidates unacceptable, but they were prepared temporarily to elect a congressman's spouse, the wife of a late friend, perhaps, because she could be persuaded to abide by the norms limiting women's roles to peripheral and auxiliary political activities. An independent, politically ambitious woman was anathema.

Outside the South, cultural limitations were not quite as detrimental to the candidacies of women, although the difference was possibly more a matter of degree than of kind. Still, widows securing nominations to succeed their husbands could anticipate a congressional career that exceeded the remainder of an unfinished term. The elaborate system of primaries and one-party politics that vouchsafed control of candidacies to orthodox aspirants in the South was not nearly so well established outside the region. And the resources and skills of nonsouthern widows, including the benefits derived from working closely with their spouses, could be exploited more effectively. In Prewitt's terms, their transition from "eligibles" to authentic "candidates"—without necessarily passing through an "apprenticeship" stage—was less likely to be inhibited by cultural and legal constraints.

True, non-Southern widows also had to contend with the aspiration of people who had been eyeing their husbands' seats. They often had to fight for party recognition, face formidable opposition in the general election, demonstrate political skills, and exhibit the qualifications constituents expected in an effective Representative. But, if this alternative form of the matrimonial connection meant a greater investment of resources than was expended by Southern widows, it also meant greater political rewards.

THE FUTURE OF THE MATRIMONIAL CONNECTION

Just how often the connection will produce future nominations of congressional spouses is, of course, difficult to say. Nevertheless, it is possible to draw some inferences from past and present patterns of widows' succession and to rely on these inferences to speculate about the future.

Although the percentage of widows among women in the House has declined, there has been an increase in the proportion of widows selected to contest their husbands' seats when vacancies caused by death have been created. As is reported in Table 2.3, 12 percent of Representatives' widows were nominated to succeed their husbands during the pre-World War II period. This figure increased to 18 percent between 1941 and 1964, and to one in four between 1965 and 1993. The table also makes clear, however, that the increase cannot be described as a national trend as much as it can be explained as a development common to Southern districts. The incidence

Table 2.3
Widows Receiving Nominations as a Percent of House Vacancies Created by
Married Members' Deaths, 1917–1993

Time Period	Total		South		Non-South	
	%	N	%	N	%	N
1917-1940	12	141	17	42	7	99
1941-1964	18	97	28	18	14	79
1965-1993	25	48	47	15	15	33

remained the same outside the South, but, from 1965 to 1993, almost one-half of the Southern districts turned to wives of deceased members when House vacancies were created by an incumbent's death.

In spite of the small number of cases occurring in recent years, it is worth noting that the circumstances under which contemporary Southern widows have been nominated have begun to resemble more closely the conditions under which widows outside the South have been selected. They are more likely to face serious competition in primary and general elections the first time they run, and, during the 1970s two congressional spouses, Lindy Boggs and Marilyn Lloyd, were renominated following their first terms in office. Moreover, in choosing Lloyd, Tennessee Democrats nominated a woman considerably younger than the average widow elected from a Southern district—a woman who could conceivably provide more than just a few years of House service.[14]

It appears that increased party competition in the South, together with a decline in the seniority and leadership roles of Southern Democratic House members, will limit the special form of the matrimonial connection so often employed in that region. This may mean either an end to the nomination of Southern widows, or party designations linked to their political skills and qualifications rather than to characteristics of their husbands' incumbency. To the extent that future widows seek the nomination in that region, they can expect stiffer competition, even if to serve only the remainder of an unexpired term.

But these findings should not obscure the strong probability that the matrimonial connection is likely to be less serviceable in the future. There are three reasons for forecasting this decline. First, fewer Representatives are dying while in office. Between 1917 and 1940 an average of seventeen members died each term. This figure declined to eleven during the period 1941 through 1964 and to below five from 1965 to 1992. Furthermore, this reduction seems to have picked up momentum reflecting a much larger percentage decrease during the latter years than between 1941 and 1964.[15]

This is not to suggest that the matrimonial connection will necessarily disappear as a pathway to Congress. The percentages reported in Table 2.3 for the most recent period may remain constant or even increase, especially if more congressional wives become better integrated into their husbands' careers. What the declining mortality rate suggests is that with the continued decrease in the number of House deaths, there will be fewer opportunities for widows to gain their party's nomination. But that does not mean that a smaller *percentage* of these women will secure that nomination.

A second reason for a likely decline in the incidence of widow's succession is that party leaders, voters, and candidates themselves seem to have altered the criteria they employ to evaluate potential female nominees. As will be made clear in the next chapter, professional training, campaign experience, and prior public office seem to have become far more important than the matrimonial connection for promoting the credibility of women's candidacies and for assessing their qualifications for House office.

This development, in turn, may be viewed as both a blueprint for and a confirmation of a recruitment process based on merit and achievement rather than one anchored in status and ascription. However able and resourceful many congressional widows have been, most have had little opportunity publicly to display their political skills *before* securing their party's nomination. That such a display is more of a requirement for women today than it was in the past may be a compelling reason to expect fewer nominations of congressional widows in the future. However, for those who, like Sala Burton, aggregate political resources while simultaneously serving as a congressional spouse, nominations to succeed their husbands continue to be a lively possibility.

Finally, we should expect fewer widows to succeed their husbands because recent years have witnessed a palpable gain in the number of women serving in the House. Judging from recent increases in the number of women nominated for House seats by the major parties, there is likely to be little, if any, retrogression in the number of female Representatives. On the contrary, they will almost certainly make up a larger proportion of the House in the coming years than they do at this writing. The larger the number of female Representatives, the smaller the number of male members—and the fewer the number of men whose deaths would occasion succession by a wife. Of course, the death of women House members may produce opportunities for "widower's succession," but the number of congresswomen has not increased so much as to suggest that this alternate form of the matrimonial connection will claim much attention in the immediate future.[16]

NOTES

This chapter is a revised and updated version of an article appearing in the August 1980 issue of *Journal of Politics*. The author is grateful to the editors for permission to reprint it here.

1. The second and third women to serve in Commons also followed their husbands, Mrs. Margaret Wintringham because her husband had died, and Mrs. Mabel Philipson because her spouse had been barred from seeking a seat in Commons for seven years. Mr. Philipson's campaign agent had been found guilty of fraudulent dealings during his successful election contest. As a result, the victory was nullified, and, in a by-election, his wife was selected to replace him. Her performance in the post was exemplary, and her constituents retained her services even after her husband regained his eligibility to run for the office.

2. The percentage declined to 37 percent between 1941 and 1964, and to 18 percent between 1964 and 1990. When the 103rd Congress convened in 1993, only 4 percent of the congresswomen had come to the House via the matrimonial connection.

3. Professional analysts who have studied the phenomenon include Amundsen 1971; Bullock and Heys 1972; Gruberg 1968; Kincaid 1978; Tolchin and Tolchin 1974; and Werner 1966. Popular treatment of the subject appears almost every time a married congressman dies, especially if his wife is nominated to succeed him.

4. The four nominated to run for their husbands' seats were Sala Burton (CA), Kathryn McDonald (GA), Catherine Long (LA), and Sheila Smith (MS). Mentioned for nomination were Lila Rosenthal (NY), Corinne Conte (MA), and Sonya Weiss (NY). McDonald's "nomination" occurred when she placed first in a primary contested by both Democrats and Republicans. She did not secure a clear majority, however, and lost the runoff primary (which was tantamount to a general election) to another Democrat who had finished second in the initial race.

5. Other cases excluded from the analysis are those in which congressmen had announced their retirement from the House, or had been defeated in a primary election before their deaths. It seemed reasonable to omit instances in which incumbents had relinquished a claim to a House seat, voluntarily or otherwise, before they expired. The wives of six suicides were considered unlikely to succeed their husbands, and congressmen whose seats were sought by a son, brother, or nephew were also defined as special cases. The inference here is that their widows would be required to defer to a male member of the immediate family (whose surname was the same) whatever their own ambitions.

6. Even this ratio is as high as it is because the term "matrimonial connection" is broadly defined. Among the women included as having been affected by it are a Representative's daughter (Winnifred Mason Huck) rather than his spouse; the wife of a House member who did not die but was jailed during Prohibition for bootlegging (Katherine Langley); two wives of nonincumbent men who died after being nominated but before the November election (Charlotte Reid and Marilyn Lloyd); two widows who, following their husbands' deaths, were denied their parties' nomination, but who contested and won the nomination for the next November election (Leonor Kretzer Sullivan and Sheila Smith); and one widow who appeared to be nominated and elected to follow her husband into the House but whose victories were successfully challenged (Lallie Connor Kemp).

Kemp was a victim of one of the most bizarre controversies in the history of the matrimonial connection. In 1933, she was caught in the middle of a factional dispute between pro-Long and anti-Long forces in Louisiana. Senator Huey Long wanted her to fill her husband's vacancy, but local community and county leaders in the district had other plans. The latter boycotted an election in which Mrs. Kemp received 99.8 percent of the vote and they managed to get the result thrown out. A second election was held a few months later, but she did not contest it.

One "widow" who might have been included in this analysis, but was not, received the nomination to replace her son. Curry Ethel Coffey, mother of Representative Robert Coffey, Jr., and a women's group activist in Pennsylvania, was persuaded by Democratic Party leaders to contest a special election after her son was killed on a 1949 training flight. The much-decorated World War II pilot was thirty at the time of his death. Curry Coffee lost the election, but she was a much more likely choice than her daughter-in-law, Eileen Mercado-Parra Coffey, who was still in her twenties, had two children under the age of five, and was a native of Puerto Rico.

Four other women who did not fit the criteria are Ruth Hanna McCormick, Clare Boothe Luce, Susan Molinari, and Lucille Roybal-Allard. McCormick's husband had been a member of the House from 1917 to 1919, before moving to the U.S. Senate. He was defeated for renomination in 1924 and died in 1925, before the Senate term expired. His spouse did not win a House seat until the 1928 election. It was Luce's stepfather, Albert E. Austin, rather than her husband, who preceded her in the House, and he did not die in office. Austin was defeated for reelection in 1940. Two years later his stepdaughter won the House seat. Molinari and Roybal-Allard sought to succeed their fathers following resignation in one case and retirement in the other. They are excluded from consideration because, unlike Winnifred Huck, each held elective office in her own right prior to seeking a seat in the House.

Congresswomen who came to the House as widows of men who never served in Congress were not beneficiaries of the matrimonial connection and, consequently, are excluded from this analysis.

7. See Kincaid (1978) on this point. Her treatment of widows' succession corrects some commonly accepted factual inaccuracies, disputes some myths implicit in the literature on the topic, and interprets the phenomenon within a fresh perspective.

8. Members who died in office after having served between one and three terms were categorized as having "low seniority." "Moderate seniority" was defined as having between four and seven terms of service. "High seniority" means eight or more terms in office. When the length of service of *all* 290 members is considered, spouses of 9 percent with "low" seniority, 20 percent with "moderate" seniority, and 16 percent with "high seniority" were nominated.

A congressman was considered to be part of the leadership if he was House Speaker, floor leader, whip, chairman, or ranking minority member of a standing committee, chairman or ranking member of a subcommittee of the House Appropriations Committee, chairman of his party's congressional campaign committee, or chairman of his party's national committee. When *all* deceased members are considered, the wives of 24 percent of the leaders were nominated to succeed them compared with 11 percent of nonleaders' wives. Corresponding figures for the South are 41 percent and 11 percent; for the non-south they are 16 percent and 9 percent.

"Safe" seats are defined here as those which were won by the deceased incumbent's party by twenty-five percentage points or more in each of the last three elections. All other seats are considered "competitive." When all 290 deceased congressmen are considered, the widows of 19 percent from safe districts were nominated to succeed their husbands, compared with 13 percent of the spouses whose husbands ran in competitive districts. Corresponding figures for Southern districts are 29 percent and 19 percent; for the non-Southern districts they are 11 percent and 10 percent.

9. The seven are Eliza Pratt (NC), Helen Mankin and Iris Blitch (GA), Ruth Bryan Owen and Ileana Ros-Lehtinen (FL), Barbara Jordan (TX), and Elizabeth Patterson (SC).

10. Sources for this information include Chamberlin 1973; *New York Times* and *Washington Post* stories; sketches appearing in *Current Biography*; and biographical information reported by *Congressional Quarterly Weekly Reports*.

11. This statement was made to the author by a Democratic Party activist from Alaska who had been a close associate of Nick Begich. The subject was explored in our conversation only after assurances were given that the source would be kept confidential.

12. Lee, a scion of what was arguably the most powerful political family in Maryland, told Byron that she would receive no support from the party if she persisted in her reelection bid. He prevailed upon her to withdraw from the race and secured the nomination for himself. Byron's public explanation centered on her need to care for five fatherless sons—a face-saving gesture that most could accept. Perhaps she believed that the score had been settled when, thirty years later, her middle son, Goodloe Byron, won the House seat that had been hers. He died suddenly in 1978 and was succeeded by spouse Beverly, thereby making the Byron family the only one to have twice employed the matrimonial connection.

13. One exception involves the congressional ambitions of Pat Lear, a former spouse of ex-Congressman James Corman. While Corman was still representing a Southern California district, his wife Pat considered the possibility of running for a House seat in a neighboring district, represented at the time by Republican Barry Goldwater, Jr. Her initial interest in the 1976 election was whetted when Goldwater began considering a race for the Senate. But even when Goldwater decided to stay in the House, Lear persisted in her candidacy—against her husband's wishes. She lost the 1976 election, as well as the one two years later, after her marriage had ended in divorce.

A more recent example of spousal ambition occurred in the 1992 election cycle, when the wife of western Kentucky Congressman Carroll Hubbard, Carol Brown Hubbard, sought the Democratic nomination for a House seat in the eastern part of the state. But both lost primary elections, he, in part, because he had 152 overdrafts on his account with the House Bank. (Mr. Hubbard was hardly the lone transgressor, and many colleagues who were implicated in the Bank scandal either retired or were defeated.) The dual losses prevented Kentucky from becoming the first state to boast a husband and wife "team" in Congress. That distinction fell to New York the following year, with the marriage of two incumbent Representatives, Susan Molinari and William Paxon.

14. Lloyd was reelected for a tenth term in 1992 and chaired a House subcommittee on nuclear energy.

15. This change can be explained in several ways. Earlier recognition of debilitating illness, more effective means of prolonging life, and other developments in medical science have surely permitted a larger number of ailing Representatives to complete their terms and withdraw from public life before their deaths. Recent improvements in retirement benefits for congressmen, along with stricter limitations on the honoraria they may earn outside of their House service, may be additional inducements for members to leave Congress while they can still do so under their own power.

16. The first attempt by a husband to succeed his wife in the House occurred in 1981, after Maryland's Gladys Spellman was reelected in November 1980, but was prevented by catastrophic illness from being sworn in. When the hopelessness of her condition was beyond doubt, the seat was declared vacant, and a new election called. Spellman's husband, Reuben, was narrowly defeated in the Democratic primary.

3

Changing Patterns of Recruitment

Decline in the number of congressional widows and their decrease as a proportion of the female population in the House are reflections of more fundamental changes in the characteristics of congresswomen. In the past, most observers recognized these changes, but until the 1992 election, they were understandably prone to highlight more obvious truths about the female presence in Congress. They noted that women were grossly under-represented in both chambers, that the gains made every two years were barely visible, that increases in the number of female state legislators were outstripping by far changes in Washington, and that, in spite of achievements recorded by the modern feminist movement, the future for women in Congress promised only incremental improvement.[1]

These were important observations, but, because they were emphasized in works published through the 1970s and 1980s, they obscured consequential changes in the life experiences congresswomen had been bringing with them to Washington. True, the number of women elected to the House had not increased dramatically, but the pool of eligibles from which they emerged had.[2] This enlarged population produced congresswomen who possessed more impressive political skills than was evident among their predecessors. As a result, when they arrived in the House, male colleagues had reason to be less skeptical about these women's efforts to adapt to the demands of congressional life. Moreover, patterns of adaptation by many recent congresswomen have reflected less inhibiting gender and legislative role orientations than were exhibited by female Representatives in the past. These latter developments will be dealt with in subsequent chapters. Here attention will be given to changes in the socioeconomic and political backgrounds congresswomen have brought to the House over time.

After inspecting these characteristics, it is evident that there has been a gradual transformation in the social, economic, and political resources that successful female candidates have been able to aggregate and exploit. The intimate association women have with their congressmen-husbands, once the principal advantage benefitting most women entering the House, is no longer as serviceable an asset relative to other resources congresswomen have been able to employ. Wives who share the name, the offspring, the values, the lifestyle, the friendships, and the organizational (or auxiliary) affiliations of male Representatives are still possible recruits for House seats, but they have lost the dominance they once had in their access to House membership. Today, female aspirants to Congress are capitalizing on other life experiences to take them to Washington, and party leaders and voters seem to be more inclined than they once were to support women who offer something other than a marital affiliation with men who were Representatives before they died.

Change in the precongressional experience of congresswomen and in the resources on which they rely means that the process by which women are recruited to the House has been materially altered, and that the accessibility of women to the House has improved markedly.[3] Criteria used to evaluate female candidates have become less particularized to women, and those elected to the House since mid-century more commonly moved through all four of the recruitment stages defined by Prewitt, not just the first and fourth. They passed from "eligible" to political "activist," to congressional "apprentice," to House "candidate," with the third stage more and more frequently taking the form of an elected office at the local or state level. At the same time that female accessibility to Congress has become more universal, a larger number of women have become "available" for House candidacy. This means they are ready to assume the risks and costs associated with conducting a professional campaign (perhaps because their chances of winning have improved); they are predisposed to subordinate other (personal and domestic) interests to those of holding a legislative seat if they win; and they are prepared to return to private callings with a minimum of disorientation should they lose (Czudnowski 1975, p. 200).

Six background characteristics of congresswomen are traced, aggregated, and examined below. Each of the six tells us something about the resources these women were able to employ to win a seat in Congress, and an analysis of each allows inferences to be drawn about changes that have occurred in "what it takes" for women to win a House contest. One of the six is great personal wealth. A second is a family with established political credentials. The importance of money in politics needs no elaboration here, although too much of it indiscreetly employed can be a liability. The value of having relatives, including fathers, brothers, uncles, and husbands who have etched the family name and reputation on the hearts and minds of voters is also obvious. Legal training and experience in elective office, the third and fourth characteristics, may also be useful resources for those who can boast of them. The first acquaints the recipient with the language of the law, hones rhetorical and reasoning faculties, and transmits other skills useful for projecting a productive legislative career. The second means that the candidate has already been a winner, that she has represented constituents, and that she is in a position to claim an exemplary public record upon which to run.

Age at the time of first election to the House is important because it says something about a congresswoman's vitality (although no formula has yet been devised to establish the relationship between chronological age and performance), and because it gives us some idea of whether she will serve in the House long enough to wield more influence than is denoted by a simple "yea" or "nay." And marital status, a characteristic all but meaningless for gauging the political assets of males, is important for women because of voter predispositions about traditional gender roles, and because of gender-related constraints politically active women often impose on themselves. A married woman, much more than a married man or a single woman, is expected to assume family responsibilities which frequently clash with goals defined by her political ambition.

There is, of course, no necessary relationship between any one of these characteristics (or all of them taken together) and electoral success. On the other hand, a person who, for example, has not held elective office is unable to rely on the political credibility that comes with winning at least one election, or on an existing, presumably approving constituency. She can claim neither a demonstrable record of achievement nor a promise of future success realistic enough to attract the attention of party leaders and campaign contributors. Potential command of a resource, then, is an important attribute of candidacy.

Discussed below are data revealing the extent to which congresswomen elected between 1916 and 1992 possessed these qualities. Inferences are then drawn about these would-be Representatives' use of the resources at their disposal and the criteria leaders and voters employed when evaluating successful women's candidacies. The patterns revealed will be interpreted in terms of changes in the accessibility women have had to the congressional opportunity structure and changes in the availability of women for House office.

CONGRESSWOMEN FROM POLITICAL AND WEALTHY FAMILIES

Being the wife of a former House member is not the only family link congresswomen have had with the world of politics. The parents and other close relatives of many of them held public or prominent party office both inside and outside of Washington. Of course this linkage is not limited to women. Between 20 and 25 percent of the men elected to the first five Congresses had relatives who had served in the Continental Congress or who had preceded them in the House or Senate (Clubok et al. 1969, p. 1043). This figure has declined considerably since those early years of the Republic, but family connections continue to be serviceable springboards to the national legislature.[4]

Substantial wealth also seems to be characteristic of many representatives, a far larger proportion than one would expect if seats in the House were filled randomly from among the adult population over twenty-five years of age. This should come as no surprise since money, like family connections, is a valuable political resource and often, even more than family ties, contributes to the electoral success of those who have it. In 1994, for example, 4 percent of House members reported a net worth of $5 million or more, with a total of 17 percent topping $1 million—a sum beyond the reach of 99 percent of the population (*Roll Call*, June 30, 1994). Over the years, the wealth controlled by well-to-do congresswomen has not always been their own, but whether it came from affluent parents, generous husbands, or their own enterprise, it must surely have been put to some use when they sought office.

One might assume, then, that the significant financial resources of future congresswomen and their families are useful in explaining their recruitment to the House. We would expect affluence and political activism to have affected the social development of these women early in their lives and, at the same time, to have reduced the impact of gender role prescriptions to which they were almost certainly exposed. These prescriptions tended to discourage women from taking an active part in politics, let alone considering a political career, and encouraged them to leave the world of politics to men (Kirkpatrick 1974, p. 15).

It would follow, then, that congresswomen who were members of wealthy or politically well-connected families, more easily than women whose families were politically inert or without significant financial resources, ignored or coped well with the social and psychological penalties that are often the consequence of nonconformity. In spite of gender role constraints, they sought and won national office. Intimate exposure to politicians and wealth probably offset, if it did not supersede, their status as females.[5]

A systematic examination of the backgrounds of congresswomen suggests, however, that while family wealth or roots in electoral politics may have once been critical to their recruitment to the House, such factors are not as important today.[6] The evidence for this inference is presented in Table 3.1. The table groups all women into four time periods, categorizing them according to the years in which they were initially elected. The columns divide them into those whose families were politically active and those whose families were wealthy, with congresswomen having both characteristics included in both columns. Congresswomen who succeeded their husbands in office are excluded from this discussion, as they are from the analyses in the remainder of the chapter.

Table 3.1
Congresswomen from Political and Wealthy Families, 1917–1993

Congresses (years)	Women from Political families		Women from Wealthy families		All* Congresswomen
	N	%	N	%	
65th-76th (1917-1940)	6	50	4	33	12
77th-88th (1941-1964)	4	17	2	8	24
89th-98th (1965-1982)	5	17	1	3	30
99th-103rd (1983-1993)	6	15	2	5	41

*Jeannette Rankin is counted twice, once in the first time period , once in the second, Chase Going Woodhouse is counted twice in the second time period, and Patsy Mink is counted once in the third period and once in the fourth. Each served nonconsecutive terms.

As the table makes clear, decline in the potential importance of family connections and private wealth in securing a House seat is precipitate. In the earliest period, one of every two congresswomen was able to capitalize on family connections. Many Floridians, for example, knew that Ruth Bryan Owen was the daughter of William Jennings Bryan, and, in Illinois, a large number of voters must have known that Ruth Hanna McCormick was the daughter of President-maker Marc Hanna, as well as the wife of the late Senator Medill McCormick.

Their successors were considerably less able as a group to take advantage of a family name. The proportions drop sharply to 17 percent between 1941 and 1982, and to 15 percent after 1982. One recent example of a congress-woman who reflected the earlier pattern is Helen Meyner. She had never served in public office before she was elected to the House in 1974. Her husband's two terms as Governor of New Jersey laid the groundwork for her success. The more common pattern in recent years was exhibited by Barbara Kennelly of Connecticut and Susan Molinari of New York. Kennelly's father, John Bailey, was Democratic State Chairman in Connecticut and a one-time Democratic National Chairman. But his daughter earned her political spurs while serving on the Hartford Court of Common Council and, later, as Connecticut Secretary of State. Molinari was a member of the New York City Council before succeeding her father in Congress after he had been elected Staten Island Borough President.

Thus, the importance of family connections is diluted when a distinction is made between well-connected congresswomen who had not held public office in the past and those who were elected to at least one such office before they obtained a seat in the House. Five of the six congresswomen sent to the House between 1916 and 1940 and whose families were involved in politics were electoral novices. During the years that followed, there was an increase in the proportion of congresswomen who could boast of both family connections and prior electoral success. Between 1941 and 1964, only Jeannette Rankin offered both. But four of the five well-connected congress-women who served between 1965 and 1982 and five of the six elected since then shared that characteristic.[7]

Consequently, the decrease in the proportion of women able to rely on family connections to gain a seat in the House does not mean that the asset is no longer usable. It is apparent, however, that recent congresswomen found additional resources upon which to build a successful campaign.

Significant wealth has been a scarcer commodity than family connections for female Representatives, although one-third elected between 1917 and 1940 had access to it. Among them were Ruth Baker Pratt and Caroline O'Day, both of New York and both privy to fabulous wealth from oil and other investments. The decline in congresswomen with abundant financial holdings is more precipitate than the drop in the proportion of women with family connections, and the former seem to have become all but a vanishing breed. The one multimillionaire among the women elected between 1965 and 1982, Millicent Fenwick, came to the House in 1975. Her net worth was about $5 million, the lower limit established here to define "multimillion-aire." Since then, only California's Nancy Pelosi and Jane Harman met that standard. Unlike Fenwick, however, they had never been elected to public office before their successful House campaigns.

THE INCIDENCE OF HOUSE LAWYERS

One of the more constant features of the American political system is the legal training of so many of its politicians. The law degree has been the most common professional credential acquired by public office holders, particu-larly those who rise to the highest levels. There is no shortage of explana-tions for this phenomenon (Czudnowski 1975, pp. 204–210), and the House of Representatives, at least as much as any legislative body in the country, has had its share of attorneys.[8]

That few women lawyers came to the House before World War II should come as no surprise, given the small proportion of females admitted to the bar during this period. After the War, however, women lawyers began to make up a larger share of female House members. The information in Table 3.2 indicates that whereas 17 percent of all congresswomen elected before 1940 had acquired legal training, the proportion climbed to one of every three serving their first terms between 1965 and 1982. The bulk of the increase occurred between 1970 and 1978, when eight of the seventeen new women coming to Washington had been to law school. Beginning in 1983, however, only five of forty-one new congresswomen were lawyers.

At first blush, this decline is puzzling. On the one hand it can be seen as a temporary drop in a long-term upward trend. With law schools admitting higher and higher proportions of women, one would expect women lawyers to approach the proportion of men lawyers in all private and public arenas—Congress included.[9] The fact that four of the five lawyers elected during the latest time period began their House tenure as recently as 1993 provides an additional sign that the percentage of women lawyers among future Representatives will grow.

On the other hand, there are three reasons why a return to an upward spiral may be more than a few years away. One is that the most recent generation of women lawyers has been receiving more attractive offers from private law firms and corporations than was available to their predecessors. The discouraging 1950s job-seeking experience of Supreme Court Justice Ruth Bader Ginsburg is well known, and it is difficult to contemplate a similar rebuff for a 1990s woman who made Law Review at an Ivy League law school. Thus, attractive opportunities in the private sector may discourage ambitious, would-be women lawyers from entering public life.

Second, women who aspire to Congress now find legal training to be only one of an increasing number of vocational pathways open to them. For many, the three years of law school and the struggle either to establish a

Table 3.2
Lawyers among Congresswomen, 1917–1993

Congresses (years)	Women Lawyers	%	All* Congresswomen
65th-76th (1917-1940)	2	17	12
77th-88th (1941-1964)	5	21	24
89th-98th (1965-1982)	10	33	30
99th-103rd (1983-1993)	5	12	41

*Jeannette Rankin is counted twice, once in the first time period , once in the second, Chase Going Woodhouse is counted twice in the second time period, and Patsy Mink is counted once in the third period and once in the fourth. Each served nonconsecutive terms.

practice or to become a partner in an existing firm sap time and energy that could be otherwise invested in community and partisan activities and in a political apprenticeship that possibly includes state or local office. These public positions, rather than legal training and experience, have become more serviceable springboards to congressional office—a finding that will be documented below. Moreover, it is conceivable that women bent on a political career will be less able than men to combine a law practice with precongressional public service until their spouses are more fully prepared to share child care and other family responsibilities.

Finally, women lawyers who seek public office may find the prospect of a judgeship—currently more attainable for women than was once the case—an option preferable to the irregular working hours and the negative election campaigns that are part of legislative life.[10]

PRIOR POLITICAL EXPERIENCE

Although prior experience in a state, county, or local public office is not a prerequisite for service in Congress, more representatives have stopped at these way stations than have bypassed them en route to the House. Analysts may differ about what exactly constitutes a "public office," but if we define it strictly as any government position to which one must be elected, we have a reasonably well-delineated, even if not comprehensive, definition of the term. And although this more specific meaning reduces considerably the number of House members who may lay claim to prior public office, the figure has not dropped below 60 percent since the end of World War II. At times, it has risen well above 70 percent.[11]

A number of reasons have been offered to explain this pattern (Czudnowski 1975, p. 187; Lasswell 1954, p. 222), but, whatever their bases, the high incidence of representatives who held prior elective offices has only recently begun to manifest itself among congresswomen. Table 3.3 reports the percentages of these women who had been elected to government office before they went to Congress. It further distributes them according to the four time periods established above. Before World War II, about two in five (42%) of the congresswomen had been elected to a public office before they were elevated to the House. Over the years this percentage has increased significantly. Among the thirty women elected to the House for the first time between 1964 and 1982, two-thirds had successfully sought voter support in a previous campaign for office. During the decade that followed, the figure rose to 73 percent.

Of course, elected office is not the only position in which would-be House members might learn and demonstrate the range of qualities making them viable candidates for Congress. Experience in appointed office and leadership positions within the major political parties may be just as likely as occupying an elective office to provide congressional aspirants with the

Table 3.3
The Incidence of Prior Election to Government Office among Congresswomen,
1917–1993

Congresses (years)	Women who held prior elective office	%	All* Congresswomen
65th-76th (1917-1940)	5	42	12
77th-88th (1941-1964)	12	50	24
89th-98th (1965-1982)	20	67	30
99th-103rd (1983-1993)	30	73	41

*Jeannette Rankin is counted twice, once in the first time period , once in the second,
Chase Going Woodhouse is counted twice in the second time period, and Patsy Mink
is counted once in the third period and once in the fourth. Each served nonconsecutive
terms.

appropriate skills, political orientations, proximity to decision-making centers, visibility, and credibility.[12]

But elective experience is clearly in a class by itself. Normally it means
that one must appeal for public support and counter the competition of
stipulated antagonists. Far more than almost any other experience that
could conceivably lead to membership in the House, elections require
public exposure; they involve greater psychic and material risks; they
normally demand more time, energy, and sacrifice of private, nonpolitical
goals; and usually the rewards are more desirable. For these reasons, an
increase in the proportion of congresswomen who have had prior experience in elected office is noteworthy, and, as will be suggested below, this
development has important implications for both their rate of integration
into the workings of the House and for the legislative behavior in which
they subsequently engage.

AGE AND MARITAL STATUS

Among the few studies that touch on the age of women in politics there
is general agreement that females normally seek elective office later in life
than do males. The phenomenon of "older women running against younger
men is especially common at the local level where male candidates in their
late twenties are not unusual but where women candidates under thirty-
five are virtually unknown" (Smith 1976, p. 67; Carroll 1993, p. 200).

The same pattern has occurred at the national level, as well. First-term congresswomen as a group have tended to be older than first-term House members generally. The median age of all new Representatives from the early years of this century until 1960 was forty-five (Oleszek 1969, p. 101). The comparable figure for congresswomen was forty-nine, an age which does not change even when women who succeeded their husbands are excluded from the calculation.

As Table 3.4 makes clear, first-term women elected to the House between WWII and the early 1980s came to Washington markedly younger than the women who preceded them. The decline was steady and relatively uniform over the forty-year period. It was reversed during the next ten years, however. Part of this most recent change can be understood as an aging trend among all first-term House members. Between 1965 and 1982, the median age of all new members was 40, compared with a median age of 43 for women. The median for all new members increased to 44 between 1983 and 1994, a period which witnessed a six-year rise among new female House members. The "spread" between all first-termers and fledgling congresswomen went from three years to five years, not a small variation, but the change mitigates the sharper, six-year shift reflected in Table 3.4.

A more comprehensive explanation for the table's irregular age variations is available, however. Female Representatives elected in the earliest years tended to be unmarried women who had reached retirement age, like 66-year-old Alice Robertson, or women who had been widowed late in life. By the 1940s, and especially by the 1970s, an increasing number of younger, married women secured House seats. They were relatively unaffected by expectations about traditional roles they should be fulfilling as wives and

Table 3.4
Median Age and Marital Status of Congresswomen Who Did Not Succeed Their Husbands, 1917–1993

Congresses (years)	Median Age	*Percent Marital Status*					
		Single	Married	Widowed	Separated-Divorced	Divorced & Remarried	N
65th-76th (1917-1940)	49	33	17	50	0	0	12
77th-88th (1941-1964)	46	17	67	17	0	0	24
89th-98th (1965-1982)	43	17	67	7	7	3	30
99th-103rd (1983-1993)	49	7	51	5	20	17	41

mothers. At the same time, the proportion of women who found congressional careers late in life, after their husbands had died, declined and were replaced by younger single women, such as Elizabeth Holtzman, Barbara Jordan, and Barbara Mikulski. Some of these patterns were repeated during the 1980s and early 1990s, particularly with respect to the youthfulness of single congresswomen. The small number of older, widowed women elected since 1982 also fits the pattern reflected during the preceding forty years.

What is different is the large increase in the proportion of new congresswomen who had been divorced and the sizable number among them who had remarried by the time they came to Washington. The figures under "marital status" in Table 3.4 document the emergence of this trend, and suggest three inferences. First, they indicate that women are elected to the House today in spite of significant disruptions in their private lives, disruptions that take the form of leaving (or being left by) a spouse, constructing ways of bringing up children in a divided household, and seeking and finding another mate.

Second, disruptions of their private lives have impeded the pace at which these women pursued their political ambitions and, as a result, they arrived in the House older than those with whom they were initially elected to Congress. And this development may help explain the recent increase in the median age for congresswomen. That age for the five divorced women elected between 1965 and 1982 was forty-three, the same as that for all women elected during those years. But the median age of the fifteen divorced women elected between 1983 and 1992 was fifty-two, four years higher than the median age of the twenty-six non-divorcees elected during the same period.

Finally, if some party leaders and voters are penalizing female House candidates for their unorthodox, sometimes rancorous, domestic lives, then these traditionalists are waging a losing battle. That divorced mothers are being elected to Congress at all means that much of the public has modified the criteria they employ when evaluating would-be congresswomen. And these women now collectively reflect roughly the same range (although not necessarily the same proportion) of marital relationships as that found in the population as a whole.

Not revealed in the table is that many of the married women elected since 1964 had a least one child under the age of seventeen, and several of the divorced women were caring for elementary school children. Based on available evidence, about 30 percent of the forty-one congresswomen elected between 1982 and 1992 were mothers of children under the age of 18. This means that more women are running successfully for House seats undeterred by responsibilities they bear as wives (or companions), mothers, and homemakers. More generally it suggests that the conflict between political and traditional family obligations has been less of an obstacle to would-be congresswomen in recent years than it was in years past.

IMPLICATIONS OF CHANGING RECRUITMENT PATTERNS

The findings presented here have accented changes in the backgrounds of congresswomen who have come to Washington during the last three-quarters of a century. The House has witnessed a gradual reduction in the proportion of women who succeeded to the seats of deceased spouses. There has been a decline, as well, in the percentage of congresswomen who could capitalize upon substantial family wealth or upon their identification with family members who had already made their way in politics. In the meantime, legal training has become a less common feature of new women House members, after a temporary upturn in the 1970s, while prior election to state and local office has become a more significant component of the credentials congresswomen relied upon to achieve their ambitions. Recently elected congresswomen are also more likely than earlier female Representatives to have current, former or alternative spouses, along with school-age offspring.

The aggregate figures upon which these conclusions are based provide neither direct nor comprehensive insight into the changing recruitment patterns of female House members. Still, some conclusions can be drawn on the basis of circumstantial evidence. Changes over time in typical social and political characteristics of congresswomen invite generalizations about the nature of these changes and about their implications.

A More Inclusive Structure of Political Opportunity

Even the casual observer of American politics is aware of the nonrandom process by which public offices are filled. While virtually all adult citizens are legally eligible to hold these offices, few have an *effective political opportunity* to do so. Most people possess neither the advantages associated with high social status nor the abundant resources by which Seligman et al. (1974) define *effective political opportunity*. These authors are concerned not with whether citizens may legally run for public office but whether they can do so as a practical matter. They state that "the boundaries of *effective political opportunity*" correspond with "the characteristics of those nominated and elected compared with the characteristics of the excluded." These characteristics are defined by the social structure, with such factors as family background, occupation and education influencing the process by which people are made aware of and encouraged to capitalize on political opportunities. They also have an impact on the extent to which people have the wherewithal to pursue their opportunities effectively.

These factors, in short, affect predispositions to political involvement and aspiration. The competition among party leaders and political groups, in turn, "creates vacancies that attract the predisposed to run" for office

(Seligman et al. 1974, pp. 16–17). When this frame of reference is applied to the groups of women who have held House seats, it seems clear that the structure of effective political opportunity has become more inclusive over the years.

Among the social characteristics and resources a candidate may convert into political success, money, family connections, professional training, and political experience are the most important. The extent to which each of these characteristics contributes to victory is likely to vary in time, place, and circumstance. But when successful candidates possessing one combination of these characteristics are regularly replaced by candidates who exhibit a discernibly different set of characteristics, it is reasonable to assume that an important change has taken place in the boundaries of the effective political opportunity structure. And the information presented above indicates that such a change has occurred.

In many and perhaps most respects, recent congresswomen do not differ markedly from earlier female House members. Almost all experienced a degree of financial security and educational training that was inaccessible to the vast majority of their female contemporaries. Almost all grew up within a milieu of social activism, if not political activism, and, if members of the earlier Congresses were initially uninterested in politics, they were likely to be alert to and knowledgeable about the world around them.

Where contemporary congresswomen tend to differ from their predecessors is in the nature of the resources that contributed significantly to their election to Congress. Most earlier congresswomen seem to have been elected to office partially on the strength of their considerable wealth or their families' political connections. These connections may have been established by either marital or kinship ties. But whatever the basis of the nexus, the political advantages these attributes generated called attention to their candidacies.

Although several women have been able to convert family connections and wealth into a House seat in recent years, most contemporary women have relied on a quite different set of resources. Until recently, many depended upon legal training to provide them with the skills and expertise helpful for securing office, and some still do. However, many more have depended upon first-hand elective experience, a career asset that promotes opportunities, habits of thought, and patterns of behavior valuable both to the candidate appealing for public support and to a House member interested in expanding upon support already mobilized.

In sum, it seems reasonable to conclude that, in the past, women Representatives relied upon those attributes of their candidacies linked to ascribed characteristics—wealth, family affiliation, and social standing. More recent female House members, by contrast, have relied more upon discernable vocational and political achievements, merits suggesting virtuosity in such political skills as organization, communication, bargaining, and policy expertise. The shift from a recruitment pattern that places a high value on achievement in place of ascribed characteristics both reflects and presages a democratization of the recruitment process. In Seligman's terms, the effective political opportunity structure today is accessible to a wider range of women than it was in the past.

Increased Availability of Women

The great majority of Americans choose not to make themselves available for recruitment to public office. They are unable either to seek or accept full- or part-time political office and they cannot contemplate returning to their occupations after filling that office temporarily. This is often the case because their principal occupations do not permit them sufficient flexibility to do so, or because the economic or psychic price they must pay for doing so is unacceptable (Czudnowski 1975, p. 200). The findings presented in this chapter indicate that the process by which women have been recruited to House office has undergone important change not only with respect to the structure of effective political opportunity open to them, but in the extent to which they have become *available* for congressional office, as well. Before World War II, congresswomen were not subject to the obligations normally borne by the female adult in a traditional nuclear family because almost all were either unmarried or widows. After the Second World War, however, the proportion of married congresswomen began to increase significantly. In the 1990s, married women with young children are undeterred from seeking office by the constraints imposed by their roles as wives and mothers.

It is evident, therefore, that the male monopoly on the flexibility needed to seek and hold office has been eroded in recent years and that the availability of House office is now devolving on larger numbers of women. The full range of maternal and domestic obligations until recently performed almost exclusively by mothers and wives has apparently come to be shared, delegated, hired-out, or indefinitely postponed by would-be congresswomen far more than was possible in the past. And the conditions under which women may become available for office have expanded no less dramatically than has the effective political opportunity structure through which they must pass.

Both of these developments are important because the recruitment process serves as a critical link between society and the polity. When a process that systematically discriminates against persons possessing clearly definable social and economic characteristics is altered to permit their inclusion in the political system, the fidelity of this link is likely to be improved. And, to the extent that the newly included citizens harbor perspectives and beliefs rarely expressed in national politics, the altered recruitment pattern becomes a more reliable channel for orderly change in a democratic political system.

Gaining seats in Congress by the formerly dispossessed is only the first step, however. There is no assurance that once in the House they will be treated as equals by other members, that they will aspire to and gain positions of influence, and that they will use that influence to articulate values and beliefs that had been ignored because people like themselves were once excluded from Congress. In the chapters that follow, attention will be given to the pace at which female Representatives have been integrated into the House over the years, and to the distinctive patterns of behavior they followed while fulfilling legislative responsibilities.

NOTES

This chapter is a revised version of an article appearing in volume IV, number 3 (August, 1979) of *Legislative Studies Quarterly*. The author is grateful to the editors of that publication for permission to reprint it here.

1. One or more of these points are developed in Werner 1966; Gehlen 1969; Amundsen 1971; Bullock and Heys 1972; Tolchin and Tolchin 1974; Lynn 1975; Diamond 1977; Lee 1977; Buchanan 1978; Mandel 1981; Rule 1981; Andersen and Thorson 1984; Benze and Declerq, 1985; Carroll 1985; Bernstein 1986; Burrell 1988, 1992; Rule and Norris 1992; and Fowler 1993.

2. One study of congresswomen's changing background characteristics is Thompson (1985). She compares these changes with shifts in the experiences of male Representatives.

3. Czudnowski (1975) provides a comprehensive treatment of political recruitment. Discussions and applications of the concept by Prewitt (1970), Seligman et al. (1974), and Matthews (1985) are also useful. The term is defined here as those experiences undergone by members of a society that contribute to their induction into the specialized roles of the political system, their training in the appropriate political skills, and their acquisition of political cognitive maps, values, expectations, and affects. Almond and Coleman (1960, p. 31) give this meaning to the term when applying it cross-nationally.

4. Hess (1966) reports that 700 families have had two or more members serve in Congress. These families account for seventeen percent of all senators and representatives who served from 1774 to the mid-1960s.

5. On these points see especially Kelly and Boutilier 1978, Chapters 4 and 5.

6. The sources for biographical information about these women include Chamberlin (1973); *Current Biography Yearbooks, 1940–1992*; Edward T. James, ed., *Notable American Women, 1607–1950* (1971); *Biographical Dictionary of the American Congress, 1774–1989* (1989); and stories about congresswomen appearing in the *New York Times*, the *Washington Post*, *Congressional Quarterly Weekly Reports*, and *Roll Call*. The amount of wealth controlled by each congresswoman is impossible to document precisely. But it can be demonstrated that the following House members, grouped according to the time periods stipulated in Table 3.1 and in order of their initial elections, were "millionaires" (the criterion by which

"wealthy" Representatives were distinguished from other congresswomen). Widows elected to succeed their husbands are omitted.

65th-76th Congresses—McCormick, Pratt, Greenway, and O'Day;

77th-88th Congresses—St. George and Weis;

89th-98th Congresses—Fenwick;

99th-103rd Congresses—Pelosi, Harman.

Among those who emerged from "political families" and listed in the same order are:

65th-76th Congresses—Rankin, McCormick, Owen, Greenway, Honeyman, and Sumner;

77th-88th Congresses—Rankin, Luce, Harden, and Kelly;

89th-98th Congresses—Hicks, Meyner, Snowe, Kennelly, and N. Johnson;

99th-103rd Congress—Patterson, Pelosi, Molinari, Roybal-Allard, Fowler and McKinney.

7. The four serving between 1965 and 1982 are Louise Hicks, Olympia Snowe, Barbara Kennelly, and Nancy Johnson. The five elected since then are Molinari, Elizabeth Patterson, Lucille Roybal-Allard, Tillie Fowler and Cynthia McKinney.

8. Putnam (1976) notes that the United States has the highest proportion of lawyers in national office among all developed countries. From 1947 to 1967, 53 percent of all newly elected House members were lawyers (Bullock and Heys 1972). There has been an overall decline in first-term lawyers in recent years, however. Their proportions topped 50 percent only twice since 1967, most recently after the 1976 election. They fell below one-third after the 1984 and 1986 elections.

9. According to the U.S. Census Bureau's *Statistical Abstract*, women made up less than 3 percent of the legal profession through the 1960s. The figure rose dramatically during the 1970s and 1980s, and by 1992 approached 30 percent.

10. In 1980, women constituted about 5 percent of federal court justices and little more than two percent of state appellate and trial court justices (Epstein 1981). Both figures increased appreciably in ensuing years, with the latter tripling between 1981 and 1991 (Baum 1994, p. 144).

11. During the years between 1947 and 1967, for example, about three of five new members of the House had served in some elective government office (Bullock and Heys 1972). In the 1970s, 1980s, and early 1990s the percentage did not drop below that figure and it frequently exceeded 70 percent.

12. Two congresswomen with formidable political skills who did not serve in elected office before coming to Congress are Nancy Pelosi and Jennifer Dunn. Pelosi served as chair of the California State Democratic Party before being named Finance Committee chair of the Democratic Senatorial Campaign Committee in 1986. Dunn was chair of the Washington State Republican Committee for twelve years before her election to the House.

Part III

Integration

4

Women in the House:
Incremental Integration

The changing pathways women have taken to get to the House and their improved preparation for legislative tasks have been accompanied by a more respectful reception from contemporary male colleagues whose own orientations toward women in politics have come to differ significantly from those of the men who preceded them. Congressmen tended to be polite and effusively deferential to congresswomen prior to World War II, demonstrating little inclination to take them seriously. Since mid-century, female lawmakers have commanded (and male members have manifested) more professional respect, and they have had more opportunities to carve out legislative reputations of their own. Yet, in spite of some dramatic changes, women are only now beginning to be fully integrated into the House.

The next three chapters consider changes in the relationships congress-women have developed with male Representatives. They describe the extent to which these women have been accepted by congressmen as equals—that is, the degree to which women have been integrated into House routines, the extent to which they have become party to deliberations in informal groups and caucuses, and the frequency with which they have gained access to formal leadership posts. This chapter explores changes in the way congressmen have perceived and related to female colleagues during the course of their daily activities. It begins with an account of how the earliest congresswomen were received by their male colleagues and discusses the transformation in male-female relationships through the 1970s and into the 1990s. The chapter also deals with the perceptions recent congresswomen have had of male behavior toward them as women and colleagues, and their reactions to discrimination based upon gender. The next chapter traces the progress congresswomen have made in securing access to informal channels of communication. Chapter 6 documents and discusses the frequency with which congresswomen have gained entry to House leadership positions.

THE EARLY YEARS

Information about the relationship between male and female House members in years past is difficult to come by, inasmuch as few scholars have devoted attention to the subject and Representatives themselves normally found little reason either to dwell on the subject or commit their thoughts on the matter to writing. Based upon the scanty documentary evidence available, before World War II, female lawmakers were seen by reporters, male colleagues, and government officals as amateurs and curiosities rather than as authentic public figures.

The press was probably the principal purveyor of this unfortunate image, although it was almost certainly catering to the well-established preconceptions of its readers. Reporters were more likely to discuss attributes of female House members associated with their being female than they were to cover women's performance as legislators. Editors and writers of the period defined as oddities women who undertook what were considered to be male pursuits and they were inclined, as was most of the public, to use different criteria to explain and evaluate both the presence and the performance of females in a field for which women were expected to have little competence (Comstock 1926, p. 379).

The press simply did not cover women politicians in the same way as they covered men in public life and congresswomen were asked questions exploring purportedly "female topics," questions that male Representatives were almost never asked. Their views on most national issues and events were rarely solicited, and their unusual status was given far more attention than anything worthwhile they had to say (Blair 1927, p. 542). Soon after Jeannette Rankin was elected, she received scores of marriage proposals in the mail, and a toothpaste company offered her $5,000 for a photograph of her teeth.[1]

Even as late as the mid-1940s, women candidates were subjected to unconventional queries. At a press conference held during her first House campaign, Helen Gahagan Douglas found attention paid to her hat (photographers said it was too large), her knees (which were revealed when she sat down in a tight skirt), the color of her eyes, and what she would wear when she addressed the Democratic National Convention. Only a few questions dealt with her political views (Douglas 1982, p. 196).

The image of the congresswoman as a curiosity appears to have influenced the treatment she received from male Representatives. She was patronized, condescended to, and ignored or dismissed by her colleagues, depending upon which of the House rituals was called for by the legislative "script." The swearing-in ceremony for women was greeted with considerably more applause and patronizing comment than was the case for men. Winnifred Mason Huck, the third woman to serve in the House, recalled how she received a bouquet of flowers from Alice Robertson, the only other woman serving at the time, and the enthusiastic reaction of her fellow House members when she was escorted up to the Speaker's Chair to take the oath of office (Huck 1923, p. 4). Of course the effusiveness of the response could be explained by the fact that she was replacing her recently deceased father, a man well known and admired by many of her new colleagues. But it is hard to imagine so festive an air if, for example, William Mason's son had been succeeding him.

After they began their legislative service, congresswomen were often treated to oratorical excesses which heaped lavish praise upon them and others of their gender. "To the ladies, God bless them; they lend sweetness and light to our somber legislative halls" was among the choicest bouquets tossed in their direction. On one occasion Mary Norton of New Jersey was so exasperated by these comments that she cried out "I'm no lady. I'm a congressman" (Porter 1943, p. 22). The New Jersey Democrat could not have been pleased when a Republican whose position she had attacked replied: "We can, dear lady, reason with you only with our hearts, not our minds" (Davis 1943).

Some House members used the advent of women in their membership as an occasion for demonstrating just how gallant they could be. Queen Guinevere could not have been attended by a more chivalrous array of courtiers. A veteran Capitol Hill writer Duff Gilfond described the scene in this way:

The courtly Speaker [Nicholas Longworth] set the precedent. Tenderly referring to the new female members as gentlewomen, he created an atmosphere in which every politician in the House turned into a knight. To greet a gentlewoman's request or recitation with anything less than applause would now cause a sensation. Some time ago . . . veterans of the rowdyish Tammany Hall actually withdrew an amendment to a tax bill so that the gentlewoman from New Jersey, Mrs. Norton, could have the privilege of introducing it; and the hard-hitting [Fiorello] LaGuardia, after a recitation by Gentlewoman Ruth Owen confessed: "If it were not for the irresistible appeal made by the charming Representative from the State of Florida, I would object; but under the circumstances, I cannot."

Gilfond added:

So gallant are these rascals on the floor that nobody would think of taking them to task for the unimportant committee assignments they hand out to the girls. (Gilfond 1929, p. 151)

Even if Gilfond may have overstated the case (some women did, after all, receive important committee assignments during this period), the moments of legitimate female glory in the 1920s, 1930s, and 1940s were few indeed. When the leaders of the House decided to permit a woman to preside over that chamber for the first time, they chose to make it while a roll-call vote was underway and, therefore, when the temporary "Speaker" was unable to exercise any of the powers accompanying the position. Feminist observers were outraged both by the patronizing manner with which the ritual was carried out and the inconsequential issue at stake. One wrote:

They were calling the roll on a vote to send a representative from the United States to the Peruvian Centennial. Momentous occasion! And "Sister Alice Robertson, the lady from Oklahoma," was allowed to stand up like a little man and hold the gavel in her hand all by herself for one brief moment! Wonderful privilege! But before anyone could address her as "Miss Speaker," it was all over. (Clarke 1925, p. 95)

Critics were anguished not only at the perfunctory nature of the event and the fact that Representative Robertson had permitted herself to be used in this way. They were incensed, as well, by the fact that Robertson had been among the strongest opponents of the 19th Amendment and they believed there were women far more deserving of recognition than she.

But most of the time congresswomen seem to have been ignored or simply dismissed as unimportant by other Representatives, as well as by official Washington. Their status as House members was devalued by men as high up in the capital's pecking order as the President and as low down as House doorkeepers, guards, pages, and elevator operators. Winnifred Mason Huck could not find a place to powder her nose, in spite of the fact that she had learned all about Capitol Hill while her father was serving in the House and the Senate (Huck 1923), and leaders of her party "took a dim view of lady members at the working level." These men "don't dispute woman's right to run for election and serve," said one Washington observer, "But they privately believe few women possess the political savvy, shrewdness and, above all, the level-headed qualities needed to function properly as a party legislator" (Lockett 1950).

Stories are legion of congresswomen who were told that they could not come on to the House floor or enter certain elevators because they were "reserved for members" (see Wiley 1947, p. 155, for example). According to Republican leader Joseph Martin, women who were not members were sometimes inadvertently permitted on the floor because the men guarding the doors to the chamber were so uncertain about who the congresswomen were. Several women of distinguished appearance and carriage were permitted to penetrate the inner sanctum, even though they were not lawmakers. Martin describes some of what he calls the "strange things" that occurred in the House during his first fifty years in politics:

I can see some of them distinctly in my memory: The woman dressed in pure white, who suddenly appeared in the center aisle, and walked majestically to the well of the House, hoping to deliver a message. Another mysterious woman dressed in pure black who slipped past a doorkeeper and took a seat on the Democratic side in such dignity that no one at first could be sure whether she was a member of congress or not, even though she had not been seen there before. (Martin 1960, p. 212)

Even an embattled President Franklin Roosevelt, seeking to mend his fences with a hostile Congress, forgot the congresswomen. Late in 1938, the White House arranged for the President to meet with all congressional Democrats to mark the close of the 75th Congress, a Congress that had been deeply divided over administration proposals to increase membership of the Supreme Court and reorganize the federal bureaucracy. The place chosen for the three-day bash was the Jefferson Island Club, situated on a Maryland Island retreat used by Senator Millard Tydings. There, about 400 Senate and House Democrats were expected to exchange pleasantries with the President, smooth over personal antagonisms developed in the last Congress, and produce the kind of party unity needed to successfully contest the imminent mid-term congressional elections.

The fact that the Jefferson Island Club excluded women was either unknown to the White House or deemed insufficiently important, and a half dozen female Democrats were unable to attend the weekend gathering. This in spite of the fact that the New Deal credentials of most of the Democratic women were among the most authentic in Congress. They kept a stiff upper lip, however, and some suggested that the slight was a blessing. "We will have a chance to give him our views another time in less crowded circumstances," one woman said, "when we won't have to compete for his attention with all those males" (*New York Times*, June 17, 1938).

As the years passed, more women were elected to the House and an increasing proportion began to speak out in a bold, independent fashion. A few exercised some influence and their aggressiveness and power could not easily be ignored. Some of the men abandoned the gallantry exhibited earlier and resorted to harsher, more pointed means of putting congress-women in their place. When the outspoken "gentlewoman from Massa-chusetts," Edith Nourse Rogers, one day during debate asked if a male colleague would temporarily yield the floor, he responded with what he doubtless considered to be humor, as well as rancor: "Not now. It's not very often that we men are in a position where we can make the ladies sit down and keep quiet" (Wiley 1947, p. 157). The attitude of some males toward assertive women lawmakers is reflected in the observations of one-time Connecticut Senator Prescott Bush when referring to Clare Boothe Luce:

Clare—I've always been a little frightened of her, because I don't deal easily with women who are severe or terribly determined. . . . I've always been afraid of women who are pithy and sharp and sarcastic.[2]

But the statement which is perhaps most revealing of both male condescension and insensitivity to the feelings of congresswomen was made during the opening weeks of the 80th Congress, the first full Congress to convene after the end of World War II. The speaker was Charles Gifford of Massachusetts, one of the more senior and, at the time, respected members of the House. The statement is all the more remarkable because it appeared in the *Congressional Record* and Gifford presumably had had an opportunity to "revise and extend" his remarks before they were published. The speech is a rambling one, covering three pages of the Record, but most of the relevant portions are included in the following excerpt:

Mr. Speaker . . . I have my anxieties about the present Congress and the future, and as an older member, I am anxious to know what the new members will bring to us in abilities and opinion. As I look to my left, I see the face of a new lady member. I wish that all other lady members were present. May I say to her, one of the greatest worries I have in Congress itself is lest we have too many of you. Although I say this in a somewhat jocular way, still I am a little serious about it. The lady members we have today are extremely satisfactory to us. But they, like all women, can talk to us with their eyes and their lips, and when they present to us an apple it is most difficult to refuse. Even old Adam could not resist. Women have a language all their own. I do not like to particularize but I should. I see the gentlewoman from Ohio [Frances Payne Bolton] is present. I read or listen carefully to everything she says on the floor. . . . Because I admire her so much I could hardly resist. I fear supporting any measure that she would propose, especially if she looked at me as such a woman can. The gentlewoman from Maine [Margaret Chase Smith] . . . never seems to have a vacant chair beside her that I could take and get acquainted with her . . . these ladies are so attractive. They are dangerous in that they may influence us too much. Suppose we had fifty of them. Seemingly, I note flirtations enough now, but what would there be with fifty of them? (*Congressional Record* 1947, pp. 631–32)

A contemporary feminist could not concoct a statement which would more cogently document male sexism in high places than Gifford's. His harangue makes explicit or implicit reference to virtually all of the female stereotypes embraced by his contemporaries. These congresswomen are "satisfactory" to male needs. But they are also manipulating, enticing, conspiratorial, unreliable, flirtatious, and objects of physical appeal. That Gifford could make these kinds of allusions without thought, let alone fear, of being challenged is convincing testimony to the "male mentality" of the House of Representatives.

A few months later, Gifford was dead, stricken while still a member of Congress. But, before long, male Representatives began to see congresswomen in a different light, in part because the qualities of the women coming to the House had changed.

THE EXPERIENCE OF CONGRESSWOMEN IN THE 1970s

Testimony offered by two dozen male and female Representatives and by thirty-six Capitol Hill staff members during the 95th Congress in interviews provides a rich array of perceptions about the relationships between women and men serving in the House during the 1970s. Although there was an all but unanimous belief that the House was a male institution, these same respondents acknowledged that congresswomen were considerably better off than their predecessors. They were given more of a chance to participate as equals in the legislative process and their views were more likely to be respected than were those of earlier congresswomen. They were consulted often, they took the initiative on a wide range of issues, and they were valued for the efforts they brought to House tasks.

In the meantime, open condescension had diminished, fewer congressmen consciously attempted to patronize female members, and achievements recorded by many women Representatives made it impossible for them to be collectively ignored or dismissed. Several House members noted that remarkable changes had taken place in these respects even during the relatively few years in which they had served. Yet, in spite of these developments, virtually all respondents defined the House as a "male institution."

Perceptions of the House as a Male Institution

In the early 1970s, Jeane Kirkpatrick was commissioned by the Eagleton Institute's Center for the American Woman and Politics to interview a national sample of women state legislators. On the basis of these women's comments, she concluded that state "legislatures share the macho culture of the locker room, the smoker, the barracks." Among the folkways of these bodies, she said, "none appears to be more widely shared than the tradition of the *masculine* legislature" (Kirkpatrick 1974, p. 106; emphasis in original). Previous studies of state legislatures had similarly characterized them as "male clubs" (Epstein 1958; Sorauf 1963).[3]

Interviews with twenty-four members of the House during the 95th Congress leave little doubt that Representatives serving at the time, male as well as female, defined their legislative body as did their state counterparts.[4] A majority of the respondents stated that the House was becoming less "male" in many respects and that women were excluded from fewer activities and discussions than they once were. Some said that women were being accepted as equals more than had been the case in the past, and several noted that an increasing number of men were apt to define the

House in ways that had nothing to do with gender. However, all but a few believed that Kirkpatrick's characterization of state legislatures applied with almost equal force to the Congress, and that the House of Representatives, too, was a "male" institution.

The comments of one congresswoman in an interview provide perhaps the most representative female response:

It is there. I don't feel it that much, but there are indications that it is a male club. But that is true of most institutions that have so many men and so few women. I don't think it affects my service, but I don't think there is any question that many of the men sort of assume that Congress belongs to them.

The reasons respondents offered to explain the House's "maleness" varied, but among these explanations, four were offered often enough to warrant explicit mention. A majority was inclined to cite the large numbers of men and the small number of women as a principal reason for the House's male orientation. When they looked around at the members on the House floor, they saw an "army" of men and barely a "squad" of women. In committee, subcommittee, or state-delegation meetings, the lone female members were "lost in the crowd." By simply being around so many men and so few women, members could not help but think of the institution as essentially male in its orientation, as well as in its composition.

Many of the House members also suggested that the attitudes and behavior that make the House "male" were rooted in "the culture." Implicit in their remarks is the view that the American culture embodies behavioral norms which influence the way in which members of society define themselves as men or women. These norms encourage members of each group to engage in different sorts of activities, just as they impose limitations on what members of each may do. According to these respondents, political decision making in the United States has been a male enterprise. When men get together within a predominantly male legislative setting, a camaraderie develops based upon a common sense of mission, as well as upon other shared "male interests." If and when women enter that environment, they are considered intruders or outsiders and they may be ignored, treated courteously but dismissed, or treated with contempt or derision. In the view of many of the House members interviewed, therefore, the House was a male institution in the same way as business organizations, industrial labor unions, and other predominantly male political and economic organizations are male. A congressman who strongly agreed with this characterization of the House asserted that "we are *representative* of the country in the *worst*, as well as the best sense of that term" (emphasis in original).

A half-dozen male and female House members had an additional culture-related reason for the masculine character of the House, attributing the warmth and sense of camaraderie that men develop for one another specifically to "male bonding." One congressman said that he would not dream of asking most congresswomen to have a cup of coffee with him to "get away and simply talk shop," even though he was very friendly with a number of them. On the other hand, he would not give a second thought to asking any one of twenty-five or more different male members to take the same coffee break. Another male respondent put it this way:

Friendships bind men together in a way that women do not experience. There is a bonding, a male bonding that does it. The language we use, the drinking we do, make it very difficult for women to enter this world.

Finally, several male House members and two female members suggested that the House was a male institution because the behavior of many of the female members left observers inside and outside Congress little alternative but to perceive it as such. The behavior referred to took several forms. Some women, these respondents asserted, overcompensate for their being women. Others define themselves as "mavericks" and act accordingly. And some women, including several in each of the first two categories, take up feminist causes. All three of these approaches to the congressional vocation call attention to women's minority status and thereby reinforce the belief that "maleness" is the norm. Each of these adaptive strategies attributed to congresswomen warrants both brief elaboration and a discussion of the rejoinders offered by House members who rejected explanations based upon female behavior.

Congresswomen overcompensate for what they perceive to be weaknesses associated with gender, said some respondents, because they fear that their constituents see them as "soft," "unassertive," and politically "ineffectual." They try to counter the image of "weakness" by projecting "firmness," "certainty," a "seriousness of purpose," and a cold "rationality." They compete with and try to destroy the stereotype of women that has been accepted by female as well as by male voters. In the process, they overcompensate for what they believe is an important political deficiency— their "femaleness."

Women who cast themselves in the role of "maverick" often seem distrustful of party leaders and of senior members of the House, against whose records they may very well have campaigned. They appear less willing to adhere to carefully balanced bargains struck in the House because of reservations about one or two decisions which they believe involve "matters of principle." And they are determined not to be co-opted by the system. From the perspective of many males, these women were unreliable, inflexible in the beliefs they hold, and incapable of engaging in the give and take that leads to compromise. They were also perceived as humorless, disloyal to their parties, and too apt to violate House norms.

A few male respondents, but no female interviewees, noted that some women demonstrated an "unfortunate tendency" to identify themselves as "women" and to become too intimately associated with "so-called women's issues." According to these informants, this inclination has diminished congresswomen's standing in the eyes of some members and has had the added effect of jeopardizing the potential influence of other women who become closely linked to these feminists. One congressman who was critical of this behavior said: "You don't see men defining themselves consciously as men. And this permits us to concentrate on other, more important, things."

To some of the male and most of the female respondents, blaming inequality on female behavior was simply another instance of making the victims of discrimination responsible for their fate. The language and styles of politicians were developed by men, not women, said one respondent, and women should not be penalized for "copying a rhetoric and a political posturing that have proved to be effective over the years." Even if women sometimes "come on too strong," the incidence of such assertive behavior is no greater among women than it is among men. Furthermore, women who sometimes depart from established political "scripts" are not taken seriously by male colleagues. Said one female Representative, "Showing uncertainty or some other human frailty means, to some men, that a congresswoman cannot make the tough decisions we all have to make from time to time."

Most respondents believed that the so-called "maverick" role attributed to many women was not limited to members of one gender. Men, too, prized their "independence" from House leadership and it was asserted that a far higher proportion of men than of women could be described as ideologically inflexible, indifferent to House norms, or unwilling to engage in compromise. Some female respondents alluded to the frequency with which male members appear as parts of minuscule minorities following lopsided roll call votes, as much a measure of ideological inflexibility as any they could think of. Women, they argued, rarely oppose overwhelming majorities of their colleagues, whether the issues were cast within partisan or bipartisan frames of reference. And several respondents held that if women are perceived as mavericks, it was because the members who see them within such a perspective were predisposed to do so. Incidents which can be interpreted to support such prejudices were used by these men to reassure themselves of the "soundness" of their bias. These males were much less inclined to pin the label "maverick" on male colleagues who engaged in unorthodox behavior.

Critics of the claim that women were mavericks challenged the alleged causal relationship between female behavior and perceptions of the House as a male institution. If there was such a relationship, one woman pointed out, the cause and effect had been transposed. Because the House is essentially a male institution, women sometimes had to remind themselves about "who they are." They had to call attention to their own identities, even if only to preserve their mental health. The patterns of social and political interaction they encountered in Congress, along with the system of rewards and punishments, the legislative priorities, and the rhetorical styles were matters about which many females felt uncomfortable when they first came to the House.

And so, if a woman occasionally felt the need to define herself as "a woman" and to act out her "womanhood," and if men did not demonstrably define themselves as men, it was because the House was already a male institution and it prescribed orientations and patterns of behavior that men had already internalized. Most women, on the other hand, were expected to "unlearn" patterns of speech, patterns of social interaction, policy priorities, and habits of thought that had grown out of the gender role they learned. "Men never need to think about their 'maleness'," said one female informant. "The frame of reference within which they operate permits them to take for granted the fact that they are male."

It would follow, then, that the women most admired by congressmen were those who had adjusted most effectively to the workways and habits of the House. They were the women who took pains to speak for their districts, their states, or some major interest groups in these geographical units, but not for other women. They were members who used the dozens of cliches that punctuate House debate, rather than employing a more individualized rhetorical style of their own. They were women who expressed a concern for saving money, or a strong national defense, or law and order, or a healthy business and banking climate, but who would not speak out conspicuously about part-time government jobs for women, the Susan B. Anthony dollar, or displaced homemakers. Accordingly, those who took up feminist causes were perceived as outsiders. And, in the words of one feminist member, "we have to put up with an awful lot of silly remarks and nastiness just because our priorities do not happen to be high up on the legislative agenda."

It is important to reiterate here that a majority of respondents did not mention the behavior of women when discussing factors contributing to the masculine character of the House. Most said that the composition of that body and the cultural orientations members brought with them were the most prominent factors leading to the "maleness" of that chamber. The character of the House, in turn, contributed to the manifestation of the four forms of discrimination described in Kirkpatrick's 1974 study. These included linguistic conventions which made reference to males only, rather than men and women collectively; a "killing with kindness" through overprotective or openly flirtatious behavior; an exclusion based upon the belief that women legislators were interested in a narrow range of issues and should not be bothered with broader, more weighty matters; and a propensity to "put women in their place" through snide or insulting remarks (Kirkpatrick 1974, p. 109). Respondents agreed that 1970s congresswomen experienced all of these "put-downs," but there was less agreement on the extent to which this treatment occurred. Furthermore, there were important differences in the impressions offered by most male Representatives and those offered by most female House members, and it is appropriate, therefore, to examine these responses separately.

Male Perceptions

While acknowledging the inequality suffered by congresswomen, most male Representatives tended to stress the infrequency with which it occurred and the change for the better that had taken place in recent years. The open discrimination they observed was relatively rare and, for the most part, unsystematic. Even covert behavior of this kind perpetrated within an all-male setting was not common. Furthermore, few could recall instances of cavalier or condescending behavior. Many male informants also maintained that the occasional incidents of discrimination were not as flagrant as they used to be.

But some noted two sets of conditions which contributed most to the isolated instances of unequal treatment. One was the presence in the House of women who had succeeded husbands who had died while serving in the House. Another was the presence in the House of men, perhaps as many as 20 percent according to most male informants, who were disdainful of all women, but especially contemptuous of women who were assertive or who gained positions of influence.

Attitudes toward specific widows who had succeeded husbands varied considerably. Some were admired, others were thought to be incompetent or "useless," and much depended upon which respondent was doing the evaluating. But the comments of some Representatives suggested that most widows fell into a category of House members who "did not make it on their own" and who, therefore, were incapable of contributing very much to House functions. They were seen as having inherited their positions, and there was some question about the legitimacy of their credentials. Two male respondents stated that they themselves tended to "write off" these women as of little consequence, a practice that was confirmed by a widow who said: "When I first got here, I think a number of members did not take me seriously. I was just a woman who would be gone after two years and I was not important enough to think about or get to know."

One congressman who was critical of women who had succeeded their husbands remarked:

Mrs. _____ sits there prettily and never says anything. People ignore her. She is strictly her husband's stand-in and has never done anything to change that impression. . . . But she succeeded her husband and there really isn't much you can expect from her. It is different for women who come here as a result of their husbands' service.

Other male Representatives said that these women were patronized by some of the older members, perhaps because of relationships formed when the widows' husbands were alive. Respondents felt that such behavior was good neither for other congresswomen nor for the House.

Congressmen who were scornful of most if not all women with whom they served tended to be senior members, although, according to some respondents, there was no necessary relationship between seniority and male chauvinism. They were quick with a wise crack, an obscene joke, or a snide reference, utterances often delivered in a stage whisper to an all-male audience. Sometimes the comment was expressed within the hearing of a congresswoman in an effort to "get under her skin." The target might be a single Representative or women in general. These men exchanged a knowing look and a smile with a male colleague when a female Representative said something which struck them as "silly," "unnecessary," "dumb," "insignificant," or "feminist." Her statement was then understood as something only a "frivolous," "disorganized," "unintelligent," "parochial," or "castrating" woman would say. According to many informants, these men believed that their insulting or derisive remarks and gestures raised their own stature in the eyes of colleagues and that their reputation as "one of the boys" was thereby confirmed.

Such House members could not always be identified from their voting records or public statements, and even most feminists found the roll call votes of some faultless. "At the substantive policy level," said on respondent, "many of these fellows seem as sensitive to, and as understanding of, women's problems as any member of the House." Political ideology or policy orientation, then, were not as useful a pair of distinguishing characteristics as were the basic attitudes these men had toward women generally.

Although several male Representatives said that a decreasing number of members were a part of this group, some also pointed out that many male members, including themselves, were sometimes critical of individual women members. But they argued that their disparaging remarks were no different from those they made about males who were guilty of similarly lamentable behavior. They pointed out that sometimes it was difficult to distinguish between criticism emerging out of hostility toward women and the same response which was rooted in some other orientation. They asserted that most congressmen were no more critical of women colleagues than they were of male Representatives, but that sometimes it appeared as if they were harsher on women.

Respondents singled out specific congresswomen for their "incompetence," or their "mediocrity," or their "perverseness," but they went on to name males whom they have criticized on the same grounds. One congressman put it this way:

It's hard to determine whether negative assessments are based on sexist or on other grounds. Some of the men here wouldn't take much of anything a woman said seriously, but it is not a general attitude. Most of us might criticize a woman for talking too much on the House floor, but that doesn't mean that we don't hold her in high regard, nonetheless. And it doesn't mean that we are predisposed to think that her weakness is a failing all other women share. And if I feel that a particular congresswoman is too "motherly," that feeling detracts very little from my assessment of her as an effective member.

Several male informants noted the difference between Representatives who held the view expressed in the above quotation and those who were contemptuous of female House members generally. The former, they argued, were not prepared to generalize about all women members on the basis of isolated indiscretions or idiosyncrasies. The latter, on the other hand, perceived and used events and personal attributes to reinforce already hostile predispositions.

Female Perceptions and Reactions

The women members interviewed in 1978 readily agreed that they were much better off than female predecessors and that they were working with more enlightened males—men more sensitive to their needs and feelings, more willing to treat them as equals, and more apt to share responsibility with them. But most of these women felt that condescending, patronizing, and, less often, insulting treatment was more frequent than most males believed was the case. Furthermore, they were convinced that instances of such behavior were more flagrant than was acknowledged by their male colleagues. One congresswoman estimated that there were about one-hundred "macho sons-of-bitches" in the House, about one-hundred "decent, sensitive guys," and about 200 "in between." "It's a normal curve," she said. Another woman, one for whom a number of male respondents indicated a high regard, would not cite figures, but felt it wasn't "quite as bad as all that." She asserted:

There is an unmistakably macho attitude among some males, but not that many. Sure, there are some leering, macho men. But most of the chauvinism we experience is unconscious; but you don't find these things in the House anymore than you find them anywhere else.

Apart from confirming some "macho" behavior in the House, these statements touch on two other ideas that were referred to frequently by other female members. The first is that such behavior was engaged in by members of the House in roughly the same measure as males displayed it in other organizations and within society in general. The second is that most of this overt behavior was "unconscious." Almost all of the women interviewed noted the "unintentional" nature of many of the indiscretions they observed.

Female reactions to what they perceived as objectionable male behavior varied, depending upon the woman, the nature of the insult, and the circumstances under which it occurred. A common response was simply to ignore the slight. One congresswoman said:

I don't feel or experience most of the macho behavior. Maybe because it is not important to me. . . . Moreover, my job is to forget the irrelevancies, such as mode or form of address, or who should get off the elevator first, and focus on the things that are really important here—my committee work, legislation, and my constituents.

Several other congresswomen indicated they had neither the time nor the inclination to make an issue of most male indiscretions. They said that there were too many more important matters that demanded their attention and their energies. Furthermore, some believed that calling these gaffes to the attention of erring males would embarrass them or make them defensive. They might also feel that a minor point was being blown out of proportion, thereby jeopardizing what might otherwise be a perfectly friendly, helpful relationship. One woman noted that sometimes sexist remarks are uttered in jest and that "you have to be a good sport to get anywhere in this House." She added:

As a matter of fact, a good deal of affection is shown through the ribbing that takes place here. Some of the jokes would drive a New York feminist up the wall, but you come to accept them. And you have to be less uptight about these things because they are meant to be funny.

Another female member reported that there was one male colleague who let out a wolf whistle whenever he saw her, adding that it was just "a little joke" between the two of them.

One legislative aide recalled an incident in which a subcommittee chairman, a courtly, Southern gentleman, called upon a young, unmarried congresswoman to make an opening statement just after their subcommittee convened and he referred to her as "Mrs. _____." She ignored the slip and was about to read her first sentence when the chairman interrupted to apologize for the error and added with fatherly affection, "We wouldn't want to chase the fellas away." By correcting the mistake and adding a patronizing comment, the chairman had made matters worse. A subsequent interview with the congresswoman involved, however, produced the following response: "But my chairman is a charming and gracious man who has behaved this way all of his life and I would be hurting his feelings more than he hurt mine if I objected to his remarks."

In this connection, another congresswoman remarked:

Several congresswomen are patronized by male members, particularly the older members. There is one woman member who is very young and is really a bright, energetic, secure woman. And the men treat her like their daughter. She is young enough to be their daughter, and they don't act that way to be deliberately impolite or condescending, but that's the way they feel. They say such things as "now listen here, young lady" or "listen here, dear" ("dear" is very often used), "you have to understand that I've seen a lot more than you and you're so young and inexperienced."

Some female members try to use this behavior to their advantage. About a half-dozen congresswomen insisted that there were positive aspects to being a woman in the House and that they are happy to take advantage of courtesies "gallant" men were inclined to dispense. Most pointed out that the help they received from chivalrous colleagues was no substitute for hard work, knowledge, and professionalism. But they believed once a woman had gained the respect of an accommodating male, there was nothing wrong with requesting his help on, say, an amendment or cosponsorship possibilities—thereby capitalizing on his experience and gentlemanly predispositions. One woman put it this way:

In some ways the deference women receive is to their advantage. I know that many younger women here, and in every profession, dismiss any special treatment as condescending, as a kind of male chauvinism. It isn't chauvinism. This male behavior is ingrained in men of certain age. It is an act of respect and most of us, at least I, accept it and make the most of it.

Although most congresswomen were willing to overlook what they considered minor annoyances produced by male behavior, some were not as forgiving and were prepared to challenge serious male indiscretions. These women did not ignore discriminatory language in proposed legislation, for example. One woman indicated that she had introduced many amendments to bills which made the language apply to both males and females. She described how she once asked a subcommittee chairman who was explaining a measure and who continually used "he" and "him," whether the legislation would apply to women. He apologized and said he would make the appropriate changes. "But," she added, "you have to remind them of these things all the time."

Several said sometimes male colleagues were so patronizing that women were forced to register their displeasure. One recalled her first appearance on the floor. The only subject some men raised was what her husband thought about her serving in Congress and how she planned to run a household while working full time. "They were nice, but they treated me as some kind of strange animal—and I finally started asking them what their wives thought of their serving in the House while there was a household to maintain and children to bring up." She added: "Some laughed and a few were embarrassed or sort of sheepish, but some had no idea of what I was getting at."

Another female Representative recalled the annoying behavior of male members during her first few months in the House.

Several said how glad they were that I didn't wear pants suits, as if it is their business. Plenty of women wear pants suits; why should that be so important to them? To their way of thinking, a woman in a pants suit was doing something wrong. But that's changed. That was five years ago. Now it's not mentioned, although some men may still think about it.

Details of an incident involving a former congresswoman were published some time ago and are relevant here. According to her account, she was riding in an elevator with a Democratic Senator whom she considered "one of God's more stupid creatures," when:

With that great condescension of which the male of the species is so guilty so many times, he literally patted me on the shoulder like a small child then took hold of my dress and said: "Myy, what a P-R-E-T-T-Y dress you have!" I couldn't stand it! . . . So I turned to him and in a voice imitating his, said: "Myyyy, what a lovely suit you're wearing. You *are* handsome." (Dreifus 1972)

But the incident which received most attention in the 95th Congress, including coverage in at least one major newspaper, occurred during a committee meeting while a male member, known for his graciousness and charm, was addressing the group. A woman committee member asked if he would yield and he responded "In just a minute, cutie pie," and went on speaking. The sound of his own voice probably obscured the bristling response from the woman, who was in the process of asking him just who he thought he was calling "cutie pie." He responded to what he thought was her continuing request for the floor with "just a few minutes, honey." The congresswoman then interrupted committee proceedings, referred to him as "Congressman cutie pie," objected vociferously to his language, and asserted her strong feminist orientation.

Some of the women indicated that they were aware of other, more vicious and more calculating insults directed toward them and toward other women, but they were the kinds of remarks uttered less frequently in the 1970s because most Representatives would not countenance them. But stories had gotten back to female members that some men felt threatened by them or that they had been characterized as "hard-nosed," or "unpredictable" or "unreliable bitches." The vulgar character of some comments made in private was revealed during the Abscam trials of House members accused of taking bribes from FBI undercover agents disguised as Arab sheiks. Secret tape recordings made of the transactions had one male Representative referring casually to a congresswoman whose "meanness" was a product of her "never [having] been laid" (Anderson and Cappaccio 1980).

The tendency of another congresswoman occasionally to employ language calculated to shock male listeners led to a well publicized exchange between her and her committee chairman. The congresswoman in question "likes to use the word 'vagina'," said one male respondent. "It stops most men cold for a moment and she slips it into conversation for effect." She used this tactic with the chairman one day when he refused to sign a travel voucher entitling her to reimbursement for committee-related travel expenses. After the argument had proceeded for a few minutes, she had become exasperated and said: "The only reason you won't sign is because I have a vagina." The chairman is reported to have replied: "Well, if you used your vagina more and your mouth less you might get someplace around here." The exchange is revealing on several counts, but perhaps the most telling is that it illustrates the alacrity with which the chairman was prepared to formulate his comeback within a flagrantly sexist frame of reference, the same framework he had doubtless employed many times before within the confines of an all male audience.

Gender-based resentment expressed by congressmen was usually directed toward women who are successful. Sponsoring a useful amendment, appointment to a desirable committee, selection for a plum by party leaders sometimes generated derisive or heated comments, comments which some respondents concluded stemmed from deeply felt jealousy. A woman Representative provided the following explanation for such a reaction:

Some men in the House feel that they are not going to let some "girl" get ahead of them. They feel that they are overburdened, harassed, and overworked, and they feel that women couldn't possibly be as overworked as they are . . . and they are not going to be out-done by a woman.

It would seem, then, that in the 1970s, congresswomen looked the other way when objectionable remarks made in their presence were unintentional or offered in jest, or perpetrated in a private, rather than a public forum, or when a response would be more self-defeating than the perceived harm caused by the action in the first place. But when the comment was mean-spirited or intentionally demeaning or uttered in public, most congresswomen would not let it go unchallenged. Responses took the forms of an angry retort, sarcasm, humor, or simply straightforward chastisement, depending upon the nature of the indiscretion and the personality and style of the woman witnessing it. Whatever the form, these reactions represented a pattern of responses which was conspicuously absent from the behavioral repertoires of most women serving in the House in the years before World War II.

THE EXPERIENCE OF CONGRESSWOMEN IN THE 1990s

Interviews with thirty-three female Representatives, twelve male Representatives, and ten staff members during the 103rd Congress revealed both continuities and changes in the level of congresswomen's integration into the House. The most important continuity is that the House was still perceived as a "male institution" by almost all respondents. The most important changes were a product of the marked increase of women in the House and of the more liberated social orientations of the men with whom they were serving.

Continuities

Among the forty-five members interviewed, forty-one affirmed the "male" character of the House. Some justifications for this characterization were related to those offered earlier. The House was male because such amenities as toilets, the gym, and the swimming pool were less accessible to women. It was male because elevator operators, Capitol Hill police, and parking lot attendants could not bring themselves to treat congresswomen as House members, and because repeated slights, though often trivial, had a cumulative effect. It was male because the daily schedule, which often called for evening sessions, and the foreshortened weekly schedule were inconvenient for female members whose household, spousal, and child care concerns competed with their legislative responsibilities. These schedules, said one congresswoman, are determined by "male leaders who believe that members have wives" to take care of their families. A few first-term congresswomen mentioned the small number of female Representatives to explain House "maleness." However much they were impressed by gains following the 1992 election, they found 11 percent female membership little different from the 4 percent present in 1978.

Most respondents adopted variations on that theme, however, offering explanations that were heard less often in 1978, when the painfully small size of the female contingent obscured other fundamental disparities. The House was male, they said, because there were no women among top leaders of either party; because none chaired a standing committee; because no more than one token woman was ordinarily appointed to fill vacancies on Boards and Commissions; and because women were often denied recognition for legislative successes by committee chairs who became principal sponsors of the measures at the eleventh hour, only after women had done the spade work necessary to place them on the agenda. "Look at the photographs taken at bill-signing ceremonies," said one senior congresswoman. "The figures in the foreground are committee chairmen, with the women who were instrumental in passing the bill either relegated to the background or absent."

A large majority of 1993 respondents alluded to the "male culture of the House" to explain the chamber's gender imbalances, just as so many Representatives had in 1978. One congresswoman noted:

Most men are more comfortable dealing with other men than they are with women, and they prefer to work with one another. There is a congeniality among men that does not include women and a congeniality among women that excludes men. Differences between us extend beyond "comfort levels" to the issues each group thinks are important.

From the point of view of some congresswomen, the difference was reflected in the way men and women defined themselves as human beings. "Being a congressman is central to most males' sense of self," said one first-term, female Representative. "Congresswomen," she continued, "define themselves as much by their family and kids as where they happen to work, and I am more excited when my daughter calls me 'mommy' than when someone else calls me "the honorable."

These gender differences affected the day-to-day interactions female and male House members had with one another. Inasmuch as many older, influential congressmen continued to be uncomfortable with women and were disinclined to work with them, the relationships they established with female lawmakers were strained, perfunctory, and unproductive. Several congresswomen described interactions with male Representatives during which they were not taken seriously, "half-listened to," or advised, through body language, that they "didn't know what they were talking about." Two anecdotes, one told by a first-term congresswoman, the other by a veteran, highlight the difficulties female members encounter. The newcomer allowed that women have not been completely ignored, as was once the case, but they are sometimes treated with subtle disdain. She said:

Men are not comfortable with us. In the cloak room, for example, a first-term woman will say "hello" to a congressman and he will be polite and say "hello," but soon dismiss her. But when that same congressman is greeted by a first-term male, he will be outgoing and friendly, sustaining the conversation. I understand that women have not spent much time in the cloak room, but I will make it a point to go there as often as possible in the future.

The second woman described a set of circumstances occurring repeatedly in subcommittee deliberations.

The men have louder voices and they talk over you, more interested in what they have to say than what you have to contribute. At some point you will make what you think is a worthwhile point, but no one will acknowledge it. It's as if you hadn't opened your mouth. Ten minutes later the same observation will be made by a male, and the others will say "what a good idea" as if they had never heard it before. We will just have to shout and be more aggressive.

The cloak room was singled out by many congresswomen as a vivid expression of the institution's "male" identity.

The more overt forms of discrimination described in 1978 continued into the 1990s, although with less frequency. Among the four forms detailed by Kirkpatrick and observed in the House in 1978, three—linguistic discrimination, overprotective or flirtatious behavior, and insulting remarks—were mentioned by members of the 103rd Congress. Their occurrence, while unusual, was not rare.

Male members occasionally referred to the "gentlemen of the House" and employed other locutions suggesting an all-male chamber. Some were accused of using women's first names during committee sessions while referring to congressman by title and surname. Early in her first term, Californian Maxine Waters stopped a subcommittee meeting dead in its tracks when the chair, Representative Joseph Gaydos, called her "Maxine," after using formal titles when calling upon males. The African-American congresswoman described the encounter as follows:

I'd never met the man before in my life, and he turned to me and said "Maxine." I stopped right in the middle of that committee meeting and said "Just a minute. What are the rules around here? We must be consistent. If he's Congressman Barton, then I'm Congresswoman Waters."[5]

This fractious exchange is a reflection of what might be a more deeply rooted division in the House, one which will be addressed below. Nevertheless, it is an example of discriminatory linguistic conventions that continue to be employed, even if heard less often than was once the case. By the 1990s, male members were more likely to use such terms as "Madam Chairwoman" when referring to a female presiding officer, and "my colleague," and "the member from California," terms they would use as a matter of course when referring to male members.

Patronizing behavior, described so vividly by earlier congresswomen, had also survived, even if manifested less frequently. Most male members, particularly junior congressmen, had had experience enough with professional women to treat them as colleagues. Such terms as "dear" or "young lady," let alone "honey," as they were once applied to congresswomen were infrequently uttered, although Marjorie Margolies-Mezvinsky describes an incident during which a committee chair responded to a congresswoman's request for the floor by saying "Well, young lady, what would you want?" (1994, p. 49). At the same time, exaggerated politeness and condescension continued to be exhibited on Capitol Hill. One congressman told a first-term female colleague how "pleasing" all the new women were and how "they certainly brightened up the place." "The subtext of his remark," she said later, "was why else were we elected except to be pleasing and brighten up the place." And a young Democratic congresswoman publicly condemned unwanted sexual attention she had received from a male Representative.

She said: "A colleague of mine complimented me on my appearance and then said he was going to chase me around the House floor. Because he was not my boss I was not intimidated, but I was offended and I was embarrassed."[6]

The corps of unreconstructed congressmen who, in 1978, were described as "macho SOBs," whose image of female colleagues did not extend beyond prevailing stereotypes, who were flagrantly insensitive to public issues central to women's concerns and who were scornful of almost any professional activity in which women engaged, was also present in 1993, albeit diminished in size. Representatives recalled a dozen or more instances when they were embarrassed by the behavior of mostly senior congressmen toward women. These men were described as "insensitive," "vulgar," "insulting" or "sexist." One congressman recalled the committee chairman who appeared at orientation session for newly elected members and spent the afternoon "leering" at the congresswomen and commenting with coarse humor on their "good looks" and "nice bodies." According to this informant, nothing was said or done about the situation because no one wanted to tangle with a committee chairman.

Another informant described the strikingly insensitive behavior of a senior Democrat following a roll call vote. The vote was on an amendment to allow Medicaid funds to pay for mammograms annually—a preferred schedule for older women—rather than biennially, as had been stipulated in the original measure. When the amendment was defeated, a disappointed congresswoman was approached by a male opponent in the debate. In a sorry attempt at humor, he said "All is not lost. Poor women can still have one breast tested this year, the other breast tested next year."

The difficulty some men had in taking women professionals seriously was reflected in the comment of a highly respected Republican congressman to a National Public Television audience. He remarked that after the 1992 election "There are so many women in Congress now that it looks like a mall." Realizing that not everyone present appreciated his comment, he quickly denied authorship of the "joke," stating lamely that it did not originate with him, and adding "I am just repeating what other members of Congress are saying."[7] On another occasion, an Oklahoma congressman referred to Margolies-Mezvinsky as "the three M girl." Even after he was taken aside and told his reference was demeaning and pathetically out-of-date, "he still didn't get it" (Margolies-Mezvinsky 1994, xvi).

Some of the incidents revealed a resistent, deeply rooted male chauvinism, even misogyny, among a small group of mostly senior males. Although almost all knew enough to avoid flagrantly sexist remarks, unusual events sometimes stripped away a fragile veneer of civility. One such event was the 1991 Clarence Thomas confirmation hearings before the Senate Judiciary Committee at which Anita Hill testified.[8] Feelings about race, sexuality, ideology, and party advantage conjoined to raise emotions to extraordinary heights. After watching the televised hearings with a group of male Republicans, one of their colleagues reported that he was appalled by the blatantly sexist remarks made by men he believed were "above those kind of comments." "If a woman were present they would not have talked that way," he said. "The vulgar remarks about Anita Hill's sexuality shocked me. I had no idea that these men had such retrograde attitudes, and maybe it took the atmosphere of the Thomas hearings to trigger gutter values that they are usually able to mask."

Virtually all congresswomen interviewed in 1993 knew that some of their male colleagues were "beyond redemption," but, like most of their 1970s predecessors, they could not be bothered thinking about them as obstacles to their legislative effectiveness. One third-term woman observed that even talking about these men in an interview was unproductive—a waste of time because it means "we are not talking about issues that are really important." And a female Republican remarked:

So much of life is reflected in the personal attitudes that you bring to a situation. I have tried to think positively and not let obstacles of this kind stand in my way. I want to establish a reputation as a hard-working, knowledgeable, conscientious, problem-solving, substantive person. I can't change the attitudes of some of these men but neither can I let these attitudes affect what I do.

Changes

The most visible change affecting female integration into the House in 1993 was their increase from twenty-eight in the 102nd Congress to forty-seven in the 103rd. Other, related changes were sparked by the unprecedented increase.

The large turnover in House members in 1992 left a correspondingly large number of vacancies on coveted standing committees and on influential party instrumentalities. Democratic and Republican leaders had little choice but to fill many of these vacancies with women. Some informants said these leaders went out of their way to showcase female members. They were sensitive to the arrival of twenty-four new women, said some, and fearful that they would lose partisan advantage if they gave inadequate attention to female members' concerns. Such highly valued committees as Appropriations and Energy and Commerce were staffed with unprecedented numbers of women. So were party policy committees and the Whip networks. Veteran women capitalized on the high turnover and the seniority system, vaulting five or more positions up their committee ladders, poised to become senior and ranking members of key subcommittees. They now had unprecedented access to influential House-Senate conference committees. And this was just the beginning of an advantageous positioning process. Said one senior male Democrat, "No amount of male chauvinism can hold back a woman who occupies a top subcommittee position and who works hard at her job. She is an integral part of the process whether people like it or not."

Increased numbers were particularly helpful for Democratic women. Twenty-one first-term Democrats joined fifteen female party holdovers to produce a critical mass of votes which could, if cast as a unit on selected issues, hold the balance of power. Female ubiquity was especially apparent among the sixty-four Democratic first-termers, one-third of whom were women. The latter used their clout to help elect African-American Eva Clayton of North Carolina President of the Democratic class for the first session of the 103rd Congress.

The augmented numbers would not have produced as much change if the new women were not as experienced or as talented as they were. With most having served in state legislatures and on city or county councils, the female class of 1993 had already built reputations as able lawmakers, and as creative, caring public servants. They were capable, confident women, prepared to work hard, take their lumps and, said one senior congress-woman, "They do not say 'poor me' when they fail to achieve their goals." Official Washington could not ignore these "agents of change." The elector-ate had sent them to Washington to purge government of waste and corruption and they were conscious of their mandate. Floridian Tillie Fowler and Utah's Karen Shepherd became co-leaders of their respective parties' efforts to reform the House. In the meantime, the new congress-women drew strength from their numbers and from highly visible, con-scious attempts by the Clinton administration to appoint women to key executive branch positions. As one senior Republican put it, "women were now being judged by their dialectical more than their decorative contribu-tions to government."

But the "decorative" was not being ignored. To punctuate their presence, congresswomen dressed in bright, feminine colors, and the pinks and reds and oranges and orchids and apricots and fuchsias accentuated the drab-ness of dark-suited congressmen when President Clinton came to the House for a televised speech to a joint session of Congress. Said one congress-woman: "We didn't necessarily plan it that way but each of us decided independently that we were going to make a visual statement and we wanted tens of millions of people to see that this was a start of a new era for the representation of women." Twenty-two of the twenty-four new women joined the Congressional Caucus for Women's Issues soon after they arrived. Caucus members and non-members, Democrats and Repub-licans, entered into an unprecedented network of mentoring relationships, with their conviviality occasionally crossing party lines. Said one senior Republican woman, "Can you imagine Democratic and Republican men arranging to break bread with one another?"

Whereas the partisan division between males was largely unbridgeable in the 103rd Congress, the social orientations of female and male Representatives were converging. This development was hastened by the whole-sale replacement of older by younger men in the 1992 election. One second-term Democrat remarked on the shift in attitudes toward women held by recently elected congressmen. He said:

My generation has been trained differently. We have become accustomed to dealing with women in professional situations. We have come to accept basic premises of the women's movement. Consequently, the proliferation of women in Congress poses no adjustment problems for us.

And several Representatives detected greater circumspection by senior congressmen in relationships established with congresswomen. Said one, "a few members of the old guard have concluded that the political liabilities of insensitivity are prohibitive."

Changes associated with increased numbers, with assignments to more valued committees, with more comprehensive networking and mentoring relationships among women, with women's greater visibility, and with new cohorts of socially aware male colleagues all had a profound effect on the level of female integration into the House. Whereas informants in 1978 frequently referred to women's exclusion from formal and informal House groups, few did so in 1993.[9]

As subsequent chapters will make clear, there were no committees and no substantive issues beyond the reach of women. Moreover, no informal group excluded women, with even the restrictive "Chowder and Marching Society" admitting two at the start of the 103rd Congress. Women's access to party leadership positions also improved, and, as will be made clear in Chapter 6, members came to believe that a congresswoman would be holding a top leadership position in the foreseeable future.

Turnover and generational change among congressmen diminished even if it did not end the open, raw hostility exhibited by some males toward congresswomen. Many of the new men were hypersensitive to the feelings of female colleagues, and contemporary congresswomen recalled fewer examples of unconscious sexism than had their predecessors. Male behavior changed markedly after the Clarence Thomas hearings. The Navy's apologies following vulgar depictions of Congresswoman Schroeder in skits produced in the wake of the Tailhook scandal also had an impact.[10] And references which gratuitously called attention to gender differences among members, once common, became occasional. One new congresswoman has since concluded "being a congresswoman is a less alienating experience in this Congress than it ever was before" (Margolies-Mezvinsky 1994, 72).

These developments paralleled change in male assessments of female behavior. Criticism based on a congresswoman's unpredictability, aggres-siveness, and feminism, offered freely in 1978, all but disappeared. It was replaced by positive observations about how effective, industrious, and productive congresswomen were. Although a few women were dismissed as "wearing their feminism on their sleeve" and as being "too strident," identifying with women's issues was not the liability it once was. The Clinton administration made women's concerns an integral part of the national agenda and feminist constituencies were better mobilized than they had been. Furthermore, many congressmen felt comfortable sponsoring feminist legislation, and congresswomen were emboldened by their numbers to determine priorities in terms of their own experience. As one senior Democratic congressman said, "For the first time it is possible to be a feminist and a 'House insider' at the same time."

It seems evident that fuller female integration into the House was linked to the change in the background and political experience of the congresswomen serving in 1993. First-term congressional women possessed more impressive political credentials than the males who accompanied them to Washington. When combined with the twenty-three women holdovers, the female House contingent contained only two members who succeeded their husbands to House office—both of whom were elected in the early 1970s and both of whom were subcommittee chairs in the 103rd Congress. This meant that one criticism of female members heard so often in 1978 went unmentioned in 1993. The charge then was that too many congresswomen exploited the matrimonial connection rather than rely on their own talents to secure a House seat. These women could not therefore be taken seriously. No one said that in 1993. Clearly change in recruitment patterns helped accelerate female integration into the House.

INTEGRATION OF WOMEN INTO THE HOUSE

Among the inferences to be drawn from the testimony of contemporary House members, the most important is that congresswomen are beginning to be accepted as equals by many male colleagues. This change has occurred in spite of the fact that the House continues to be perceived as a male institution by congressmen as well as by congresswomen. Much of the discrimination suffered by female members by virtue of their gender is unintentional. Congresswomen believe these slights are often of insufficient importance to warrant a response, or that it is self-defeating to call attention to them. None said the discrimination she suffers is harmful enough to prevent her from serving as an effective House member.

Almost all informants agreed there continued to be instances of serious male indiscretions and sexism. This behavior is engaged in by a comparatively small group of men who are disinclined to take female members seriously. They have little difficulty creating justifications for ridiculing congresswomen behind their backs, and they sometimes treat women condescendingly in face-to-face encounters. When offensive behavior is exercised openly, however, contemporary congresswomen, far more than their pre–World War II predecessors, are likely to challenge it.

The increasing professionalism contemporary congresswomen have brought with them to the House has contributed to their integration into that chamber. Male members cannot help but be aware of the political experience, professional competence and legislative savvy more and more congresswomen exhibit while performing House tasks. These women command treatment as equals, a development explored more fully in Chapter 12. Men who treat them lightly run the risk of looking foolish in the eyes of male, as well as female, Representatives.

The addition of twenty-four new congresswomen has expedited the integrative process. Increased visibility, selection for strategically valuable committees, creation of new mentoring and communication networks, and aggressive promotion of neglected issues, including issues directly affecting women, have made congresswomen less marginal to life in the House. Their growing influence has magnified perceptions of their influence, and fewer congressmen view women as outsiders than was the case in the 1970s.

Female Representatives have been helped by an increasing number of male allies. Turnover in recent years produced male Representatives whose life experiences differed markedly from those of their predecessors. Some attended colleges, graduate schools, and law schools after traditional gender roles and the cultural values underlying them had come under attack. Many matriculated with women whose educational and vocational aspirations mirrored their own and whose achievement levels approximated or surpassed their own. Some of these soon-to-be congressmen married women who supported the women's liberation movement, and it is reasonable to assume that these spouses raised their husbands' consciousness about discrimination based upon gender. As a result, the number of congressmen who are uneasy about their professional relationship with female Representatives is declining, even though their disappearance is not imminent.

Not all change occurring between 1978 and 1993 reflected a more fully integrated House. Comments from several Black congresswomen described dismissive or high-handed treatment by white male members. Discrimination based upon race was not much discussed by congresswomen in 1978 interviews, probably because only four of the eighteen female Representatives were Black and because three of the four had established enviable reputations. Lawyers Barbara Jordan and Yvonne Brathwaite Burke were known as experienced, skilled women, and Shirley Chisholm was months away from appointment to the House Rules Committee. If members of this tiny minority of a minority were less readily accepted by male colleagues than other women, it went unreported. By 1993, the number of Black women had grown to eight, including two in their second term and five in their first. Their visibility had increased and their marginality was more obvious. Their status as House members was regularly challenged by Capitol Hill staff, and they presented congressmen with images these men could not easily reconcile with visions they had of themselves and of Congress.

Difficulties encountered by African-American congresswomen were reflected in Maxine Waters' emphatic objection to the white chairman who called her "Maxine" after referring to everyone else by title. In 1993, a first-term Black woman said she knew her color was not helping her among white male colleagues, and she believed that her gender prompted Black congressmen not to take her seriously. She said many men, including the leadership, were indifferent to women of color. Her observations could be attributed to her youth, her inexperience in the House, and her gender, as well as her race. But the comment of a second-term Black congresswoman lends credence to her concern.

African-American women are ignored on Capitol Hill. They are not seen; they're invisible to the male power structure in the House. You can see it in small ways, as well as large. When a white congresswoman is waiting for an elevator, the men stand back and allow her to get on first. When a Black woman is waiting it's like she isn't there and the men rush ahead of her. Black women are the most discriminated against people in the United States and it's true in the House, as well.

Although contemporary congresswomen are not fully integrated into the House—and some believe they have a long way to go—they have made demonstrable gains. The routine relationships they establish with males have come to resemble more closely the past working relationships congressmen maintain with one another. Today, it is difficult to imagine a male Representative rising to "bless the ladies," and it is all but impossible to envision a speech appearing in the *Congressional Record* similar to the one given by Congressman Gifford in 1947. If, by some stretch of the imagination, a congressman delivered one, it is safe to assume that the *Record* would reflect appropriate rejoinders.

Just as the character of women's routine interaction with men has changed, so, too, has their access to the House's many informal groups. By the 1990s virtually all such groups included at least one woman, a circumstance not fully anticipated in 1978. This development is explored in the next chapter.

NOTES

1. Possibly the richest brief biography of Jeannette Rankin is Kate Walbert's Op Ed piece in the *New York Times*, April 2, 1993, marking the 76th anniversary of Rankin's arrival in the House.

2. Bush, the father of former President George Bush, was at one time challenged by Luce for the Republican nomination to the Senate. Prescott Bush, Co-

lumbia University Oral History Project, 1966, as quoted in Garry Wills, "Father Knows Best," *New York Review of Books*, November 5, 1992, p. 38.

3. None of these works explicitly defines the term "male institution." Questions posed to House members did not ask for a definition of such an institution, but answers to other queries (see Appendix C) suggest that a "male institution" has some or all of the following characteristics: a preponderant proportion of its membership is male; its members define the institution as "male"; the routine treatment accorded to males by one another is advantageously different from the routine treatment accorded to females by male colleagues; the institution's basic and subsidiary facilities satisfy the needs of males more fully than they satisfy the needs of females; and the institution's influence structure is more accessible to males than it is to females.

4. Thirteen of the twenty-four House members interviewed were female— eighteen women were in the House at the time. A total of thirty-six administrative and legislative staff aides were also interviewed, all but six of whom served on members' office staffs. The remainder were attached to committee and House staffs.

5. This exchange was reported in *Congressional Quarterly Weekly Report*, November 23, 1991, p. 3,461.

6. The statement was made by Indiana Congresswoman Jill Long and reported in *Congressional Quarterly Weekly Report*, October 12, 1991, p. 2,950.

7. The speaker was Congressman Henry Hyde of Illinois while appearing on a PBS debate on the religious right. The program aired on September 17, 1993. Harriet Woods of the National Women's Political Caucus was a panel participant and she was not amused.

8. Hill had testified before television cameras that Thomas had harassed her sexually while she worked under him at the Equal Employment Opportunity Commission. What incensed many viewers, male as well as female, were the efforts of Republicans on an all-male Committee to attack and humiliate her in order to save Thomas's confirmation. In critics' eyes, the woman who was allegedly wronged became the victim.

9. Almost all of those interviewed mentioned the men's gym and hunting excursions as milieus within which women are absent, but these are exceptions and the significance of female exclusion will be discussed in the next chapter.

10. The Tailhook scandal arose after dozens of women were molested and sexually assaulted at a 1991 convention of naval aviators in a Las Vegas hotel. The Navy was delinquent in its investigation of the matter—the Secretary of the Navy resigned and several officers were disciplined or forced to resign early—and Patricia Schroeder, a member of the House Armed Services Committee, had been particularly critical of the Navy for not finding and disciplining the scores of Navy airmen believed to be responsible for what happened. The Congresswoman became the target of Navy personnel and their defenders.

5

Access to Informal Channels of Communication: Women and House Caucuses

Informal discussions House members have with one another do not lend themselves to ready observation, and relatively little has been written on the subject. Representatives communicate among themselves informally in many settings—on the House floor, in the cloak room, and in House corridors, to mention just a few. These conversations take place on thousands of occasions each day and they collectively embrace the entire range of matters of concern to social beings who also happen to be elected public officials.

Accordingly, congressional observers undertake a formidable task when they try to determine informal interactions sufficiently significant to warrant systematic attention, and when they attempt to analyze the patterns of influence Representatives exert upon one another. Those who follow the behavior of female House members bear the additional burden of learning the extent to which variations in these patterns are gender-related. Among other things, they want to know the extent to which women are an integral part of informal communications networks.

The approach adopted here is to concentrate upon the informal groups that operate within the House. These groups were chosen as a focus because they are among the most important crucibles within which, hidden from public scrutiny, information and ideas are exchanged, legislative tactics and strategies formulated, coalitions and majorities mobilized, and confidences shared (Stevens et al. 1981). At the same time, they affect and are affected by the structure of influence within the House, the range and nature of public policy options open to the House, and the effectiveness and influence of individual House members. This approach has its drawbacks, inasmuch as some important relationships are established and decisions made in ways that have little to do with group life. The approach is appealing, nonetheless, because the House possesses a rich array of active caucuses, and because exchanges within them often have an important impact on the behavior and careers of House members.

Male and female Representatives in the 95th and 103rd Congresses were asked about their membership in informal groups and about the extent to which one or more of these groups excluded congresswomen. Respondents were also asked about the extent to which group affiliation had anything to do with the legislative and institutional success of group members. What follows is a distillation of the answers to these questions. Inferences are drawn about changes in women's accessibility to small groups during the last thirty years, and about the disadvantages congresswomen suffer by virtue of their being excluded from some of these groups. But first the groups must be defined.

INFORMAL GROUPS IN THE HOUSE

The House of Representatives, like many other large organizations, contains a number of informal groups, most of them small, a few containing more than 125 members. These coteries have no sanction in law and were recognized only recently by House rules.[1] They are created by Representatives who decide that they have enough in common with like-minded members to meet with one another on a more or less regular basis and share information, common problems, lawmaking possibilities, and ideas for improving their performance. Members are attracted to each other because of party, ideological, geographic, ethnic, or racial ties, or they unite because of economic concerns their constituents share. Some have simply developed a personal rapport with one another, a bond which induces them to meet, compare notes, and enjoy camaraderie.[2]

Groups of this kind have always been present in the House, but only after World War II did they begin to proliferate. Their greatest surge began in the mid-1970s. From 1977 to 1980 their number doubled, and by 1984 they exceeded one hundred.[3] Some of the caucuses formed during these years reaped membership bonanzas, with the Congressional Arts Caucus swelling to 166 in three years, and the Tourism Caucus reaching 180 during roughly the same period (*New York Times*, January 15, 1983).

The rise of small groups has been linked to greater heterogeneity in the composition of House districts, an increase in the number and complexity of problems which constituents concluded Washington should solve, a decline in party loyalty among voters, and the absence of serviceable ideological frameworks to give order to the broadened range of contemporary issues. Decentralization of the House's power structure and continued parochial concerns of its committees also contributed to their increase (Stevens et al. 1981).

All of these changes made lawmaking and representational tasks more difficult for Representatives. The more varied character of their districts and the declining usefulness of formal House instrumentalities increased members' uncertainty about the problems faced by constituents and possible remedies for these problems. They were also more likely to be unsure about the impact legislative proposals would have on the nation and their districts, and about the extent to which enacted measures were fulfilling intended proposes.

Members created informal groups to reduce this uncertainty. Among the groups' most important functions is to provide information about pending legislation. They are also a source of voting cues, and they constitute deliberative arenas for shaping legislative, political, and institutional strategies. In addition, they offer opportunities for members to highlight issues, to develop expertise, and to promote integrated consideration of policy proposals unlikely to receive the attention of committees shackled by narrow jurisdictional constraints (Stevens et al. 1981). Apart from enriching the social and political lives of their members, these groups also tend to facilitate the congressional decision-making process (Fiellin 1962; Stevens et al. 1981; Hammond 1989; Loomis 1988, p. 150).

Some groups are "structured" in that they possess an established leadership hierarchy, a well-delineated division of labor among their members, a more or less exclusive communications network, a reasonably descriptive title or designation, or enough of these features in sufficient measure to warrant such a classification. Other groups may have relatively little formal structure in that they have no designated leaders, no subgroups to which tasks may be allocated, and no communications system other than that which is available to all other House members. Such a group is less likely to have a name which defines its character and by which members and outsiders can readily refer to it.

Group meetings may be carefully organized, with an agenda and list of speakers, or they may encourage a free-flowing exchange of views among participants. Membership may be taken seriously or viewed casually. It may be permanent or temporary; constant or intermittent. And membership may be conferred only by the group as a whole or it may be contingent upon the needs of the Representatives who float in and out of them, depending upon whether affiliation happens to suit their goals at the time.

Over the years, there has been sufficient variation in the character of the groups to warrant their placement in one of three categories.[4] The categories are not mutually exclusive and distinctions among them are often blurred. Nonetheless, they are useful here for analytical purposes. The most formal of the three before its elimination in 1995 was the Legislative Service Organization (LSO). The Congressional Black Caucus, the Democratic Study Group, and the Republican Study Committee were among the better known LSOs. Each of the House delegations from California, New York, and Pennsylvania supported its own LSO. These service organizations were distinguished from other structured groups in that members' fees were ordinarily drawn from clerk-hire funds to pay a staff which was separate and distinct from members' office staffs. They were allocated office space in House facilities, but they could not accept outside funds (from special interest groups, for example) to support their activities. In 1995, members of the twenty-eight LSOs were required to stop using clerk-hire funds to pay LSO staffs and to relinquish office space and equipment devoted to caucus activities. Most LSOs reorganized and joined scores of other caucuses as Congressional Membership Organizations (CMOs).

Caucuses included in this second category of structured groups charge no fees and possess no staff. CMO members shift in and out of leadership roles, their communications networks are unsophisticated, and they do not typically form durable subgroups to perform research or other tasks. Nevertheless, most meet regularly, and possess definable membership boundaries. Many have been uncommonly durable, with Representatives placing a high value on affiliation. Some of the most influential House groups fall into this category, including the Chowder and Marching Society—more about which below.

Unstructured groups make up the third category of informal House agencies. By their very nature their memberships are not easily identified and their boundaries are difficult to define. Included under this heading are groups of Representatives who use the gym, who hunt or golf together, or who often sit with one another on the House floor. Members are hard put to provide a name for their group—other than, say, the "skeet-shooting" group—and they may not be consciously aware they are a part of a clique. Their opportunities to consort with one another may be regular or intermittent, planned or spontaneous, and the duration of their meetings may be extended or brief. Whatever the group's characteristics, congressmen exploit the private, informal setting of group sessions to discuss their priorities and the business of the House, to organize their thoughts about matters that are important to them, and to talk about ways and means of affecting the flow of legislative events. Of course conversation touches on many subjects, social as well as political, but a common interest in these matters reinforces the rapport members have already established with one another and provides additional occasions for exchanging ideas, frames of reference, and political support.

The best known and most durable unstructured House group was the "Board of Education."[5] The Board had its roots in the friendship of two men who would later become House Speakers, Republican Nicholas Longworth and Democrat John Nance Garner. During World War I, the two often met for drinks in a Capitol hideaway called the David Webster Room. Later they moved to an office on the third floor of the Cannon Office Building and began to invite colleagues there to discuss House business over cocktails.

When Longworth became Speaker, he moved the meetings to a room under the Capitol dome, and it was then that the sessions were given a name. House members were invited to the inner sanctum, not to be lectured to by House leaders, but to report what they knew about legislative developments and to indicate by their behavior whether they had leadership potential. Garner explained one of the Board's purposes: "You get a couple of drinks in a young congressman and then you know what he knows and what he can do. We pay the tuition by supplying the liquor" (quoted in McNeil 1963, p. 82).

Other goals of the Board were to expedite congressional business, negotiate disputes, reach accommodations and gentlemen's agreements, distribute patronage, and provide occasions for camaraderie among men who genuinely enjoyed one another's company. Garner continued the tradition when he became Speaker, as did Sam Rayburn after Garner became Vice President. Rayburn moved the meetings to a small room on the first floor of the Capitol, H-128, and for two decades he and his intimates, including John McCormack of Massachusetts, swapped stories, sipped bourbon, and discussed affairs of state.

According to McNeil:

These private sessions were one of the most useful tools of the Speaker's leadership in the House. . . . Other influential men of the House were invited to these sessions, particularly when their expert knowledge of specific problems was needed, and they, too, would participate in developing the Speaker's strategy. (1963, pp. 83–84)

CONGRESSWOMEN AND INFORMAL GROUPS

In 1969, Frieda Gehlen reported that, with the exception of such groups as state delegations and freshmen classes—groups to which members were granted automatic membership—and, apart from the Democratic Study Group, which admitted all Democrats who cared to join, women were denied admission into those "informal groups made up of friends and acquaintances who meet more or less regularly to discuss current legislation, general politics, and whatever else comes to mind" (Gehlen, 1969). She went on to point out that no woman had ever been invited to attend "the Board of Education."

By 1978, much had changed. There were many more groups than when Gehlen conducted her interviews, and, although none had gained access to a group comparable to the Board of Education, virtually all women had become members of LSOs and CMOs. One congresswoman explained why:

A conscientious effort has been made to make congresswomen an integral part of the process. This has happened for two reasons. One, the women's movement has raised men's consciousness about past discrimination against women. Two, women members have been assertive, so assertive that we will simply not stand for being excluded.

House informants did not make a distinction between structured and unstructured informal groups, but there are compelling empirical and analytical reasons for emphasizing their differences. More than three-quarters of the women in the 95th Congress belonged to one or more of the former, even when affiliations with class groups, the Democratic Study Group, state delegations and, of course, the Congresswomen's Caucus, are excluded.[6] Many said membership in these groups was important to them, and several congressmen referred approvingly to contributions women had made to group deliberations. One Republican congressman praised the leadership of a woman who had chaired the Republican Study Committee and another stated:

I belong to the Wednesday Group, which is made up of moderate and progressive Republicans. There are two women members in the Club at the present time and they participate aggressively and are listened to. They are most welcome and attractive members and they are treated as "one of the boys."

A female member commented in general terms about the access women had to House groups:

With few exceptions, members are not excluded from groups if they want to be in them. The informal groups around here are as old as the House itself . . . and from my experience I would say that women are not so much excluded because of their sex as they are included because they have a shared interest with the other members that make up the group.

Widespread acceptance of women by informal groups did not extend to many unstructured groups or to a few caucuses whose membership was by invitation only, and congresswomen acknowledged their exclusion from groups of this sort. One said:

There is one problem area insofar as exclusion is concerned. When males get together in a group and drink together and talk together informally, women are never present. And you can't do that with female members. You don't have the "buddy-buddy" system among women. When the day's business is over, we don't have the time to stay around. We have to rush and take care of the other things we have to do because we have no "wives" to help us.

Congressmen confirmed this observation. Several referred to settings in which male members established the bonds that defined their group. Some talked about the "gym fellowship." Users of the gym made up not one but a congeries of groups with shifting memberships and attendance. They had in common the all-male environment, the locker-room language and banter, and the opportunity to exchange ideas of mutual interest in an atmosphere embodying the physical activities that they saw as natural extensions of their male identities. Relationships of the sort established in the gymnasium were reflected in other settings. Members mentioned after-hours parties, thrown principally by lobbyists who themselves were trying to improve their rapport with influential congressmen. The nature of the entertainment provided on those occasions, along with the stag-party ambience that prevailed on hunting trips, golfing weekends, or cocktail receptions, presupposed that no congresswomen or wives would be present.

House informants gave a number of reasons for barring congresswomen from these settings, reasons which are not mutually exclusive. Many suggested that the presence of women within these informal groupings would force male members to alter their behavior. The men, they noted, would have to do and say things which were inappropriate to the circumstances which prompted the gathering (and, perhaps, the formation of the group) in the first place. They would have to give excessive concern to their appearance, their demeanor and language, and many believed that the nature of the conversations would be affected, as well.

Several male informants stated that women were excluded because they were "different." They were not the same as men because they had not been around Capitol Hill as long as most men, and because they had not established a rapport with male members which permitted or encouraged candid, trusting exchange of confidences. Even if women were accepted by the male fraternity, said one congressman, there were many men who would never be at ease with women. These men found affiliation with unstructured groups worthwhile precisely because they were able to cast aside the inhibitions that mixed company normally required them to sustain.

Some congressmen noted that gatherings in someone's office, a House dining room, or a downtown hotel were social as well as political occasions, and they found socializing with women colleagues when husbands were not present awkward. The absence of spouses in these circumstances risked the accusation that a male and a female Representative were more friendly than was good for the reputation of either. One congressman said that he was very careful about preserving a formal, businesslike relationship with women colleagues, even when meeting with them socially—which, he said, "was not very often."

One described the setting for such a group and offered a commonly heard view of why women were excluded.

This room right here [an office in one of the House Office Buildings] is a meeting place. Different members come by and we sit and drink and rap and talk about how things are going. I have great difficulty imagining a woman coming in and joining the group. She would alter the entire atmosphere. Congressmen ———, ———, and ——— [a committee chairman, a subcommittee chairman, and an aspiring floor leader] and a few others come by and we rap. These men don't have the political rapport with women in the same way that they have it with one another. It would be awkward with women present. The men would feel constrained to straighten their ties, to watch their manners, and to stop themselves from saying "go fuck yourself" when the kidding touched a sensitive nerve.

In 1978, at least two prestigious CMOs contained no women, SOS, and the Chowder and Marching Society. SOS was created in 1953 by future House minority Leader John Rhodes and about twenty other, mostly freshmen Republicans. These members were conservatives who believed they could roll back the liberal excesses of the Roosevelt and Truman administrations. The title of the organization was variously translated as "Save Our Souls," "Help," or "Shit on a Shingle"—the last referring to an all too common meal served in military mess halls.

The Chowder and Marching Society is the older and more prestigious of the two. The origin of its name is uncertain, but it appears to have been chosen whimsically, in the absence of a consensus on alternative titles. The CMO was begun in 1949 by Congressmen Glenn R. Davis of Wisconsin and Donald Jackson of California. The two conservative Republicans were disturbed because a costly veteran's pension bill had been rammed through committee, and they were determined to block its passage on the floor. They summoned thirteen, mostly young, Republicans to meet with them one Wednesday afternoon to consider how to defeat the measure, and the group's members have been meeting weekly ever since. The Society is dedicated to cutting federal spending and reducing the national government's intrusion into the lives of Americans. Among the thirteen charter members were such notables as Richard Nixon and Gerald Ford (Jones, 1964, p. 28).

Membership in C and M grew to between thirty and forty, with one or more members inducted in each Congress, depending upon the number of Society members who did not return from the last Congress. Republican floor leaders and ranking party members on influential standing committees are, with few exceptions, affiliated with the group. All enjoy membership for life, and Representatives who go to the Senate, Cabinet posts, the White House, or back to private life, may continue to attend Society meetings. Presidents Nixon and Ford hosted White House parties for Society members.

The group has no staff and members pay no dues. Until recently weekly meetings were held in the offices of members, with the site rotating among them. The sessions were chaired by the person in whose office the meeting happened to be taking place. When House debate became more contentious, protracted and unpredictable, C and M members moved their meetings to the Minority Leader's conference room, just off the House floor. Only members are permitted to be present, with staff barred—a prohibition more stringent than the one followed on the House floor itself. Members discuss pending legislation, legislative strategy, or other congressional or political matters. Someone who feels strongly about an issue, for example, is free to speak to it and try to influence others to adopt a like point of view.

The political importance of the group is disputed. According to one member, its role in shaping policy is limited. He conceived of it as a social, rather than a political, association, something akin to Rotary or Kiwanis. He acknowledged that members do, indeed, discuss what is going on in their committees, but claimed that no one tried to gather support for a bill or, like the Wednesday Group, relied upon prepared studies and recommendations as a basis for building consensus. Nevertheless, he volunteered that his affiliation with Chowder and Marching was the most valued of all his associations with Washington groups. Another Republican said Society meetings were an important opportunity for influencing colleagues and for establishing frames of reference and impressions which give meaning and weight to future events. The things that are done at these meetings, he noted, are later reflected in the behavior of Society members, as well as in the decisions of other Republicans and in the actions of the House itself.

In 1978, no congresswoman was a member of C and M nor had any woman ever been a member.[7] More surprising was the response of two Republican women, and a much larger number of female Democrats, who had never heard of the Society. One of the two Republican congresswomen added agitatedly, "And what's more I don't care about the Chowder and March on Society [sic], or whatever it's called. Groups like that have nothing to do with what's really going on here and it gives me a headache to think that you people [social scientists] are even interested in it." Several male members said they knew little about the group, responses difficult to reconcile with the claim of one Society member who believed it was among the most influential caucuses in the House. This was especially so, he said, since the Society began to hold breakfast meetings with SOS.

Another Republican woman, one who said she knew no woman was a member at the time, was nonetheless astonished to learn that no woman had ever even been asked to join. She reasoned that given the talent of many past and present Republican women, the exclusion of all clearly suggested that they were discriminated against because of their gender. Society members may have been reacting to bias charges when they later formed a Chowder and Marching Auxiliary. However, membership was limited to Representatives' wives (*New York Times*, March 15, 1982).

While both male and female House members acknowledged the systematic exclusion of women from unstructured groups and recognized, as well, their absence from the more visible Chowder and Marching Society, they did not agree about whether, as a result, congresswomen were less effective. A majority of male members said that women Representatives were not handicapped by their absence from such groups, and that they had just as much of an opportunity as male members to help their constituents and to affect legislation. Several congressmen pointed out that women were members of other informal groups, and therefore, had many opportunities to make behind-the-scenes contributions.

Female respondents were divided about equally between those who believed exclusion limited the usefulness of their House service and those who did not. One Democratic woman said the meetings of these groups were little more than "bull sessions," and she would decline to attend even if invited. Another Democrat was indifferent. Membership was irrelevant to her because she and other female Representatives had learned how to achieve their goals without being part of such groups. "And besides," she added, "the Congresswomen's Caucus gives us our own group now. We get together and do our own thing."

Some congresswomen, on the other hand, agreed with former Representative Edith Green who asserted in 1972 that women do not play an important role in Congress. She added:

In the days of Sam Rayburn, the most powerful group here was something called the "Kitchen Cabinet [sic]." They were Rayburn's male buddies who got together evenings . . . drank bourbon, talked, and decided the course of the nation. John McCormack was the same way. I guess his clique didn't drink bourbon, but over card games the males chose to make the big decisions that counted. (Dreifus 1972)

Other female Representatives said they were unable to be as effective as they might be because they did not have the sounding boards and communication networks unstructured groups provided for male members. One congresswoman said members lose something when they cannot participate in groups of this kind, something which is difficult to define. She put it this way:

Members who don't or can't participate in them are like the kid in college who has no one to study with; no one to exchange ideas with to get a broader idea of what's going on in the class; no one to work with to get the right kind of "vibes" about the course and the teacher. It takes longer for that kid to understand what is going on and often that student is never as good as he or she could be.

The absence of a consensus about whether congresswomen were seriously handicapped by exclusion from informal groups suggests that members differed not only about what they hoped to contribute to the legislative process but also about what they expected to derive from their service in Congress. They differed, as well, in their perceptions of what phases of the decision-making process were important. This tendency to minimize the influence of informal groups may be partly a reflection of the unwillingness of people who are excluded from an activity to attribute much significance to it (Gehlen 1969, p. 39).

WOMEN AND GROUPS IN THE 1990s

Group life by 1993 had become richer and more differentiated. In 1983, Republicans had formed the Conservative Opportunity Society (COS), a caucus headed by Georgia's Newt Gingrich. By 1985 COS had forty members, and it served as a springboard for Gingrich's rise to party Whip in 1989 and to Speaker of the House in 1995. In the meantime, more moderate Republicans formed the "92 Group," a caucus they hoped would help them become a House majority after the 1992 elections. In 1989, dozens of members combined to form the Congressional Sportsmen's Caucus, which, by 1993, numbered 182 Representatives and thirty-five Senators. All of these groups invited congresswomen to join, and by 1993 they were all integrated.

Ultimately, even the two principal bastions of male exclusivity, SOS and the Chowder and Marching Society, changed their membership rules. In 1988, SOS asked Olympia Snowe and Lynn Martin to join its ranks, and, by 1993, at least one-third of the twelve Republican women were affiliated. Following the 1992 election, C and M inducted its first congresswomen, Ileana Ros-Lehtinen and first-termer Tillie Fowler—both from Florida.[8] This step by the oldest of elite Republican caucuses was unknown to many House members months after it had been taken. Reactions of those later informed ranged from surprise to disbelief. One moderate Republican congressman exclaimed, "By God, that hoary old group has finally come around." And a conservative Republican congresswoman refused to accept the news, saying "I cannot imagine who they could possibly have admitted," implying that if C and M admitted any woman, it would have been she. A motive for the shift in membership policy was suggested by a Republican congresswoman:

They did it very late and reluctantly. The increased number of women in the House made "the old boys" vulnerable to questions and charges in the press about why they excluded women. They were being "politically correct."

At the same time, some unstructured groups became accessible to women, while others diminished in number and importance. Two congresswomen, Barbara Kennelly and Barbara Vucanovich, joined male colleagues on the golf course, and others appeared at nearby gun clubs for skeet shooting. Congresswomen who were joggers sometimes joined similarly disposed congressmen, and more women began to attend informal evening gatherings and supper meetings. Groups of congresswomen agreed to meet among themselves, independent of the regularly scheduled sessions of the Congressional Caucus for Women's Issues. In the 102nd Congress, Republican women dined together once a month, occasionally accompanied by high-ranking female members in the Bush administration. The practice was continued in 1993, with from six to eight of the GOP women participating

each evening, an attendance level belying the consensus that congresswomen have a harder time getting together than men do.

There is evidence, as well, that many all-male, late afternoon and evening
cliques have fallen victim to a more burdensome legislative workload and
an increasing number of "Tuesday to Thursday" House members resolved
to spend more time at home with angry and distrustful constituents. "The
'after hours' groups are a thing of the past," said one congressman. He
added:

The days of Sam Rayburn's Board of Education are also over. That was when a small
group of men could dictate congressional decisions and the fate of the country. Now
things are too decentralized. And the influence of groups that exclude women is
minimal. Things are wide open now and there are many people in the House who
influence policy. . . . The fact that women are excluded from some groups varies in
significance from the trivial to the inconsequential.

The one type of unstructured group that persists and to which women
may never gain entry are the "gym" groups. Dozens of congressmen play
basketball or racquetball daily, often with the same cast of colleagues. The
rapport they establish with one another and the social and political ideas
they exchange in a locker room setting are available to congresswomen only
at significantly greater opportunity costs, if at all. Several males who were
not part of the gym culture said they regret not being able to make use of
yet another occasion to make friends and influence people. The importance
of such groups was highlighted by a senior Democratic congresswoman.
She recalled having reached an agreement with two male members about
a language change they would jointly offer to legislation being considered
by their subcommittee. When the proposal was introduced by one of the
two men the following morning, it varied somewhat from the language
upon which they had initially agreed. She remembered the incident this
way:

I supported the new language, but after the subcommittee meeting I went up to
Congressman _____ and asked him what had happened to the language the three
of us had agreed to. He said that he and the other fellow had thought up the second
version while working out in the gym and, he kiddingly said, that I ought to take
up paddle ball before I miss out on anything else. Now that happened just last week,
and if you had asked me about the importance of these groups before then I would
probably have said that they were unimportant. But I can see now that they matter,
not so much in terms of whether major legislation passes or does not pass, but in
terms of what's in a bill and what's not in a bill.

Gym cliques aside, congresswomen have become more fully integrated
into the life of the House since the 1960s and especially during the last
decade. Their increased numbers and formidable political skills have made
them indispensable additions to congressional groups, structured and un-

structured. One consequence of this development is that they are now better positioned to place women's concerns—priorities growing out of their private, gender-related experiences—on the legislative agenda. To succeed, congresswomen must first persuade male Representatives that these priorities are legitimate and that they are shared by a national constituency. Their access to previously all-male groups offers new opportunities to promote the "ripeness" of their causes in politically useful settings. The informality, intimacy, and exchange of trust obtaining in such settings provide an ideal atmosphere in which to alter preconceptions about what the country's goals ought to be and which of our often conflicting values ought to prevail. Consequently, to the extent that congresswomen with a feminist orientation are able to alter the mind sets of their male colleagues, problems such as domestic violence may become congressional priorities. More will be said about this in Part IV, "Behavior."

A second consequence of fuller House integration for women is that they are now strategically placed to seize top party leadership posts. In 1993, the highest positions were filled by men able to capitalize on relationships cultivated in elite sub-groups. Women's difficulties in ascending the leadership ladder is almost certainly linked to past exclusion from these groups. But, as will be made clear in the next chapter, they recently began to claim more than a handful of secondary leadership roles, and they are poised to penetrate the highest levels—not least because they have established better developed informal relationships with male colleagues.

NOTES

1. Late in 1981, the House Administration Committee ordered legislative service organizations (which make up a large component, but not a majority of the groups discussed here) that accept funds from extra-congressional sources either to stop the practice or give up publicly supported staffs, office space, and other facilities. The ruling also required regular reporting procedures and stricter accountability in the use of office staffs and public funds. See *Congressional Quarterly Weekly Report*, Vol. 39, October 24, 1981, p. 2074. The new guidelines also had an important impact on the Congresswomen's Caucus, as is made clear in Chapter 10. In 1995, House rules were changed to prevent caucuses whose activities were underwritten by public funds from continuing to rely on such support. Legislative Service Organizations were thereby eliminated. Members of most continued to meet regularly, however, and took on the properties of Congressional Membership Organizations. LSO staffs moved out of public facilities and began to rely on private funding to support publications and activities, which until then had been financed by public funds.

2. The Democratic Study Group and the Republican Study Committee are two groups anchored in party affiliation. Ideological groups include the Conservative Opportunity Society and the Progressive Caucus. The Northeast-Midwest Congressional Coalition is an example of a group based on regional interests, and the Hispanic and Black caucuses are the two best known ethnic and racial group-

ings. The Steel, Auto, and Textile caucuses are made up of members whose constituencies share common economic concerns.

3. An exact count of caucuses is difficult to come by, but the figure of one hundred is certainly a conservative estimate if partisan and bipartisan state delegations are included. Hammond (1989) found 120 active caucuses at the end of 1987 and noted that forty others had become inactive.

4. Hammond's (1989) six-part typology—national constituency, regional, state/district, industry, party and personal interest—is based upon members' motivation for joining. The three categories offered here are based on degree of structural differentiation.

5. Some characteristics of the Board of Education correspond closely to those possessed by structured groups, but the changing cast of characters attending its meetings (apart from the party leaders themselves), the small number of members present, and the secret, almost conspiratorial nature of its deliberations distinguish it from most caucuses.

6. The Congresswomen's Caucus was formed in 1977, and it observed a prohibition on male membership until late in 1981. When men joined the group, it changed its name to the Congressional Caucus for Women's Issues. The former title is used when referring to group activities through 1981, the latter when alluding to events after that year. See chapters 10 and 11.

7. A Chowder and Marching Society membership list was not obtained, and members do not readily volunteer the names of other members. The group's failure ever to admit a congresswoman through 1978 was learned in interviews with two Society members in the 95th Congress.

8. C and M's selection of two women from the same state is puzzling, given its interest in maintaining geographical balance within its membership. A Florida Representative opined that since South Florida (in which Ros-Lehtinen's district lies) and North Florida (Fowler's region) are like two different states, the Society was getting more economic and cultural diversity than was immediately apparent.

 6

Access to Leadership Positions

Until recently, selecting a woman for a country's highest government positions was so uncommon that when such a choice was made it occasioned a response otherwise reserved for landing a man on the moon. The anemic ranks of twentieth-century female leaders that included Indira Gandhi of India, Sirmavo Bandaranaike of Sri Lanka, and Israel's Golda Meir were augmented in 1979 by British, Portuguese, and Bolivian leaders. Since then, voters and legislators in Norway, Iceland, the diminutive Caribbean island of Dominica, Yugoslavia, Denmark, the Philippines, Pakistan, Poland, Canada, and Turkey have followed suit.[1] But each of these instances constitutes for these countries the one and only case of female success at the highest level, and their novelty punctuates the limited progress women have made to date. Writing in 1955, the esteemed political scientist Maurice Duverger observed that however much women in government received the support and respect of male colleagues, equality deteriorated when keen competition for legislative leadership developed between them. The French scholar said he saw no sign of change in these conditions (Duverger 1955, pp. 123–125).

NO ROOM AT THE TOP

Duverger might well have been describing the predicament of women in the House of Representatives. For, unlike their sisters in American state legislatures, congresswomen have been unable to penetrate the highest ranks of their party hierarchies.[2] No woman has ever served as House Speaker, floor leader, or Chief Whip, and no female Representative has presided over her party's caucus, or chaired her party's Policy, Steering, Campaign, or Personnel Committees. None has directed the proceedings of a Committee on Committees, and few have served on, let alone headed, any of the four most sought-after standing House committees—Appropriations, Budget, Rules, and Ways and Means.

Consequently, describing and analyzing the progress congresswomen have made in securing leadership positions means focusing on secondary party posts—those to which their parties assign either limited or token responsibilities. Although not nearly as influential as, say, the Whip, they are important because top leaders have recently delegated more power to them and because they frequently serve as springboards to higher party positions.

SECONDARY AGENCIES OF PARTY LEADERSHIP

Most members who hold secondary leadership positions carry out a narrow range of responsibilities. Their opportunities to exercise influence are normally shared with more than a few colleagues, and the deference and perquisites they receive are minor when compared with those enjoyed by top leaders. Nonetheless, they affect selected decisions more markedly than do representatives who hold no party positions at all. Currently, these members serve as caucus or conference officers below that of chair, and as chief deputy, deputy, regional, assistant and at-large whips. They are also members of policy committees, campaign committees, committees on committees, personnel committees and the Republican Research Committee.

Several secondary positions are of token importance. Many representatives on the Democratic Campaign Committee, for example, do little to contribute to party fortunes. The committee is made up of representatives from each state sending at least one member of the party to the House. It contains an executive subcommittee, however, and the subcommittee monopolizes the decision-making process. Other members do little more than rubber stamp agreements hammered out in executive sessions—sessions often dominated by the committee chairman and by party leaders who are committee members *ex officio*. Until 1989, the Republican Committee on Committees was similarly constituted and many of its members held "token" positions (Bone 1956, p. 118; Jones 1965, p. 97; Peabody 1976, p. 271; Rohde 1991, p. 137).

The number of secondary party positions has increased substantially in recent years as Democratic and Republican leadership structures have become more institutionalized. Democratic positions have grown from 87 to 226 since 1949, reflecting an effort to integrate junior representatives into middle-level leadership ranks. Marked changes have taken place in the size of the Democratic Whip network as well as in the size of that party's Campaign Committee—changes that more than offset the Democrats' elimination of their Committee on Committees and the absorption of that panel's functions by a reorganized Steering and Policy Committee (Rohde 1991, p. 86).

Proliferation in Republican positions has been almost as great, with growth in the size of its Policy Committee and the addition of a Research Committee contributing appreciably to its overall increase. These new positions have augmented the opportunities available to representatives interested in capitalizing on party service at an intermediate level. At the same time, the more sharply etched division of labor within the leadership structure and the *ex officio* additions of leaders to party panels have permitted these secondary agencies to exercise more influence than they once did.

Modest though their responsibilities have been, the importance of serving on them should not be underestimated. Party conferences and policy committees have been revitalized within the last thirty years, and leadership of the former and service on the latter have become more desirable (Peabody 1976, pp. 294–295; Ripley 1983, p. 219). Former Speaker John McCormack began regular meetings of the Democratic Caucus in 1969, a practice continued and strengthened by his successors (Jones 1964, p. 104; Dodd 1979, p. 29; Rohde 1991, p. 24). Congressional Campaign Committees, too, have become more important, in part because of the increased sums needed to run a successful campaign and because public financing of presidential elections has had the effect of funneling larger private sums into House contests. Contributions of in-kind assistance by these panels, particularly by the National Republican Congressional Committee, have become more important (Jacobson 1992, p. 74). The specialized skills now needed to contest House seats have given these Committees unusual opportunities to contribute to the political futures of those who run under their labels. Between 1976 and 1986, spending by the Democratic Congressional Campaign Committee increased from $1 million to $13.5 million. Comparable National Republican Congressional Committee expenditures were $9.2 million and $41.2 million (Herrnson 1988, pp. 32–34).

The greater size and significance of the whip organizations is also worth noting. The addition of chief deputy whips, deputy whips and, for the Democrats, at-large whips, have made these networks more hierarchical. At the same time, recorded votes on floor amendments and electronic voting have required assistant whips to stay in closer touch with rank-and-file members and to attend more strategy sessions with party leaders (Dodd 1979, pp. 29–40). The Democratic whip network has been augmented by party task forces. Since 1977, a task force has been created for virtually every important legislative measure. Each is chaired by a representative appointed by the leadership. Most other members emerge from the committee having jurisdiction over the bill in question and from interested members of the party whip organization. Once formed, a task force proceeds to do all it can to persuade colleagues to support the bill around which the group has coalesced. Thus task forces have become an integral component of the Democratic whip operation (Loomis 1988, p. 177; Rohde 1991, p. 88).

Affiliation with secondary party agencies is valuable because conscientious service on them has frequently led to a top leadership position (Peabody 1976, p. 12). Massachusetts Congressman Joseph Martin was an assistant whip when named Republican floor leader in 1938,[3] and one year later John McCormack was promoted from Caucus Chairman to majority leader when Sam Rayburn became Speaker (Peabody 1976, p. 280). In 1961, four ambitious Republicans, California's Bob Wilson, Michigan's Gerry Ford, Wisconsin's Melvin Laird, and Arizona's John Rhodes, sought the chairmanship of their party's Campaign Committee. Wilson's victory did not deter the other three from later securing other intermediate party posts, positions from which Ford and Rhodes later vaulted to floor leader. More recently, Democrat Tom Foley was elected House Speaker after many years of apprenticeship in lesser party posts.

Another reason for focusing on these secondary agencies is that accepting an appointment to them signals at least a modest desire to assume party responsibilities. The service itself, in turn, provides opportunities to demonstrate leadership qualities, to establish friendships and rapport with colleagues whose support may later be called upon, and to acquire knowledge about people and issues which may subsequently be employed to persuade others of one's personal and political prowess.

Of course, not all House members want a leadership position, and many of those who serve on party instrumentalities do not intend to use them as stepping stones to more important posts (Peabody 1976, p. 4). But experience on one or more of these agencies has come to be an all but necessary condition for selection as party whip, floor leader, and Speaker, and it seems appropriate therefore to note the changing frequencies with which female representatives have served on them.

CONGRESSWOMEN IN SECONDARY LEADERSHIP POSITIONS

In her analysis of the 87th Congress, Frieda Gehlen found that few female representatives serving in 1962 were members of their party's leadership hierarchy. Furthermore, the male House members with whom she spoke gave women no chance of being elected to senior party positions. The most common reason for this view was that women were unable to establish the informal relationships upon which would-be leaders must rely. Some congressmen thought that their female colleagues were too emotional or too idealistic; others that they were too subjective or too rigid. Accordingly, they saw little chance of a woman receiving enough votes from male members of her party, and some believed that leadership roles should, as a matter of course, be reserved for men (Gehlen 1969, pp. 39–40).

A count of the women holding secondary leadership positions from the end of World War II to 1964 corroborates the observations of Gehlen's informants. As is evident in Table 6.1, which aggregates positions held by each woman serving in each Congress within each of three time periods, a Democratic woman had yet to be appointed to her party's whip network or the House Rules Committee, and none had served on the Democratic Patronage Committee. On the other hand, women had regularly been Secretary to the Democratic Caucus, several had been appointed to the Democratic Committee on Committees, and a few had served on their party's campaign committee. Occasional ex officio service by the caucus secretary on the Steering Committee also occurred.

Republican congresswomen had fared about as well as female Democrats. To be sure, none had been tapped for Conference Secretary, a niche that was more important to Republicans than to Democrats,[4] and none had served on the Congressional Campaign Committee. But several had been members of their party's Policy Committee, a more significant body than the Democratic Steering Committee (Jones 1964, pp. 104–105), and Katharine St. George had been appointed to both the executive subcommittee of the Committee on Committees and the House Rules Committee. The influential New Yorker also served as one of three regional whips, a distinction shared by Washington state's Catherine May. (See Appendix D for a listing of congresswomen who have held secondary leadership positions from 1947 to 1994.)

In the years since Gehlen's study, Democratic women have steadily increased their presence within the expanding whip network and they have been tapped regularly for positions on their party's policy and campaign committees. Perhaps more important is their success in securing seats on the coveted Rules Committee, even though no more than one woman has been on the panel at any given time. The figures in Table 6.1 for the most recent period approach or exceed those recorded between 1965 and 1984, even though the former period includes five Congresses and the latter embraces ten. Republican women generally outpaced their Democratic counterparts. Their improved fortunes are reflected in Lynn Martin's two terms as Vice Chair of her party's Conference, her term on the Rules Committee and the frequent selection of Nancy Johnson and Olympia Snowe as members of the Republican Whip network. These same women, along with Barbara Vucanovich, Jan Meyers, and Ileana Ros-Lehtinen, have periodically served on the influential Policy Committee. (See Appendix D.)

These data do not distinguish between more important and less important leadership positions, however. Neither do they take into account the total number of congresswomen serving during each of the stipulated time periods, a factor which would obviously affect how many could have possibly been elevated to secondary roles. The first of these limitations has been addressed by separating leadership positions into categories reflecting the nature of the responsibilities each is expected to fulfill. A category of *strategic* positions includes both parties' chief deputy, deputy, regional and

Table 6.1
Congresswomen in Secondary Leadership Positions, 1947–1993[a]

Democratic Women

Congresses (years)	Caucus Officers	Whip Network	Steering and Policy Comm.	Campaign Comm.	Comm. on Comms.	Rules Comm.	Patronage Comm.
80th-88th (1947-64)	10	0	2	8	4	0	0
89th-98th (1965-84)	10	15	14	21	5b	3	0
99th-103rd (1985-93)	2c	31	9	22	-	3	NA

Republican Women

Congresses (years)	Caucus Officers	Whip Network	Policy Comm.	Campaign Comm.	Comm. on Comms.	Rules Comm.	Personnel Comm.	Research Comm.
80th-88th (1947-64)	0	5	8	0	3	2	0	-
89th-98th (1965-84)	0	2	5	11	17	0	2	2
99th-103rd (1985-93)	2	10	14	35	14	1	d	8

a) Each Term's service for each Congresswoman in a secondary leadership position is counted separately.
b) In 1975, Committee on Committees responsibilities were removed from the Democrats Ways and Means Committee and given to the Democratic Steering and Policy Committee.
c) The Democrats eliminated the post of Caucus Secretary in 1988. Until then it had been routinely held by a Congresswoman
d) Eliminated after the 100th Congress.
Sources: Congressional Record, Congressional Quarterly Almanac, Congressional Staff Directory.

assistant whips, Democratic at-large whips, Rules Committee appointees, and executive subcommittee members of the campaign committees. Steering and Policy Committee members also fall under this heading. The positions are defined as strategic because Representatives holding them normally help to shape and implement their party's legislative or campaign strategies. Decisions that affect schedules of committee and floor deliberations, the framework of debate, mobilization of party strength, and distribution of campaign contributions all have the character of partisan combat. They reflect efforts to gain legislative, political, and electoral leverage for partisan purposes.

Leadership positions defined as *integrative* are found most prominently on the Committees on Committees, the personnel committees, and the Republican Research Committee. Secondary caucus and conference officials also play integrative roles. The functions of these positions are to reconcile individual aspirations with organizational goals, and to promote cooperation and unity among party members. Representatives filling them distribute rewards in ways calculated to satisfy members' needs and to encourage them to seek consensus.[5] Integrative leaders facilitate intraparty discussion, invite expression of many points of view, distribute patronage, promote policy-oriented research and formulate long-term policy goals. Distribution of committee assignments is among the most important integrative tasks performed within each party.

The third type of secondary leadership category is defined here as *token*. It refers to positions which carry little responsibility, and which reflect a recognition for their occupants which is more apparent than real. Selection to either of the two campaign committees and, before 1989, to the Republican Committee on Committees, but not the executive subcommittees of these three panels, means that House members will make little more than token contributions to their parties' electoral, legislative, or organizational goals.

Of course, some party instrumentalities undertake both strategic and integrative tasks. Whip networks, for example, distribute information which could lead to consensus, just as they try to mobilize party members to do combat with the opposition. Policy committees, particularly the minority party panel, seek to formulate legislative options which are both acceptable to their members and subversive of opposition party unity. Accordingly, the categories are not mutually exclusive and, for purposes of analysis, Democrats serving on the Steering and Policy Committee since 1975, when that panel began to determine committee assignments, are considered as exercising both strategic and integrative leadership roles. Republicans on the party's Policy Committee are treated similarly, inasmuch as they devise policy options as a strategic tool while simultaneously shaping party consensus and internal harmony. The distinctions made here help shed light on the nature of the responsibilities parties have assigned to congresswomen, as well as the frequency with which each type of responsibility has been distributed.

To determine the progress congresswomen have made in obtaining secondary leadership posts, use has been made of a statistical measure which takes into account the number of secondary positions to be filled and the number of women serving in the House. Infrequent appointments may be as much a reflection of the small number of women elected to the House as it is an indication of leadership reluctance to elevate women to reasonably weighty party positions.

The measure, an "Index of Female Representation," has been calculated for each of the three categories of positions.[6] A score of 1.00 indicates that women hold leadership positions equal in proportion to that which they would have secured if these positions were awarded randomly. If, for example, a total of ten Democratic congresswomen were eligible for 100 leadership positions also available to 190 Democratic males, the Index of Female Representation would be 1.00 if five of the ten filled leadership positions. If, on the other hand, only two positions were assigned to women, the Index would be 0.40, indicating that they held two-fifths of the positions that their number alone (as a proportion of the total number of Democrats serving in the House) suggests they should hold. An Index of 2.0 means that twice as many positions were filled by women than they would hold if the vacancies were distributed randomly.

The figures appearing in Table 6.2 are Indexes of Female Representation scored by Democratic and Republican women from 1947 to 1993. This period has been divided to permit comparison of female success rates over time, as well as between the two parties. Thus, from 1947 to 1964, Democratic congresswomen were only about one-half as likely (0.53) as one would expect to serve in strategic positions, while holding their own in integrative leadership positions. They were almost four times more likely to be found on token party agencies than their numbers and chance would suggest. In subsequent years they first improved substantially their level of representation in the first two categories, only to fall back to more modest proportions during the last ten years. In the meantime, the rate of assignment to token party instrumentalities declined significantly, an indication, perhaps, that Democratic women became increasingly unwilling to accept positions whose potential influence is scant.

Republican women serving from 1965 to 1984 found themselves in strategic and integrative roles comparatively less often than was the case in earlier years. During this middle period, only two GOP congresswomen were selected to serve as a deputy, regional, or assistant whip, or as a Rules Committee member, and even the selection of Marjorie Holt, Nancy Johnson, and Barbara Vucanovich as Campaign Committee Vice Chairwomen in the 97th and 98th Congresses raised the strategic Index to a relatively feeble 0.41. (See Appendix D.) Republican women went from a

Table 6.2
Index of Female Representation for Strategic, Integrative, and Token Leadership Positions, 1947–1993

| Congresses (years) | Type of Position | | | | | | Average Number of Women serving per Term | |
| | Strategic[1] | | Integrative[2] | | Token[3] | | | |
	Dem.	Rep.	Dem.	Rep.	Dem.	Rep.	Dem.	Rep.
80th-88th (1947-1964)	0.53	1.09	0.95	1.18	3.94	0.00	7	6
89th-97th (1965-1984)	1.35	0.41	1.80	0.80	1.55	1.56	10	5
98th-103rd (1985-1993)	0.99	1.55	1.18	1.02	0.89	2.13	19	11

1. Includes Democratic positions in the whip network and on the Rules Committee, the Steering Committee (later the Steering and Policy Committee), and the executive subcommittee of the Campaign Committee; Republican positions in the whip network and on the Policy Committee, the Rules Committee, and the executive subcommittee of the Campaign Committee.

2. Includes Democratic positions on the Committee on Committees, the Steering and Policy Committee from 1975-1994, and the Personnel (Patronage) Committee, and caucus officers who were *ex officio* members of the Steering (or Steering and Policy) Committee; Republican positions on the Policy, Research, and Personnel (Patronage) Committees, and the executive subcommittee of the Committee on Committees. Republican Caucus officers are also included.

3. Includes Democratic and Republican Campaign Committee members and Republican Committee on Committees members who did not serve on these panels' executive subcommittees.

slight overrepresentation to a slight underrepresentation on integrative positions.

The most recent period has witnessed a substantial turnaround for Republican women, however, and they can claim greater success in securing strategic secondary leadership positions than can Democratic congresswomen. The steady increase in their presence on token committees suggests a continued willingness by Republican women to undertake relatively innocuous responsibilities, but the change is probably insignificant inasmuch as the augmented tokenism has been accompanied by appointments to party agencies that really matter.

The broadest inference to be drawn from the Table is that Congresswomen have, for the most part, held their own when secondary leadership positions were apportioned. True, fluctuations have occurred, but during the last thirty years, Democratic women have secured as many positions in all three categories as their numbers would entitle them to. Republican women experienced a "drought" between 1965 and 1984, but during the last ten years, they have generally been as successful as Democratic congresswomen.

What the table does not reveal is that, until recently, a literal reading of Duverger's observations has been borne out. Equality between men and women has deteriorated when they contested leadership positions. The operative term is "contested." From 1947 to 1984, virtually all positions held by women in both parties were conferred on them by leaders rather than wrested from men in intra-party battles. With one exception, none competed successfully with one or more male colleagues in an up or down vote.[7]

The women who served on the Democratic Steering and Policy Committee during this period included such stalwarts as Julia Butler Hansen, Leonor Sullivan, Barbara Jordan, Gladys Spellman, Geraldine Ferraro, and Patricia Schroeder. Each was selected by the Speaker and his close advisors, not in an open contest with ambitious male Democrats. Sullivan and Ferraro were *ex officio* members because of their position as Secretary of the Democratic Caucus. But the secretary's position was, until its elimination in 1987, reserved for women members and had never been held by a male. Among the many women who were part of their parties' whip network, none secured the position in an intra-party election.

During the last ten years, this pattern has begun to change significantly in ways not fully revealed by Table 6.2. Lynn Martin's election as Vice Chair of the Republican Conference came only four years after she first arrived in Washington. She subsequently lost a race for Conference Chair by three votes.[8] Other congresswomen, including Democrats Mary Rose Oakar, Marcy Kaptur, and Barbara Kennelly, broke new ground when they contested, albeit unsuccessfully, similar leadership positions. In 1992, Nancy Johnson challenged but lost to incumbent Republican Vice Chair Bill McCollum, the first time a congresswoman had been so bold as to seek a high party post that was not vacant. In the meantime, female Democrats, including Nancy Pelosi, Elizabeth Patterson, and Anna Eshoo (in her first term) have been elected assistant whips by colleagues from their regional zones. In 1993, Patsy Mink became the first woman elected, rather than appointed, to the Democratic Steering and Policy Committee.

Greater progress by congresswomen is also reflected in the choices made by both parties to fill Rules Committee vacancies. When Katherine St. George, the first woman ever to serve on the Rules Committee, was named to the panel in 1961, she had been in the House for sixteen years. The three Republican men simultaneously appointed to the Committee with her had served an average of six years. Shirley Chisholm, who in 1977 was the next woman selected for the Committee, had been in the House for eight years. But the three women elevated to the Rules Committee during the last ten years averaged fewer than five years of House experience.[9]

Reliance on this formal record, valuable though it may be, offers only a two-dimensional account of the elusiveness and frequency of leadership opportunities available to congresswomen. It says little about the perceptions members have about the accessibility women have to leadership positions, their beliefs about the extent to which women are discriminated against in this regard, and their expectations about the prospects women have for future leadership opportunities. What follows is an account of changing views members have held about each of these matters. The account rests on two sets of interviews. The first, conducted in 1978, sought the observations of thirteen congresswomen and eleven congressmen. The second was completed in the summer of 1993, and involved thirty-three female and twelve male Representatives serving in the 103rd Congress. The two groups were asked identical questions about the accessibility congresswomen have to leadership positions, the gender-based obstacles they may encounter, and future prospects women have for obtaining a top leadership position. (See Appendix C, items 21–26.)

Responses to these questions add a perceptual dimension to the questions addressed in this chapter. They also provide useful anecdotal evidence. Perhaps most important, a comparison of observations made in 1978 with those offered in 1993 allows inferences to be drawn about the extent to which fifteen years have made a difference in the integration of congresswomen into their parties' leadership structures.

PERCEPTIONS OF LEADERSHIP OPPORTUNITIES FOR CONGRESSWOMEN

Attaining a leadership position in the House is a product of many factors, some of which defy precise definition.[10] First, members must aspire to leadership responsibility and purposively work to obtain it. They know that these positions are neither awarded by default nor conferred on the timid. Normally, a person becomes a leader only after privately testing the waters, requesting support from the party colleagues most likely to give it, publicly announcing an intention to seek the post, and then working to muster the votes needed. But few House members actively seek these positions. Most are content to "cultivate their constituencies" and "make their contributions through participation in committee and floor activity" (Peabody 1976, p. 4).

A member's ability to penetrate the leadership hierarchy is also related to his or her qualifications. Legislative and political skills, a knowledge and understanding of the House, and personality characteristics which are either appealing or which do not repel a large number of colleagues are of considerable importance. Other telling factors are length of House service (floor leaders in recent years served an average of eighteen years before their elevation to that post; whips an average of nine years [Ripley 1983, p. 213]); the type of district and the state represented; policy orientations (although one study suggests that "moderateness" and party loyalty have not been particularly important criteria affecting leadership selection [Sullivan 1975, pp. 33 and 41]); the extent to which an aspirant has supported successful contestants in previous leadership battles; and the particular mix of members who happen to make up the bulk of the leadership when a Representative attempts to be inducted into its ranks.

A good many House members are winnowed out of the leadership pool because they do not possess "a set of more or less intangible traits labeled 'leadership potential.'" They are unlikely to succeed unless they believe that they have that potential and unless they act on their belief "in characteristic ways" (Peabody 1976, p. 472). Finally, a leadership candidate's gender is an attribute of which House members are likely to be aware (even if they discount it) when deciding which colleague warrants their support.

Most of these factors were mentioned or referred to indirectly by informants who were asked about the degree to which the last of these considerations, gender, affected leadership choices made by House members. Although a few male and female Representatives said that they had once or twice voted for a woman because she was a woman, it should come as no surprise that most respondents pointed out the difficulty of explaining selection decisions in terms of a single, isolated variable. All interviewees were nonetheless prepared to comment on the importance of gender in the calculus of leadership choice, and these responses make it possible to draw inferences not only about the willingness of House members to select congresswomen to lead them, but also about the attitudes that contribute to women's handicaps in this regard.

Male Perceptions, 1978

In 1978, most congressmen interviewed were disinclined to choose a congresswoman for a top leadership position. Selection of a woman for a secondary party role was one thing—elevation to a major leadership role quite another. Some respondents said that they themselves might vote for a woman, but each added that male colleagues were not ready to do the same. A few mentioned specific female Representatives whose future leadership prospects were bright. But more alluded to women who they believed would never attain a position of party responsibility, citing personal liabilities for the most part. They concluded that, given the attitudes of current colleagues, the emergence of a female floor leader or whip or caucus chairman was many years away.

One congressman expressed directly the view only hinted at by others when he observed that it is unrealistic to expect a woman leader to be chosen before women become a larger proportion of the House membership. Only then, he asserted, are the chances of a woman being chosen significantly increased. He added:

When you're dealing with a population that is so predominantly male, selection of a female leader would be inconsistent with the laws of probability. The leadership is likely to be representative of its constituency, and the overwhelming percentage of its constituents is not female.

Some informants speculated that if a woman were extraordinarily able, better qualified than her male competitors, she could conceivably be elected. But she would have to have demonstrated in unambiguous fashion that she was hard-working, reliable, and flexible, and that she possessed both sound judgment and had the interests of her party (and not only of her constituents and her ideological following) at heart. One Democratic congressman echoed the views of many other respondents when he said that "no woman is likely to be elected to a leadership position in the near future." What does seem possible, he continued, is that a female might be selected Democratic Whip since that is an appointive rather than an elected position. Her performance as whip might then permit her to develop the coalition she would need to be elected floor leader and, perhaps, one day, Speaker. But, he added, "there is just no way a woman could make it today."[11]

Congressmen varied in the reasons they gave for reaching this conclusion. Some attributed it to the attitudes of those making the selection, others suggested that it had to do with the qualities of specific female members and women in general, and some offered both kinds of explanations. A few noted that many of their colleagues believed it was "in the nature of things" for men to have authority over women, not the other way around. Some added that House members were unaccustomed to working with or for a woman before they came to Congress. They saw themselves as the principal authority figure in their own households, and they were not prepared to accept a sharp departure from such arrangements in Congress. Informants also suggested that some congressmen never even entertained the idea that they were the equals of the women with whom they were serving, and the possibility of their looking to a congresswoman for leadership was, for them, unthinkable. Several of these same respondents said that many congressmen would find dealing with a woman leader awkward. These members, informants intimated, would not know how to adjust to conflicting role prescriptions. Their role as males who are supposed to demonstrate masculine respect for and deference toward a member of the "weaker" sex would clash with their role as subordinates who are expected to exhibit political respect for and deference toward a powerful House member who happened to be a woman. "There are some men in the House," noted one Congressman, "who simply cannot handle that kind of situation, and they would try to avoid it."

But about one-half of the male respondents suggested that the reasons women are unlikely to be selected for a leadership position in the near future inhere in the attributes of women generally and in qualifications of specific women serving in the 95th Congress. Several male informants said that most women do not want the kind of responsibility that goes with leadership. Women, they said, are accustomed to leaving management to men and they are happy to do that in the House. According to these members, women lack the drive and ambition needed to "position" themselves and win a battle for a leadership post. They are much less concerned about "getting ahead."

A few respondents maintained that the vast majority of women do not have the qualifications to perform successfully in a leadership position. They implied, for example, that floor leaders must be calm, rational, and firm, and often had to act aggressively and ruthlessly. They felt that most women were too emotional and too "soft" to manage the problems that develop in the House and that many would either go off "half-cocked" or passively permit the actions of others to shape political and legislative strategies and outcomes.

Almost all respondents were ready and even eager to discuss the shortcomings of specific female colleagues, after their anonymity was reaffirmed. Some women were described as third- or fourth-rate, others as "not smart enough." One congresswoman would never make it because she was so "threatening" that she was "hated," and another would never get anywhere because she was a "maverick" and always "needled" the leadership. Some women who succeeded their husbands were dismissed as not experienced or competent enough to warrant service in the House, let alone a leadership position. And two women were ruled out because they talked too much and said too little.

A few female members were singled out because they were "unrealistic" in their understanding of how a member achieved a leadership post. One informant said:

There are some congresswomen who have strange ideas about how leadership positions are gained around here. They think that top jobs are handed out like badges. If you are here long enough, and if you are a good girl, one will be given to you. They think that a position should be reserved for at least one woman on the leadership roster. . . . Maybe that's true for some things, but for positions that really count around here they would have to have much more going for them than a desire to be the "token" woman.

Interviews with congresswomen revealed that most did not hold so simplistic a view of how leadership positions are obtained. Almost all believed that hard work, intelligence, and ability are, and ought to be, more important than gender in securing the rewards distributed in the House.

Female Perception 1998

Few women in the 95th Congress were optimistic about leadership possibilities for female colleagues. Most agreed with the males serving with them and with the women interviewed by Gehlen in 1962. Among the thirteen congresswomen volunteering their views, four thought that a woman could be selected for a major leadership position in the foreseeable future. But two of the four, and almost all of the others who speculated about this hypothetical prospect, agreed that a woman candidate for a leadership post would have to be "twice as good" as any male even to be considered seriously for the position.

The most optimistic view came from a Democrat who had experienced some measure of party recognition and was almost euphoric in her expectations about women assuming leadership roles. This congresswoman recalled that when she first came to the House she never thought she would be as successful as she had been. In response to a question about discrimination based upon gender, she remarked:

I personally don't experience obstruction. I have the complete acceptance of the men in my party. I have had my share of successes and who is to say where I can go from now on . . . I have gained the respect of my colleagues but when I first came to the House I wouldn't have dreamed that such things could happen.

The buoyantly positive tone of this response was shared by no one else. Most congresswomen believed either that women would continue to be barred from leadership positions or that they would avoid leadership opportunities in order to give more attention to constituency and policy concerns—concerns which they were convinced had a more legitimate claim on their energies.

In 1978, Republicans tended to be less sanguine than Democrats, and, given the absence of notable success among female Republicans who may have coveted secondary party positions, their gloom is understandable. One said simply that "Women will never get anywhere in the Republican party because the men in the House in my party cannot conceive of the prospect of sharing power with a woman or of taking directions from her." Another allowed that perhaps an "extraordinarily exceptional woman might get somewhere in Congress, but the rest of us are shut out."

Several women in both parties explained that their goals in the House were not entirely compatible with the tasks one performs when either seeking or exercising party leadership. They said that they came to Washington to represent the people who voted for them and that they would just as soon leave partisan concerns and political advantage to others. These women would not accept the charge that their goals were more modest than those who sought leadership positions. They argued that their goals were "different," and that by giving undivided attention to the legislative programs that mattered to them, by reaching out and helping people, they were engaging their intellect and emotions in those activities from which they derived the most satisfaction.

For some women it was not so much a lack of interest in gaining the kind of influence leaders normally exert, as much as it was a distaste for the kind of behavior in which they would have to engage if they decided to make leadership responsibility one of their House goals. One highly regarded Democratic congresswoman, a member who believed that women could be selected for major leadership positions, said:

Putting up with the process of cultivating colleagues, of getting them to like you and place their trust in you—which is what you have to do if you're going to seek a leadership position—is absolutely abhorrent to me. I can't imagine ever doing that. I become ill just thinking about it and I think a lot of other people, men and women, do also.

This woman's response refers to a process that was either explicitly articulated or implicitly alluded to by a majority of the congresswomen interviewed. One called it a process of "cultivating people," of getting them to "like you and trust you." These women agreed that people who groom themselves or who are groomed for leadership roles must establish close personal and professional relationships with Representatives upon whom they will depend when they seek political support. Developing such relationships takes time, they pointed out, and requires an investment of enormous energy by would-be leaders. To be successful, they had to exploit all available channels, formal as well as informal, through which to interact with party colleagues. Those who found such activities distasteful, but went after a leadership role nonetheless, were handicapped, and were likely to fail.

Several women also discussed the need to be aggressive in order to make party leaders sit up and take notice, a style which some women were unwilling to adopt. Those who actively sought recognition, the informants continued, risked the enmity of men who believed that women should not behave in so castrating a fashion. Said one congresswoman:

But you have to be that way in order to survive in the House. If you come on like Caspar Milquetoast, they'll trample all over you. On the other hand if you push aggressively for your goals, you are seen as a "pushy" woman, and they'll react with hostility.

A majority of women who were pessimistic about the future of would-be female leaders attributed their gloomy assessment less to female proclivities and personalities, factors congressmen thought were important, and more to established patterns of interaction in the House. They noted that women were systematically denied opportunities to deal with male colleagues in informal, unstructured settings. They had fewer occasions, therefore, to demonstrate legislative and political skills, salutary personal qualities, "good fellowship," and those human frailties which party members could decide to overlook because sometimes they were virtues. As a result, the males with whom they would have to compete for leadership positions were likely to be better known, even if not necessarily more able, supplicants for their colleagues' support.

One other handicap mentioned by several congresswomen was that none of the female members in the 95th Congress had been around long enough to make a legitimate claim to a top leadership position. Republican Margaret Heckler, the senior congresswoman, was in her sixth term at the time. The senior Democrat, Shirley Chisholm, was serving her fifth term. And all female respondents agreed that no House member could realistically expect to achieve top leadership status until he or she had been in Washington for fifteen years or more. They acknowledged that would-be leaders had to spend many years "paying their dues" before they could hope to obtain the recognition they sought.

A few congresswomen pointed out factors affecting leadership selection over which members had little control. Luck and happenstance, they noted, often separated the successful from the unsuccessful. One Republican speculated that these were the kinds of considerations that induced Barbara Jordan to retire from the House at the end of the 95th Congress. In July 1978, just months before her retirement, Jordan was asked in a television interview whether the reasons she decided to leave Congress resided in the House or in herself. She replied:

It's a little bit of both. Now, if the Congress had offered me, let us say, an opportunity to work through the politics of Congress to a leadership role, I suppose that I could have been induced to forgo this tug of conscience [to leave Congress and do something else] for a little longer. But House politics did not seem to make it possible that I would be able to do that. There is also a sense—a sense that I have—of a diminution of my personal efficacy in the House. Now stated another way, I did not feel that I could further impact, dramatically or moderately, on the course of events personally as they moved through the Congress.[12]

Thus, institutional and personal considerations contributed to her decision. Among the former were the fact that Jordan had served in the House for a relatively short period of time and that her opportunities to exert substantial influence were several years away. But she could not have been oblivious to the fact that Jim Wright of Texas already had the number two position within the leadership hierarchy and was all but certain to succeed House Speaker O'Neill. Other Texans were, therefore, unlikely to move into one of the five or six major leadership positions very soon. But even if through sheer force of personality Jordan could have overcome this obstacle, a prospect entirely within the realm of the possible, she would have had to "jump over" Democrat Shirley Chisholm, a Rules Committee member and the Secretary of the Democratic Caucus. Another congresswoman who also happened to be black would have had to have displayed coalition-building skills more impressive than even those at the command of the redoubtable Barbara Jordan to have penetrated the topmost ranks of the leadership hierarchy.[13]

The dilemma faced by Jordan is experienced by male as well as female Representatives. But from the vantage point of many congresswomen, this difficulty is a transitory one for men—one which is not likely to be accompanied, as it is for women, by gender-related bias. For about one-third of the female respondents, however, lack of sufficient seniority represented the most important obstacle standing between a qualified, able, and ambitious woman on the one hand, and a major leadership post on the other.

Male Perceptions, 1993

Congressmen in the 103rd Congress were much more optimistic about leadership possibilities for female colleagues than their 1978 male predecessors had been. Fifteen years earlier, no male anticipated the elevation of a congresswoman to a top leadership post in the foreseeable future, and events proved them prescient. In 1993, however, more than three-quarters of the male Representatives interviewed believed such an event could occur by the end of the century, or at least "within the next ten years." One highly respected senior Democrat believed it could happen in both parties.

Many of the congressmen interviewed distinguished between whether a female Representative would gain a top leadership post in the foreseeable future and whether she could secure such a position. Almost all believed it *could* happen, while one-half believed it would happen. Reservations expressed by the latter group were based upon the "insufficient seniority" commanded by women with the best chance of winning a top party position and the relatively "long line" of ambitious men whose seniority was higher and who were better positioned to penetrate the highest party echelons. More important, however, was the belief held by more than three-quarters of the congressmen that if women are not party leaders by the turn of the century it will not be because they are women. Gender, several observed, "will not stand in women's way."

The confidence reflected in forecasting female success was based partly on the increased number of congresswomen. One senior Republican predicted that the number will at least double by the year 2000 and that males will be forced by the sheer size of the female contingent—perhaps as much as 25 percent of the House—to relinquish their monopoly on top leadership positions. Several congressmen added that by the year 2000, many of the already diminished attitudinal barriers inhibiting women's advancement will have all but disappeared. By then most men will have worked comfortably with women both outside and inside of Congress; they will have come to recognize that women are as capable as men of making positive contributions to the legislative process; and they will have concluded, consciously or otherwise, that the premises underlying traditional gender roles are bankrupt.

Whereas congressmen in 1978 went out of their way to deprecate the leadership qualities of their female contemporaries—fastening on stereotypical female weaknesses to explain their judgments about the future—congressmen interviewed in 1993 readily volunteered the names of women who could be chief whip or floor leader in ten years or less. The names of Democrats Barbara Kennelly, Nancy Pelosi and Louise Slaughter came up regularly, as did that of Republican Nancy Johnson. Along with the names came praise for their "political savvy," their reputations as hard working "team players," and their acceptance by current leaders as "insiders." They and other congresswomen were singled out for their "standing up" for what they believed was right (a "stand-up guy" is a favored accolade in the House), and for effectively pursuing policy goals on the floor and in committee, while at the same time, demonstrating a willingness to compromise and to support their party leaders when the chips were down. Finally, unlike a few of their female colleagues, said one admirer, these congresswomen did not "*always* wear their gender on their sleeves. They are women for all seasons."

All acknowledged that Democratic women were better positioned than Republican women, partly because the former outnumbered the latter three to one. Several also believed, however, Republican women suffered from the presence in their party's ranks of a small but active coterie of "unreconstructed" social conservatives. Said one senior Republican, "It is an embarrassment to my party that we have no women in top leadership slots." He added that Nancy Johnson's 1992 loss in the race for conference vice chair was a disappointment to him, and that the Republicans missed an opportunity to show that their party is more hospitable to women's aspirations.

Reluctance to promote women was not peculiar to members of one party, however. One southern Democrat expressed what he believed were views reasonably common among lawmakers from his region. He confidently asserted that "there is no way" that a woman would become a leader in his party in the near future. "Many of the men I know from my part of the country in both parties would never vote for a woman." This was clearly a minority opinion, but if it persists and is held with sufficient intensity by enough men, it could delay considerably the arrival of a woman leader in the House.

Female Perceptions, 1993

In 1993, Congresswomen were much more sanguine about their leadership opportunities than their predecessors in the 95th Congress had been. Whereas fewer than one-third of the women interviewed in 1978 anticipated female leaders in the foreseeable future, twenty-eight of the thirty-three women interviewed in 1993 thought one of their own could be among the top leaders by the turn of the century. Several said "yes" reflexively, adding terms like "right on" and "absolutely"—indicating at least as much hope and faith as reasoned belief in the prospect. Several said that if the legislatures of Canada, Mexico and Turkey can name female leaders, so can the United States. Responses from seventeen first-term women differed little in this respect from those of the sixteen women who were at least in their second term, although the newcomers seemed to say "yes" with greater alacrity and enthusiasm.

Unlike many of the women interviewed in 1978, none in the 103rd Congress expressed distaste for the activities in which would-be leaders must engage while building coalitions—the hours spent "schmoozing," getting colleagues to like and respect you, cultivating support of skeptics, and showing colleagues that a woman "has what it takes." Several noted that women now had access to virtually all of the informal groups in the House, and that opportunities for improving rapport with male colleagues had vastly increased. Few invoked the familiar dichotomy distinguishing between the ways males and females define their legislative roles—a power orientation vs. a policy orientation—as a deterrent to women's success. According to most respondents, ambitious congresswomen would not allow their attentiveness to constituency concerns and their strong policy preferences prevent them from working their way up the leadership ladder.

On the other hand, many noted the importance of turnover in the present leadership, the need for more seniority among women, and strategic "positioning" of viable female leaders. A few mentioned that such women would have to be people with whom the male leadership could feel comfortable, but the vast majority of congresswomen interviewed stated that whatever factors might delay the elevation of a woman to a top leadership position, gender was not one of them.

Much of their optimism was based on the unprecedented number of women elected in 1992. But increased numbers was only part of the reason for their positive outlook. At least as important were the personal and political strengths of the twenty-four first-termers. Most had recorded notable political achievements before they came to Washington and several had already accomplished a good deal in their first few months as Representatives. All congresswomen agreed that this class of women would furnish outstanding lawmakers in the twenty-first century. In the meantime, their numbers and talents validated the aspirations harbored by senior women, women whose ambitions were now more difficult for the all-male hierarchy to ignore.

Barbara Kennelly's appointment as Chief Deputy Whip was mentioned frequently by women in both parties as a precursor to greater successes yet to come. True, she had been appointed, not elected to the post, and she shared the title with three other Democrats. But the decision reflected the party's recognition of Kennelly's capability, and its realization that women had to be admitted into important party councils. Several Democrats asserted that the decision was forced on the leadership—"they had no choice." But they also noted that Kennelly had taken the route traditionally followed by would-be leaders. She established rapport with House leaders, particularly Speaker Tip O'Neill. She took her cues from these leaders on most matters and was a team player. She sought and secured a seat on the Ways and Means Committee, later justifying the confidence placed in her by the leadership. She risked her reputation by taking on Maryland's Steny Hoyer for the vice chairmanship of the Democratic Caucus. And, although she lost, she received a respectable eighty-two votes in a contest she was never expected to win. For many, Kennelly's selection as Chief Deputy Whip was simply one more step toward the "charmed circle." And if she did not make it, other capable and persistent women surely would.

Imminent though female leadership may seem, most congresswomen recognized just how difficult would be what one member called "the last few laps around the track." She added that members of the House compete at a level which puts women at a disadvantage.

The stature of the men, their size, the volume of their voices, the level of intimidation they can project during debate all make a major difference. Women are placed at a disadvantage in the competition for leadership. The House is a very noisy place; sometimes it witnesses a yelling match. A good deal is decided through bullying and shouting and loud exchanges among members. Decisions are often made not on the basis of the intellectual integrity of the arguments or on reasonable, objective merit, but on the physical size of the combatants and the decibel level their voices reach.

For this member, a woman able to obtain a top leadership position must be able to compensate for the disadvantages of smaller size, weaker voice and less intimidating presence. Nevertheless, she was as confident as any of her colleagues that they could be overcome.

Although there were no sharp differences in views along party lines, one senior Republican was less hopeful about leadership prospects than any of her colleagues. She said that being a member of a party that had been in the minority for so long complicated what was already a daunting quest. She said that the men in her party were especially jealous of positions of influence, given unabating Democratic hegemony in the House. She volunteered the view that there had been no significant change in women's leadership opportunities since she arrived in the House, but added almost wistfully that perhaps next term, with the likely turnover in Republican leadership in the 104th Congress, women will get the recognition they deserve.

DISCRIMINATION ON THE BASIS OF GENDER:
THREE CASE STUDIES

The problem of disentangling and weighing the factors contributing to the distribution of leadership positions has already been noted. A member's qualifications, goals, and seniority, along with many concrete and symbolic characteristics of incumbency, all affect leadership prospects. That no women have served in the top half-dozen leadership positions of either party provides circumstantial evidence of discrimination based upon gender. Statements offered by informants in the 95th Congress justify taking that evidence seriously, although by 1993 discrimination had become infrequent and less consequential, even if it had not been eliminated completely. Nevertheless, accounts given by both groups yield three reasonably clear cases in which congresswomen making claims to leadership roles were rebuffed because they were women. Two of them were witnessed in the 1970s, the third in 1993.

One involved Edith Green of Oregon and it was mentioned by both male and female informants in 1978, as well as by Green herself in a published interview (Dreifus, 1972). The Oregon Democrat was serving as Assistant Whip for the western zone when she received a call from Congressman Wayne Aspinall, Chairman of the Caucus of Western Democrats. Aspinall regularly attended meetings of the Democratic Steering Committee, but, since he would be unable to attend the next scheduled meeting, he asked Green if she would attend in his place. He had decided that since she was the Whip for the Western Region, she was the appropriate person to substitute for him. She agreed to attend.

Before the meeting, however, Green received a telephone call from the Steering Committee Chairman, septuagenarian Ray Madden of Indiana. Madden told her that he would not allow her to participate in the meeting and if she appeared he would cancel it. In recounting the incident, Green added:

It was disgusting, really disgusting. No male member got up and said Madden's behavior was ridiculous, that I was representing the western region as a Democrat and had the right to attend. No one said that Ray Madden had no right to bar me. (Dreifus 1972, p. 19)

Few women served in Congress longer than Edith Green and fewer still were able to play so influential a role on their committees. During her years as Chair of Education and Labor's subcommittee on higher education, Green served as sponsor and floor manager of many important bills enacted into law. Neither these successes nor her selection for secondary leadership roles, however, gave the Oregon Democrat reason to believe that leadership opportunities for women were equal to the opportunities available to men.

When in 1972 she was asked whether she would consider running for a top leadership post, she replied:

You know the saying: "Negroes are fine so long as they know their place." The same goes for women in Congress. A woman is fine as long as she knows her place. If a woman were to announce she was running for a party position, she would be considered an "uppity female." (Dreifus 1972, p. 20)

Green's bitterness was partly a product of the running battles she had had with other Democrats on the Education and Labor Committee and the unusually hostile comments regularly uttered by other members of her party—particularly John Brademas and Frank Thompson (Gladieux and Wolanin 1976, pp. 118–152). Her critics believed that she sought to dominate committee decisions affecting higher education while, at the same time, undermining proposals championed by other liberal Democrats. One congresswoman who observed Green's behavior and treatment in the committee setting remarked:

When Green presided during markup sessions of the full committee and led the discussion, two things happened. First, the men, some of them, demonstrated their awe of her. They were in awe of her intellect and ability. She was so good at clarifying the issues—she was a real teacher, which is what she was before she came to the House. . . . And this intellect and ability really threatened some of the men—which leads to the second thing that happened. I saw hostility toward her. It was expressed in the inane and ridiculous remarks they made. And sometimes they were so exaggeratedly condescending it was disgusting.

In 1973, Green gave up eighteen years of seniority on the Education and Labor Committee and accepted a position on the Appropriations Committee. She explained the move by noting that national attention was then on the House "money" committees because of President Nixon's increasing impoundment of funds, his veto of appropriation measures, and his efforts to terminate important programs. That she had few allies left on the Education and Labor Committee must surely have made her decision easier.

The frustration of Congresswoman Marjorie Holt's bid for a leadership position at the start of the 95th Congress may be more to the point. After Republican Louis Frey of Florida announced he was giving up the chair of his party's Research Committee to become a candidate to head the Republican Policy Committee, Holt, who was perceived as a conservative, announced her candidacy for the vacancy left by Frey. She was opposed in that contest by Congressman William Frenzel of Minnesota, a member of the moderate wing of his party.

When Republicans caucused to choose their leaders for the 95th Congress, the names of Holt and Frenzel were introduced for consideration, with nominating and seconding speeches presented in behalf of each. Just before the vote, however, the second ranking Republican, Minority Whip Robert Michel of Illinois, asked for the floor and urged his party colleagues to support Frenzel. He argued that since three of the top four leaders already chosen (floor leader John Rhodes, himself, and newly elected Policy Committee Chairman Del Clawson) were conservative and only one (Conference Chairman John Anderson) was a moderate, another moderate would give the party the ideological balance needed to make Republicans more effective in the new House. The vote was then called and Frenzel won, 77–53.

Reactions of Republican respondents to Michel's action were mixed. Some felt that following Clawson's victory over Frey, the concern for ideological balance was a genuine one, even though Frey was no less a conservative. Some of these same informants noted that Frenzel was a capable, hard-working House member and deserved all the support he received, a sentiment they said was shared by many who did not vote for him. But several Republican members considered Michel's behavior unusual at the very least and outrageous at worst. They said they could not recall a leader ever intruding just before a vote to try openly to influence the outcome of this kind of contest. Naturally, leaders worked behind the scenes to try to affect the election result, but these members had never seen behavior similar to that engaged in by the Republican Whip. One Republican said:

Michel's behavior was unforgivable. Marjorie had the votes all locked up until he spoke out. He probably turned around the votes of a dozen freshmen—many of whom Marjorie had gotten commitments from—because he spoke up. After all, Michel's the party whip. That's what he's supposed to do, round up votes for the leadership position. He certainly seemed to succeed this time.

A Republican congresswoman voiced similar sentiments, and added:

I remember when it happened. A lot of people were stunned that he would do such a thing. . . . I voted for Marjorie and felt at the time that it was inappropriate for him to have spoken as he did.

Several respondents observed that Holt's unsuccessful effort to secure a leadership position foundered because she was a woman, although they mentioned other factors that may have been controlling. They alluded to her "inflexibly" conservative outlook, to Frenzel's longer House service and, without denigrating Holt, to the enormous respect in which the Minnesotan was held. But the belief by some at the time that a party leader would not have gone to these lengths to defeat a male candidate with Holt's record suggests that some House members perceived the act as one which reflected bias based upon gender. Said one female informant:

Those fellows just couldn't have been as relaxed with Holt as they were with one another. Frenzel is good, but I think that the leadership would have supported Ivan the Terrible rather than be saddled with a woman in that position.

Those who deny that Holt had been discriminated against and who accept explanations based on Frenzel's seniority and the party's quest for ideological balance could be given more credence were it not for the outcome of subsequent leadership contests. There is no evidence, for example, that Republican leaders applied the seniority rule or the principle of ideological balance when one of the most conservative House members, Pennsylvania's Bud Shuster, defeated the more senior Frenzel 90–55 for the GOP Policy Committee chair in the 96th Congress; or when, at the same time, Mississippi Republican Trent Lott won the Research Committee chair in a contest with the more senior and more moderate Lawrence Coughlin of Pennsylvania. The resulting line-up of Republican leaders, save for Anderson, was more conservative than ever. And Holt was defeated again before the 97th Congress convened when she challenged Richard Cheney, a former Ford White House aide who was about to begin his second term, for the GOP Policy Committee chair. She secured 68 of the 167 votes cast.

Disclaimers of bias are also made questionable by observations offered in a comprehensive study of congressional leadership selection.

The Republican . . . rather monolithic voting structure is skewed heavily in the conservative direction. Little attempt seems to be made by conservatives, who outnumber liberals by six, or seven, to one, to tolerate dissent or elect liberals to the party leadership. . . . Republican leaders are almost universally selected from the conservative mainstream of their party. (Peabody 1976, pp. 307, 470)

The party made an exception in 1976 when it chose Frenzel over Holt. Had it not been the only occasion during that period when a vacancy was denied a conservative and filled by a moderate, the disclaimers could be given more weight.

The most recent case of gender-based discrimination did not involve the filling of a leadership position, but rather an appointment to the chair of a House select committee. The particulars are nonetheless relevant because the decision artlessly to circumvent a congresswoman's legitimate claim to the chair was made by top Democratic House leaders.

The woman in this case was Marilyn Lloyd, a Tennessee Democrat who had just been reelected for a tenth term. She and New Jersey Congressman William Hughes had both come to Washington in 1974 and they later joined the House Select Committee on Aging at the same time. The committee was the largest of the five select panels, but like the others, it was barred from bringing legislative measures to the floor and, consequently, it exercised little legislative or political influence. Even so, many representatives found good reason to serve on the committee. Membership increased their exposure to issues facing the country's elderly population and allowed them to respond more insightfully to problems encountered by older constituents. Congresswomen in particular were drawn to the select committee and ten of the twenty-eight female representatives were members in the 102nd Congress.

When the 1992 election left Lloyd and Hughes the most senior majority party members, she decided to pursue the committee chairmanship. The Tennessee Democrat already occupied an important position on a House standing committee. She headed the energy subcommittee of the House Science, Space and Technology Committee and she had used her influence to improve the economy of a congressional district that included Oak Ridge. But the opportunity to lead the Aging Committee seemed at least as appealing as her other committee responsibilities, even though it was legislatively toothless. Lloyd was entering the twilight of her career and by leading the fight on the problems of aging she would be addressing the needs of a rapidly growing national constituency—a segment of the population that dwarfed in size and visibility any constituency she had ever represented.

Lloyd advised Democratic leaders of her intentions to seek the Aging Committee chair, conducted an active lobbying campaign among fellow Democrats, and solicited and received a letter of support from members of the Congressional Caucus for Women's Issues, Republican as well as Democratic. According to some Capitol Hill sources, she appeared to have the overwhelming support of rank and file Democrats and her appointment seemed assured. To the extent that Congressman Hughes was working for the assignment, his efforts were considerably less public than were Lloyd's.

Before the 103rd Congress convened, Speaker Tom Foley told Lloyd that he had decided to award the Aging Committee chair to Hughes. The criterion used to make the decision, he said, was "the alphabet," inasmuch as the two enjoyed equal seniority. Since "H" came before "L" in the alphabet, Hughes would chair the committee and Lloyd would be next ranking Democrat. None of the members interviewed in 1993 could remember when the alphabet was used to decide a contest for a chairmanship, and Lloyd was reported to have been outraged by both the arbitrariness of the decision and by the failure of the leaders to tell her the grounds for the decision before it was made so she could plead her case anew. She later told one colleague that it was a major disappointment to her, among the most discouraging experiences of her congressional career. Several congresswomen attributed Lloyd's setback to her gender, with one female Representative explaining her conclusion this way.

It is not only gender that was at work, although gender was very important. The Democratic leadership was not happy with Lloyd. She often voted against them and they were uncomfortable with her temperament and style. But I cannot imagine them telling a male member that he was not getting a committee chairmanship because his last name began with a "Z." Tossing a coin would have been a better way of deciding the issue if they wanted to leave it to chance, but that was too risky—Lloyd might have won.

The irony in these events is that the House eliminated all select committees soon after Hughes became chair, partly as a cost-cutting measure, partly because several chairs of standing committees saw them as unworthy competitors for scarce House operating funds. Months later, Lloyd announced she would not run for an eleventh term.

Allegations of gender-based discrimination against congresswomen aspiring to leadership positions are difficult to confirm. The problem of disentangling gender bias from other possible explanations for denial of a leadership post, and the absence of hard, documentary evidence are just two factors contributing to that difficulty. Many respondents in the 95th Congress, especially staff members, reported instances of discrimination, but investigations at least as exhaustive as the ones relied upon here would have been necessary if reasonable doubts were to be allayed. Nevertheless, the experiences of Green, Holt and Lloyd are consistent with circumstantial and attitudinal patterns revealed elsewhere in this chapter, and they suggest that, in spite of some progress, female Representatives have had to survive all of the trials faced by male colleagues when seeking a major leadership post in the House—plus the one to which they are subjected by virtue of their being female. That discriminatory practices seem to be diminishing provides hope for contemporary congresswomen even if it offers little solace for their predecessors.

WOMEN AND HOUSE LEADERSHIP

The pace at which women have gained access to leadership positions has been incremental, and none has secured one of the major posts in her party. On the other hand, some advances have been made and members' perceptions about the status of women in the House have undergone a corresponding change. Whereas virtually no Representative interviewed in 1962 expected a woman floor leader or whip in the foreseeable future, and whereas a large majority of them drew the same conclusion in 1978, a sizable majority of interviewees were able to conceive of such a prospect fifteen years later. Many respondents went so far as to name specific women who they believed would make excellent leaders.

Earlier forecasts can be traced to the anemic size of the total female contingent, and this insuperable condition overwhelmed the more subtle explanations detailed above. Yet, a dramatic increase in the number of congresswomen is only the most prominent of five important circumstances needed to lay the groundwork for their selection to leadership positions. An increase in the number of women serving apprenticeships is a second condition facilitating the climb to the top. Almost as important as numbers and apprenticeship is length of service. No floor leader since World War II served as few terms as the most senior woman in the 95th Congress, and it would be unreasonable to have expected a woman to have occupied a major party post in 1978. In the 103rd Congress, eight women had served ten years or more, roughly the length of time it has taken to become party whip, and by the year 2000, the number of congresswomen with that much seniority is likely to be twice as large. Lengthy service is a precondition for leadership not only because time is required to learn the trade, but because seniority itself is valued by some and it permeates decision rules. Time is also needed to build a coalition large enough to elect would-be leaders and to compete with ambitious male members who have both long service and the other valued qualities that accompany realistic aspirations.

A fourth and related condition facilitating a member's selection to a leadership position is access to the House's informal influence structure. As was noted in Chapter 5, women have been more fully integrated into this network and many have been accepted as equals by those with whom they interact. Consequently, women who aspire to a major party post can rely upon the exchanges of trust and support that affiliation with such groups encourages. Admission of Republican women to the Chowder and Marching Society has practical as well as symbolic consequences for would-be women leaders. It allows them to interact regularly with the most influential males in the Republican party and it signifies their having overcome one of the last hurdles to integrated House membership.

Service on a significant standing committee is neither a necessary nor a sufficient condition for advancement within one's party, but it, too, can expedite achievement of such a goal. Increased expertise in important policy areas, opportunities to help other members, and occasions for demonstrating political skills are three of the more important by-products of service on these committees. It should come as no surprise that an unusually large proportion of leaders saw prior service on the Appropriations, Rules, or Ways and Means committees before they rose to a high party office.

In sum, the prospects of would-be female House leaders are linked to an increase in the number of women colleagues within their own party and in the House, generally; to service in secondary leadership positions; to youth, good health, constituency appeal, and stable district boundaries sufficient to permit a return to the House often enough to acquire considerable seniority; to entry into informal groups and communications networks which give them opportunities to establish a camaraderie and rapport with those over whom they will exercise leadership; and to performance on a major House committee which calls attention to their mastery of the legislative process, and the personal and political skills that House members expect leaders to possess. As all five of these conditions become more prominent in women's House experience, their leadership opportunities at the highest levels are all but certain to materialize.

For many of the congresswomen interviewed, the implications of such a change are far-reaching. Several alluded to the different leadership styles employed by men and women. "When you have an all male leadership," said one senior Republican, "it is harder for women to get their attention." She added that "when women are included in the leadership, then women who are not part of that group are more likely to be heard." She continued:

Men and women have different ways of moving through the decision-making process. A mixed leadership team allows for better access for rank-and-file members. Women tend to be more open and accommodating to those with whom they disagree. They are more conscious of the implications their decisions have for groups of people who are not in the room with you when you're making decisions that affect them. Men don't realize as much as they should that different people with different backgrounds—ethnic, gender, racial—should be taken into account when crafting proposals.

If this Republican congresswoman is correct, the increased leadership opportunities that so many anticipated are likely to have profound consequences for the policy agenda Congress will help shape in the coming years. Just how women will influence that agenda can be adduced by examining opportunities congresswomen have had to shape policy in the past, and by tracing the legislative priorities they have established over time. These subjects will be addressed in the next five chapters.

NOTES

1. In 1979, Conservative Party Leader Margaret Thatcher was made Great Britain's Prime Minister, Maria de Lourdes Pintassilgo became (for a short time) Portugal's first woman Premier, and Bolivian leaders temporarily conferred the Presidency upon Lydia Gueiler Tejada (only to force her resignation in a military coup a year later). The same year also saw appointment of France's Simone Veil as President of the 410–member European Parliament. The 1980s and early 1990s witnessed selection of Vigdis Finnbogadottir, Iceland; Mary Eugenia Charles, Dominica; Corazon Aquino, the Philippines; Gro Harlem Brundtland, Denmark; Benazir Bhutto, Pakistan; Kim Campbell, Canada; and Tansu Cillar, Turkey.

2. Githens and Prestage (1978, p. 267) found that 14 percent of women state legislators responding to questionnaires held leadership positions. When they took seniority into account, however, they concluded that women were underrepresented. Kirkpatrick notes that female legislators have been successful in securing leadership positions partly because they have been willing to fight for them (Kirkpatrick 1974, p. 127). By the early 1990s, six women had served as the highest-rank-

ing members of state senates; seven had been speakers of lower chambers (Center for the American Woman and Politics, "News and Notes," Winter, 1991, p. 3).

3. Martin's position was more important than its title in contemporary usage suggests. He was one of two Assistant Whips and ranked immediately below the floor leader.

4. The Republican Conference Secretary is a more sought-after position than was the same post among Democrats, inasmuch as it has sometimes been a springboard to Conference Vice-Chairman, an office Democrats did not create until 1987, when they simultaneously eliminated the position of Caucus Secretary.

5. According to Jones (1964, pp. 72–73), this is one of the central tasks of the Republican Policy Committee.

6. The equation employed to determine the Index of Female Representation for women in each party was derived as follows:

$$x = x_m + x_w$$

$$n = n_m + n_w$$

Where x equals the number of leadership positions available within the party; n equals the number of Representatives in the party; and where m signifies men and w signifies women. Thus, if $x_w/x = n_w/n$, then the Index of Female Representation = 1.00.

7. Edith Green is the lone exception. She was elected Assistant Whip for her region in the 91st, 92nd, and 93rd Congresses.

8. Martin trailed eventual winner Jerry Lewis by a single vote on the first ballot, and was finally defeated by three votes, 85–82, on the second ballot.

9. The three women most recently appointed to the Rules Committee are Republican Martin and Democrats Sala Burton and Louise Slaughter.

10. The best treatment of this subject appears in Peabody 1976, chapters 10 and 16. Part of the discussion that follows draws generously on Peabody's work.

11. The Democrats subsequently made the Whip's office an elected one.

12. See transcript of "The MacNeil/Lehrer Report: Barbara Jordan Interview," July 4, 1978, Educational Broadcasting Corporation and Greater Washington Educational Telecommunications Association, Inc., 1978.

13. In a letter to the author written on November 17, 1978, Congresswoman Jordan stated, in response to a request to explain her retirement from the House: "in House politics, you get in at the bottom and await your turn to move up. The line is long." She also noted that her statement on the "MacNeil/Lehrer Report" had nothing to do with race, sex, or state of origin.

Part IV

Behavior

7

Changing Legislative Opportunities

Most women legislators around the world have specialized, willingly or otherwise, in substantive issues believed to be of peculiar interest to their gender. They have been active in such policy domains as education, health, welfare, local government, and domestic relations, and many have sought avenues to promote peace and international harmony, as well. By contrast, few women have had opportunities to shape tax laws, hammer out appropriations measures, or fashion rules to govern commercial and financial practices. They have also had little to do with writing civil and criminal codes or with creating military and defense policies.

This pattern was well documented for West European parliaments in 1955, when Maurice Duverger noted that the small number of women in the German Bundestag occupied as many as one-half of the positions on committees dealing with public health, welfare, and juveniles, and one-quarter of the seats on labor and social welfare panels. Few women sat on committees dealing with the nation's budget and taxes, however, and none was a member of an economic policy committee. One-half of the motions, reports, and speeches offered by female members of that body related to social issues—welfare for mothers, equal pay for women civil servants, and domestic relations. Similar findings emerged when Duverger examined the subject matter of speeches given by women in the French National Assembly (1955, pp. 95–97).

Matters were much the same on the other side of the Channel. In the 1920s, it was unusual for female M.P.s to speak out on economic issues during debate in the House of Commons (Brookes 1967, p. 53). Even in the years following World War II, they were inclined to limit their attention to legislative measures touching on health, education, matrimony, pensions, widows, and orphans (Mann 1962, p. 34). When asked if he would like to see more women in politics, Conservative Party leader Edward Heath replied: "Yes . . . *so long as they are providing what women can do and not just duplicating what men can do*, which would lead to them not making a woman's contribution" (Brookes 1967, p. 267. The emphasis is Brookes's).

One explanation for this pattern holds that women are by nature, experience, and interest better able to deal with some issues and less adroit when addressing others. Accordingly, they gravitate toward the former. A second maintains that questions of taxation, government spending, national security, the administration of justice, and business and commerce are the most consequential matters with which a polity must come to grips and, since men, after all, determine the national agenda and apportion substantive responsibilities among lawmakers, they relegate female colleagues to policy areas of secondary importance. In his analysis of European legislatures, Duverger embraces the latter explanation. He concludes that his findings are less a product of men and women possessing different interests and competencies than they are a function of male unwillingness to permit women to serve on legislative instrumentalities that shape fundamental policies.

THE SPECIALTIES OF EARLY CONGRESSWOMEN

The legislative experience of congresswomen serving between the World Wars was similar to that of their European counterparts. Moreover, many Americans who otherwise bristled at discrimination against women saw nothing wrong with female lawmakers concentrating on subjects with which by nature and training they were believed to be most comfortable. Even those who decried the limited political opportunities available to women believed that politics had a natural division of labor. Sophonisba Breckinridge, for example, argued that women should enter legislatures to fashion governmental policies that are domestic in character—to transfer to the public arena those skills and services which women normally exhibited in the home (1933, p. 295).

These views were shared by even the most liberated of the early congresswomen. When asked why a woman should serve in Congress, Jeannette Rankin replied:

There are hundreds of men to care for the nation's tariff and foreign policy and irrigation projects. But there isn't a single woman to look after the nation's greatest asset: its children. (Quoted in Chamberlin 1973, p. 5)

And Ruth Bryan Owen maintained:

Through thinking, training, experience, the woman in politics has a most definite original contribution to make in such fields as child welfare, education, the removal of inequalities of women before the law, and international relations. More women assisting in the delicate contacts between country and country would mean, I firmly believe, more surety of world peace. (Owen 1933, p. 30)

It should come as no surprise, then, that most congresswomen who served between the wars were assigned to standing committees dealing with issues deemed appropriate to their gender. The pattern began to change in the 1940s, however, particularly after passage of the 1946 Legislative Reorganization Act. Female Representatives gradually gained positions on the House's most valued committees and subcommittees at a pace similar to that of their male colleagues. As will be demonstrated in the pages that follow, women today are as likely to shape policy in nontraditional domains as they are in domains considered to be female preserves.

EXPANDING COMMITTEE AND SUBCOMMITTEE OPTIONS

In order to demonstrate the extent to which congresswomen have achieved access to nontraditional policy domains, subjects dealt with by Congress were first categorized as being either more or less amenable to female treatment. Congresswomen's committee assignments were then aggregated by time periods—1917 to 1946, 1947 to 1964, 1965 to 1984, and 1985 to 1993. Deciding which policies (and the committees responsible for them) were more compatible and which less compatible with women's interests strains the imagination. The observations of those who perceived such distinctions (Breckinridge, Owen, and Gehlen [1969, p. 36], among them), are useful, however, and, for the purposes of the discussion that follows, "women's" committees and subcommittees are those which consider health, education, welfare, and family matters. They also oversee measures affecting members of disadvantaged groups (Indians, women), local government (the District of Columbia, territories), and veterans' and civil service benefits. Housekeeping details, concern for foreign (but not defense) policy, and the efficient and ethical running of government are also matters in which women have been reputed to possess unusual interest and competence.

Committees dealing with issues considered peripheral to women's concerns focus upon defense policy, internal security, manufacturing and trade, business and finance, agriculture, taxation, public works (and other subjects that encourage horse trading for palpably parochial benefits), civil, criminal and constitutional law, and the appropriations process. The artificial nature of distinctions between traditional and nontraditional areas of alleged female interest becomes clear when policies are interpreted within a perspective broader than is customarily brought to bear. Matters of war and peace, the sufficiency and quality of agricultural products, street crime, the size and source of tax revenues, the distribution of these revenues among the poor and the ill, and allocations of resources generally can be construed as "health" and "welfare" issues. Political and social conventions in both Congress and the country have discouraged this broader view, however.

If, then, we accept the more narrowly conceived differences among issues, the information in Table 7.1 is revealing. It indicates first of all that almost two-thirds (64%) of the initial assignments distributed among congresswomen serving between 1917 and 1946 were to committees concerned with "women's" issues. Among them were those dealing with Indian affairs, women's suffrage, education, pensions and other benefits for veterans, civil service, and the manner in which executive agencies are organized to expend appropriated funds, a subject which should not be confused with the appropriations process itself.

A few congresswomen were awarded seats on Banking and Currency, Rivers and Harbors (a major pork-barrel committee), and Military or Naval Affairs. They were among the little more than one-third assigned to panels dealing with issues traditionally defined as male. The table does not show that no woman was placed on such weighty House committees as Ways and Means, Agriculture, Interstate and Foreign Commerce, Appropriations, and Judiciary.

Since the implementation of the 1946 Reorganization Act, the pattern has changed markedly. Between the 80th and 88th Congresses, first-term congresswomen were appointed to such previously all-male preserves as the Judiciary, Merchant Marine and Fisheries, and Agriculture committees, and

Table 7.1
Initial Assignments to Committees and Subcommittees Whose Subject Matter Is of Traditional Interest to Women, 1917–1993

Time Period (Congresses)	Total Initial Assignments of Congresswomen	Number of Assignments to Traditional Comm. and Subcomm.	Percent of Assignments to Traditional Comm. and Subcomm.
1917-1946 (65th-79th)	73	47	64%
1947-1964 (80th-88th)	59	33	56%
1965-1984 (89th-98th)	129	64	50%
1985-1993 (99th-103rd)	188	76	40%

Note: When women were assigned to two or more committees, each was categorized separately.
Sources: Schwemle *(1982), Congressional Quarterly, Inc., Congressional Quarterly Almanac, 1955-1993; Congressional Directory, 1917-1993.*

a few gained assignments to the new panel on Science and Astronautics. Change between 1965 and 1984 may have been more important than is indicated by the six-percentage-point shift recorded in Table 7.1, inasmuch as congresswomen were assigned seats on virtually all remaining nontraditional committees. Neophyte Barbara Mikulski, for example, penetrated the previously all-male Interstate and Foreign Commerce Committee in 1977. The ten-percentage point change occurring between the mid-1980s and the mid-1990s reflects increasing success among congresswomen seeking initial assignments to committees on Agriculture, Armed Services, Energy and Commerce, and Public Works.

Evidence of this shift is reinforced when considering committee choices made by women after completing their first terms. As Table 7.2 makes clear, almost three-quarters of the relatively few transfers and additional assignments undertaken by congresswomen prior to 1947 sent them to panels whose subject matter was stereotypically suitable for them. The figure decreased significantly during the post–World War II period, however, and the point has been reached where no House committee or subcommittee is beyond the reach of a congresswoman. Subcommittees devoted to advanced technology, the latest developments in weapons systems, tortuous commercial regulations, and intricate tax and banking arrangements are now routinely made up of at least one congresswoman.

Table 7.2
Post–First Term Transfers and Additional Assignments to Committees and Subcommittees Whose Subject Matter Is of Traditional Interest to Women, 1917–1993

Time Period (Congresses)	Total Transfers and Additional Assignments of Congresswomen	Number of Assignments to Traditional Comm. and Subcomm.	Percent of Transfers and Additional Assignments to Traditional Comm. and Subcomm.
1917-1946 (65th-79th)	17	12	71%
1947-1964 (80th-88th)	59	30	51%
1965-1984 (89th-98th)	191	51	51%
1985-1993 (99th-103rd)	56	25	45%

Note: When women were transferred or subsequently assigned to two or more committees, each was categorized separately.
Sources: Schwemle *(1982), Congressional Quarterly, Inc., Congressional Quarterly Almanac, 1955-1993; Congressional Directory, 1917-1993.*

At the same time, female House members continue to serve on committees devoted to subjects of traditional interest—veterans, hospitals, health care, education and the environment. In fact, they have occasionally been grossly overrepresented on committees dealing with these issues. Bella Abzug suspected ulterior motives when she called attention to the fact that as many as five of the twelve women in the 92nd Congress served on the Education and Labor Committee (Abzug 1972, p. 26). But the precongressional experience of the five, along with their policy and political orientations surely must have contributed to the skewed distribution to which Abzug alluded.[1] As recently as 1982, however, Shirley Chisholm remarked: "When you talk about . . . the different kinds of programs that deal with human beings, it's women who will have to be leaders on those issues because the gentlemen find other issues more exciting" (Payne 1982, p. 132).

Another committee to which contemporary congresswomen flocked is the now defunct Select Committee on Aging. Since it was not a permanent standing committee it is excluded from the tabulated findings. But the issues with which it came to grips have been extraordinarily salient in recent years. Its size ballooned to more than sixty in the late 1980s, making it the largest committee in the House. Between 1987 and 1990, more than 40 percent of women Representatives were members. But the continued attraction congresswomen have for committees treating issues that are stereotypically "female" does not alter the fact that many more are addressing nontraditional subjects.

A compelling explanation for this development is attitude change about female interests and skills within the larger society. The House may simply be recording changes already reflected in the private choices made by women throughout the country. Contemporary congresswomen may also be more aggressive than past congresswomen. They may be more insistent in their demands for a committee assignment compatible with their nontraditional interests and more determined to be where important decisions are being made. Although they have not penetrated the House's top leadership structure (as was demonstrated in the preceding chapter), they seem to be securing access to a wider range of policy domains than was available to their predecessors.

ACCESS TO EXCLUSIVE COMMITTEES AND CHAIRS

Recent congresswomen have begun not only to specialize in subjects formerly regarded as more suitable for males, they have also begun to gain seats on the most prestigious House committees. Access to these critical arenas supplies participants with uncommon tactical advantages. For one thing, colleagues who do not serve on them often seek committee members' support and, when help is proffered, the latter are able to capitalize on the gratitude their favors elicit. For another, reciprocal benefits exchanged among members of each of these coveted committees are likely to nourish the political and electoral fortunes of them all.[2]

Congresswomen have been more successful in securing assignments to valued committees than they have been in becoming chairs or ranking members of committees. While they have held their own with males when it comes to being named chairs and ranking members of subcommittees, their success in this connection has not been evident on the House's most prized committees, as will be made clear below.

Assignments to Exclusive Committees

There is overlap between committees whose subjects were deemed unsuitable to female talents and those considered most prestigious by the House. But the two categories are not identical, and the rates at which congresswomen have been awarded the two types of assignments have not been the same.

The figures in Tables 7.1 and 7.2 indicate that about one-third of the female Representatives serving between 1917 and 1946 filled vacancies on committees whose subject matter was considered inappropriate for women. Table 7.3, on the other hand, makes clear that a significantly larger proportion of these early congresswomen sooner or later found themselves on exclusive House committees.[3] Six different women, including Ruth

Table 7.3
Male and Female Representatives Serving on Exclusive Standing Committees during Their First Five Terms, 1917–1993

Time Period in which First elected	Gender	1st Term	2nd Term	3rd Term	4th Term	5th Term
1917-1946	Male	33%	55%	66%	69%	70%
(65th-79th)	Female	27%	43%	50%	57%	67%
1947-1964	Male	3%	11%	16%	22%	28%
(80th-88th)	Female	0%	5%	12%	14%	23%
1965-1984	Male	5%	14%	28%	30%	30%
(89th-98th)	Female	8%	24%	30%	31%	33%
1985-1993	Male	6%	15%	29%		
(99th-103rd)	Female	5%	18%	36%	a	a

a) Too few women for a useful comparison.
Source: U.S. Congressional Directory, 1917-1993

Bryan Owen, Effiegene Wingo, Edith Nourse Rogers, Frances Bolton, Emily Douglas Taft, and Helen Gahagan Douglas served on the Foreign Affairs committee, and Margaret Chase Smith saw initial service on Post Office and Post Roads, both of which were defined as "exclusive" at the time.[4]

Nonetheless, the earliest congresswomen as a group did not do as well as their male contemporaries. Whereas little more than one-quarter (27%) received exclusive assignments in their first terms, one-third of the freshmen congressmen were similarly successful. Furthermore, the women seem never to have caught up with (although they approached) the rate of exclusive committee assignments males with comparable service received during their first five terms. For example, two of three male Representatives (66%) in their third term during this time period were assigned to exclusive committees, compared with only one of every two congresswomen. The three-percentage-point difference between men and women in their fifth terms seems to be of little importance, except that the delay congresswomen experienced almost certainly diluted the effect their House seniority could have on committee seniority, inasmuch as committee influence depended upon the latter rather than the former.

The House career of California's Florence Kahn reflects the difficulties some congresswomen experienced in the years before World War II. Kahn sought to replace her husband on Military Affairs, a committee which he had chaired before his death, but she received, instead, three minor committees, one of which was Indian Affairs. The San Francisco Republican refused to accept this last assignment, noting that the only Indians in her district were in front of cigar stores and beyond any assistance she could provide. The Republican leadership then awarded her a vacancy on the more appealing Education committee (Gilfond 1929, p. 159). But Kahn had to wait until her third term before securing a Military Affairs seat and two more terms before being given a vacancy on the Appropriations Committee.

These early cases may not be strictly comparable with assignments distributed following committee reorganization in 1946, but the disadvantages congresswomen suffered relative to their male colleagues did not abate between the 1940s and the 1960s. Not a single female Representative was initially assigned to an exclusive committee—then defined as including only Appropriations, Rules, and Ways and Means—as compared with three of every one-hundred fledgling congressmen. The difference may not be a significant one, but it seems formidable if only because the percentage for women simply could not have been lower. And their failure ever to equal the success rate of males with comparable service underscores their handicap.

Contemporary congresswomen have reversed the pattern. A larger proportion of first-term women than men have been appointed to exclusive committees (expanded since 1975 to include the Budget Committee), and, as their terms of service progressed, they maintained their advantage over males who were elected to the House when they were. The small size of the female universe makes one hesitant about placing too much confidence in the comparison, but the fact remains that Carrie Meek (Appropriations), Martha Keys (Ways and Means) and Lynn Martin, Bobbi Fiedler, and Lynn Woolsey (Budget) received prestigious committee assignments as soon as they arrived on Capitol Hill. And other females elected since 1965 transferred to exclusive committees at a generally more rapid rate than males with equal years of service.

Thus, women elected to the House since the mid-1960s have been more successful than their predecessors in securing prestigious assignments, and they have fared better as a group than the males whose House careers began when theirs did.

Committee and Subcommittee Chairs

Before passage of the 1946 Reorganization Act, five women had headed standing House committees. Mae Nolan led the Committee on Expenditures in the Post Office Department and Caroline O'Day chaired the Committee on the Election of the President, Vice President, and Representatives in Congress. Leadership of so inconsequential a pair of committees gave neither woman an important policy-making role. On the other hand, when Mary Norton chaired first the District of Columbia Committee and then the Labor Committee, she gained national recognition. The chair of the first earned her the designation "Mayor of Washington," that of the second gave her the opportunity to sponsor and manage important legislation—notably the Wages and Hours Act of 1938. But when the Labor Committee was combined with the Education Committee in 1947, Norton moved to the House Administration Committee. Her considerable seniority soon elevated her to the chair of that less prestigious House panel.[5]

In 1947, Edith Nourse Rogers chaired the nonexclusive Veterans' Affairs Committee, and in the 93rd and 94th Congresses, Leonor Sullivan led the similarly nonexclusive Merchant Marine and Fisheries Committee. No congresswoman has led a standing committee since Sullivan left the House, but many chaired subcommittees or served as ranking minority party members both before and after the Missouri Democrat retired. They number close to fifty, but that figure reveals little about whether women Representatives secured subcommittee leadership positions proportionate to their total number in the House.

To determine the extent to which this has been the case, a count was made of women elevated to top subcommittee positions beginning in 1955—a time when most, even if not all, standing committees had established subcommittees.[6] Their number was analyzed in terms of how many subcommittee chairs existed on the full committees to which they were assigned and the number of male Representatives with whom they were competing for such positions. The calculations produced an Index of Fe-

Table 7.4
**Index of Female Representation* for Subcommittee Chairs and Ranking
Minority Positions, 1955–1993**

Time Period (Congresses)	Democratic Congresswomen	Republican Congresswomen	Total Congresswomen**
1955-1964 (84th-88th)	1.54	.90	1.24
1965-1974 (89th-93rd)	1.51	1.94	1.73
1975-1984 (94th-98th)	1.16	.80	1.02
1985-1993 (99th-103rd)	.59	1.08	.80

*See Chapter 6, Note 6 for a description of how the Index was derived.
**Women serving on committees that did not have subcommittees are excluded.

male Representation, with the Indices in Table 7.4 reflecting the degree of success congresswomen achieved collectively. An index of 1.00 denotes a level one would normally expect to occur by chance, a figure of 2.00 indicates that the women were twice as successful as their numbers and opportunities would permit on average, and anything less than 1.00 implies women were underrepresented in subcommittee leadership positions.[7]

The table indicates that the rate of female representativeness has fluctuated over time, but that, except for recent Democrats, congresswomen have generally held their own. Between 1955 and 1974, female Democrats were more than 1.5 times as likely as male Democrats to be elevated to a subcommittee chair. Their rate of success during the next period was little more than one would expect if chairs were distributed randomly. Since 1985, however, they have been about one-half as successful as their male colleagues. The frequency with which Republican congresswomen have been ranking members of subcommittees has been erratic, with their high success rate between 1965 and 1974 especially noteworthy. In recent years, however, they have been about as likely to secure ranking subcommittee positions as GOP men.

Explanations for the decline in the Democratic index reside partly in the unusually large number of Democratic women elected for the first time in 1990 and 1992. Since 1983, forty three new female Representatives were sent to Washington, thirty-four Democrats, nine Republicans. The 1990 and 1992 elections alone accounted for twenty-six Democrats and three Republicans. Most of the new Democrats and all of those elected in 1992 had not yet secured a subcommittee chair after the 103rd Congress convened and their numbers diluted the positive contribution to the Index of Female Representation recorded by women Democrats elected to the House before 1990.[8] The smaller number of newer Republican women and their more gradual appearance in the House during the last decade did not similarly offset positive contributions to the Republican Index made by senior GOP congresswomen.

Another reason for the decline in the Democratic Index is linked to an increase in the proportion of Democratic women appointed to committees that are highly valued and which experience relatively little membership turnover. Subcommittee leadership on these panels normally requires more seniority than is needed for leadership status on lesser committees. Thus, the low seniority of an unusually large number of Democratic women on desirable committees has, for the time being, depressed their most recent Index of Female Representation.

In sum, congresswomen have expanded the range of issues to which they give their attention and, as a result, they have augmented their potential for leading the House in all policy domains. Since the 1970s, they have served on subcommittees that dealt with such matters as interstate and foreign commerce, nuclear energy and weaponry, communications and transportation, international law, and criminal justice, subjects all but inaccessible to female Representatives in years past. They have also gained seats on those committees that most influence fiscal decisions, with almost all Congresses convened in the last two decades having at least one woman on each of the money committees—Appropriations, Budget, and Ways and Means. Female membership on the powerful Rules Committee has been more intermittent, although the Democrats appear committed to having at least one woman member on Rules as long as they remain the majority party.

In the meantime, few women have been chairs of standing House committees, with the handful who have heading relatively unimportant panels. The frequency with which they have claimed top positions on subcommittees, however, has varied over time. Republican women have generally held their own. Until recently, so did the Democrats. The sharp decline suffered by the latter during the last ten years is partly due to the significant increase in new women members elected in 1990 and 1992—members whose minimal seniority made subcommittee leadership all but impossible. The lower Democratic Index is also a product of an increase in the proportion of women appointed to the House's most valued committees, panels whose large size and low turnover prolong their climb to the top.

Failure of congresswomen to rise to subcommittee leadership positions on highly prized committees has thus far limited their opportunities to shape policies on the weightiest of issues. On the other hand, the pace at which they have been assigned to prestigious panels has been greater than that of men in recent years, and current congresswomen are likely to have a better chance through the seniority rule of capturing a subcommittee chair or ranking membership than either their female predecessors or their male contemporaries.

Recent years have witnessed an increasing number of congresswomen sensitive to the demands of the feminist movement, and many have begun to champion measures calculated to affect women directly. As the remaining chapters in this section make clear, congresswomen have begun to alter their representational role orientations and to influence the disposition of legislative measures affecting contemporary women. They have concluded that American women need champions in Washington who are prepared to define and speak for their collective needs.

NOTES

1. Two of the five, Edith Green and Shirley Chisholm, shared an interest in education which predated by many years their election to the House. Louise Day Hicks had built a political reputation on her opposition to school busing for purposes of racial integration and had served on the Boston School Board before coming to Washington. Ella Grasso, whose husband was a school superintendent, had established a record of achievement in the field of education while holding public office in Connecticut, especially through programs to help the retarded and blind. And Patsy Mink's close ties to organized labor made her assignment to the Committee a reasonable one. If those controlling the distribution of assignments meant to isolate the influence of these women by putting them on the same committee, as Abzug suggested, they were assisted by the relatively narrow range of interests which women were expected to develop in their formative years.

2. Democrats serving on the Ways and Means Committee before 1975 were in a particularly advantageous position inasmuch as they constituted their party's Committee on Committees (Manley 1970, pp. 76–78). They continue to exercise influence on minor tax provisions of special interest to colleagues whose constituencies are likely to be directly affected in ways which the rest of the country will not be. Unusual opportunities to help another Representative's standing with constituents are similarly available to Appropriations Committee members (Fenno 1966, pp. 87–88).

3. The following committees were defined as "exclusive" between 1917 and 1946: Agriculture, Appropriations, Banking and Currency, Foreign Affairs, Interstate and Foreign Commerce, Judiciary, Military Affairs, Naval Affairs, Post Office and Post Roads, Rules, and Ways and Means (Galloway 1953, p. 281). After 1946, the term applied only to Appropriations, Rules, and Ways and Means. The Budget Committee, established in the mid-1970s, has also been included in that category, even though service on it in no way precludes assignment to other committees.

4. Smith was not satisfied with her assignments, preferring a seat on Naval Affairs to one on the once important but by then overrated Post Office and Post Roads Committee (Lamson 1968, p. 11). On the other hand, the House increased the size of the Foreign Affairs Committee in the 71st Congress to accommodate Owen (Paxton 1945, p. 6).

5. Norton's decision to move from a more to a less prestigious committee was apparently voluntary, prompted by the shift in House control from Democratic to Republican after the 1946 election, and the elevation of New Jersey's Fred Hartley, Jr., to the chairmanship of the Education and Labor Committee. At first Norton explained her shift to the House Administration Committee as motivated by the Democrat's loss of a New Jersey Senate seat and her need to "take over a great

amount of work for my state . . . somewhere I can be most useful" (*New York Times,* January 4, 1947). But during House debate over what later came to be called the Taft-Hartley Act, Norton was asked to explain her departure from the Labor Committee. She replied:

Frankly, in one sense I regret that the gentleman has asked me that question because I have never knowingly hurt a member of Congress on either side of the aisle. I have a very great respect and affection for the members I have served with, but I regret to say I have no respect for the present chairman of the Labor Committee. And I could not serve with a chairman for whom I hold no respect. My reason for that is that during the ten years I was chairman of the Labor Committee, the gentleman from New Jersey, who is now the chairman of the Labor Committee and who comes here before you and talks about labor as if he knew something about it, attended exactly six meetings in ten years. That was my reason for leaving the Committee on Labor (*Congressional Record*, 80th Congress, 1st Session, Vol. 93, Part 3 [April 15, 1947]: p. 3432)

6. Standing committees that had established subcommittees by the 84th Congress (1955) included Agriculture, Appropriations, Armed Services, District of Columbia, Foreign Affairs, Government Operations, House Administration, Interior and Insular Affairs, Interstate and Foreign Commerce, Judiciary, Public Works, and Veterans' Affairs. Banking and Currency, Education and Labor, Merchant Marine and Fisheries, and Post Office and Civil Service adopted formal subcommittee systems in the 85th Congress; Ways and Means in the 93rd; Small Business (as a permanent committee) in the 94th; and Rules in the 96th. The Budget Committee created "Task Forces" in the 95th Congress and they are treated here as if they were subcommittees. Congresswomen assigned to committees having no subcommittees were excluded from the analysis. Information about assignments was gathered from *Congressional Quarterly Almanac*, 1955–1993.

7. See Chapter 6, footnote 6 for a description of how the index was derived.

8. The Democratic Index rises to .83 if subcommittee appointments in the 103rd Congress are omitted. It increases to .89 if appointments in both the 102nd and 103rd Congresses are excluded from the calculation.

8

Issues Affecting Women: Changing Legislative Priorities

Before World War II, most bills introduced by congresswomen either ignored women as a class or spoke to a narrow range of their concerns.[1] Reasons for this neglect included a lack of interest in issues impinging directly on women, a determination that a public display of such interest would be politically damaging, a conviction that the problems women face should be resolved at the state level or without benefit of governmental intervention, and a belief that a congresswoman associating herself with such issues would weaken her effectiveness among House colleagues. In fact, most legislative proposals directly affecting women were introduced by male lawmakers.

By the mid-1960s, female Representatives had all but abandoned the reservations of their predecessors, introducing scores of bills crafted to help women. This shift in representational role orientations was accompanied by growth in the number and types of women's issues addressed in proposed legislation. These issues were not new in the sense that they had never been broached before. On the contrary, many had been raised by nineteenth-century feminists. What had changed was their newfound political saliency. An increasing number of American women recognized that they were being overwhelmed by problems men did not encounter, that the private sector and state and local governments had dealt with these problems inadequately, or not at all, and that the difficulties women faced were on a scale large enough to warrant responses from Washington.

Most of the newly visible concerns centered on women's opportunities in the marketplace, their vulnerability to abuse, the contributions to family life they were expected to make, and the extent to which private, personal choices were limited by private and public institutions. Decisions to try to place these issues on the national agenda grew out of the changing social and economic status of American women, the life experiences of women elected to Congress after World War II, and the resolve of the latter to do right by the former.

Thus, the increased readiness of congresswomen to stake out positions on matters of concern to women was accompanied by an expansion in the repertoire of women's issues capturing public attention. In the discussion that follows, congresswomen's changing policy priorities will be examined within the context of the politicization of women's private and public relationships—relationships once considered inappropriate for consideration by the national government.

WOMEN'S ISSUES AND CHANGING PRIORITIES

Over the years, most proposed legislation directly affecting women has generally fallen into one of three categories. Legislative measures, first of all, reinforce traditional gender role performance. Such bills address women's needs in terms of their roles as mothers, wives, homemakers, and dependents. Other measures are egalitarian in intent, seeking to elevate women to positions of equality with men in the marketplace, government, and the academy, as well as in the public consciousness.

A third category of bills is affirmative in character. Affirmative measures facilitate women's claims to the resources and recognition available to men as a matter of course, and free them from the social, economic, and cultural constraints under which they have customarily labored. Affirmative measures are those which recognize the importance of women's role in history and society, which support and reinforce women's claims to economic independence, and which assist them in overcoming the sexism embedded in a male-dominated social structure. This broad range of measures may be classified further into three subtypes: symbolically affirmative, economically affirmative, socially affirmative. Examples of traditional, egalitarian, and affirmative legislation are presented in Table 8.1.

Not all legislative initiatives fall under these three headings, and some satisfy criteria for at least two of the three. But the typology is useful for classifying most bills affecting women directly, and it helps provide a conceptual framework within which to describe and interpret changes in emphasis given to selected issues affecting women. Moreover, the behavior of congresswomen is better appreciated when it is understood as an expression of shifting legislative priorities.

Between the two world wars, a significant majority of the bills female Representatives introduced reinforced the roles women traditionally performed. Under the provisions of these measures, women were defined in terms of their relationships to men. Following World War II, congresswomen turned to legislative measures designed to make women the equals of men. These bills sought to eliminate barriers to women's vocational, financial, and academic achievement. Since the early 1970s, congress-

Table 8.1
Types of Women's Issues

Issue Type	*Legislative Examples*
Traditional	Pensions for widows of military veterans
	Social Security benefits pegged to husband's earnings
Egalitarian	Equal Pay Act of 1963
	Title IX of the 1972 Education Act Amendments
Affirmative	
1. Symbolic	Establishing a "Working Mother's" Day
	Creating a Susan B. Anthony Silver Dollar
2. Economic	Federally-funded day care centers
	Support for displaced homemakers
3. Social	Aid to victims of domestic violence
	Prevention of unnecessary mastectomies

women have increasingly championed proposals affirming the initiatives of women pursuing goals which their traditional gender roles once placed beyond their reach. Such measures attempted to use the national government to help circumvent the limitations of role expectations.

Proposals in all three categories were offered by House members during all three periods, but, as will be demonstrated, the trend from traditional to egalitarian to affirmative is a clearly observable one.

Reinforcing Traditional Role Performance

Between the world wars, the overwhelming majority of House proposals designed to assist women were submitted by men and were traditional in nature. Many congresswomen elected during the period, particularly those who succeeded their husbands or who served for a short time, introduced no measures directly affecting women. Most of the remaining female Representatives confined their attention to bills whose treatment of women was linked to their status as spouses and mothers. Alice Robertson urged that pensions be paid to retired U.S. deputy marshals (or their widows) assigned to the federal district court in Oklahoma. And Katherine Langley urged an increase in the pensions of widows whose husbands had served in the Mexican, Civil, and Spanish-American Wars.

Dozens of other bills allocated economic and symbolic rewards to World War I veterans and their surviving spouses, often extending benefits to wives of veterans whose disabilities and deaths were not service-connected. Several proposals provided assistance to widows of foreign service officers, to Gold Star Mothers, and to veterans' widows who, after remarrying, became single again. Many of these measures were not enacted into law. Nevertheless, the aid they promised to mothers and female spouses was pegged to the experience and status of men, with the affected women considered legal extensions of these men.

Labor laws protecting women workers were proposed during this period and they, too, were traditional in character. State and local governments, more than Congress, dealt with protective measures in the years between the wars, but the House and Senate regularly received petitions to enact national protective labor legislation. Shorter hours, better working conditions, minimum wages, and bars to dangerous occupational tasks were among the work rules sought. As the funding body for the District of Columbia, Congress was asked to enact protective measures for women employed in the capital. Mary Norton considered many such bills while chair of the District of Columbia Committee, but most congresswomen gave the subject little attention.

Nonetheless, the issue was a controversial one and bitter battles were waged between representatives of most women's groups on the one hand, and employers' groups (and the National Woman's Party) on the other. The former were interested in humane work rules and saw them as harbingers of more enlightened employment arrangements for men. Management saw these laws as infringing on their right to hire employees under conditions of their own choosing, and as undermining the sanctity of contracts. The courts found a middle ground, interpreting protective labor legislation as an unconstitutional violation of the free market in the case of men, but permissible for women. One Supreme Court justice noted that because of their delicate physical stature and maternal responsibilities, women workers required government protection from "the greed as well as the passion of men" (quoted in Lemons 1973, p. 143). While protective legislation for women drew a wide range of reactions, the major premise of its judicial justification averred that women would be unable to perform their traditional roles without it.

Some bills introduced between the wars penalized women because their behavior violated traditional role expectations. During the recession that followed World War I and again in the depths of the Depression, working married women were threatened with diminution of pay or, worse, unemployment, in order to increase the number of jobs for men. Married women who were civil servants and whose husbands were also government employees were especially vulnerable. In 1932, Congress passed the Government Economy Act, a law designed, in part, to cut the size and cost of the bureaucracy. Section 213 of the act provided that among those employees to be dismissed first were people whose spouses also worked for the federal government. The language of the act did not specify which spouse should be fired or furloughed, but, inasmuch as wives were almost always earning less than husbands, the former were more likely to give up their jobs. Some civil servants whose husbands were in the armed forces were required to relinquish their positions even though they earned considerably more than spouses whose enlistments still had several years to run.

Although a relatively small number of married couples were ultimately affected by the law (about 2,000 federal employees were forced to leave their jobs under this provision of the act), three-quarters of those terminated were married women. A large proportion of them held low-paying jobs in the Treasury and Commerce Departments and in the Veterans' Administration (Becker 1981, p. 203). The hardship experienced by these women was considerable and no one knows how many affianced couples, both of whom were civil servants, delayed their marriages rather than risk a significant cut in their collective income.

Congress repealed Section 213 five years after its passage. Arguments for repeal included claims that it discriminated against married women in practice, even though either spouse could have been affected; that it resulted in dismissals based on marital status rather than on job performance, with negative consequences for morale; and that its implementation affected unskilled and semiskilled rather than high-salaried workers, thereby reducing expected economies. Whereas no female House member had argued against Section 213 when the act was passed (Edith Rogers and Mary Norton criticized other portions of the measure), and whereas all but Norton supported its final passage, each of the women serving in the House in 1937 spoke out for its recision. This reaction constituted one of several exceptions to the general rule followed by congresswomen between the wars—that of confining their support for women's issues to measures reinforcing traditional gender roles. Apparently the flagrant discrimination against married women in this case was more than even the most circumspect female Representatives could countenance.

The Drive for Equality: Early Years

In the years before World War II, some congresswomen abandoned their traditional outlook on a narrow range of subjects. When they did, the initiatives undertaken were unmistakably egalitarian in conception and purpose.

Women serving in the military and related services were the category of females most often singled out for equal treatment. After World War I, attempts were made to confer belated military status (and, therefore, the benefits associated with such status) on women who had served overseas. Abortive efforts were made to award the Congressional Medal of Honor to some women, as well. When World War II began, the Women's Auxiliary Army Corps, the country's first female military unit, and other women's military and defense services were established. Later, permanent commissions were conferred on army and navy nurses, and a Medical Specialist Corps was created, giving officer status to dieticians, and physical and occupational therapists. Their recognition as professionals constituted an important departure in principle, even if not always in practice, from the statutory treatment women customarily received.

Women working in the civil and government-related service and female aliens were also intended beneficiaries of egalitarian measures during this early period. Several unsuccessful bills attempted to equalize the pay scales of men and women employed by the federal government. Others sought to do the same for private-sector workers engaged in war-related jobs. One measure made a modest effort to end discrimination based upon gender in awarding government contracts, and some proposals were designed to increase the number of government service opportunities for women. Caroline O'Day sought unsuccessfully to help alien women by sponsoring a bill to give female ministers and professors who emigrated to the United States under the nonquota provisions of the 1924 Immigration Act the same privileges available to alien men in the same vocations. Under the 1924 statute, the latter could bring dependents, the former could not.

But perhaps the most important immigration bill affecting women at the time was sponsored by Ruth Bryan Owen. Before 1922, an American woman marrying a foreign subject lost her citizenship, even though the marriage was later dissolved through divorce or death and she returned to the United States for repatriation. Legislation passed in 1922 eliminated that problem for women marrying non-Americans *after* adoption of the Act, but provided no remedy for those who had done so before 1922. As someone who had married a British subject, lived abroad, and then returned to the United States to nurse an ailing spouse, Owen identified closely with women in the same predicament, and she worked to give women not covered by the 1922 Act the same options as those married after that date. The proposal had special significance to her because her unsuccessful opponent in the 1928 congressional election challenged her right to serve on the grounds that she was not a citizen. The House decided otherwise.

Other egalitarian, and some affirmative, measures introduced during this period included a proposal to extend suffrage to all American women (offered, of course, before the adoption of the 19th Amendment), as well as to women residents of U.S. territories; a bill recognizing women's interests in aviation; a proposal to establish a federal Department of Home and Child, an affirmative step to elevate the role of homemakers and recognize the special problems they faced; and legislation offering federal funds to states which provided instruction on the hygiene of maternity and infancy. This last proposal was enacted in 1921, but was permitted to lapse in 1929.[2] At the same time, scores of resolutions were submitted calling for an Equal Rights Amendment to the Constitution. None was sponsored by a woman House member until 1945, however.

The egalitarian impulses of House members introducing these measures put them ahead of their time, although the few female Representatives contributing such proposals usually served on the committees which claimed jurisdiction over the bills' subject matter. Thus, many of the attempts to confer veterans' status on women were authored by Edith Rogers of the World War Veterans' Legislation Committee. Margaret Chase Smith used her position on the Naval Affairs Committee to secure passage of her bills to permit Women Accepted for Volunteer Emergency Service (WAVES) to see overseas duty and to establish a permanent Nurse Corps. And Caroline O'Day's membership on the Committee on Immigration and Naturalization added credibility to the measures she introduced extending equal benefits to male and female aliens.

In spite of these efforts, congresswomen demonstrated much less concern than male Representatives about issues affecting women directly, egalitarian or otherwise, even after taking into account the former's significantly smaller numbers.

The Drive for Equality: Post–World War II

While most of the congresswomen serving through World War II were inclined either to say nothing about women's issues or to propose measures reinforcing their traditional roles, many serving in the postwar period made public commitments to end discrimination based upon gender. Among the most popular of their proposals was one calling for equal pay for equal work, an idea ultimately embedded in the Equal Pay Act of 1963. The legislation received early support from Helen Gahagan Douglas, Margaret Chase Smith, and Chase Going Woodhouse, and even the more cautious Frances Bolton introduced a bill authorizing a study of discriminatory pay practices. By the late 1950s, almost one-half of the women House members had introduced measures requiring the federal government or private companies involved in interstate commerce to provide the same compensation to men and women employed in the same capacity.

The congresswoman who played a critical role in persuading the House to consider the measure was Oregon's Edith Green. Green's membership on the Education and Labor Committee gave her immediate access to consideration of an equal pay bill, and for years she had unsuccessfully tried to convince Labor Standards subcommittee chair Phil Landrum, an opponent of the legislation, to clear it for committee and floor debate. On one occasion she approached Landrum and asked the Georgia Democrat to introduce a "minor" bill which she wanted to sponsor but, for political reasons, could not. Landrum, happy to oblige, agreed before knowing what Green had in mind. He was appalled when she proposed reducing the salaries of congresswomen by $5,000. Green argued that the bill was needed because congressmen worked so much harder, put in longer hours, introduced so many more bills than did women lawmakers, and, therefore, deserved more pay. The Georgian demurred, insisting that women worked just as hard as men and withdrew his offer to sponsor the proposal. Whereupon the Oregon Democrat said that she was happy he felt that way because she had an "equal pay for equal work" bill in his subcommittee and she would be grateful if he would schedule hearings on it (Dreifus 1972).

Landrum never did oblige. But, in 1960, Education and Labor Committee Chair Graham Barden of North Carolina retired and was replaced by New York City's Adam Clayton Powell—a Representative sympathetic to the Equal Pay bill. Landrum lost his subcommittee chair, and it was New Jersey Democrat Frank Thompson's Special Subcommittee on Labor that reported out the measure. He was supported in the debate by veterans Frances Bolton, Katharine St. George, Edna Kelly, and Green, among others.

One reason the bill passed was because it was tame in comparison with another proposal for which support had been growing—the Equal Rights Amendment. The ERA had been introduced in the House as early as 1923. It had attracted the support of an increasing number of male Representatives over the years. Many women's groups opposed the Amendment, believing it would deprive women of some of the benefits they enjoyed in the workplace by virtue of their gender.

The manner in which congresswomen coalesced to support the ERA had a logic all its own. In the pre–World War II period, no female House member publicly identified with the Amendment. The opposition of most women's groups and support for the measure by the suspect National Woman's Party doubtless encouraged congresswomen to distance themselves from it. Most women leaders saw ERA as a threat to protective labor legislation, laws in which they had a significant investment and which had been difficult to pass in a climate hostile to the labor movement (Lemons 1973, p. 142).[3] They believed the Amendment would force women workers to abide by the more forbidding work rules governing male employment.

Most labor organizations also opposed the ERA. Union leaders feared the Amendment would provide an excuse for employers to reduce benefits received by male workers when more generous emoluments were extended to women employees. They also believed that jobs held by men would be lost to women. Many employers, on the other hand, hailed the measure, construing it as a way of undermining the integrity of labor unions and of ending protective legislation for women. Among the Equal Rights Amendment's earliest supporters was the National Association of Manufacturers (Lemons 1973, p. 191).

The first congresswomen to support the ERA, therefore, were not New Deal, prolabor Democrats who generally took the lead on issues promoting political and economic equality, but conservative, probusiness Republicans. In 1942, Jessie Sumner, arguably the most conservative Republican in the

House, male or female, expressed strong support for the ERA, although she did not go so far as to introduce an ERA Resolution. Three years later, Republicans Margaret Chase Smith and Edith Nourse Rogers broke the ice and became the first female House members to cosponsor the Amendment. Soon thereafter, it was another Republican, conservative New Yorker Katharine St. George, who led the ERA battle. For several years she had only male Representatives to keep her company. Seventy-nine of them joined her in signing a petition to force a House vote by discharging the Judiciary Committee, led by Brooklyn Democrat and ERA antagonist Emanuel Celler, from further consideration of the Resolution (Lockett 1950). In the meantime, such progressive Democrats as Chase Going Woodhouse and Helen Gahagan Douglas worked actively to stall the Amendment. In 1953, two other conservative Republicans, Ruth Thompson of Michigan and Margaret Stitt Church of Illinois, added their support and, two years later, additional Republicans and the first group of Democrats signed on as ERA cosponsors.[4]

As women's groups began to change their positions on the Amendment, leadership among congresswomen shifted to liberal Democrats. Martha Griffiths, Gracie Pfost, and Julia Butler Hansen, among others, began to champion the measure. In the end, it was Griffiths who, in August, 1970, led a drive to discharge the Judiciary Committee from further consideration of the Amendment and force a floor vote. She was also a prime mover when the resolution was passed in the next Congress. Democrat Leonor Sullivan was the lone woman among the twenty-four Representatives voting against the Amendment.

The ERA, of course, was a comprehensive measure, one which was calculated to impose an egalitarian stamp on virtually all economic, social, and political relationships. Its adoption by the Senate in 1972 occurred during a decade of more modest efforts to pass legislation validating women's claims for equal rights under the law. Congress passed measures establishing task forces and commissions to study the legal status of women. It also approved Title VII of the 1964 Civil Rights Act prohibiting sex discrimination in employment; the Equal Employment Opportunity Act of 1972; and Title IX of the 1972 Amendments to the Education Act, which required equal treatment of women in education.

Congress later enacted the Equal Credit Opportunity Act of 1974; the equal opportunity provision of the Career Education Incentive Act of 1977 (to help overcome sex stereotyping in employment); the Women's Educational Opportunity Act of 1978; and the Defense Appropriation Act of 1976, one provision of which authorized the admission of women to the military service academies. In 1977 veterans' status was conferred on 850 surviving members of the World War II Women Air Force Service Pilots and, one year later, the time period for passage of the ERA was extended. Unlike the pattern revealed between the Wars, the congresswomen who introduced these egalitarian measures did not necessarily serve on the committees having jurisdiction over them—partly because the House began to permit joint sponsorship of bills during this period and partly because a new generation of female Representatives was less willing than their predecessors to compartmentalize women's concerns.

The drive for equal treatment almost always focused upon women, rather than men, as the victims of discrimination. From the outset, however, congresswomen were sensitive to the extent to which laws and practices discriminated against males. A number of bills provided for the appointment of men as armed forces nurses, and Margaret Stitt Church was among the first female Representatives to offer amendments to the Railroad Retirement Act, the Civil Service Retirement Act, and the Social Security Act to give husbands and widowers the same benefits that had been awarded to wives and widows. These proposals paved the way for similar bills, among them Millicent Fenwick's proposal to apply the Mann Act, prohibiting the transportation of women across state lines for immoral purposes, to males.

Not all of the measures offered by congresswomen during this period were traditional or egalitarian in intent. As early as 1949, bills had been introduced to provide a tax deduction for the costs of a housekeeper or a day care center to look after dependents while taxpayers were at work. The measure would apply to both single and married parents and, while the law was designed to benefit both men and women, the latter were far more likely to be single parents. They were also likely to be the more dispensable wage earner when both wife and husband were employed. Thus began the drive to pass affirmative legislation, a trend which burgeoned in the last quarter of the century.

The Shift Toward Affirmative Legislation

Success in sponsoring egalitarian measures, along with the realization that equal opportunity under the law did not necessarily mean equal opportunity in fact, emboldened Representatives to introduce affirmative proposals. Many of these bills did not even mention gender, and some applied explicitly to men, as well as to women. But all were expected to help the latter far more than the former in practice. Several were perceived as necessary *because* earlier egalitarian measures had been passed. Some women could take advantage of equal job opportunities and equal pay for equal work only if adequate day care centers were available for their children, and only if there were enough part-time or flextime jobs accessible to permit them to fulfill domestic, as well as career, responsibilities.

The range of affirmative legislative measures is broad, with each proposal addressing at least one of three general goals—symbolic, economic, and social. Symbolic measures place a higher value on women's traditional role performance, reinterpret more positively contributions women made in the past, recognize these contributions with appropriate ritual, and, in the process, seek to make the public aware of their significance. Economically affirmative laws compensate women for socioeconomic limitations under which they labored while they fulfilled traditional gender role responsibilities. These measures help make women independent of such restraints, and provide both the material and moral support needed to achieve that independence. Bills falling into the socially affirmative category are more difficult to define. They lift the social and cultural limitations imposed upon women by men—husbands, lawyers, physicians, bureaucrats, local, state and national lawmakers among them—who are ignorant of, or insensitive to, women's needs and who reflect these shortcomings in the rules they create (or fail to create) and implement.

1. Symbolically Affirmative Measures. The easiest affirmative measures to trace are those which sought to commemorate the achievements of female leaders and to institutionalize rituals celebrating the skills, courage and devotion of American women. More than a half-dozen congresswomen sponsored measures to establish Eleanor Roosevelt and Mary McLeod Bethune historic sites; and Margaret Heckler took the lead in naming a hospital in Bedford, Massachusetts, for Edith Nourse Rogers. Mary Rose Oakar succeeded in passing a bill to put Susan B. Anthony's profile on a newly minted silver dollar, but only after beating back efforts to use the anonymous "Miss Liberty" on the coin. In a March 22, 1978 letter to the Treasury Department, a group of congresswomen, led by Margaret Heckler and Elizabeth Holtzman, opposed selection of a mythical female figure. They said, in part:

> Although we applaud your decision to place a woman's face on the coin, we don't think the choice of the mythical figure, "Miss Liberty," is particularly appropriate since there are many female American historical figures who could certainly qualify for the honor. Moreover, "Miss Liberty" has previously graced numerous coins— several Liberty dollars, the Liberty dime, and the winged Liberty head (Mercury) dime, among others.
>
> We can't recall an instance where a male mythical figure was placed on a general circulation coin solely to avoid controversy over which male should garner the honor—Kennedy, Roosevelt, Jefferson, Washington, Lincoln, and Eisenhower made it over Father Time, Uncle Sam and Neptune.
>
> There have been many women whose mark on American History is such that they could appropriately be placed on a general circulation coin: Susan B. Anthony, Betsy Ross, Eleanor Roosevelt, Helen Keller, Amelia Earhart, Harriet Tubman, Jane Addams, Alice Paul, Nellie Ross, and Molly Pitcher, to name a few.

Scores of Representatives and Senators joined forces to restore the Congressional Medal of Honor to the only woman ever to have received it but from whom it had been stripped fifty years after it had been conferred. Mary Edwards Walker had been a Civil War surgeon attending Union soldiers on

Virginia and Tennessee battlefields. She was captured, spent four months in a southern prison, and was exchanged "man for man" for a confederate major. Generals William T. Sherman and George H. Thomas recommended that she be awarded the medal, President Lincoln agreed, and President Andrew Johnson performed the ceremony on November 11, 1865. However, in 1916, a military review board recommended that Walker's medal, along with similar awards to 911 servicemen, be revoked. Congress approved the recommendation. Nevertheless, Walker wore the decoration until her death in 1919.

Her descendants claimed that the revocation was based upon the physician's gender and her unorthodox life style and beliefs. Walker had been an ardent suffragist. She wore men's trousers and frock coats, and gave feminist lectures attired in men's evening dress with the Medal of Honor on her lapel. On June 10, 1977, the medal was posthumously restored by Army Secretary Clifford Alexander, following congressional demands that the 1916 revocation be overturned. Shortly thereafter Walker was the subject of a commemorative stamp issued by the U.S. Postal Service.

Among other affirmative measures of this type were bills acknowledging women's collective achievements and their civil rights. Proposals to establish a "Women's Equity Day," and a "Women's Rights Day" were introduced. Laws were passed designating an International Women's Year and establishing a Women's Rights National Park in Seneca Falls, New York, site of the 1848 Women's Rights Convention. A "Working Mother's Day" was approved, and Barbara Mikulski successfully spearheaded the drive to establish a "Women's History Week." Finally, some congresswomen proposed that the House impanel a select Committee on Women, lest women's problems and contributions be relegated once again to the darker recesses of the legislature's (and the public's) consciousness.

One purpose of these bills was to resurrect and burnish the reputations of women who had made significant contributions to society, but who were either forgotten or consigned to a footnote in history. Another was to provide young girls, and women generally, with female role models. Many of these measures sought to elevate the importance of the routine tasks that were part of women's traditional roles, but which were undervalued by society precisely because the work was done cheaply, routinely, without complaint, and by women. One goal was to make these activities valuable not because they were done to complement traditional male responsibilities, but because women did them so well. Some measures had important social and economic consequences, but their principal function was to attach new and renewed value to the uses to which women's efforts have customarily been put, and to increase the worth of all of their activities, traditional and otherwise.

2. Economically Affirmative Measures. A second type of affirmative legislation sought to lift or ameliorate economic constraints on women, whether manifested in the law, in practice, or in public expectation. Egalitarian measures passed in the 1960s and 1970s were intended to overcome barriers to independence and achievement, but many women were neither trained nor otherwise prepared to capitalize on the new statutes. Others were impeded by prior commitments to home, children, and spouse—commitments which could be broken or bent only at considerable emotional cost.

Thus, something more than legal equality was needed if women were to realize their potential. By the end of the 1970s, congresswomen had introduced scores of bills to relax the circumstantial squeeze in which women found themselves. Mention has already been made of tax credits for child care costs incurred by working parents. Other proposals increased the number and quality of day care centers for children of welfare recipients and low-income families, a considerable number of which featured women heads of households. And Shirley Chisholm sponsored bills to reimburse relatives, including grandparents, for child care costs incurred at home (not just at a day-care center) while the children's parents were working. Later bills proposed programs to train women in occupations traditionally dominated by men; to promote women's business ownership; and to increase the number of federal contracts received by female entrepreneurs.

Many of the measures falling within the category of affirmative legislation made little or no mention of women. When introduced, however, House debate made clear that they were expected to apply to women far more often than to men. Other bills calculated to help women take advantage of economic opportunities sought to establish part-time and flextime employment within the federal government and to provide incentives to employers interested in creating similar opportunities in the private sector. Further to preclude already illegal discrimination on the basis of marital status, Bella Abzug led an effort to prohibit the use of prefixes "Miss" or "Mrs." before the names of persons applying for jobs.

An increased divorce rate, together with the continuing tendency of wives to outlive their husbands, stimulated concern for the predicament of "displaced homemakers." These were women who lost their financial security because of a spouse's death or estrangement, and who had either never acquired marketable skills or had been too long out of the labor pool. When divorced, they were usually deprived of the pension and health benefits upon which they had once counted as spouses of gainfully employed males.

Economically affirmative legislation offered some remedies. Several bills called for a government-funded network of centers throughout the country to help displaced homemakers become economically self-sufficient. Related proposals held out incentives to employers who might hire these women. In the meantime, measures were introduced treating the homemaker as an independent wage earner, with the size of her social security payment determined not by her spouse's income, but by the number of years she was married. Just as controversial were bills which guaranteed a portion of a former husband's pension and health benefits to a divorced homemaker even after the ex-husband had remarried. Other proposals gave homemakers the opportunity to allocate household allowances to individual retirement accounts, regardless of whether their spouses were eligible for such accounts.

But the most comprehensive effort to compensate women for the socioeconomic limitations imposed upon them was introduced first in the 97th Congress and in every Congress thereafter. Called the Economic Equity Act,[5] it contained many of the affirmative measures to which allusion has already been made. The omnibus bill was sponsored by scores of Representatives over the years in an attempt to counter policies in the public and private sector that were at odds with work patterns determined by the realities of women's dual wage-earning and parenting roles.

Its provisions made it easier for women to secure the pensions and annuities of retired, deceased, or estranged husbands. It also gave tax credits to employers who hired displaced homemakers. Other provisions made dependent care financially more viable for women who worked; barred discrimination on the basis of gender when determining insurance premiums; and encouraged bureaucrats to implement laws already on the books in a nondiscriminatory fashion. Throughout the 1980s and early 1990s, many of the Economic Equity Act provisions were defeated, if they did not languish in committee. Even when passed, some went unfunded, which meant their reintroduction in the next Congress.

3. Socially Affirmative Measures. The third form of affirmative legislation embraced proposals calculated to lift those restraints on women which were a product of male insensitivity to women's noneconomic needs. The males in question were husbands, bureaucrats, lawmakers, and physicians, among others, who established public and private priorities and who shaped the national agenda.

In 1975, a provision of the Public Health Service Act established a National Center for the Prevention and Control of Rape. The law created an advisory committee (a majority of whose members were required to be women) to advise the Secretary of Health, Education and Welfare on such matters as the treatment and counseling of victims. It also addressed the development and maintenance of a clearinghouse for information on prevention, control, and treatment of victims, the rehabilitation of offenders, and possible assistance to local mental health centers. Elizabeth Holtzman successfully sponsored an amendment to the Federal Rules of Evidence which made inadmissible under most circumstances the introduction of evidence about past sexual behavior of an alleged rape victim. A related measure was introduced to eliminate spousal immunity to a charge of rape. In the meantime, many congresswomen cosponsored bills dealing with domestic abuse, with some containing funds to provide training for judges who regularly heard cases involving battered women.

Often neglected medical needs were addressed in bills to prevent unnecessary mastectomies; to provide explicit social security, medicare, and medicaid coverage for diagnostic tests for uterine and breast cancer; to authorize the Public Health Service to provide counseling and aid to pregnant women, especially teenagers; and to establish centers for research in infertility and contraception. One measure would make abortion a constitutional right. Another established an Office of Research on Women in the National Institutes of Health.

Affirmative proposals offered through the early 1990s represented a political response to the social, economic, legal, and cultural dependence that a male-dominated society had imposed on women—a dependence which many women and men accepted as natural and just. The bills sought to allow women to reject traditional tasks if they so chose, to make such rejection less costly, to give greater priority to problems they believed to be peculiarly their own, and to force policy makers to adopt a more universal perspective when framing the national agenda.

The categories of traditional, egalitarian and affirmative measures are not mutually exclusive, and introduction of each type was not confined to only one of the time periods defined here. All three types of measures were introduced in each of the three periods, although few affirmative proposals were broached before the 1940s. Moreover, recent years have witnessed sponsorship of bills that are throwbacks to an earlier era. Constitutional amendments to overturn the Supreme Court's 1973 abortion decision have been proposed. Efforts to extend the time period for passage of the ERA barely survived, and attempts to revive it were defeated.

But these developments have not significantly changed the dominant character of women's legislation considered by Congress in the 1990s. They may have slowed the pace at which affirmative legislation has been accepted, but they have not fundamentally altered its course. The Family and Medical Leave Act was among the first measures passed in 1993. Later consideration of comprehensive measures addressing women's health, domestic abuse and sexual assault, among other issues, made the 103rd Congress more sensitive to women's personal, private needs than any that had preceded it. (See Chapter 11.)

CHANGING REPRESENTATIONAL ROLE ORIENTATIONS

Accompanying these variations in the type of proposals congresswomen were prepared to introduce were related changes in the way these women defined their role as representatives. Most who were elected to the House between 1916 and World War II rejected the claim that they were in Washington to represent American womanhood, and most who served through the 1960s echoed these sentiments. Jeannette Rankin was an important exception, and several of her contemporaries maintained that they wanted to inject a woman's point of view into the legislative proceedings. But most early congresswomen were unprepared to represent the interests of women as a discrete group.

One of the more perceptive political activists of the earlier period, Emily Newell Blair, deplored the absence of a feminist orientation among women seeking public office. Blair had been a leader in the suffrage movement and had expected women who gained positions of influence to provide instrumental support for women's causes. She tried to live up to that promise during her seven years as Vice Chairman of the Democratic National Committee, but was discouraged to find that she was part of a distinct minority. "Women today," she said, "do not have the feminist point of view." Once they received the right to vote, she continued, they dropped their feminist orientation. A woman who runs for office makes "no appeal to women to put a woman in office, no argument as to her right to hold office, but [there is] a minimizing always of her sex. And yet, thousands of votes were cast against her, for no other reason than that she was a woman" (Blair 1931, pp. 21–22).

Blair maintained, moreover, that once in office, women ignored other women. Those who serve on party committees "give their proxies at committee meetings to men by whose influence they have been elected," and they "do what they are told by these men to do." She recognized that the heart of the problem was that rank-and-file women did not mobilize their resources behind women's candidacies. As a result, congresswomen "owe their election far more to the support of men than to the backing of women, and . . . they must give recognition to men rather than women . . . if they expect to get reelected" (Blair 1931, pp. 21–22).

Another commentator of the period, diplomat-lawyer George Anderson, reached a similar conclusion, but, unlike Blair, he saw no alternative.

A member of Congress, whether man or woman, is responsible for the legislative interests of the district he or she serves, representing men as well as women. . . . The result is that, in the practical work of legislation, a woman member of Congress finds herself associated with or pitted against men and women similarly representing group interests. . . . Accordingly, legislation for women becomes no more important to most women members of Congress than legislation for men. They become immersed, perforce, in the general problems of the country and of their respective districts. (Anderson 1929, p. 533)

Anderson believed that the most successful congresswomen were those who ignored their gender and who operated upon the same representational premises as male members of Congress. He may have had Ruth Baker Pratt in mind when he made this observation. Pratt had served two terms on the New York City Board of Aldermen and was later elected to the

House. The New York Republican sponsored no measure directly affecting women, but was, instead, a zealous partisan.

As I see politics, it is a game—like any college football game. Once a man has selected his college and joined a football team, in the heat of the game, even though the opposing captain seems abler, cleverer, more apt to win, he doesn't slacken his efforts or do anything to help the other side win—he puts his back into the game harder than ever. It is just this sort of courageous, fighting spirit that is going to strengthen party machines and make them better. (Pratt 1926, p. 23)

Other women serving in the early 1930s may not have been as ardent partisans, but most were no more likely than Pratt to champion women's causes. Florence Kahn, Katherine Langley, Virginia Jenckes, and Isabella Greenway scarcely mentioned the interests of their gender, with one of Kahn's few contributions coming in her first term when she submitted a bill authorizing a cloakroom attendant for women Representatives. Even Margaret Chase Smith, who left the House in 1948 to go to the Senate, eschewed a feminist orientation. She said:

In my service in the U.S. House of Representative, I was perhaps identified more with WAVES [Women Accepted for Voluntary Emergency Service] legislation than any other. It left the impression, I'm afraid, that I was a feminist concentrating on legislation for women. And if there is one thing I have attempted to avoid it is being a feminist. I definitely resent being called a feminist. (Lewis 1972, p. 85)

By minimizing their identification with women's issues, early congresswomen were doubtless following a prudent course. If they wanted to be taken seriously by constituents and colleagues, they were obliged to assign high priorities to the same matters that concerned constituents and colleagues. Women lawmakers serving in subsequent years operated under the same constraints. Kirkpatrick reports that in the early 1970s female state legislators did not emphasize women's issues when campaigning in the same way that "a black might articulate group demands of blacks" (1974, p. 100), and that "women who otherwise worked harmoniously with male legislators met with hostility from these same men when championing women's issues" (1974, p. 124).

It is clear, however, that an increasing number of women elected to the House have been feminists. Bella Abzug, about whom more will be said below, was surely the most vocal and visible of these Representatives. Her bold positions probably made the relatively restrained feminism of other congresswomen more acceptable to male House members. But a half-dozen years before Abzug took her House seat, Patsy Mink made clear that she planned to represent women as a class. "With so few women in Congress, I feel an obligation to respond to the needs and problems of women" (Lamson 1968, p. 107).

Emulating Mink in the House later were such self-proclaimed feminists as Margaret Heckler, Shirley Chisholm, Elizabeth Holtzman, Patricia Schroeder, Barbara Mikulski, Barbara Boxer, Olympia Snowe and Susan Molinari, among others. While campaigning for her first term, Mikulski told a group of garment workers she would give special attention to women, adding, "If I don't, who will?" (*Washington Post*, November 1, 1976). Later, Geraldine Ferraro wrote:

The Congresswomen carry a special responsibility, as do all "minority" politicians. They are called upon to speak with a single voice for the cause of "women's issues." The women of America are a diverse population and the women in Congress reflect that diversity. . . . Nonetheless there are areas of mutual agreement which allow us to formulate a common legislative agenda. (Ferraro 1979)

A few contemporary congresswomen have pointedly declined to adopt a feminist representational orientation—either because they are generally unsympathetic to feminist goals or because they have rejected its political efficacy. Congresswoman Barbara Vucanovich is among the former; Marilyn Lloyd is among the latter.[6] For some women, the political risks of such an orientation are substantial, and they may express feminist views on only a few, carefully selected issues. Margaret Roukema's mixed feelings are evident in a statement she made soon after arriving in Washington.

I do feel a special responsibility to women. But I wasn't sent here for women's issues. I was sent here for all the people in my district. I'm troubled by the isolation of women. Unless we mainstream, we're losing the opportunity to earn policy-making positions. (*Washington Star*, May 27, 1982)

The rise in the number of congresswomen investing their resources in women's issues was a product of several factors. Among the more obvious were changes in social and economic relationships occurring nationally, an increase in the number of politically active women seeking House seats, and the emergence of an electorate prepared to accept, if not actively support, female candidates for whom women's issues are salient. But these circumstances probably would not have produced the outpouring of affirmative women's legislation had it not been for an additional development in the House—the formation in 1977 of the Congresswomen's Caucus. The activities and goals of the Caucus did not necessarily encourage all of its members to adopt a feminist orientation. But they did serve as a magnet for female representatives interested in issues directly affecting women. The Caucus was a source of positive reinforcement for those who wanted to politicize incipient women's concerns which had not yet become part of the national agenda. Thus, the adoption of a feminist orientation and the ascendancy of egalitarian and affirmative legislation were linked to the creation and development of the Caucus.

NOTES

1. The act of introducing a bill is not the only indication of a member's interest in a subject, and it is not necessarily the best evidence of such interest. Measures are often proposed or cosponsored simply to relieve constituency pressures or to support the initiative of a colleague. Nevertheless, introduction of a bill is a public act. It bears a reasonable relationship to a member's interests and priorities and, at the very least, it means that a Representative is prepared to have constituents and colleagues identify him or her with its substance and consequences. Failure to sponsor *any* bills on a subject is as revealing as introducing many measures addressing that subject. Legislative proposals need not have become law to merit their inclusion in the discussion that follows.

2. The Sheppard-Towner bill occasioned much controversy before it was passed in 1921. It authorized $1.25 million to be distributed over a five-year period among those states creating programs to instruct residents in the hygiene of maternity and infancy. The states were eligible for the funds if they devised a plan for transmitting the health information, and if the plan received the approval of the Department of Labor's Children's Bureau. The legislation was allowed to lapse in 1929, but was reborn in the 1935 Social Security Act. A history of the act appears in *Lemons* (1973).

3. The National Woman's Party had been instrumental in passing the 19th Amendment, but its later activities alienated even some of the most devoted suffragists. Its membership never rose above a few thousand and it was stigmatized as "radical," not least because of the righteous, uncompromising style of its leader, Alice Paul. The most prominent women's lobby of the period, the Women's Joint Congressional Committee, established a subcommittee to work for the defeat of the ERA (Breckinridge 1933, p. 270), and the National League of Women Voters, the National Women's Trade Union League, the YWCA, and the General Federation of Women's Clubs were among the more formidable organizations opposing the measure.

4. The names of the women claiming sponsorship of the ERA in the 84th Congress appear on page 2922, of the *Congressional Record*, 2nd Session. The Index to the *Record* for that year (1956), however, indicates that many of them failed to introduce ERA resolutions of their own, perhaps a not unusual occurrence in a period during which the House prohibited joint sponsorship of bills. Five years later as many as ten of the eighteen congresswomen introduced ERA resolutions.

5. See Chapters 10 and 11 for a discussion of the role played by the Congressional Caucus for Women's Issues in promoting components of this Act.

6. Lloyd was the only congresswoman expressing opposition to the August 1978 Resolution to extend the period of time during which states might approve the Equal Rights Amendment. She did not vote against extension (no congresswoman did) but she was absent when the Resolution was considered and was "paired against" it. Years later, she said she would support the Amendment if given another opportunity to do so.

9

The Congresswomen's Caucus: Preliminaries

When Congresswoman Patricia Schroeder came to the House in 1973, she assumed female members of Congress met regularly to discuss the status of women. Her expectation was a reasonable one, given the ease with which informal House groups form whenever a handful of Representatives believe issues important to them are not being addressed effectively through established congressional channels (Stevens et al. 1981, p. 432).

But Schroeder was surprised and disappointed to find that there was no women's group (*Washington Post*, April 25, 1978). Not that no one had tried to create such a caucus. Republican Margaret Heckler and Democrat Bella Abzug had separately tried to organize one, but neither had achieved notable success. A tentative beginning was made in 1975, when Democratic congresswomen met to talk about committee preferences. The most senior member among them, Leonor Sullivan, agreed to channel committee requests to the Speaker, but she was opposed to calling the group a "caucus" and she limited discussion to committee choices. It was not until April 1977 that the Congresswomen's Caucus became an official House group.

The event took place after the feminist movement had gained momentum, several years after similar caucuses had been formed by women in state and local government (Margolis and Stanwick 1979), and well after such women's groups as the National Organization for Women and the National Women's Political Caucus had begun to establish avenues of access to Congress. It is reasonable to ask, therefore, what took congresswomen so long to create a specialized instrument to dramatize and respond to women's concerns?

The answer is not a simple one. Part of it resides in the anti-caucus orientations of a few senior congresswomen whose support was crucial to formation of a women's group. Even though the House paid less obeisance to seniority in the 1970s than it did in earlier years, its members normally could do little that was innovative without at least the tacit support of veteran Representatives who had a stake in the venture. Personality differences between senior and junior women members were a factor, as well, as was the questionable legitimacy some felt such a group would have in the House. Would-be members were uncertain of its purposes and feared the ambiguity of its goals. Finally, no broad-based women's caucus was likely to be established as long as Bella Abzug was a member of the House. Each of these explanations is explored below.

OBSTACLES TO CAUCUS FORMATION

In the 1960s and 1970s, Leonor Sullivan was a formidable presence in the House. When she retired in 1976, the Missouri Democrat headed the Merchant Marine and Fisheries Committee, chaired the Banking, Currency, and Housing subcommittee on Consumer Affairs, and was a high-ranking member of the subcommittee on Housing. She had also acquired a national reputation for "truth-in-lending" and other consumer protection measures.

But Sullivan harbored traditional views about the role of women. Although she acknowledged there was room for women in public life, she believed that their involvement in politics should come only after they fulfilled family responsibilities. She held further that women could make important contributions to public policy precisely because they brought to bear viewpoints different from those shared by males (Dudar 1967). She maintained, however, that these contributions would be jeopardized if women called attention to their gender by uniting for policy-making purposes.

Furthermore, Sullivan was contemptuous of the feminist movement. She was the only woman in the House to vote against the Equal Rights Amendment; she insisted on being identified as "Mrs. John Sullivan"; and she urged that the House adopt a dress code that would prohibit women from wearing pants suits in the House chamber. Her opposition to forming a women's caucus, then, was a product of deeply rooted social orientations (Lamson 1979, p. 105).

Sullivan probably would have held these views even if she had not occupied leadership positions in her party and within the House. But, as Secretary of the Democratic Caucus and as a committee chair, she had iron allegiances to those mainstream Representatives who had helped her achieve her status and great confidence in those agencies through which she and they exercised influence. A women's caucus would too easily be construed as divisive or marginal by male colleagues and affiliation might cause her to lose the support of congressional leaders and members of her committees. Sullivan's reluctance to single out women for special treatment was reflected in her decision as chair of the Consumer Affairs subcommittee to extend provisions of the Equal Credit Opportunity bill to social groups other than women—to minority groups and the aged. Organized women's lobbies resisted, however, because such action would obscure the issue of gender discrimination and endanger passage of the measure. She eventually backed down (Gelb and Palley 1987, p. 73).

Sullivan also concluded that differences in district needs and in the partisan and ideological orientations among congresswomen would make an all-female policy coalition unmanageable. This is why, when she met informally with other congresswomen at the start of the 94th Congress, she refused to call the gathering a "caucus" and limited its business to helping to secure useful committee assignments for its participants.

Sullivan was not the only veteran congresswoman responsible for delaying formation of a caucus. Neither Julia Butler Hansen, who served from 1960 to 1974, nor Edith Green, who retired in 1974 after twenty-two years in the House, saw participation in a caucus as a worthwhile expenditure of their energies. Hansen, considered by many as the most "professional" woman in the House, had served in the Washington state legislature for many years before coming to Congress. Said one male Representative with visible admiration, "Hansen was a pleasure to watch. She did her homework, had the respect of the members, and never gave a thought to the fact that she was a woman." Like Sullivan, the Washington Democrat was too intimately associated with the prevailing House power structure seriously to consider affiliating with a women's caucus, even though, unlike Sullivan, she was sympathetic to most of the goals of the women's movement.

Although Green believed that her House career suffered because of discrimination by male colleagues, she, too, rejected prospects of a congressional women's group. In fact, Green may have been the least enthusiastic of the three. Since her success in promoting higher education legislation could never be surpassed by any victories she might win as a member of a women's caucus, there seemed little reason for joining, let alone championing, such an organization. She had helped produce such ground-breaking measures as Title IX of the 1972 amendments to the Higher Education Act, and had been instrumental in passage of the 1963 Equal Pay Act. Green had also helped Martha Griffiths pry the Equal Rights Amendment out of the House Judiciary Committee, and no one could fairly accuse her of being unresponsive to gender inequalities. Nevertheless, she believed that a women's group in the House would do more to call attention to social and political divisions within the country than it would do to ameliorate those divisions. Her distaste for the Congressional Black Caucus grew out of the same conviction.

The institutional and role orientations of these women contrasted sharply with those of younger congresswomen, and the differences prompted occasional clashes between members of the two generations. Interviews with women members of the 95th Congress revealed bristling exchanges between Sullivan and Schroeder, for example. "They were at each other all the time," said one House member. Another suggested that Sullivan and Abzug saw things so differently that their disagreements took on a personal dimension. Said one observer, "each had a firm idea of what a woman should be and the gulf between these views simply couldn't be bridged." And, when a younger congresswoman who had served in the early 1970s was asked why birth of the caucus took so long, she replied "because Leonor Sullivan was against it and before her Julia Hansen and that woman from Oregon whose name I'm blocking because she made me so angry. That's why we couldn't get anything going."

Although the caucus was not established until after these senior women left the House, their opposition to its formation was not the only factor contributing to the delay. A second is associated with disagreement among congresswomen about the functions a caucus could serve and whether concentration on women's issues was an appropriate investment of time for House members elected to represent men, as well as women. When the idea of a caucus was broached in the early 1970s, some women envisioned a group which would define important women's issues, fashion legislative language needed to address these issues, mobilize support for its initiatives inside and outside the House, create a united front to enact its proposals into law, and ensure that the new rules were vigorously enforced.

Many congresswomen were simply unwilling to submit to the discipline of such a group, however, not least because they anticipated fundamental disagreements with other women on what constituted a fit subject for caucus deliberation, and because they anticipated insoluble disputes on complex issues. Recalling these earlier days, one congresswoman said:

Some of the younger women wanted to use the group as a real "caucus," but we couldn't do that given the different points of view among us. I was opposed to calling it a "caucus" because the disparities of our districts made it impossible to unite or take action in concert.

But for some of these women a caucus based upon gender was unacceptable no matter how much consensus members reached. They believed a women's caucus would lack the legitimacy granted other informal groups. Most saw nothing wrong, and much that was right, with caucuses based upon economic, ideological, or district commonalities. But they were unwilling to conceive of or classify women's issues in the same way. Part of this predisposition inhered in the political realities they faced. Women's organizations in their districts might applaud association with a caucus, but these groups were either weak or unlikely to offset negative reactions affiliation with a women's caucus might trigger in men's circles and among traditional women. Identification with such an organization would call attention to a feature of their biographies whose accentuation could increase their liabilities in the next election.

Even some of these women may have been willing to affiliate with a limited, loosely structured, barely visible congresswomen's group had it not been for an additional obstacle with which they had to contend—the presence in the House of Bella Abzug. Before her election in 1970, Abzug had gained national recognition as a champion of liberal causes. She had been an attorney for the American Civil Liberties Union, an organizer of the Women's Strike for Peace, a celebrated speaker on feminist issues, and among the most charismatic leaders of the civil rights and antiwar movements. She had been relentless in articulating her views, unyielding in the belief that they were right, impatient with delay in their adoption, and critical of whoever opposed them.

Abzug did not alter her behavior after she won her House seat, and she came to be one of the most controversial individuals ever to serve in Congress. Although the Manhattan Democrat spent only six years in the House, she was better known and occasioned more comment than colleagues whose service was three or four times as long. To understand fully why the presence of a single person was so important a factor in retarding the formation of the Congresswomen's Caucus, elaboration of her orientations, her goals and her personal style is useful.

THE BURDENS OF BELLA ABZUG

In the House, Bella Abzug was *sui generis*. She evoked strong responses from colleagues, reactions which varied from approbation and respect to ridicule and contempt. Those who agreed with her policy preferences nonetheless acknowledged that she was sometimes harder on her allies than on her enemies, and that she was a difficult person with whom to get along.

Some have argued that there were two Bella Abzugs: a "good Bella" who worked hard, fought for what she believed in, and forced the House to grapple with the most pressing issues facing the country; and a "bad Bella," who harassed her colleagues, violated the norms of the House, and could not accept the fact that those with whom she disagreed were just as interested as she in representing constituents (Auletta 1975). But it seems evident that the same set of forces produced both the "good" and the "bad" Bella. For Representative Abzug was an unusually bright, energetic, and resourceful House member. She believed passionately in the justice of the causes she embraced and had little patience for human and procedural obstacles that got in the way. The intensity, righteousness, and imagination that fueled her behavior contributed to both the positive and the negative vibrations she transmitted.

It was impossible not to form an opinion about her. The unconventional way in which she defined her role as a congresswoman, the hostility she often displayed toward House leaders and toward Congress as an institution, and the distinctive style which spiced her personal relationships made her stand out from other members. These features of her House service combined to discourage other congresswomen from associating with an incipient group whose most visible member could make caucus affiliation a political liability.

The Nature of Her Constituency

Abzug never forgot that she represented a Manhattan district, but she insisted that she spoke for a national constituency, and she was inclined to infer national sentiment from district attitudes. She believed that the country's powerless people—women, the young, minorities, the poor, and those who opposed the Vietnam war—looked to her to redress their grievances. Moments after she officially took her house seat she moved out to the Capitol steps and was sworn in again, this time by Brooklyn's Black congresswoman, Shirley Chisholm. Inside the Capitol she had promised to defend the Constitution of the United States. Outside, in front of hundreds of women who had come to Washington to see her, she pledged to work to end the war and to redirect the country's resources toward peaceful purposes.

Once in office, she found it impossible to ignore the demands made by scores of national groups with whom she was sympathetic. When thousands of young people came to Washington in May 1971 to protest the war, she was among a handful of Representatives to address them—and was understandably upset by the haste with which they were being arrested, even as she was speaking to them. She was equally attentive to women's groups from states and districts other than her own, and when delegations from the Women's Strike for Peace, or the National Women's Political Caucus beckoned, she was unable to turn away. Overworked, overcommitted, underorganized, she sometimes told those who came to her office to contact their own representatives. But her inclination to serve as a champion of society's underprivileged was reinforced when they told her that other political leaders were not nearly as committed to their cause as she (Abzug 1972, p. 150).

Of course all House members occasionally claim to speak for the American people when they know full well they are expressing sentiments peculiar to their districts. But, save for those members of Congress who were orchestrating presidential campaigns in the early 1970s, Bella Abzug, more than any other legislator, acted as if her constituency were continental. She genuinely believed that she was the country's first national congresswoman. Looking back at her record at the end of her first year she highlighted her role as a representative of the nation's women, its youth, its minorities and its poor. She claimed she symbolized the priorities of these groups because of her "action inside and outside of Congress" (Abzug 1972, p. 301).

Inside the House she missed few opportunities to force members to take a position on the war; to compel administration spokesmen to explain why there were not more women in the bureaucracy; and to urge both representatives and administrators to appropriate more money for social services. She believed that an organization like the Democratic Study Group should relentlessly raise the issue on the war on the floor until Congress finally acted (Abzug 1972, p. 53). And, when she was asked to summarize rather than read her complete statement on the Equal Rights Amendment before the House Judiciary Committee, she replied that she would either present it in its entirety or not read it at all (Abzug 1972, p. 79).

Outside the House she traveled around the country speaking before peace rallies, women's organizations, and minority groups, frequently moving them to tumultuous responses by her passion and eloquence. But Abzug was so consumed by her mission that she was unable to establish and maintain close personal relationships. She acknowledged this void in her life soon after she took office, observing "on the surface I appear to be very involved in a lot of social relationships. But inside I'm not relating to anybody" (Abzug 1972, p. 103).

Later she lamented the fact that she had cut herself off from other people, but she concluded that there was no alternative. If she allowed her personal feelings and needs to claim her attention, she would be unable to look after the people who regarded her as their champion: young people, the poor, blacks, people opposed to the war, and women.

Relations with House Leaders

Abzug's distraction from those human relationships which ultimately energize all institutions and her obsession with political and social goals produced a chasm between her and congressional leaders. During the 1970s, most representatives were affable, undoctrinaire, accommodating people in private. They respected the views of their colleagues even when these views differed significantly from their own. But they expected partisan and ideological opponents to treat them similarly. Abzug appeared systematically to violate this expectation, speaking out as if she were the only member who knew the truth and implying that those who disagreed with her were misinformed, stupid, or ill-intentioned. When her colleagues were reluctant to accommodate her, she made congressional leaders the targets of her frustration and the House the object of her scorn.

Abzug had the energy and zeal of a crusader and, like most crusaders, she was uncomfortable with the deliberate pace of the legislative process. As an ardent reformer, she was distressed, as well, by the gentlemen's agreements entered into by most veteran House members who believed that public policy should be changed incrementally or not at all. She saw other members as pursuing careers, bargaining, negotiating, compromising to avoid today what might be embarrassing tomorrow. She saw herself as part of a people's movement, a movement that demanded change now, immediately, before more lives were lost or wasted and more injustice perpetrated.

Her criticism of the House hierarchy left few leaders untouched. She railed against those who permitted the Pentagon, big business, and war contractors to take over the power structure. She condemned Democratic leaders for not trying to get legislation passed, even though a majority of the party was behind it. They seemed to her more interested in building unconscionable coalitions with members of the right wing (Abzug 1972, p. 299). And she excoriated a Speaker of the House whose bipartisan foreign policy was crafted as if he were still fighting World War II (Abzug 1972, p. 299). Her answer was to try to figure out "how to beat the machine and knock the crap out of the political power structure" (Abzug 1972, p. 209).

Abzug defined the country's problems within an "us against them" perspective, and most Democratic celebrities were "them." Less than two months after taking her seat she openly berated House Speaker Carl Albert for preventing the Democratic Caucus from taking a position on the Vietnam War. She accused him of being in league with President Nixon in wanting to prolong the war and, when he began to anger before her onslaught and to counterattack, she reminded him of the movement that had sent her to Washington to end the war. Even after tempers cooled she warned the Speaker that she would force a vote on continuation of the war (Abzug 1972, p. 64).

The following day, during a roll call vote on government financing of a supersonic transport plane (a project she opposed but which most party leaders supported), Democratic Whip Hale Boggs passed her on the floor and said, "We're losing by ten votes." She responded "What do you mean *we're* losing by ten votes. *You're* losing, not *us*" (Abzug 1972, p. 68; the emphasis is Abzug's).

In front of Government Operations Committee members, she denounced Chairman Chet Holifield for placing her on the Conservation subcommittee rather than the one dealing with military operations. "Had you had the guts to put new members, like myself, on committees which have something to do with our mandates . . . you might have helped the whole rotten Congress" (Abzug 1972, p. 59).

Her reputation for baiting the leadership prevailed throughout her six years in the House and, when she left in 1976, her staff remembered her pugnacity in verse, part of which read:

With hat firmly planted
She never recanted
On the stump, on the floor, in committee
Standing up for the weaker,
Standing up to the Speaker,
A symbol of people and city. (*New York Times* December 11, 1976)

But Abzug had mellowed during the later years of her congressional service. She seemed to get along better with Tip O'Neill than she had with Carl Albert, and the Speaker from Massachusetts made her an at-large Whip. As she was about to leave the House in 1976, he asserted that she was "one of the most knowledgeable legislators in the House" and "without a doubt the hardest working Member." O'Neill added:

Bella Abzug has been a breath of fresh air. . . . While three years ago she probably held the title for maverick of this Chamber, she has now become an effective, hardworking and productive Member of the "establishment" whip organization. . . . I appointed her to the whip organization because I respected her abilities, talents, and real legislative acumen. (*Congressional Record*, vol. 122, September 30, 1976, p. H 12060)

But not all Democrats agreed with O'Neill, partly because they had been victims of her wrath and partly because her reputation as a maverick was unaltered.

Relations with Colleagues

Just as congressional leaders were assaulted by her acerbity, so, too, were the customs and practices of the institution itself. She was impatient with the deliberative process, with the establishmentarian views of House members, with the wheeling and dealing in which they engaged, and with the propensity of members to compromise their principles (Abzug 1972, p. 6). She condemned the unwritten rule which holds that "to get along you have to go along," and she did neither.

During debate to extend the draft she outraged her colleagues on the House floor by threatening members who planned to support the measure with retribution at the voting booths. The women of this country and their sons, she claimed, would never forgive those Representatives who sent young men to an illegal war. She said:

I urge you to consider the full power of this combined group; seventy-three percent of the people [those opposed to the war] have been trying to get through to you, and these women and young people will lead them against you unless you vote against the draft bill which is before you today. (*Congressional Record*, vol. 117, April 1, 1971, p. 9022)

Fellow Democrats were appalled when she inserted in the *Congressional Record* a supposedly secret roll-call vote taken in the party caucus. The vote was on a Resolution to set a date for withdrawal of U.S. troops from Vietnam. In spite of the fact that the yeas and nays had already been printed in a Baltimore newspaper—it was this news item that she had inserted—many Democrats were furious with her for violating the secrecy of the Caucus and for creating a source of potential political embarrassment. They were upset, as well, by her unremitting effort to force the Caucus and the House to deal with the war—to call a halt to U.S. involvement in the war, to bring American forces home, and to reduce military appropriations. Some thought her requests for time-consuming roll call votes were counterproductive because they resulted in lopsided majorities against whatever she proposed.

She managed to annoy even hardened House veterans by finding inappropriate occasions to champion her causes. During time set aside to pay tribute to Emanuel Celler on his 84th birthday, for example, Abzug was among a dozen members to take the floor to recognize the House's longest-serving Representative. But, after briefly lauding her fellow New Yorker, she praised groups of antiwar activists who had come to Washington and were then choking House galleries, and she asked Speaker Albert to tell the House what President Nixon had told him about the war in a White House meeting that day (*Congressional Record*, vol. 118, May 9, 1972, p. 16,292). There is no evidence that Albert complied with her request, but the galleries roared their approval. Celler may not have resented the indiscretion, but other House members must have deplored Abzug's judgement and her violation of two of the chamber's honored constraints—suspending political dialogue when celebrating a member's personal, private achievement, and avoiding references to people seated in the galleries.

While her unorthodox methods did not often lead to legislative victories, they nonetheless attracted the notice of the Washington press corps. Frequent national exposure was a mixed blessing, however. It irritated House members who resented the attention she received and pleased her ideological adversaries because she was portrayed as a person with whom responsible Representatives from conservative districts should have little to do. Furthermore, some liberal members felt that she should be spending more time doing her legislative homework and less time finding ways of making news. Abzug acknowledged the ease with which she received national exposure and attributed it not to conscious courting of headlines but to saying what was on her mind. During her first year in office she found it impossible to keep up with her appearances on television or radio (Abzug 1972, p. 131).

House members who were concerned about her attacks on Congress, her willingness to reveal publicly what they considered to be private political acts, her resort to dilatory tactics, and her inclination to be what students of Congress call a "showhorse" (as distinct from a "workhorse")[1] could not ignore, as well, Abzug's doubts about the responsiveness and the efficacy of Congress. Early in her House career she noted that she had no wish to be a member of the House elite at the expense of those she believed she represented. If she could not achieve her goals working from within Congress, she asserted, she would "go back outside again—to the streets—and do it from there" (Abzug 1972, p. 7).

Personal Style

It is possible that many of Abzug's colleagues would have been prepared to accept her policy orientations, her unorthodox behavior, and her low regard for their institution if her style were ingratiating. But that was not the case. She often personalized her attacks. During the draft debate, for example, she criticized the older members for sending young men to be killed in battle.

But her personalized criticism probably did the most damage in dealings with people who were natural allies—her own staff, members of the New York City delegation, liberals, and Democratic leaders of the Committees on which she served. Her relations with those she hired to serve her in Washington were often stormy. Capitol Hill observers reported frequent shouting matches between Abzug and her aides, with the latter publicly abused and often denied even a scintilla of self-respect. One assistant who left the Washington office stated:

She is supposed to be a great humanist, and yet she's very cruel to people. At staff meetings, she'll say, "Oh, shut up, you never had any sense. Stupid, why are you saying this?" Her face gets all tight and you see the rage. (Winfrey 1977, p. 14)

A staff member who called in sick was told, "I don't give a damn. As long as I'm paying your salary, you'll show up" (Brenner 1977).

Staff turnover, relatively high in most congressional offices, was a way of life in Abzug's office. During her first four years in office, she went through five chiefs of staff (four administrative assistants and an executive assistant) and six personal secretaries—even more if a woman who was on and off the payroll on three different occasions is counted more than once (Auletta 1975). Said a former campaign manager: "The people who stay with her are either masochists or ideologues" (quoted in Brenner 1977, p. 56). When trusted aides announced that they were leaving, she felt betrayed. Abzug named a major campaign advisor as her first administrative assistant, but when she quit because the job was too difficult, Abzug was furious. She condemned the assistant for not staying on while at the same time demeaning her performance as office manager (Abzug 1972, p. 158).

Democrats in the New York State delegation are hardly known for their unity, but Abzug proved to be a notably discordant force within a group plagued by personal animosities and petty political squabbling. During her first two weeks in office, she managed to insult and exasperate veteran Hugh Carey, New York's representative on the Democratic Committee on Committees. She told Carey that she wanted a seat on the Armed Services Committee, a panel whose legislative subject matter would give her a platform for denouncing U.S. involvement in the war. She was not optimistic about securing the seat, but she believed (rightly, as matters turned out) that even if she was unsuccessful her campaign would make it possible for another liberal ultimately to gain the assignment (Abzug 1972, p. 21).

Carey later called Abzug while the Committee on Committees was meeting to tell her that she had not been placed on Armed Services. There were already four New Yorkers on that panel, he said, two Democrats and two Republicans, and the Committee had decided not to add any more Representatives from the state. Abzug was incensed.[2] When Carey asked what he should do about recommending her for another committee, inasmuch as she had listed no other choices, she replied: "I don't give a damn what you do. . . . You have no power" (Abzug 1972, p. 22). Carey was reported to have said later that "if the Second Coming were tomorrow, even He couldn't get Bella Abzug on the Armed Services Committee" (Abzug 1972, pp. 28–29).

Toward the end of her first year in the House she was accused of sabotaging a delegation luncheon by encouraging other New York Democrats to boycott it. The charge produced a strenuous denial from her, along with denunciations of Congressmen Ed Koch and Ben Rosenthal because they believed she had leaked a story about the alleged boycott to the New York City newspapers. Abzug knew she had detractors among the delegation and that they had no compunctions about damaging her politically. But she was prepared to work without them.

Later she found that few New York Democrats would support her when she ran in the 1976 Senate primary. Congressman Jerome Ambro of Nassau County said that having Abzug at the top of the ticket in his district was like running with Mao Zedong. She was outraged by Ambro's comment, asserting that if he could not support her at least he should not criticize her. The Long Island Democrat apologized for the remark, but neither he nor any other Democrat, with the exceptions of Bronx Representatives Herman Badillo and Jonathan Bingham, endorsed her candidacy. And when she lost the primary to Daniel Patrick Moynihan, she lashed out at fellow Democrats in characteristic fashion, calling Brooklyn Congressman Stephen Solarz a "coward," and Harlem's Charles Rangel "corrupt."

Abzug wore out her welcome among most liberals, just as she did among her neighbors. She was unrelenting in her efforts to make the Democratic Study Group adopt a strong position on ending the war, believing that inasmuch as the Democratic Caucus would not vote on the issue she could at least force the House's most important liberal bastion to take a stand on it. DSG members discussed the matter, but took no action (Abzug 1972, p. 53). Even when cautioned that she was irritating some of the group's members with her persistence, she rejected the warning (Abzug 1972, p. 119).

When some of the most liberal members of the DSG (including fellow New Yorker William Fitts Ryan) were considering the possibility of forming a smaller, ideologically purer House group, they were uncertain about including Abzug. Although they agreed with her on most issues, they felt that she was too aggressively compulsive about her own concerns and that she would affect deleteriously both the new group's effectiveness and the rapport of its members. According to one congressman, she was finally invited to join. But the group soon disbanded, partly because it had become too large, thereby making ideological unanimity all but impossible.

Abzug's relations with her committee chairmen were not uniformly poor. She got off to a bad start with Holifield on Government Operations, but Public Works Committee chairman John Blatnik of Minnesota was more sensitive to her skills and her political goals. Blatnik left the House when the 1974 session ended, however, and Robert Jones of Alabama succeeded him. Jones was not nearly as patient with Abzug as his predecessor had been and, according to one member of the Committee, he had little liking for her. Unfriendly exchanges punctuated panel discussions and Jones began to call her "Bella Donna," a term which sounded enough like "prima donna" to suggest part of Jones's meaning, but which he must have known was the name of a poisonous herb.

In sum, Abzug left a trail of distrust, frustration, hostility, ridicule, and personal animosity in her dealings with people whose help she might normally have expected. She terrorized her staff, exasperated her New York colleagues, scared off fellow liberals, and alienated her committee chairmen often enough to strip herself of the few allies upon whom she should have been able to rely. Said one former aide, "Half of working for Bella is repairing the damage" (Brenner 1977, p. 57).

Abzug's Effectiveness

But, for all of her liabilities, many members of the House regarded her as an effective congresswoman. In the first place, she did not always behave irrepressibly. Most of the time she was a reasonable, diligent, intelligent House member. Second, her attendance on the Floor and in committee meetings was good. She did her homework before attending these sessions and her questions to witnesses were thoughtful and informed. Furthermore, her relations with other committee members were often friendly and cordial. One House member with whom she served on the Public Works Committee said, "Bella has been given a bum rap. Sure she came on strong.

She could really dish it out. But she could take it, too. She could deal and compromise with the best of them and she was one of the ablest people in this place."

Three congresswomen with whom she served acknowledged that she had a problem in "human relations," but each concluded that her contribution to the House was considerable. "Bella Abzug was an abrasive person but, still, I think she was one of the most effective people we had here and her defeat (for the House seat given up by Ed Koch when he was elected Mayor in 1977) was a great shame." The second admiringly alluded to Abzug's skill and purposiveness in getting sex discrimination prohibitions added to House bills. And, in defense of the "abrasiveness" label pinned on the New York Congresswoman, another member asserted: "Why should you have to be nice if you disagree so fundamentally with someone on matters that are as important as the ones Bella concerned herself with?"

Abzug's awareness of her reputation and her conscious effort to amplify components of her image indicates that she exercised greater control over her behavior than her seeming irrepressibility suggests. The journal she published after her first year in office reveals more guile and self-knowledge than critics acknowledge. The wide-brimmed hat that became her trademark, the forceful, irreverent, antiestablishment speech, the persistent calls for change were features which she assiduously cultivated and which defined her persona. In a Los Angeles appearance before the California Democratic Councils she chose a dress only because it could be worn with a hat ("How could I deprive them!" she explains). Her introduction was followed by a tumultuous demonstration, after which, she reports with considerable detachment: "I went into my song and dance and moved them to a five-minute standing ovation . . . it happens everywhere I speak across the country" (Abzug 1972, p. 99).

She knew that she was a proselytizer and that she could lecture people for hours if they would let her. She knew that she was sometimes a "bully" and that the biggest bully in the House, Wayne Hays of Ohio, might not prevail if they started bullying each other. And she knew that she was often "pushy" and could sympathize with "pushiness" when she saw it in others. She knew, in short, that she was not an easy person to live with. Speaking at a Women's National Press Club dinner soon after taking her House seat she quoted a daughter's statement at an election night celebration: "'Thank God we're getting her out of *our* house and into *their* House'" (Abzug 1972, p.18; the emphasis is Abzug's).

But, most important, she believed that the liabilities accompanying her style constituted a price she had to pay to get what she wanted. For she was, above all, an activist. "You can't just sit around and *think*," she said. "I go around *doing* . . . prepared to take risks" (Abzug 1972, 166–67; the emphasis is Abzug's).

Reputation and Legacy

She took the risks and she paid the price. For those who believed in her causes she was a dynamic, courageous, oratorically gifted, and effective leader. For those who did not, she gained a reputation in Washington as an abrasive, uncompromising, irresponsible, unpleasant, and fanatical woman whose support could be the kiss of death, whose behavior was subversive, and whose image was a source of ridicule.

And, in Washington, reputation is everything. Hundreds of political and social calculations are made on the basis of startlingly imperfect knowledge, and decision-makers are forced to rely on the stereotypes of which they happen to be aware. Once an image is created, it is difficult to alter—and Abzug's image was indelibly burned into the minds of Washington opinion leaders.

After-dinner speakers, looking for a laugh from their audiences, needed only to mention her name to evoke the desired response. Her stout figure was a frequent target of men who were trying to be funny. Abzug quotes Vice President Spiro Agnew speaking at a fund-raising dinner as saying Republicans should work for adoption of "welfare, revenue sharing, and *most importantly, we have to keep Bella Abzug from showing up in Congress in hotpants*" (Abzug 1972, p. 49; the emphasis is Abzug's). When Governor Nelson Rockefeller testified before the Public Works Committee and his dollar figures were contradicted by the Manhattan congresswoman, he responded: "The distinguished Representative from New York has questioned my figures, [yet] she has none to substitute, except a very beautiful figure of her own" (Abzug 1972, p. 285). And, when two vacancies simultaneously occurred on the Supreme Court and President Nixon was reported to be considering a woman for one of them, *Washington Post* columnist Morris Siegel urged Nixon to appoint Bella Abzug to both seats (Abzug 1972, p. 251). It is difficult to imagine Agnew, Rockefeller, and Siegel making the same remarks about a stout male Representative.

When Abzug left the House there remained a legacy impossible to ignore—even by those who did not serve in Congress until after she gave up her seat. One liberal Democrat who had never met her noted (in response to a question about the reception given congresswomen by their male colleagues) that all congresswomen were treated as equals. "Perhaps things are this way," he added, "because there is among the women in the House no one like Bella Abzug." A conservative Republican, whose service overlapped Abzug's, commented on her loss to Republican William Green in the 1978 race to fill Koch's vacancy: "Abzug . . . was the most unpopular member of the House. She was so abrasive that even some Democrats were happy when she lost last month." And, when President Carter created a National Advisory Committee for Women a year after Abzug left Congress and appointed her codirector, Kentucky Democrat Carroll Hubbard remonstrated on the House floor:

I can assure President Carter that ninety-nine percent of the taxpayers in the Commonwealth of Kentucky are opposed to any new Federal agencies or committees, and 99.9 percent of Kentuckians are opposed to Federal tax dollars being spent by Bella Abzug. . . . It is difficult to believe that President Carter interprets the taxpayer revolt in this country to indicate that what we need now in Washington is Bella Abzug giving advice. (*Congressional Record*, vol. 124, June 13, 1978, p. H 5354)

It is no wonder, then, that the New Yorker's presence in the House retarded the development of a Congresswomen's Caucus. Other women members would have difficulty enough explaining affiliation with a group which called attention to their nontraditional roles and whose legitimacy was in doubt. To be associated, at the same time, with a woman who had a reputation for radical views, flamboyant behavior, and incendiary speeches was politically unacceptable.

Before she left the House, Abzug met occasionally with a small group of women liberals (Patsy Mink, Patricia Schroeder, Elizabeth Holtzman among them) to discuss common interests. The difficulty such a group would have had in expanding while Abzug remained a House member was underscored in 1978 when she was nominated to replace Koch. Prospects of her return sent waves of trepidation through not only conservative groups that had little use for her combative admonitions, but also among women Representatives who, following the establishment of the Congresswomen's Caucus, had come to believe that affiliation was politically useful. There was concern that she would "take over" the Caucus without even trying, and thereby destroy it. Some privately feared that Abzug's powerful personality would again command the attention of the press and that she would dominate the life of the Caucus, perhaps reversing the acceptance it had begun to receive in its early months.

These fears proved to be premature, of course, inasmuch as Abzug lost. But the loss was viewed with mixed feelings by several Democratic congresswomen whose legislative objectives differed little from those of the redoubtable New Yorker. They regretted the result because Abzug was so forceful a champion of causes in which they fervently believed. But they did not lament it as deeply as they might have because the viability of their fledgling organization was, for the time being, secure.

At the same time, they realized the profound effect that Abzug had on the House, on congressional consideration of women's issues, and on the propensity of other congresswomen to adopt feminist orientations. Abzug's forceful, often strident advocacy of women's rights and women's needs paved the way for House acceptance of the same sentiments when offered in a manner House members found less offensive.[3]

NOTES

1. Donald R. Matthews employed these terms when discussing what he called the "folkways" of the Senate. Senators interested in generating publicity, in

making the headlines, were "showhorses" and their behavior violated Senate norms. "Workhorses" were too busy mastering the details of proposed legislation to attract the attention of the media. Thus, the latter gained the respect of their colleagues while the former were suspect (Matthews 1960, p. 94).

2. One reason Abzug was upset was that the Committee on Committees had decided to rescind its appointment of freshman Herman Badillo to the Agriculture Committee after the Bronx Democrat heatedly refused to accept it, and to recommend him for the Education and Labor Committee, instead. Two years before, the committee had done the same for Shirley Chisholm, shifting her from the Agriculture Committee to the Veterans' Affairs Committee when the Brooklyn congresswoman strenuously objected to an assignment she believed had little relevance to her black constituents in Bedford-Stuyvesant. Abzug saw the Committee's failure to alter its decision in her case as a personal affront (Abzug 1972, p. 22).

3. Geraldine Ferraro later paid tribute to Abzug for her contribution in this regard. The onetime Vice-Presidential candidate wrote:

Like many institutions, Congress was stuck in its old, all-male ways. It had taken women like Bella Abzug to break through the front lines of defense. . . . Without women like her, my female colleagues and I would still be fighting to get in, instead of concentrating on the work at hand. (Ferraro 1985, p. 41)

The Congresswomen's Caucus: Early Years

Departure from the House of both Sullivan and Abzug left the way clear for remaining congresswomen to create a caucus. And the opportunity was seized by Elizabeth Holtzman and Margaret Heckler.[1]

THE RIGHT CONDITIONS

Holtzman was, like Abzug, an extraordinarily bright, intense lawyer who defined herself as a liberal and a feminist and who had an unshakable belief in the justness of her causes. She was a conspicuously conscientious House member as well, and her tenacity and strength of will were endowments she shared with her Manhattan neighbor. Moreover, both women had been part of a mini-group of liberal Democrats which met periodically over coffee and lunch to sign letters and issue statements supporting women's rights and demanding an end to the Vietnam War. But the styles of the two New Yorkers could not have differed more fundamentally. Whereas Abzug was irrepressibly spontaneous, extroverted, thick-skinned, and confident, Holtzman was deliberate, introverted, sensitive, and insecure.

To some observers, the Brooklyn Democrat was a cold, humorless perfectionist who lacked the human relations skills needed to persuade strikingly diverse female House members to join forces. Critics believed she was too inflexible and strong-willed to exercise the restraint required to build a women's coalition. But they failed to recognize that the same dogged determination and penetrating intelligence that sometimes alienated colleagues could also craft a caucus framework women found acceptable. According to Betty Dooley, the first Executive Director of the Caucus, "If it hadn't been for Liz, it would not have gotten off the ground at all." Someone with her "dynamic interest" was needed to animate the whole program (Lamson 1979, p. 105).

Holtzman's efforts were a necessary condition for forming a caucus, but they were not a sufficient condition. Among the other women willing to lead the endeavor, Margaret Heckler was especially important. Heckler's earlier interest in organizing a caucus made her an ideal partner in the venture. This savvy, moderate Republican gave the enterprise the bipartisan orientation needed to convince outnumbered Republican congresswomen that the new group would not be an instrument of the Democratic party's liberal wing. Moreover, she and Holtzman worked well together and complemented one another's strengths. Heckler was accepted by the business community, while the Brooklyn Democrat had excellent access to labor organizations. They would later turn to both for support.

Also important to Caucus formation were the efforts of national feminist groups seeking access to Congress. Lobbyists from the National Organization for Women (NOW), the National Women's Political Caucus (NWPC), and the Business and Professional Women's Clubs (BPWC), among others, encouraged their female contacts in the House to organize a group to which they could communicate their objectives and through which they could make their goals part of the national agenda. Said one congressional aide when interviewed in 1978:

Formation of the Caucus came about almost as much because of the pressure from outside Congress as it did from pressure within. Women's groups wanted more formal entree to the House and they saw a caucus as giving it to them.

Two other congresswomen played key roles in getting the caucus off the ground. One was Shirley Chisholm, the other Barbara Mikulski. Chisholm took an early interest in forming a congresswomen's group and participated actively in preliminary discussions of its structure and purposes. Her involvement assured observers in and out of Congress that the group's attention would not be confined to the interests of middle-class, white women. Mikulski was an important link to outside interest groups. The former Baltimore City councilwoman, an intelligent, energetic feminist, had an impeccable credit rating with women's organizations. She was highly regarded by professional politicians in both Baltimore and Washington, as well, and her identification with the Caucus gave it the ballast it needed to withstand the suspicion and hostility it was certain to encounter from mainstream Representatives.

Mikulski also contributed a pragmatism and a flexibility to the group— characteristics which permitted continued viability of an organization whose members held radically different views on women's issues. Said one Caucus member:

The Caucus got off the ground because we recognized that we were going to be a pluralistic group. We don't have a shared idea of what women should be. However, we recognize that we are different and because we have decided not to develop a united front on every issue—abortion, for example—we have an effective group in this [the 95th] Congress.

Accordingly, determination to search for a consensus and acceptance of the prospect that one would not be found on some volatile issues were the strategic premises guiding Caucus development.

The energies of these women would have been invested less productively had it not been for the support of a White House sympathetic to most of their goals. President Carter and his aides were receptive to Caucus initiatives and they took new and unorthodox ideas seriously. True, the President did not give women's issues the highest priority, and communications breakdowns did occur between Capitol Hill and his advisors. But the relationship between Caucus members and the White House was cordial. More important, scores of cabinet and sub-cabinet-level Carter appointees were prepared to go out of their way to accommodate Caucus needs.

LAYING THE GROUNDWORK

Creation of the Caucus proceeded on two overlapping tracks, one principally inside the House, the other mainly outside. Soon after the November 1976 election, a Steering Committee made up of Holtzman, Heckler, and Chisholm was created. Its members discussed the goals a congresswomen's caucus could fulfill and worked out a structure it might adopt to help realize these aims. At the same time, an Ad Hoc Coalition of Women's Groups, made up of representatives of more than forty organizations, began to meet with Cabinet nominees of the newly elected, but not-yet-sworn-in Carter administration. Coalition lobbyists from NWPC, NOW, and BPWC, among other groups, urged that women be given responsible positions in the new administration, and expressed concern about the disproportionately large number of women then filling low-level government ranks.

In the meantime, Mikulski sent a questionnaire to the seventeen other congresswomen asking them to assign priorities to women's issues they thought should receive attention during the 95th Congress. Thirteen responded, and a majority attached highest priority to creating more jobs (and more responsible jobs) for women in the federal government. A less-discriminatory social security system was second, with other members' concerns including child care, displaced homemakers, and health care for women. While the Maryland Democrat was gathering the data, Holtzman and Heckler were sounding out these same women about their interest in a caucus.

In late January, the Steering Committee discussed services a Congresswomen's Caucus could offer and issues women House members should address. They explored the possibility of placing more female Representatives on major standing committees, and agreed to reintroduce feminist measures that had died in the last Congress. They also discussed new bills that should be submitted in the 95th Congress. Perhaps the most important product of the meeting was a shared belief that the caucus, whatever its structure and functions, would be a catalyst for like-minded women, rather than a disciplined unit trying to forge unanimity on women's issues. The three women agreed that each Representative would decide for herself whether to support other members on an issue-by-issue basis, with action taken in the name of the caucus only when all congresswomen agreed.

The Steering Committee created the skeleton of an organization in a series of three meetings held in March. It stipulated the uses to which the caucus would be put. Among them were keeping one another informed about committee discussions affecting women's issues; monitoring floor action; developing legislative proposals to help women; endorsing and supporting these bills with testimony before committees; lobbying colleagues; and monitoring the administrative behavior of executive branch officials.

The group would have two "chairs" (the term "chairpersons" was rejected as being awkward), and an executive committee made up of the co-chairs, a treasurer, and three other congresswomen. Inasmuch as the Democrats were the majority party, they would hold a committee majority. Later, Heckler and Holtzman were selected as co-chairs, Yvonne Brathwaite Burke was named Treasurer and Mikulski, Chisholm, and Shirley Pettis became members-at-large. The Steering Committee gave the group's officers two-year terms, coinciding with the beginning and end of each Congress, and settled on its formal designation—"The Congresswomen's Caucus."

The first meeting of the Caucus was held in the Capitol at 12:30, Tuesday, April 19, 1977. Four congresswomen discussed "battered women" and remedies the Caucus might pursue to deal with the high incidence of spousal abuse. Through the remainder of the 95th Congress an average of nine of the fifteen members appeared for each meeting. Executive Board members were almost always present, with Holtzman and Heckler alternately presiding. The group conducted three types of meetings. At the start of the year, sessions were often devoted to establishing a list of legislative priorities. Members stated, sometimes through staff aides, the matters important to them and tried to enlist the support of other women. Unanimity was neither sought nor reached, but consensus emerged on most matters, and members left the sessions better informed about the concerns of others and more fully aware of the extent to which their own preferences were shared by colleagues.

An alternative format was followed when administration officials spoke to the Caucus. During the 95th Congress, the Caucus met with Commerce Secretary Juanita Kreps, HEW Secretary Joseph Califano twice, Attorney General Griffin Bell twice, Labor Secretary Marshall, and Bert Lance and James McIntyre, successive Directors of the Office of Management and the Budget. Sometimes speakers began with a preliminary statement on a subject in which Caucus members had an interest, but more often congresswomen began the questioning at once. Administrators went out of their way to be responsive, and attendance at these meetings was slightly higher than it was for those devoted to legislative priorities.

A third type of meeting centered on Caucus administration. These infrequent sessions touched on fund-raising, staff and equipment needs, and Caucus procedures, and they were likely to be less well attended. Two factors explain the lower turnout. First, most congresswomen were simply not interested in the mechanisms that kept the Caucus going, even though most were satisfied with the information and camaraderie affiliation brought with it. Second, administrative matters were normally dealt with at the biweekly Executive Committee meetings and by the group's Executive Director.

The meeting site, H235, encouraged informal, thoughtful, unhurried exchanges among Caucus members and between them and invited Cabinet officials. The "Congresswomen's Suite," as it was officially called, or the "Women's Reading Room" as it was otherwise known, is made up of three rooms—a drawing room which can fit about twenty-five people in chairs around its periphery if they don't mind sitting close to one another, and two small rooms, one of which contains kitchen facilities, the other writing desks and telephones. The Suite was set aside for congresswomen in 1962 to give them a place to handle correspondence, tape broadcasts for use in their districts, hide from constituents, lobbyists, and staff, and kick their shoes off and relax, something which congressmen did in the cloak rooms.[2] Thus it was as much of a "retiring room" as a "reading room" before the women began to use it for their meetings, with issues of the *Congressional Record* being the only printed matter available on a regular basis.

The Suite is just a few steps from the House floor, across the hall from the working office of the House Speaker. It is an ideal meeting place for members called on to answer quorum calls or vote midway through their meetings, and its proximity to the Speaker's office has obvious symbolic virtues. These same factors prompted the Congressional Black Caucus leaders to use the room for their sessions until asked by the congresswomen to convene elsewhere. In 1990, its name was changed to the "Corinne 'Lindy' Boggs Congressional Women's Reading Room" to honor the then retiring Congresswoman. Initiative for the change came from the Louisiana delegation and other female Representatives. Boggs was a much beloved colleague but tactical as well as commemorative reasons may have prompted the name change. Not long before, the Speaker had tried to appropriate the room for the Democratic leadership and the co-chairs reasoned that by attaching Boggs' name to the Reading Room, only the most insensitive and mean-spirited House patriarchs would take it away from the Caucus.

The drawing room's quiet elegance provides a pleasant atmosphere for Caucus discussions. Its most distinctive piece of furniture, a couch to which former President and Congressman John Quincy Adams was allegedly carried and on which he died of a stroke minutes later, gives the room historical cachet.[3] One wall of a corridor leading to the drawing room is covered by photographs of each woman who has served in the House, with pictures of current congresswomen appearing on drawing room walls.

Caucus membership was reasonably stable throughout the 95th Congress, but did not include all eligible women. Fifteen of the eighteen Representatives joined soon after it was established.[4] Some, notably Barbara Jordan, were members largely in name only, however. The number increased to sixteen when, early in 1978, newly appointed Senator Muriel Humphrey was invited to join. Senator Maryon Allen, another appointee to the 95th Congress, declined to affiliate with the group.

From time to time the Caucus had an impact on policy. Attention it gave to a bill prohibiting employer discrimination against pregnant women contributed to the measure's passage. And the spotlight it threw on gender disparities in federal employment and social security arrangements helped the discriminatory character of these practices penetrate the consciousness of many who had given little thought to altering either policy. But Caucus leaders had limited success in shaping the legislative agenda and in persuading colleagues that women's issues were not only linked to one another but also intimately interwoven among programs which, on their face, seemed unrelated to women's needs. During the 95th Congress, they tried to establish the position that welfare policy was connected to the availability of child-care services, job-training programs for women, rural development, part-time and summer jobs, counseling for pregnant teenagers, and food stamp distribution. This approach had little effect at the time. An attempt to treat social security and women's private pension rights within the framework of rapidly changing trends in spousal relationships met an even less auspicious fate.

There was one important exception to this generally unimpressive record, however. In 1978, the Caucus mobilized colleagues to extend the life of the Equal Rights Amendment. Their success was a tour de force, and Holtzman, Heckler, and other Caucus members scored a victory many thought impossible when they first undertook the battle.

BUYING TIME FOR THE ERA

When Congress approved a constitutional amendment granting equal rights to women in March 1972, there seemed little doubt that three-quarters of the state legislatures would approve it within the stipulated seven-year limit.[5] The votes in the House and Senate were overwhelming, 354 to 24 and 84 to 8 respectively, and most believed the sentiment expressed in these huge margins would be reflected in the states, as well. Before 1972 ended, twenty-two states had endorsed the amendment, and, in 1973, eight others followed suit. Although only eight more were needed, legislatures in remaining states, most from the South and West, were less enthusiastic. Three agreed to the measure in 1974, and one each acted favorably in 1975 and 1977. But, in the meantime, four states which had supported the amendment (Idaho, Nebraska, Tennessee, and Kentucky) rescinded their earlier approval.

With two years left, affirmative votes in only three more states would make the proposed amendment part of the Constitution—assuming that the action taken by rescinding states was discounted by Congress. Yet, in spite of intensive efforts by pro-ERA women's groups and support by the new Democratic administration, adoption by three additional states before the March 1979 deadline was considered unlikely. Much opposition to the amendment had crystallized since its early string of successes. The Eagle Forum, an organization created and administered by Phyllis Schlafly, was the most visibly active force working against the amendment, but it was joined by many conservative groups throughout the country, groups able to exercise influence with legislators in less urban, less industrialized states who represented constituencies holding a more traditional view of women's place in society (Mansbridge 1986, pp. 163–164). As a result, ERA proponents decided to seek an extension of the seven-year limit to permit additional pressures to be brought to bear in the remaining fifteen holdouts. In October 1977 Elizabeth Holtzman introduced a Joint Resolution adding seven years to the period during which states could endorse the measure. A companion Resolution was introduced in the Senate by Indiana Democrat Birch Bayh.

Obstacles to the resolution were formidable. In the first place, there was no precedent for extension of a proposed amendment's time limit. Ever since 1917, when Congress began to impose such limits, none had been seriously challenged. Even some lawmakers who supported the ERA regarded the proposed extension skeptically. Second, many conservatives in Congress believed approval of the Holtzman resolution should require a two-thirds vote in both House and Senate, the same extraordinary majority needed for all constitutional amendments and, of course, for ERA passage in 1972. Third, some House and Senate members concluded that if Congress gave the states which had not voted for the amendment more time during which to do so, it ought to give states which had adopted the measure the option of rejecting it upon reconsideration. Permission to rescind an endorsement would implicitly recognize the decisions reached by the four states nullifying earlier approval, although many argued that Congress should honor only those rescissions passed during the extended time period.

The potentially killing effect of any one of these objections left most ERA proponents pessimistic about its chances. Even Holtzman was uncertain about her resolution's fate, and, while the Speaker and House Majority Leader pledged their cooperation, they told Caucus members they were not hopeful. For a time, it appeared as if the measure would be rejected by the House Judiciary Committee, and doubtful Senate leaders considered bypassing their own Judiciary Committee because that panel was unlikely to produce an ERA majority.[6]

In fact, the House Judiciary Committee reduced the proposed extension from seven to little more than three years, giving additional states until June 30, 1982, to approve the amendment. Otherwise it reported out a measure which met its supporters' terms. The Committee rejected the demand that legislatures which had approved the proposed amendment be given the opportunity to rescind it during the extension period, and it asked the Rules Committee to adopt a rule permitting passage by a simple majority, rather than by two-thirds vote. The Rules Committee complied. Efforts to change the rule and the Resolution on the House floor failed, and the House passed the extension, 230–189. Days before the 95th Congress adjourned, ERA supporters scored a 60–36 Senate victory. Inasmuch as the Senate Resolution was identical to the House-passed measure, a House-Senate conference was avoided. Late as it was in the session, prolonged attempts to reconcile differences between the two chambers could have prevented the Resolution's passage before adjournment.

The shifting sentiment in Congress was as much a product of Caucus leaders' efforts as it was of any other factor. Once the House Judiciary Committee called for hearings, Caucus members launched an intensive drive to build support for extension. They called in women's groups leaders and pleaded with them to become involved. According to one source, they "nagged and cajoled and literally begged some who didn't think the drive would succeed."

Some militant women's organizations did not need much prodding, and they participated in massive demonstrations on Capitol Hill. But it was Caucus members primarily who mobilized and gave direction to the outpouring of energy and emotion generated by the issue. Holtzman, Heckler, Schroeder, Mikulski, and Spellman, particularly, met with women's groups in their own offices, in the Caucus office, and elsewhere in Washington, although Holtzman's Longworth Building suite was the principal hub of activity. They coordinated the efforts of the groups, explored legislative strategies, and suggested lobbying tactics. Before the battle was over, they were meeting with women's groups three and four times a week. Leaders from such feminist organizations as NOW and NWPC appeared regularly on Capitol Hill, but so, too, did leaders of associations less identified with feminist causes, including the Girl Scouts of America and the YWCA.

Caucus members had not met formally and determined they would work to pass the Resolution. No such formal decision was necessary. The ERA was one of a handful of measures on which they all shared enthusiastic, even passionate, agreement. Some were prolife, others prochoice on the abortion issue. And they might disagree on how much federal money to spend to aid victims of spousal abuse. But the ERA was the litmus test of whether you were for women or against them, and only four congress-women expressed reservations about unrestricted extension of the time limit, three of whom were not Caucus members. Only one of the four, Marilyn Lloyd, did not vote for final passage. She was "paired against" the resolution.[7]

Caucus leaders pursued standard practices in building a winning coali-tion. They counted the number of "sure" votes, designated which House and Senate members were either undecided or capable of being persuaded to alter negative predispositions, and adopted tactics calculated to reach each cluster of holdouts. They lobbied face to face when personal rapport with members permitted, and they pressured colleagues indirectly by encouraging delegations of women's groups to visit members' offices. They also asked other Washington lobbyists to urge clients they represented to request their own lawmakers to support the Holtzman-Bayh Resolution. Holtzman capitalized on her access to labor leaders, Heckler on her ac-quaintances in the business community, and Spellman on her contacts among state and local government officials. Before long, the Resolution's prospects brightened. Legislators from states with powerful labor unions announced in favor of the measure, and even some from states that had not approved the ERA came around.

The White House played a role, as did House and Senate leaders and representatives of women's groups. But the successful coalition was largely the product of a campaign orchestrated by Caucus activists. It was a consequence of shrewd legislative maneuvering. Congressmen concerned about anti-ERA sentiments in their states and districts would have to vote against the measure to satisfy constituency opinion—no matter what their personal feelings about the women's movement. But they did not necessar-ily have to vote against the rule permitting passage by a simple majority, or in favor of a floor amendment allowing states on record supporting the ERA to rescind actions already taken.

Accordingly, Holtzman and other Caucus leaders pointed out the oppor-tunity these lawmakers had to retain constituency support while, at the same time, helping female Representatives pass the most important women's measure they would address in the 95th Congress. "Vote against final passage if you must," they told male members, "but support us with votes to bar rescissions by state legislatures and vote down the motion to require a two-thirds majority." Among the 189 congressmen voting against final passage, fifty supported the pro-ERA positions on at least one of the three roll call votes that preceded it. The closest tally was on a motion by Illinois Republican Tom Railsback to allow states to rescind their earlier approval of the ERA. Thirty-four of those voting against final passage also chose to reject the Railsback proposal. More than half of that number, eighteen, were Southern and Border Democrats. A switch of sixteen votes would have changed the result.[8]

Adoption of ERA extension was the legislative high point of the 95th Congress for most Caucus members. First, they had forced the White House, as well as Congress, to deal with an issue many believed was, if not dead, then not a high public priority. Second, they had turned a problematic outcome into a signal victory, and they had done it on an issue which more than any other reflected their raison d'être. Third, it was a legislative success for which they could take much of the credit. As women, they represented, more than any other lawmakers, the intensive, pervasive pro-ERA sentiment throughout the country. Fourth, against formidable odds, they had built a congressional coalition sufficient to extend the time limit, and they had devised a legislative strategy to permit that coalition to work its will.

The victory was short-lived, however. The additional time bought by the Resolution saw not a single state added to the thirty-five that had already approved the ERA. But, for the time being, Caucus leaders saw their success as a portent of better things to come.

ORGANIZATIONAL GROWING PAINS

Soon after the Caucus got underway, three problems emerged to haunt its activities. One had to do with the unanimity rule, a requirement that all members had to agree to support letters, statements and proposals before they could be distributed as official Caucus positions. Second, the process devised to determine whether pronouncements did, in fact, have unanimous support was cumbersome and time-consuming. The third and most serious source of concern was the group's difficulties in raising money to pay staff and to support research on women's issues.

Differences in the political and ideological orientations of Caucus members often meant there were times when consensus, not to mention unanimity, could not be reached. Fundamental disagreement over abortion had made that subject off limits at the outset. But even when members were in general agreement, they sometimes differed on such matters as what action spoke most effectively to a problem and how much money should be spent to finance a program. Most decisions were reached by a handful of officer-activists, but, in the process, Caucus positions were narrowly drawn and more cautious than many believed they should have been. Furthermore, some issues about which members felt deeply remained unaddressed.

The second problem, the drawn-out process of trying to reach agreement among members, was also a product of the unanimity rule. Early Caucus practice was to circulate all documents among the entire membership for their signatures. If one or more members refused to sign, the statement could nonetheless be issued in the names of the signatories, but not as a Caucus document. Unconscionable delays resulted when some members neglected to pass material to other congresswomen in a timely fashion. Caucus staff were forced to call members' offices to learn on whose desk the document was gathering dust. Later, identical copies were sent to all members simultaneously to hasten the process. An additional difficulty inhered in the tendency of some members to alter the language of a statement, producing changes which, if not agreed to, would induce them to withhold their support. This practice forced recirculation of the document and further delay. Elizabeth Holtzman was a stickler for detail, and, even after submitting a proposal of her own, she often modified it later.

But the unanimity rule and the delay it produced were minor compared with the funding problem. The Steering Committee had established an annual dues of $50, and it expected members periodically to allocate a portion of their clerk-hire money, funds used to pay their office and district employees, to compensate Caucus staff. The practice was a common one and it permitted members of Legislative Service Organizations collectively to bear the costs of maintaining these agencies. But each woman was expected to determine how much of her staff funds, then about $340,000 exclusive of stationery and equipment allocations, would be set aside for Caucus needs, and no mechanism was established to guarantee payment of either the clerk-hire contribution or the annual dues. Only the good faith of the members and their sense of responsibility to one another and to Caucus goals would generate salaries and operating revenues for the Caucus staff.

From April to July 1977, the size of the Caucus treasury was of little consequence, inasmuch as the office staffs of congresswomen affiliated with the organization, especially Holtzman's, carried out administrative tasks. But the need for funds crystallized quickly in July when the Caucus placed Betty Dooley on the payroll as Executive Director. Dooley was an excellent choice for the position. She had, herself, been a candidate for a Texas House seat, a fund raiser for Robert Strauss when he was Treasurer of the Democratic National Committee, and a lobbyist on health issues in state capitals and on Capitol Hill. Her knowledge of Washington and connections with socially progressive organizations were precisely the qualities the Caucus sought. One of her first acts was to hire as Deputy Director Susan Scanlan, a bright and able young woman who had more than three years' experience on Capitol Hill. Before long, the two were sharing a mammoth work load. They recruited and supervised Caucus interns, directed research on women's issues, established and coordinated a network of liaison persons in each Caucus member's office, developed research proposals to submit to foundations for financial support, issued press releases, prepared statements and speeches, learned members' positions on legislative proposals, arranged for Caucus meetings with Cabinet and other administration officials, attended all meetings, and followed up on directives and suggestions generated by these sessions.

While Dooley and Scanlan were normally able to secure the in-kind services and equipment needed to run their office, money to pay their salaries was another matter. In 1977 and 1978, some congresswomen neglected to pay their dues, and only eight of the fifteen House members contributed clerk-hire funds. Months passed during which Dooley and Scanlan were either not compensated or paid far less than the monthly rate called for by the $25,000 and $16,500 annual salaries each was told she would receive. A sum of $12,500 had been initially budgeted for a Secretary/Bookkeeper, but no one bothered seriously to suggest filling that slot. In fact, several congresswomen were either oblivious to the staff's financial needs or simply did not care about them. Feelings ran the gamut from those of Shirley Chisholm, who allocated more than twice the amount of any other Caucus member, to those of Millicent Fenwick, who told the staff that if they really believed in the value of what they were doing they should not want to get paid.

The growing financial problems prompted Caucus members to establish a corporate entity separate and distinct from the Caucus. This was the Congresswomen's Caucus Corporation (CCC). The CCC charter named the six-member Executive Committee of the Caucus as the Corporation's Board of Directors. The new organization was defined as a charitable and educational agency designed to conduct research, educate the public, and maintain the administrative overhead needed to support these ends. This designation brought the organization within the meaning of paragraph 501(c)(3) of the Internal Revenue Code and permitted it to collect tax-deductible contributions. Dooley was named the CCC's Executive Director and Scanlan became Executive Director of the Caucus.

Thanks to a series of fund-raising parties, more than $200,000 was collected to pay Caucus debts and to hire experienced researchers for the CCC. The staff then sought grants from the Ford Foundation and the Rockefeller Family Fund to support salary and other overhead expenses. But both Foundations rejected these requests because grants were normally awarded for specific research projects, rather than to satisfy general budgetary needs. Ford's decision was also based on the political character of the group requesting the money. True, the Congresswomen's Caucus had put some distance between its members' political identities and the research and educational functions of the CCC. But the Corporation's Board of Directors was the same group of congresswomen making up the Caucus Executive Committee. Furthermore, the Caucus staff and the CCC staff overlapped and occupied an increasingly crowded, top-floor room in the Rayburn building.[9] Thus, if the Caucus hoped to launch its research and coordination activities, it would have to make a more palpable distinction between its political and educational arms. This it did in October 1978, when it created the Women's Research and Education Institute (WREI) to replace the CCC.

The Institute was given a Board of Directors, no member of which was a congresswoman; the terms "Caucus" and "Congress" were conspicuously absent from its title; it was assigned a staff distinct from that of the Caucus; and, at the first opportunity, it moved from the Rayburn Building into private quarters elsewhere in Washington. As we shall see, the decision to separate the Caucus from its nonprofit educational offspring turned out to be a fortunate one.

The congresswomen who had made up the CCC Board of Directors were replaced on the Board of WREI by nonpolitical (or no-longer-political) women with national reputations. Former Representative Martha Griffiths was named its President.[10] In spite of the fact that the WREI Board was responsible to the Caucus, with the latter influencing the former's agenda, sufficient distance had now been established between the two to lay to rest trepidations harbored by foundations about providing funds to "political" organizations. And the money began to come in. The Ford Foundation reacted favorably to a second proposal and gave the Institute a $150,000, two-year grant to hire a research coordinator. The grant was renewed for an additional two years in 1982 and increased to $250,000. A $25,000 grant was awarded by the Rockefeller Family Fund to permit the Institute, in cooperation with George Washington University's Women's Studies Program and Policy Center, to undertake a study of the economic problems of older women. This grant, too, was later renewed.

But the largest single sum, $300,000, came from the Charles H. Revson Foundation. The award financed one-year fellowships for ten women interested in Capitol Hill's policy-making process. Funds were subsequently made available for additional fellowships by R. J. Reynolds Industries, the Philip Morris Company, and the Helena Rubinstein Foundation. By 1982, the Institute had increased its staff to a half-dozen. It continued to function as a link between researchers and policy makers, serving as an information clearinghouse for lawmakers and women's research centers. However, the financial solvency it gained in the early 1980s contrasted sharply with the fragile fiscal state of the Congresswomen's Caucus during that same period.

DECLINE OF THE CAUCUS

When the 95th Congress adjourned in the fall of 1978, Caucus leaders looked back on two years of reasonable success. They had created an organization to represent women's interests; they had established a small, if underpaid staff to sustain the organization's activities; they had made progress in identifying some pressing women's issues; they had played a major role in extending the time period for state consideration of the Equal Rights Amendment; and they had developed a camaraderie among members that served their professional and personal needs.

But the next three years saw prospects for successfully pressing women's issues deteriorate and the Caucus lost much of its momentum. Reasons for the change had to do with the departure of members from the House, an unfortunate tactical decision by Caucus leaders at the start of the 96th Congress, difficulty in recruiting new members, political and personality clashes among members, insufficient financial resources, and the 1980 election of Ronald Reagan.

Retirements, a bid for another public office, and 1978 election defeats meant that six women who had been members of the Caucus in the 95th Congress would not be back for the 96th. One of the missing had lent prestige to the group simply by having her name on the letterhead, but a lack of interest in most women's issues had minimized her contributions to the Caucus. This was Barbara Jordan. Retiring Republican Shirley Pettis took her cues from party leaders as a rule, but her membership on the Caucus Executive Committee improved the group's bipartisan image. Helen Meyner had also been a faithful Caucus supporter, and her unsuccessful reelection campaign deprived the Caucus of an eminently sensible, intelligent, even-tempered foreign policy specialist with a keen insight into discriminatory practices affecting women. Yvonne Burke's decision to run for California Attorney General meant that the Caucus would have to find a new Treasurer, and that it would lose a politically experienced, articulate lawyer.

In some ways, the defeat of Martha Keys was the most damaging to the Caucus. Keys, only the second Democratic woman ever to serve on the Ways and Means Committee, had become the Caucus specialist on social security. Her loss was also difficult to accept because many attributed it to her marriage to another House member, Andrew Jacobs of Indiana. Some of her Kansas constituents apparently believed she was abandoning them in favor of her new husband's district residents. True, she had won reelection two years earlier, after Kansans were already aware that this mother of four had divorced her husband upon coming to Washington and had remarried soon after arriving there. But 1976 was not a strong Republican year, and the residual ill-feeling about her domestic life, when coupled with the GOP tide in 1978, was probably a powerful enough issue to make the difference.

These losses were offset in part by the election of three new congress-women, two of whom, Democrat Geraldine Ferraro and Republican Olympia Snowe, lost little time in affiliating with the group. The third, Beverly Byron, eventually joined, but as will become evident, Caucus membership was unimportant to her. Another addition was the lone woman Senator, newly elected Nancy Kassebaum. The Kansas Republican was not known for dramatizing women's causes and she had opposed extension of the time period for approving the Equal Rights Amendment. But she favored the ERA itself and took moderate positions on most issues. Kassebaum was appointed to the Caucus Executive Committee.

Thus, the loss of loyal and constructive members was partly offset by the arrival of a few reinforcements. But the gains were diminished by a serious miscalculation on the part of Holtzman and Heckler. It occurred when they decided to persuade the three women who had declined Caucus member-ship in the 95th Congress—Marjorie Holt, Virginia Smith, and Marilyn Lloyd—to join the organization in the 96th. From the time the Caucus had been established, the co-chairs had been uneasy when answering questions from the press about why some congresswomen were not members. They drew the obvious conclusion that affiliation by all congresswomen would end the need to make defensive replies to these queries. It would also present the House, the public, and monied foundations with a united front, and end lingering doubts about the organization's viability. And so, they set out in January 1979, to bring the remaining congresswomen into the fold.

Acting in tandem, they approached Holt, Smith, and Lloyd and asked them to join. The three conservative congresswomen were told about the unanimity rule—that nothing with which they disagreed would be en-dorsed by the Caucus—and that they would be under no obligation to attend even a minimum number of meetings. They were further advised that they would not be pressed for financial contributions (after all, even women who were already members had managed to ignore this require-ment), and that their names would be on the letterhead. In the meantime, they could identify with the Caucus to a greater or lesser degree, as their political needs dictated.

The co-chairs also noted the group's positive features. They pointed out that Speaker of the House Tip O'Neill had been impressed with the CC's contributions, that many male colleagues looked favorably on its efforts, and that Senator Kassebaum had joined the Caucus at her first opportunity. Holtzman and Heckler added that in its first two years the Caucus had done nothing radical, and had not damaged a member's standing with her constituents. Apparently the three women found the arguments persuasive, inasmuch as they accepted the offer. But it was an offer hard to resist. They were asked to join an organization whose meetings they did not have to attend, whose financial needs they could ignore, and over whose collective decisions each exercised an absolute veto. And should the Caucus score a notable achievement, they could join in claiming credit for it.

Caucus activists soon found the benefits of 100 percent female membership offset by the difficulties of trying to lead a more diverse group of congresswomen. The three new members rarely attended meetings, even when administration representatives were scheduled to speak. They introduced few ideas for Caucus leaders and staff to develop, and they were notably reluctant to try to persuade colleagues to support Caucus positions. Unsurprisingly, they allocated no clerk-hire funds to pay Caucus expenses. But they did exercise the right to veto proposals, refusing to sign letters and statements that had been drafted for membership endorsement. They were especially disinclined to support measures costing money. True, Caucus leaders could now claim that all women were members, but their chances of securing consensus on most women's issues and of generating an innovative legislative program were sharply reduced.

As the 96th Congress progressed, meetings were held much less frequently than they had been in the 95th, and a legislative agenda simply never emerged. The Caucus invited Cabinet and sub-Cabinet officials to talk about subjects falling within the jurisdiction of the agencies they headed, but these appearances slowed to a trickle. One reason for their decline was the inertia gripping the Caucus. It was able to dramatize few policy priorities, social security and the plight of aging women being notable exceptions, and Caucus leaders felt no overwhelming pressures to invite other speakers. A second reason was diminution of the Caucus's reputation. The difficulty leaders had in persuading the Chairman of the Joint Chiefs of Staff, General David Jones, to meet with the group reflected this loss of influence. When the General was asked to discuss discrimination against women in the armed forces, an aide phoned to say that the General did not feel qualified to talk about the subject because "he does not favor discrimination against servicewomen." When the Caucus persevered and established a specific meeting date, a colonel called the Executive Director to say that "the General is unable to come to your party." After Betty Dooley repeated the reply to Marjorie Holt, ranking Republican on the Military Personnel subcommittee, Holt called Jones directly and the General changed his plans.

Caucus leaders were aware of the lost momentum and some expressed their frustration openly. Mikulski and Schroeder complained bitterly to other members and to the CC staff. But still the Caucus seemed rudderless. It recorded some successes, persuading the Small Business Committee to hold hearings on "women in business," and it helped enact legislation providing ex-wives of Foreign Service officers with a pro rata share of their husbands' pensions in divorce settlements. This Caucus-backed effort was particularly significant in that the law became a model for subsequent pension reforms, including benefits for former wives of military personnel

and civil servants. But these achievements fell far short of the gains anticipated by Caucus leaders and their staff when the 96th Congress had
convened.

Another factor leading to the decline of the Caucus was rooted in
differences in the personal and political styles of its members. Partisan,
ideological, and regional difference explain a good deal of what happens in
Washington, but important developments also turn on personality differences. Thus, Caucus malaise during the 96th Congress was partly the result
of Margaret Heckler's hesitant leadership and the annoyance it provoked
among CC activists. Having co-chairs promoted a bipartisan spirit, but it
inhibited expeditious, decisive action. The unanimity rule was a drag on
CC initiatives, but even before a statement was circulated for members'
reactions, the two chairs had to approve it. And Heckler was notoriously
slow about making decisions.

Her hesitancy on Caucus matters was a reflection of the same uncertainty
she exhibited on the House floor. During roll calls, for example, she was
often among the last to cast a vote, waiting to see what other members of
the mostly Democratic Massachusetts delegation would do, and concerned
about the consequences of breaking ranks too frequently with Republican
colleagues. She agonized over roll call votes and often struggled to beat the
fifteen minute time limit before which a "yea" or "nay" had to be cast. One
observer said that he could not blame her. She was a moderate Republican
from a liberal state and represented a politically marginal district. Consequently, she had to be circumspect when casting votes on issues salient to
her constituents. But her caution carried over into Caucus activities and the
only time limit she heeded was the one dictated by her internal clock. As a
result, she delayed for days signing even the most innocuous letters,
thereby frustrating staff members, and especially Patricia Schroeder when
the Colorado Democrat replaced Elizabeth Holtzman as co-chair. On one
occasion it took her six weeks to sign a luncheon invitation to labor leader
Douglas Fraser, so long, in fact, that the date of the luncheon had to be
changed.

It was during the 96th Congress, as well, that an open break developed
between Caucus leaders and one of their peripheral members. Relations
between them had not been good during the 95th Congress, but the differences seemed unimportant because Caucus members were engaged in
many constructive activities. Few achievements emerged during the 96th
Congress, however, and the congresswomen began to magnify irritants
they had ignored in the past. The woman who was seen as out of step was
Millicent Fenwick, and her adversaries included almost all Caucus members who were carryovers from the 95th Congress.

For many people inside and outside the House, Millicent Fenwick was
the model congresswoman. Tall, slender, and with aristocratic bearing, her
statements on and off the floor addressed the moral and ethical dimensions

of important issues. She established a reputation for being scrupulously honest and for shunning behind-the-scenes deals that often precede congressional decisions. She believed in social justice with all her heart, but was terrified about the possible excesses of a too-powerful government and she frequently resolved conflicts between admirable social goals and limited government in favor of the latter.

If her imposing stature, penetrating wit, noble causes, and pleas to do "the right thing" annoyed her less-patrician colleagues, that, she concluded, was their problem. She was much admired by others, not because she was an effective legislator—she neither excelled nor wished to excel at the skills useful for creating legislative majorities—but because she sometimes served as the conscience of the House. She chided other members for accepting campaign contributions from political action committees, and vigorously opposed the salary increases they voted themselves (one critic noted that he would have voted against the increase if, like Fenwick, he, too, had inherited $5 million). These actions endeared her to voters who thought politicians were venal and who believed the honor and opportunity of serving the people are reward enough for conscientious legislators. While campaigning, she was refreshingly candid and unequivocal. When she later ran for a Senate seat, she supported busing for racial integration before an audience of conservative Republican suburbanites; she called for reduced government pensions at a meeting with postal workers; and she opposed the death penalty, school prayer, and tuition tax credits, staples of the conservative Republican's diet, in an address to a small town Republican club (Geist 1982). Perhaps this behavior cost her the election, but she had never lost one before and, given the strength of her convictions, she would have had it no other way.

From the time she joined the Caucus, the New Jersey congresswoman had been uncomfortable with her affiliation. In fact, Fenwick believed that all caucuses divide lawmakers more than they unite them. Social and economic problems have to be worked out for the society as a whole, she contended, and caucuses institutionalize special, rather than national, interests. It should come as no surprise that this attitude adversely affected her relations with other Caucus members. They wanted to define, dramatize, and address women's needs. She was preoccupied with national problems which she believed were not divisible by gender. Thus, her colleagues sometimes saw her as subverting Caucus goals. At meetings, she raised subjects not on the agenda, and had to be reminded regularly to stick to the topic. She asked visiting officials questions having little to do with the reasons they had been invited, she patronized other members, and she was loath to support most spending proposals, regardless of how favorable an impact they might have on women. On one occasion, she astounded some congresswomen by criticizing the Caucus for supporting female beauty shop employees in the House who were asking for the same fringe benefits already available to men who worked in congressional barber shops.

One of the first to take offense to Fenwick's behavior was Shirley Chisholm. The circumstances under which the break between the two occurred have been reconstructed from the accounts of three witnesses. One day at a Caucus meeting Fenwick expressed her dislike for caucuses and the divisiveness they produced. Chisholm remarked that they were useful for groups that had not yet been integrated into the society. For Blacks, especially, said Chisholm, caucuses mobilized resources which otherwise might never be brought to bear. "When we have a completely fair society," the Brooklyn Democrat continued, "we won't need caucuses." When asked by Fenwick what achievements the Congressional Black Caucus could claim, Chisholm mentioned legislation requiring the Small Business Administration to set aside loans for firms owned by members of minority groups. Fenwick dismissed the example as insignificant, told Chisholm that she, personally, did not discriminate against people because of their color and that she had been active in the civil rights movement since Brown v. Oklahoma [sic], longer, in fact, than Chisholm had. The assertions may well have been true, but Chisholm was incensed by Fenwick's patronizing manner and made it a point thereafter to avoid meetings at which she believed Fenwick would be present.

Fenwick's attack on Helen Meyner further alienated her from other Caucus members. When congresswomen traveled to China together, most invited a spouse or some other companion. Elizabeth Holtzman, for example, was accompanied by her mother. Meyner brought her husband, former New Jersey Governor Robert Meyner, and Fenwick paid the way of her physician, inasmuch as a pacemaker had recently been implanted in her chest and its efficacy had not been fully tested. While traveling in China, the Meyners had been particularly solicitous of their New Jersey neighbor, remaining behind with her when she did not keep up with the rest of the group and generally being helpful to a tour member who was less agile than other travelers. But when they returned to the United States, Fenwick publicly denounced Meyner for taking her husband to China at the taxpayer's expense. Whatever the merits of the claim, Fenwick's behavior was viewed as unnecessarily mean-spirited and she further lost the respect of Caucus members.

The strained relations continued to surface from time to time, but Fenwick did not mention them when she finally resigned from the organization in 1981. Instead, she chose to emphasize the source of the group's financial support to explain her decision. Fenwick questioned the propriety of House members soliciting funds from special interest groups to support the Women's Research and Education Institute. The objection was a reasonable one and, in fact, had been raised earlier by the Ford Foundation when considering a grant proposal from the CCC. The same demurrer would lead in 1981 to significant changes in House rules governing Legislative Service Organizations. But even after WREI replaced the CCC and set up separate quarters with a separate staff and a Board of Directors containing no congresswomen, the fact that it sought tax deductible contributions from groups affected by legislation on which congresswomen who were served by WREI had voted was unacceptable to Fenwick. She said "I don't think it's appropriate for members of Congress to form a group and get deductibility for contributions made to that group" (*New York Times*, July 16, 1981).

Fenwick's departure was only the first of several occurring during this period. Other women left the Caucus in the 97th Congress, defections which its leaders encouraged, and which were followed by the CC's transformation.

STALEMATE AND PURGE

When the 97th Congress convened in 1981, Caucus leaders were intent on increasing their membership. The preceding months had witnessed the loss of two former Caucus officials, Elizabeth Holtzman and Gladys Spellman. Holtzman had given up her House seat to run, unsuccessfully, for the Senate, and the CC was forced to carry on without one of its founders and moving spirits. A more devastating blow, because it was unexpected and tragic, was struck when Spellman, on her way to easy reelection, suffered a heart attack and became comatose. She won the contest in spite of her condition, but the House later declared her seat vacant after physicians concluded that there was no hope of recovery.

Spellman's loss was hard to overestimate. She had served as Caucus Secretary in the preceding Congress, and her excellent rapport with colleagues was matched by valuable contacts with public officials all over the country. While serving as Prince George's County Commissioner, the Maryland Democrat was appointed to the Advisory Commission on Intergovernmental Relations by President Lyndon Johnson. She was active in national organizations of local and state officials and was later elected President of the National Association of Counties, the first woman to hold the position. When she came to the House, she already knew a good many of her new colleagues, inasmuch as they had been state and local officials before serving in Washington and had participated with Spellman in national conferences. She was chosen Vice Chairman of the 94th Democratic Class when that swollen group of "Watergate babies" met to organize themselves,[11] and she was active in planning the ouster of three Democratic committee chairmen who had been unresponsive to the policy preferences of rank and file party members. Thus Spellman's illness and Holtzman's defeat deprived the Caucus of two of its ablest women.

The 1980 elections sent four new Republican women to the House, Bobbi Fiedler, Lynn Martin, Marge Roukema, and Claudine Schneider, and one,

Paula Hawkins, to the Senate. Heckler and Schroeder lost no time in calling a Caucus meeting to brief the newcomers, but only Fiedler, Martin, and Schneider attended. The co-chairs were joined by Lindy Boggs, and the three veterans highlighted the virtues of Caucus membership. The first-termers were also told that each member was expected to contribute $2,500 annually from clerk-hire funds to support the CC staff, a requirement ignored by some in past years. Later, the names of the four new House members appeared on the Caucus letterhead. But neither affiliation on paper nor the earlier sales pitch persuaded any of them to join at the time.[12]

Rejection by all four came as a surprise to many observers and as a disappointment to Margaret Heckler. It was a surprise because they had seemed interested in women's issues, and none appeared to represent a district in which CC affiliation would be viewed as a liability. Moreover, they all supported the Equal Rights Amendment, and Martin and Schneider, especially, had run with strong support from women's groups. It seemed only natural, therefore, for them to have become a part of the Caucus, even if unable initially to take an active role.

Heckler's reaction grew out of a belief that these other Republican women would help her maintain the Caucus as a bipartisan organization. Republicans Olympia Snowe and Nancy Kassebaum had helped promote the Caucus as a vehicle for protecting women's rights. But as one of its founders and as co-chair, Heckler, much more than they, was torn between the conservative orthodoxy of her party and the liberal orientations of Caucus activists who believed, as she did, in aiding women. The prospects of recruiting four other moderate Republicans who would move the Caucus consensus closer to the political center were enormously appealing.

The explanations the four gave for not joining were clear enough, although each woman probably weighed the reasons differently. First, they believed the financial contribution was larger than was warranted by the advantages they could expect to derive from Caucus membership. The sum of $2,500 was simply more than they were prepared to part with in their first term. Second, they said their preoccupation with other projects would leave insufficient time and energy to do justice to Caucus affiliation. Third, unstated, but implicit in their explanations, was a reluctance, shared by most new members, to identify with groups and issues when the political consequences of such associations are uncertain. Electoral vulnerability is greatest during the first few terms and many members delay affiliation with organizations deemed marginal to their service until they have established a stronger political base in their districts.

Fourth, at least one of the four was disinclined to view issues as "women's issues." She may have believed that separate economic and regional interests lent themselves to explicit representation, but the same was not true about gender. There were no "men's" or "women's" issues. These same sentiments were shared by Paula Hawkins, who maintained that she did not believe "in a women's caucus, black caucus, or any special interest caucuses," and she too, declined to join (*New York Times*, July 16, 1981).

Fifth, some of the Republican women were concerned about the political style and motives of Patricia Schroeder. Although she and her predecessor as co-chair, Elizabeth Holtzman, were both Harvard-trained lawyers, they had very different legislative styles. Whereas Holtzman was deliberate and painstaking in preparing herself on issues, Schroeder worked quickly and spontaneously. At times, she appeared impulsive. She spent little time agonizing over the precise language to use to express her views and gave minimum attention to considering the appropriate time to introduce them into discussion. Holtzman believed in slowly, systematically building her case and then overwhelming the opposition with a mountain of evidence; Schroeder in using her ammunition as soon as it became available. The Denver Democrat also invested her energies in many different causes, thereby gaining the reputation of being unable to master the subtleties of more than a few.

As a result, critics concluded that Schroeder did not do her homework and was predisposed to shoot from the hip. She was also seen as a publicity seeker—more because she readily agreed to requests for interviews and was always good for a creative, publishable wisecrack than because she con- sciously sought the exposure—and some first-term Republicans voiced reservations about being identified with an organization led by a liberal Democrat whose legislative behavior was not always predictable and whose goals seemed inextricably linked to generating press coverage. Said Lynn Martin when asked why she decided not to join the Caucus: "The dues were too high, and I don't need to pay that for a Pat Schroeder show" (Glaser and Elliot 1983, p. 160).

But casting a shadow over all of these explanations was another concern these women shared, a concern more important than any they offered publicly. It was a fear that affiliation with the Caucus would place them at odds with the Reagan administration. Ronald Reagan was opposed to the Equal Rights Amendment and had persuaded a Republican national con- vention to deny support for the Amendment after forty years of calling for its enactment. He had also promised to reduce the federal government's role in promoting the public welfare and to cut back programs and dollars directed toward that end. By contrast, the Congresswomen's Caucus nor- mally called for a greater federal role and larger expenditures of federal funds. The four first-termers were too new seriously to consider opposing the administration on social welfare issues, and they turned the Caucus down rather than chance offending the President and his constituency. Margaret Heckler, they reasoned, might have the seniority and the electoral security to risk opposing the White House on issues affecting women. As newcomers, they had neither.

Having missed a golden opportunity to replenish its membership, the Caucus, nonetheless, had some reason for optimism as the 97th Congress began. True, the new women had not accepted the invitation to join the group, but their names would appear on the letterhead for a few months, and there was always the chance they would affiliate later in the session. Furthermore, some CC members believed the new administration would be more sympathetic to women's needs than most critics had predicted. Before his inauguration, the President-elect, accompanied by Vice President-elect George Bush, Max Friedersdorf, who would head his congressional liaison office, former Ambassador Anne Armstrong, and Jeane Kirkpatrick, who was about to become U.S. Ambassador to the United Nations, held a reception for congresswomen. Mr. Reagan made clear he opposed the ERA because he preferred other ways of ending discrimination against women, and he said he would work diligently toward achieving that goal.

The Caucus referred to the event as a "working" luncheon and, indeed, some important items of business were explored. The President-elect assured the women they would have regular access to Cabinet members, and told them to let him know with whom they would like to meet. He also listened to the congresswomen spell out their priorities and, in a press release issued later that day, Caucus leaders observed that the President elect was "obviously open to suggestions and ideas." The meeting showed his "sensitivity to the role of American women and the problems we face." Skeptics called this reaction unrealistically optimistic, but many of the women were prepared to give the President, this charming, gentle man, the benefit of the doubt.

A second reason for the upbeat mood among Caucus members was the improvement in the administrative and financial arrangements governing Caucus operations. During the early months of 1980, the staffs of the Caucus and the Women's Research and Education Institute occupied the same cramped quarters in the Rayburn Building. The space and facilities were simply insufficient for both simultaneously to hold meetings, conduct briefings, and carry out administrative and clerical functions without getting in one another's way. In February, the Caucus hired Ann Charnley Smith to succeed Susan Scanlan, who moved over to WREI, and office overcrowding produced a highly charged atmosphere. Staff members of both agencies had difficulty keeping their responsibilities, facilities, resources, and interns straight. In April, WREI moved out of the Rayburn Building, settling in private quarters, and Smith had a better opportunity to deal with the increasing difficulties facing the Caucus. She brought to her task a rich background of teaching, foreign travel, and administrative, organizational, and public relations experience—qualifications useful for a Caucus Director who had to be a self-starter. The most vexing and persistent problem she had to confront was that of financing staff activities. Some members continued to withhold or delay clerk-hire contributions.

It was partly in response to these financial difficulties that Smith worked with Caucus leaders to create *Update*, a biweekly newsletter. The principal objective of this new organ was to provide timely information on the status of legislation affecting women, information which until then was unavailable in a single, easily accessible source. *Update* summarized recent bills, announced pending hearings, alerted readers to action taken by House and Senate committees, provided special reports on issues that had ripened in recent months, and reported federal regulations adopted by government agencies.[13] The newsletter was conceived to keep Caucus members, their liaisons, and other interested parties informed about current and pending developments. But the publication was also expected to solve the Caucus's financial woes. *Update* would be free to members, but other lawmakers, along with interest groups active in women's issues, would be charged an annual fee. If enough subscribers signed on, the newsletter could be the CC's salvation. Cost of the biweekly was set at $125 per year, but corporate recipients were asked to pay $1,000.

By December, 1980, with the distribution of the second issue, more than twenty Representatives, two Senators and one subcommittee (on Civil and Constitutional Rights) had subscribed, and all congressional offices had begun to receive it. Soon after, business, labor, philanthropic, and public interest lobbyists sent checks. By devising a means of transmitting information more effectively, the Caucus simultaneously took a step closer to solvency. *Update* subscriptions could yield up to $20,000 annually, which, together with help from interns, and funds from those congresswomen who fulfilled their financial responsibilities, would be enough to sustain staff activities.

Possible support from the newly elected President, a resourceful staff director, and financial viability were the three most important reasons for Caucus leaders' optimism, but they were not the only ones. Another good sign was the scores of women's bills introduced in the House. These measures called for social security reform, changes in pension systems that discriminated against women, protection of reproductive rights, aid to women specializing in math and the sciences, creation of a breast cancer task force in the National Institutes of Health, an economic equity bill, and more rigorous enforcement of Title IX and other anti-discriminatory provisions passed in the last fifteen years. At the same time, congresswomen were receiving strong moral support from women's groups. Late in January, the National Women's Political Caucus and the Capitol Hill Women's Political Caucus held a luncheon reception to honor the twenty-one women in the House and Senate, and the CC later joined with representatives of women's organizations to hold a briefing on legislative highlights in women's issues from 1973 to 1980.

But as the 97th Congress wore on, the fragile optimism initially characterizing Caucus members' spirits began to crumble. Failure to reach consensus on many issues, a serious problem in 1979 and 1980, arose again in 1981. Fenwick resigned from the group and the three Caucus members whom Heckler and Holtzman had successfully recruited in 1979—Holt, Lloyd, and Smith—refused to support measures objectionable to the new administration. Members gave up trying to convene regularly and meetings fell off sharply. Especially dispiriting was the refusal of administration officials to honor Caucus requests for briefings. Only two high-ranking administrators accepted invitations throughout 1981, Health and Human Services Secretary Richard Schweiker, and Social Security Administrator John Svahn. David Stockman, Director of the Office of Management and the Budget, ignored repeated calls to appear. When Carter advisors had come to Capitol Hill, a candid, free-flowing exchange of ideas took place, with administrators agreeing to conduct a survey, write a report, look into a questionable practice, consider counterproposals, and come back for another session. The meeting with Schweiker was useful, but the one with Svahn generated hostility. Caucus members pointed out that Social Security reform to help women was not a partisan issue, but Svahn did little more than express regret that it had become one.

If the infrequent meetings with the President's top advisors were a disappointment, the President's budgetary priorities were a calamity. After he released his proposed 1982 budget, the Caucus asked WREI to prepare a report detailing the budget's impact on women. WREI distributed its study at the end of March and Caucus leaders found it sobering (Rix and Stone 1981). Cuts in Aid to Families with Dependent Children, more than 90 percent of whose recipients were women and children, would affect 650,000 families. Proposals to place a cap on Medicaid, reduce eligibility for food stamps, shrink the Women, Infant and Children program, cut the Social Security minimum benefit program (three-quarters of the 2.3 million recipients were female), and vitiate the Legal Services Corporation (two-thirds of whose clients were women) were expected to have a disastrous impact. What was clear to Caucus leaders was that this President, who had promised to be sensitive to women's needs, had fashioned a budget which would harm those women least able to protect themselves—the poor, the elderly, the widowed, and the isolated. The President was accused of accelerating the feminization of poverty.

There was little the Caucus could do, however, inasmuch as a strong negative response would be vetoed by more conservative CC members. Consequently, criticism of the Reagan administration was issued either individually or through the collective voices of smaller combinations of women. For Caucus liberals, these circumstances were intolerable, and they reacted in two ways. First, they placed some middle-class, egalitarian women's issues on the back burner and began to give undivided attention to securing financial viability for millions of economically disadvantaged women. Said one staff member, "You can't think much about more vigorous enforcement of Title IX when medical benefits for women and children are being threatened." Second, they changed the ground rules defining the obligations of members and their organization's mode of doing business.

The economic equity bill was the centerpiece of the first response. The bill was a comprehensive one, targeting women whose traditional roles and responsibilities had left them economically disadvantaged. They were deprived of pensions and annuities, employment opportunities and wages, capital for investment, and Social Security and insurance benefits. The bill reflected an affirmative effort by lawmakers to respond to the deprivations women suffer because society asks them to perform certain social roles, because they dutifully carry out these roles, because little or no monetary value is attached to the tasks they fulfill, and because they usually live longer than men. Caucus leaders joined three senators in cosponsoring the bill and they made it their highest priority during the remainder of the 97th Congress.

For liberals, inability to use the Caucus as a positive force had persisted too long. The inertia was especially galling in the face of the Reagan administration's efforts to blunt many of the victories women had won since the 1960s. "We had no idea, " said one Caucus activist, "just how creative they [the Reagan administration] would be in undoing rights for women." In July, the Executive Committee met and decided to change the guidelines governing Caucus operations and member responsibilities. They put an end to the unanimity rule, limited to seventy-two hours the length of time members could take to approve or reject a document circulated for Caucus endorsement, and required (rather than simply "urging") each member to contribute $2,500 to the Caucus annually. They also agreed to require rejection by two persons, rather than a single member, before withholding the Caucus imprimatur on a letter.

The reaction was immediate and predictable. Republicans Marjorie Holt and Virginia Smith and Democrats Marilyn Lloyd and Beverly Byron resigned. Byron asserted that the fee was excessive relative to the services the Caucus provided. Schroeder, on the other hand, explained why the decision had been made: "The ten of us carrying it [the Caucus] said 'this is really aggravating. They [those who make no contributions] run on the fact that they belong to the Congresswomen's Caucus and they ask us to write speeches'" (*New York Times*, July 16, 1981). Caucus leaders also ended the pretense that the four new Republican women were members, and their names were dropped from the letterhead. With the adoption of new rules and the purge of marginal members the CC entered a new phase. It became more aggressive and more predisposed to reveal its progressive orientation. Its smaller size made consensus more likely and unanimity easier to engineer.

Rapport between the co-chairs became more problematical, however, because the pressures on Heckler's middle position between liberal Democrats and orthodox Republicans intensified once the organization was reduced to ten members. The indecision and delay characterizing her past behavior worsened, and Schroeder and the Caucus staff sometimes waited weeks for her to sign a letter. The most exasperating instance of this behavior occurred when the Senate approved the nomination of Sandra Day O'Connor to the Supreme Court and Caucus members agreed to send her a congratulatory note. The staff drafted a simple letter to that effect and forwarded it to Heckler for approval. Concerned about the vigorous opposition to O'Connor's nomination by pro-life forces, and anticipating a difficult reelection campaign in 1982, Heckler revised the draft stating that the Caucus took positive note of the new justice's "strict constructionist, conservative views." The change was unacceptable to other Caucus leaders, and Heckler produced a second version which suggested that the Caucus would be reviewing with interest O'Connor's judicial record in Arizona. This, too, was unacceptable and, ultimately, the initiative died. Individual congresswomen did, indeed, extend best wishes, but none conveyed sentiments on behalf of the Caucus.

In the end, Heckler's devotion to the Caucus and her belief in its usefulness as an instrument for helping women were not as appreciated as she and her supporters had hoped. Critics who thought she was being used to give a bipartisan facade to what was really a Democratic sideshow must have felt vindicated when, during the 1982 campaign, Caucus Democrats campaigned for her opponent. Democratic Congressman Barney Frank and she were placed in the same district as a result of reapportionment, and Geraldine Ferraro, Barbara Mikulski, and Schroeder told Massachusetts residents "You don't have to be a woman to be a feminist." Women's groups, too, supported Frank. But Heckler's difficulties and dilatory behavior became less important when, toward the end of 1981, the Caucus was faced with a crisis. The organization's survival was threatened and its leaders were forced to change its structure and composition.

TRANSFORMATION: THE CONGRESSIONAL CAUCUS FOR WOMEN'S ISSUES

The decision requiring the Caucus to change its character was made official on October 21, 1981, but members had been expecting it for weeks. It was issued by the House Administration Committee and it changed the rules governing the operations and funding of all Legislative Service Organizations—the twenty-six caucuses officially registered with the House. Under the old guidelines, they could occupy space in House office buildings, use congressional office supplies and equipment, lay claim to House telephone numbers, and raise funds from sources both inside and outside of Congress. Under the new rules, these organizations could receive office space, furniture, furnishings, telephones, and other goods and services from the House. And they could be financed by contributions of members through dues and assessments from clerk-hire and expense allowances. But they could not receive outside funding from, say, corporations and foundations, and, at the same time, retain their entitlement to public benefits.

The Congresswomen's Caucus was, for the most part, already in compliance with the new rules. When it set up the Women's Research and Education Institute, moved the corporation out of House facilities, established it as an entity separate and distinct from the Caucus, and made it the sole recipient of foundation and other grants, the Caucus had insulated itself from direct, outside funding. But one of the new rules affected indirect contributions, including newsletter subscriptions. With *Update* subscriptions defined as an outside source of revenue, the Caucus could no longer sell the biweekly to private customers and, at the same time, rely on House resources and facilities and on members' financial contributions.

Under the new rules, all caucuses had to inform the House Administration Committee by no later than January 1, 1982, whether they planned to give up sources of outside income. If not, they had to vacate public premises by January 1, 1983. Anticipating the Committee's decision, the Caucus met the day before it was handed down to consider its implications. Members agreed that if *Update* subscriptions were discontinued, the Caucus would have to be disbanded. On the other hand, if the newsletter moved off Capitol Hill in order to keep its outside funding, it would become a less accessible resource. Faced with the unpleasant choice, the Caucus decided to expand its membership by admitting male Representatives. Funds generated until then by *Update* subscriptions would be replaced by the annual dues of congressmen who joined the Caucus.

The idea of permitting men to affiliate had been broached when the Caucus was in its infancy, and had been considered intermittently ever since. Many congresswomen had acknowledged that some male colleagues were more authentic feminists than some female Representatives, that women, one-half the country's population, deserved to be represented by more than a handful of House members, and that by inviting men to join, the Caucus would gain better access to the House power structure. Nevertheless they had rejected male membership, believing a male presence would dilute Caucus concerns about women, and that men might try to seize control of the organization for their own purposes. The subject was raised again after male Representatives helped bail out the Caucus by subscribing to *Update*. But with newsletter fees from corporate, labor, and other interest groups now ruled out, the Caucus decided it had no alternative but to permit male members to make an even greater contribution—this time as members.

On March 2, 1982, the organization changed its name to the "Congressional Caucus for Women's Issues" and, by the middle of the month, sixty-six congressmen had signed on. Before long, male membership reached 100 and included House Speaker Tip O'Neill. What kind of "members" they might become was not immediately certain. When the transformation was being considered, Schroeder and others supported "auxiliary" membership, allowing congressmen to pay something less that the full $2,500 dues and giving them a reduced role in determining policy. One proposal suggested charging men $1,000, allowing them to attend quarterly meetings, and permitting participation in press conferences and hearings sponsored by the caucus.

Those who were less enthusiastic about admitting men held out for a smaller role, and Caucus members finally decided to charge males an annual fee of $600, for which they would receive *Update*.[14] Furthermore, their names would appear on press releases and all correspondence. However, they were ineligible to hold Caucus office or vote for officers or on policy matters, and none would be invited to join the Executive Committee, now made up of all congresswomen belonging to the CCWI. In fact, many congressmen who affiliated were members in name only. They paid their dues, but delegated to their staffs the responsibility for keeping informed about Caucus matters.

One Caucus critic commented: "The men are allowing themselves to be used. They are adding their names but they have no power in the Caucus. It's tokenism in reverse." But a staff person close to the Caucus said:

The men would have been admitted sooner or later. When they were taken in, it was out of financial necessity, but it was politically expedient, as well, and the men will reap some benefits among women's groups in their own districts. Some congresswomen were invited to these districts in 1982 to campaign for fellow Caucus members.

Shortly after male Representatives affiliated, Co-chair Pat Schroeder commented: "We've known for some time that we had to broaden our base of support. We knew that separatism was not the way to go. We need partnership with men in the women's movement" (*New York Times*, December 14, 1981).

These observations reflected the limited progress the Caucus had achieved before its transformation. Apart from extending the time period for passage of the Equal Rights Amendment, the CC had been unable to build majorities in Congress, effectively devise political strategies, or significantly affect the legislative agenda. One reason for these failings was its size. Until membership went beyond a handful of activist congresswomen, its value as a voting bloc and as a reference group for House leaders was bound to be limited. Moreover, few of its members had sufficient seniority to control legislation within their committees' jurisdictions or the leverage to exchange such control for favorable treatment of measures supported by the Caucus. Their numbers and their peripheral positions within the structure of influence often left them at the mercy of colleagues who were disinclined to view women's problems as legitimate concerns of Congress.

But the characteristic which made short-term success problematic was the organization's principal criterion for membership. Unlike the great majority of other House groups, the CC recruited members because of who they were rather than because of the nature of their constituencies. House members joined the Steel or Textile Caucuses, for example, because their districts rely on the manufacture or processing of these products. Regional, ideological, partisan, ethnic and racial groups similarly united House members whose districts' residents shared a demonstrable geographical, programmatic, political or cultural orientation. The CC, on the other hand, was made up of people whose membership depended on their womanhood, rather than on commonalities shared by their districts. Since its priorities were often incompatible with policy preferences in some members' districts, its viability was always in doubt.[15]

Still, admission of men gave feminist congresswomen potential allies who were well placed within the House power structure. The change increased their opportunities to persuade colleagues to consider matters which its women members thought were important. One instance of Caucus clout occurred weeks after the transformation. In December 1981, a federal district court in Idaho declared the extension of the ERA time period unconstitutional, and upheld the right of states to rescind prior approval. At the time, six months remained during which three additional legislatures could have acted to bring to three-quarters the number of states approving the proposed Amendment. When NOW asked for an expeditious appeal of the judge's verdict, the Justice Department demurred and announced it would ask the Supreme Court to allow the case to follow "the normal appeals process." The Department's response virtually assured high court inaction until after expiration of the extension period.

Incensed by the decision, Caucus leaders helped frame a telegram to President Reagan urging the Department to reconsider its position. The telegram, signed by eighty-eight Representatives and thirty-one Senators, had the effect sought by the signatories. It is worth noting that among the seventy-eight male House members whose names were on the telegram, fifty-nine, more than three-quarters, soon became or were already members of the Congressional Caucus for Women's Issues.

NOTES

1. Information in this chapter and the next was gathered from interviews with congresswomen and staff members, and from the Caucus minutes, memoranda,

letters, press releases, and newsletters they provided. The interviews were conducted in 1978, 1979, 1981, and 1993.

2. Prior to 1962, female members searching for a room of their own had little choice but to use H311, the "Ladies' Retiring Room" located on the relatively inconvenient gallery floor of the Capitol and accessible to the wives and families of all members of Congress.

3. According to a fact sheet prepared by the House historian and available in the Suite, there is some doubt about whether the couch is actually the one on which Adams expired. Visitors are told that it is and when a Reagan Cabinet official seated on the couch was informed of its historic role, he looked around the room uneasily, rose, and occupied an empty chair.

4. Congresswomen declining Caucus membership at the time were Republicans Marjorie Holt and Virginia Smith, and Democrat Marilyn Lloyd.

5. The text of the proposed amendment read as follows: "Equality of rights under the law shall not be denied or abridged by the United States or by any state on account of sex. The Congress shall have the power to enforce, by appropriate legislation, the provisions of this article. This Amendment shall take effect two years after the date of ratification."

6. Legislative events and decisions relating to the extension resolution appear in the following *Congressional Quarterly Weekly Reports*, vol. 36: May 27, 1978, p. 1347; July 15, 1978, p. 1833; August 19, 1978, pp. 2214, 2226, 2227; October 7, 1978, p. 2724; and October 14, 1978, p. 2983. Information about the role played by the Caucus in extending the ERA time limit was developed through interviews with several Caucus members and with staff aides of both male and female House members in 1978 and 1979, and through observation of two meetings of representatives of women's groups in 1978, during their most intensive lobbying efforts.

7. The one Caucus member to vote in favor of states being allowed to rescind earlier ERA approval was Republican Shirley Pettis of California. Pettis voted for final passage, however. Non-Caucus members Marjorie Holt and Virginia Smith voted as Pettis did.

8. The Railsback motion was rejected 196–227. Among the sixteen other Representatives voting against both his motion and final passage, eight were Republicans and eight were Northern Democrats.

9. The uncertain status of the Caucus was embarrassingly clear. The space for its staff had originally been designated as a lounge for congresswomen. The office was windowless and its door had no permanent number on it. (A piece of cardboard taped to it with the number "2471" seemed to suffice). Memoranda distributed to announce meetings in the room often stated: "Room 2471 Rayburn Building is directly across the hall from 2400. PLEASE NOTE THIS LOCATION as room is hard to find."

10. Shirley Pettis (who had just retired from the House) was named Vice President, and Dorothy Height, President of the National Council of Negro Women, became Secretary. Washington activist Esther Coopersmith was made Treasurer, and members of the Board included Radcliffe President Matina Horner, Sloan-Kettering biochemist Mathilde Krim, AFL-CIO official Jane O'Grady, actress Jean Stapleton, and Sharon Percy Rockefeller, the only woman in the United States whose husband was a Democratic Governor and whose father was a Republican Senator. Betty Dooley, who had been Executive Director of the CCC,

was named Director of the Institute. Early in 1980, the Institute staff moved out of the Rayburn office it had been sharing with the Caucus staff and settled in a southeast Washington townhouse, blocks from the Capitol.

11. When the 94th Class of Democrats met to select officers, Berkley Bedell of Iowa nominated Spellman for Secretary, but she reacted with mock horror, saying that "the Women's Liberation Movement would not approve" her filling a position typically reserved for women. Spellman then nominated Bedell as Secretary and Max Baucus of Montana submitted her name as Vice Chairman, adding that he thought women's liberation would approve of her serving in that office.

12. Caucus leaders generally listed congresswomen on the letterhead unless and until they were asked explicitly to remove a name. Claudine Schneider eventually joined the Caucus, but Lynn Martin, who paid 1981 first quarter dues, discontinued her affiliation soon after. (Thompson 1993, p. 10)

13. *Update* was not the first House newsletter specializing in issues affecting women. Several years before, Congressman Charles Rose of North Carolina launched "The Congressional Clearinghouse on Women's Issues." Rose's staff wrote it, printed it, and published it without aid of other members, and it was more of an advocacy periodical than *Update* became. In 1978 he decided that it was draining his resources and he decided to give it up. He approached the Caucus staff to see if they wanted to assume its publication, but when they learned that production costs, including in-kind expenditures, were $140,000 a year, they told him that they could not possibly accept his offer. During this period, Caucus staffers considered themselves fortunate if they were paid on time.

14. By the early 1990s, male contributions had risen to $900 annually, while congresswomen's dues had declined to $1,800. About seventy percent of Caucus operations were financed by the former (Thompson 1993, p. 20).

15. The now defunct Blue Collar Caucus bore a similarity to the Congresswomen's Caucus. Its membership was limited to those who had worked in blue-collar jobs before being elected to the House. Begun by house painter Edward Beard of Rhode Island, it never exceeded more than a half-dozen members and it disbanded after Beard was defeated for reelection. During its short life, the Blue Collar Caucus was sustained by the shared vocational background of its members rather than by the common experiences and orientations of a preponderant, sharply visible proportion of district residents. The same fate may well have been in store for a painfully small caucus made up of Representatives whose only qualification for membership was based on their gender.

11

The Congressional Caucus for Women's Issues: Survival and Growth

Following transformation of the Caucus, its survival was no longer in doubt. By admitting scores of congressmen as dues-paying associate members and by scrupulous collection of annual fees from female members, the Caucus assured its financial viability. The funds raised were used to pay the small staff needed to carry out daily routines, publish *Update*, coordinate activities of members, and generate legislative, public relations, and organizational initiatives for consideration by the Executive Committee. The co-chairs' unwavering commitment to the organization's goals added further to its integrity.

Organizational viability was accompanied by a shift in the focus of Caucus attention. When, before the purge, Caucus leaders were uncertain about members' shared commitment, valuable resources were invested in a search for consensus. When, before the admission of men, they were unable regularly to pay their staff, time and creative energies were devoted to a search for dollars. However, once membership was pared to like-minded women and men prepared to pay for their affiliation, the Caucus was able to concentrate exclusively on promoting their priorities. Between 1983 and 1992, CCWI members championed hundreds of legislative proposals calculated to advance women's economic, social, and cultural interests. Most were not enacted, but several were. Although some that passed represented a reclaiming of gains nullified by hostile Republican administrations, the period also witnessed a few legislative innovations. These years also saw the groundwork laid for policies and programs that would bloom one day in a more favorable political climate.

MARKING TIME, 1983–1992

Few House caucuses are powerful in and of themselves. Influence ultimately turns on the talents and political opportunities of individual members. Consequently, caucuses are effective if they are blessed with strong, persistent, purposive leaders and if a devoted rank and file is well placed within the leadership and committee structures. The Congressional Caucus for Women's Issues was amply endowed with the first of these characteristics even if deficient in the second. Its vitality during this period depended upon the commitment and energies of its co-chairs, the sense of direction they imparted to the CCWI staff, and the doggedness with which its members demanded action on women's issues from an often intractable Congress and from unsympathetic Reagan-Bush administrations.

Early in 1983, Congresswomen Schroeder and Snowe began a partnership that proved to be more harmonious and effective than any shared by previous CCWI cochairs. Differences in their style and temperament produced irritants unavoidable in competitive political relationships between strong personalities, and people close to one co-chair often complained about the behavior of the other—Schroeder because she received "too much" press, because she was too liberal, and because she was insufficiently endowed with a spirit of bipartisanship; Snowe because she took too long deciding whether she and other Republican women should support pending CCWI initiatives. Moreover, both were intermittently reproved by female colleagues because policy goals were not being achieved quickly enough or at all. From time to time antagonists also objected to the amount of control the co-chairs exerted over the Caucus.

Snowe bore the additional burden of trying to reconcile loyalties to Republican administrations with her feminist convictions. During this period, the Executive Committee maintained an official neutrality on the abortion issue, even though all of its Republican and most of its Democratic members were pro-choice. Snowe proved to be more critical of administration social policies than Heckler had been, but she had to be judicious about when, how, and how often to confront the White House and House GOP leaders. Her circumspection sometimes led to a delayed Caucus response and, on one occasion—involving the Family and Medical Leave Act—to a watered-down legislative substitute. In response to her critics, a staff assistant said "Snowe was in an awkward position because Bush vetoed our entire agenda." Nonetheless, dissatisfaction with the co-chairs was neither persistent nor acute, and the two adopted common positions on most issues affecting women directly. In fact, their joint support of legislative proposals increased over the years (Thompson 1993, p. 40). According to a former Caucus aide:

The members were competitive with one another, just as all members of Congress are. But they realized that they were only twenty people and they needed to overcome the petty stuff in order to achieve their goals. They were a small group, and not many people paid attention to them. They were reminded of their common ground when Speaker Foley tried to take over the Women's Reading Room for members of his staff. The members went nuts, and he backed off.

The CCWI staff played an important role in soliciting, aggregating, and disseminating ideas for Caucus initiatives. Proposals for new projects came from many sources—including the co-chairs, other Caucus members, women's interest groups, and staff members. Decisions to distribute "Dear Colleague" letters, letters to the administration, and other written communications were approved by the co-chairs and carried out by the staff so long as their messages were consistent with existing Caucus positions. All legislative initiatives, bill endorsements, and key strategy decisions were brought to the Executive Committee for its consideration. If both co-chairs endorsed a proposal, the Executive Committee usually approved it. Once approval was given, the staff set in motion what was referred to as a "Caucus Event" or "Action." Such an "Event" or "Action" could take the form of a press conference, a "Dear Colleague" letter, testimony before a committee, an invitation to an official to meet with the Caucus, or an endorsement of a legislative measure. If approval was not obtained, members would have to pursue the initiative in their individual rather than in their collective capacities. They introduced legislation of their own, appeared at hearings, lobbied other House members, and tried to get the attention of the press.

Executive Committee meetings were held about once a month with the co-chairs alternately presiding. More than one-half the members attended most sessions, a respectable number given the competing demands on their time. The co-chairs were the most active participants, but Congresswomen Boxer, Johnson, Lowey, Morella, Oakar, Pelosi, and Slaughter were among those who spoke up frequently. The CCWI began each year with a list of legislative goals and spent the remaining months trying to realize them. Members saw themselves as advocates and facilitators who were trying to make their priorities a part of the national agenda. *Update* and a three- to four-page Weekly Report were the principal means by which members and their staffs were informed about past and future committee and floor developments.

The precipitate growth in Caucus membership in the early 1980s after admission of congressmen was followed by more incremental gains through the remainder of the decade. Table 11.1 traces the change. Most Democratic women had readily joined the Caucus in the past, with their Republican counterparts slower to follow suit. By 1992, however, all nineteen Democratic and two-thirds of Republican congresswomen had joined the organization. Male Democrats had also increased their membership, to the point where more than 50 percent believed they were helped by identifying with the CCWI. This meant that Caucus leaders could count on at least the lip service of a growing number of colleagues who were well placed in the House power structure. The great majority of Republican men, Representatives who had never shown much interest in the Caucus, declined to affiliate. Their refusal to join both presaged and exacerbated

Tabled 11.1
Caucus Membership, 98th–103rd Congress (1983–1994)*

	% of Democrats		% of Republicans		% of House	
Congress	Female	Male	Female	Male	Female	Male
98th	85%	42%	33%	5%	64%	28%
1983-84	(11)	(107)	(3)	(8)	(14)	(115)
99th	83%	39%	36%	6%	61%	24%
1985-86	(10)	(94)	(4)	(5)	(14)	(99)
100th	92%	33%	55%	7%	74%	23%
1987-88	(11)	(83)	(6)	(12)	(17)	(95)
101st	93%	42%	55%	8%	77%	28%
1989-90	(14)	(102)	(6)	(13)	(20)	(115)
102nd	100%	53%	67%	8%	89%	35%
1991-92	(19)	(130)	(6)	(13)	(25)	(143)
103rd	97%	49%	58%	3%	87%	30%
1993-94	(34)	(111)	(7)	(5)	(41)	(116)

*Note: The count was made midway through the Second Session of each Congress.

difficulties the Caucus encountered when dealing with the Reagan and Bush administrations. Because Republican men in the House, the Senate and the executive branch blocked or diluted most CCWI legislative proposals, the Caucus was able to claim few important victories during this period.

President Reagan and his appointees did much to derail the Caucus agenda, and attempted to roll back feminist gains recorded during the preceding twenty years. One of the President's principal targets was affirmative action and other equal employment policies. He was partly successful in firing critics on the Civil Rights Commission, replacing some with conservative allies. And a Federal Communications Commission dominated by his appointees abandoned affirmative action guidelines when granting broadcast licenses, turning against a woman to whom an earlier FCC had granted a license.[1] The Reagan Justice Department sought to reopen affirmative action consent decrees entered into by more than fifty cities and counties with the object of weakening or eliminating negotiated agreements. A similar effort was made to dilute affirmative action rules followed by contractors who did business with the federal government. In the meantime, the chair of the Equal Employment Opportunity Commission, Clarence Thomas, abandoned the use of numerical guidelines and timetables to settle employment discrimination cases, and fewer claims were resolved.

The Justice Department also filed a series of briefs in Supreme Court cases supporting narrow interpretations of egalitarian and affirmative legislation and urging that other such laws be overturned. With the help of Reagan Supreme Court appointees, Title IX of the 1972 Education Act was construed narrowly so as to prohibit discrimination only in those educational activities receiving direct federal aid. Shortly after this decision—Grove City *v.* Bell—the Education Department announced it would stop enforcing institution-wide coverage of the Act. Later the Office of Management and the Budget declared it would save money by eliminating in 1990 many of the traditional census questions about housing, employment, and social services. Critics charged that OMB was motivated by policy, not financial considerations, noting that if the socioeconomic data were not collected, there would be no information base upon which to justify remedial legislation. Within weeks, OMB had second thoughts and restored most of the disputed questions.

Even though the Caucus took no official position on abortion, it supported family planning and efforts to prevent unwanted pregnancies. When President Reagan decided to stop family planning clinics from mentioning abortion as an option for pregnant women (the so-called "gag" rule) and to prevent international family planning organizations receiving U.S. financial aid from funding or encouraging abortions (the so-called Mexico City policy), the Caucus attempted, unsuccessfully, to reverse both. It filed a "friend of the Court" brief to overturn the gag rule, and it distributed a "Dear Colleague" letter calling for abandonment of the Mexico City policy. Some of these rear-guard efforts were temporarily successful. But even when they prevailed, Caucus members were required to invest scarce resources in battles they believed had already been won, and they had little left in reserve to undertake new legislative initiatives.[2]

Caucus leaders recorded a few successful "economic equity" initiatives affecting the tax code, child support enforcement, distribution of private and public pension and retirement funds, commercial credit, and child care. But these gains represented success at the margins, with more fundamental equity bills left to languish in committee or stymied in the Senate. Bills to equalize private insurance premiums and benefits for men and women, to conduct a comprehensive study of federal wage and classification systems, and to require businesses to provide family and medical leave to employees failed—largely because of administration resistance. Even some of the enacted proposals were left unfunded.

When measures designed to help women did succeed during the Reagan years, most were symbolic, inexpensive or both. Thus, Congress proclaimed a National Women's History Week, established a memorial to

"Women in the Armed Forces," approved a statue of Jeannette Rankin in the Capitol Rotunda, and authorized $500,000 to make the former residence of Alice Paul a National Historic Site. At the same time the House created a Special Committee on Children, Youth and Families,[3] and established a child care center for offspring of House employees.

These modest achievements did little to assuage the growing frustration felt by Caucus members and staff. They chafed under Gramm-Rudman appropriation caps that limited or eliminated funding for the few economic equity programs they had managed to pass, and they fumed as the Reagan administration used the appointment process, executive orders and administrative rulings to eviscerate feminist achievements recorded in the 1960s and 1970s. Toward the end of the Reagan years, the Caucus staff anguished over whether to concentrate on urging adoption of new programs or to try harder to salvage the old ones. For some, neither seemed achievable.

Caucus initiatives during the Bush administration fared a little better. The President's appointees made themselves available to CCWI leaders, even if Bush himself did not.[4] Between 1989 and 1992, dozens of executive branch officials from the National Institutes of Health, the Food and Drug Administration, the Small Business Administration, and the Surgeon General's office met with the Caucus. Secretaries and Assistant Secretaries of the Departments of Health and Human Services, Labor, Defense, State and Justice also appeared, in marked contrast to the unavailability of most officials in the Reagan administration. Apart from the President himself, only Secretary of Education Lamar Alexander refused (or left unanswered) Caucus requests for meetings.

The Bush years also saw fewer administration attacks on past feminist gains, but the President was particularly unyielding on abortion-related issues. Bills which permitted research on fetal tissue, which allowed funding for family planning organizations whose referrals and counseling included an abortion option, or which countenanced abortions in military hospitals and the District of Columbia were certain to be vetoed. On the other hand, Mr. Bush was more sympathetic than his predecessor to other Caucus-sponsored initiatives. Among the major successes of the period was passage of a Child Care Development Block Grant. The legislation authorized a five-year, $10.5 billion program to help the states improve the quality and availability of child care and to help low-income families pay for it. A second legislative triumph was realized only after prolonged resistance from the Bush administration. The 1991 Civil Rights Act overturned a half-dozen 1980s Supreme Court decisions that made it more difficult for women and minorities to prove they suffered job discrimination when bringing suit against employers. The Act also allowed claimants to collect compensatory damages if their suits were successful, although the Caucus was unable to eliminate ceilings on just how much plaintiffs could be awarded to compensate for damages suffered.

Passage of a handful of economic equity measures received less national attention, perhaps because most required little by way of new expenditures. Each addressed a specific discriminatory practice women faced as home-makers, employees, professionals, business entrepreneurs, and consumers. Caucus members agreed to take this incremental approach to achieve economic equity after the ERA was defeated. They reasoned that separate bills addressing discrete inequities were their only recourse once a broad-gauge constitutional amendment was no longer viable. And so the Small Business Administration was authorized to assist low-income women and minority entrepreneurs to gain credit, and the Department of Education was given a mandate to encourage women and minorities to enter the math and science professions. Congress also created a commission to study the "glass ceiling," attitudinal and economic barriers that prevented women from rising much beyond middle management level in the workplace no matter what their qualifications and performance records.

But these modest achievements were obscured by major defeats the administration dealt to the Family and Medical Leave Act (FMLA). Bush vetoes were twice sustained on a measure providing twelve weeks of unpaid leave to workers facing new parental responsibilities or medical emergencies at home. The Caucus had invested all available resources in the FMLA inasmuch as it saw the measure as central to its agenda. To have the bill passed twice by both the House and the Senate after bitter floor battles only to be vetoed by the President were losses difficult to endure.

The most dramatic Caucus accomplishment in the early 1990s was successful advocacy of women's health legislation. Until then, little atten-tion had been given to federal support of research on breast and cervical cancer, clinical tests on women's diseases, studies of osteoporosis and other bone disorders, and research on infertility. Among the most important developments during these years was issuance in June 1990 of a General Accounting Office report requested by the Caucus indicating that women had been systematically excluded or underrepresented in scores of clinical studies whose subjects ranged from heart disease to the overuse of prescrip-tion drugs. GAO's startling findings were not lost on Caucus members, and the following month they introduced more than a dozen bills aggregated under the general heading of the Women's Health Equity Act (WHEA). Most were largely ignored by Congress, but Caucus leaders began to get the attention of the Surgeon General, Antonia Novello, NIH Director Bernadine Healy, and Secretary of Health and Human Services Louis Sullivan.

In subsequent Congresses, the drive for women's health equity took on a life of its own. Early in 1991, the Caucus endorsed a package of 20 bills under an expanded, more ambitious WHEA rubric. Some were eventually vetoed by President Bush, but among those passed was a measure to increase low-income women's access to mammography and pap smears, authorization of more than $300 million for breast cancer research at the National Cancer Institute, and a bill to create an Office of Women's Health Research in the National Institutes of Health.[5]

WOMEN AND THE 103RD CONGRESS

The unprecedented increase in congresswomen elected to the 103rd Congress—from twenty-eight to forty-seven—and the large number of first-term women—twenty-four—had a dramatic impact on the composition of the CCWI. When twenty-two of the new women joined the Caucus, its Executive Committee increased by almost 70 percent.[6] In addition, the number of African-American women members went from three to eight, and, for the first time, the Executive Committee included Hispanic women. Among the former was Florida's Carrie Meek, who had once worked as a domestic, cleaning white women's homes; among the new Caucasian women was Lynn Woolsey, a former welfare mother. These additions brought to twenty-seven the number of states with women in the House and they provided a diversity unknown to the Caucus until then. Its members were now better able to craft proposals and map strategy likely to appeal to broader coalitions of women than was once the case.

Few of the nearly ninety first-term males joined the Caucus, partly because, as in the past, new members were discouraged by mentors from joining any LSO or other caucus until they were better adjusted to congressional life. Scandals associated with the House Bank and Post Office, together with growing distrust of public officials, prompted many of these same members to turn back to the federal treasury as much as twenty-five percent of their clerk-hire funds to demonstrate their probity and fiscal responsibility. This cost-saving action further discouraged new congressmen from parting with the $900 CCWI associate membership fee. Nevertheless, the CCWI totaled 157 by early 1994, eleven short of its 1992 record.

The qualifications and experience of the new women affected the stature of the Caucus. Almost all had served in public office before arriving in Washington—a larger percent, in fact, than the fledgling men who had come with them—and they needed relatively little time to learn how to make the most of legislative and institutional opportunities. They also benefitted from the willingness of party leaders to lean over backward to help them.

Almost two-thirds of the seventeen first-term women interviewed said they had asked for seats on the Appropriations, Ways and Means or Budget committees, not always because they thought they had a chance of securing such positions. For many, these initial expressions of interest would give credibility to the same requests in subsequent Congresses. Moreover, two Democratic women succeeded in their quests, three more were assigned to the coveted Energy and Commerce Committee, and the collective pressure exerted by the new female Representatives strengthened the hands of veteran women seeking these same, highly prized committees.[7] The sharp increase in the number of congresswomen assured their representation on all committees, thereby allowing perspectives and experiences peculiar to women to find expression on virtually every issue raised in the House.

The rise in Executive Committee membership had consequences for the group's organizational structure, leadership opportunities, and policy orientation. Increased numbers allowed the Caucus to establish five task forces.[8] This division of labor would allow members to focus more narrowly on selected priorities and to make more efficient use of their energies. It also changed the dynamics of the Caucus, allowing a larger number of congresswomen to create and exploit leadership openings. Task forces on Women's Health, chaired by Louise Slaughter, on Violence Against Women, chaired by Constance Morella, and on Economic and Educational Equity, led by Patsy Mink, were among those formed. Maxine Waters, who during her first term had been unhappy with the absence of CCWI leadership turnover and with the co-chairs' leadership styles, volunteered to chair a task force on Caucus Bylaws.

Creation of a fifth task force, on Reproductive Rights, reflected a fundamental shift in the group's stance on abortion. From its inception, Caucus members had agreed to disagree on this highly volatile issue, and the CCWI had never taken an official position on legislation construed as having pro-choice or pro-life implications. The retirement of Lindy Boggs in 1990, the 1992 election defeat of Mary Rose Oakar (two vocal opponents of abortion), and the election of twenty-four new congresswomen who went on record in support of the Freedom of Choice Act changed all that. When twenty-two of these women joined the Caucus, the group's pro-life voice was reduced to a whisper, and Caucus leaders pushed through Louise Slaughter's motion declaring the CCWI unequivocally pro-choice. A Reproductive Rights Task Force was approved minutes later. That no pro-life members of the Caucus, male or female, resigned from the Caucus as a direct result of the decision indicated they valued affiliation with a CCWI made more robust by the 1992 elections than they did ideological purity. Congresswoman Marcy Kaptur, for example, who generally opposed use of federal money to fund abortions for poor women, retained her position as Caucus Secretary.[9]

But it was not only its numbers, its diversity, its distribution among House committees, its increasingly active task forces, or its newly articulated pro-choice position that strengthened the Caucus's hand in the House. At least as important as any of these developments was the election of a President who was sympathetic to CCWI priorities. Caucus phone calls to the Clinton White House and to executive branch agencies were reliably returned—an experience almost unknown during the Reagan years. Issues of common interest to the President and the Caucus occasioned scores of meetings between representatives of the two. Hillary Clinton's staff met regularly with Caucus members while the President's ill-fated health care reform package was being hammered out. And Clinton appointees were far more familiar with the particulars of the Caucus's legislative agenda than members of preceding administrations had been.

The CCWI decision to support reproductive rights preceded by a few weeks President Clinton's executive orders reversing Reagan-Bush rulings on abortion-related policies. A day after taking office, he overturned the Reagan gag rule, the regulation prohibiting counselors at federally assisted family clinics from discussing abortions or referring clients for the procedure. He also lifted the ban on fetal tissue transplantation research; directed the Food and Drug Administration to reconsider import restrictions on the abortion pill, RU-486; reversed the so-called Mexico City policy, which proscribed federal grants to international family planning organizations that also performed abortions; and eliminated the Defense Department ban on privately funded abortions performed at overseas military medical facilities. Later Congress passed an appropriation bill allowing the District of Columbia to use locally raised revenue to pay for abortions for poor women, a practice prohibited since 1988, and restored to federal workers and their dependents abortion coverage under the Federal Employees Health Benefits Program, an option denied them since 1983.

Yet, the abortion issue triggered the most humiliating moment for many Caucus members, particularly first-term, pro-choice congresswomen. It occurred when the House attached the Hyde Amendment to a Health and Human Services appropriation measure late in June. Since 1976, Illinois Congressman Henry Hyde had successfully sponsored an Amendment denying women eligible for Medicare from using federal funds to pay for abortions. Early in the 103rd Congress, the Caucus's Pro-choice Task Force began to map strategy to prevent its passage once again. Task Force Chair Nita Lowey was a member of the Appropriations Committee, the panel that would bring the bill to the floor, and, after consultations with colleagues and the House Parliamentarian, she and her allies were confident House rules would prevent a vote on the Amendment. But Hyde used a little known procedure, sanctioned in advance by the Parliamentarian, to force a House vote and the Amendment was approved by a comfortable margin.

For some, adoption of the Amendment, though devastating, was not as galling as the debate preceding the vote. Some senior members described it as the most acrimonious they had ever witnessed, with one congresswoman told to "shut up," and African-American Cardiss Collins advised by Hyde that she had little understanding of the needs and wishes of her own constituents. Charges of racism and sexism were leveled at Hyde and others who spoke, charges which poisoned the atmosphere in the weeks that followed, in spite of Hyde's apology to Collins the next day. Afterward, Caucus leaders scheduled a series of meetings with Speaker Foley to express their anger and to advise him that they believed the Parliamentarian had been less forthcoming with them than he should have been. Many interpreted the events as a personal affront and the debate produced tensions between white and African-American Caucus members. The press described the outcome as a decisive loss for pro-choice forces and as a clear sign that the Freedom of Choice Act, codifying Roe *v.* Wade, was in trouble. Some reporters said the 1992 bumper crop of pro-choice women members had not had the anticipated impact. That the Hyde Amendment had been mildly weakened—allowing Medicare funds to pay for abortions in cases of incest and rape, as well as when the mother's life was in danger—was small consolation to those who were confident they would defeat it altogether (Margolies-Mezvinsky 1994, pp. 111–112).

Pro-choice forces recouped some of their losses when, in May 1994, the President signed a bill barring the threat or use of force outside abortion clinics and establishing criminal and civil penalties for those physically obstructing persons providing or obtaining abortion-related services. Yet, from the perspective of some pro-choice congresswomen, few of these positive developments broke new ground. Most simply lifted what they regarded as unconstitutional barriers to women, especially poor women, who decide to have an abortion. Some of the obstacles removed had been erected by the Reagan-Bush administrations and engendered by the antichoice atmosphere they fostered. Both Presidents had been supported by formidable pro-life constituencies, and their policies had been sustained because Congress was sharply divided on the issue and because the extraordinary majorities needed to override presidential vetoes could not be mobilized. Election of a pro-choice President altered the strategic framework within which the issue would be considered, however, and the CCWI decision to adopt a pro-choice stance removed all doubt about how this women-led group would allocate future resources.

But the struggle over reproductive rights was only part of the story of the 103rd Congress. After it convened, Caucus leaders believed they could reclaim ground lost during the preceding twelve years and devote more of their energies promoting new initiatives. They were no longer obliged to fight rear-guard actions to preserve policy victories won before 1980. Accordingly, they pressed for passage of measures vetoed or vitiated by hostile administrations and unsympathetic congressional colleagues. The Family and Medical Leave Act, introduced by Patricia Schroeder in 1985 and vetoed twice by President Bush, was signed by President Clinton weeks after his inauguration. A related act allowed federal employees to donate accrued annual leave time to a "leave bank," from which co-workers may draw when faced with a family or medical crisis.

In June, 1993, Congress passed the National Institutes of Health Revitalization Act, a measure responding to unresolved issues addressed by the 1991 Women's Health Equity package. The Act authorized development of infertility and contraceptive research centers and encouraged health professionals to enter these fields. It also provided for significant increases in research on breast, ovarian, and other cancers of women's reproductive systems. One provision authorized $40 million for research on osteoporosis, another required the National Institute on Aging to conduct research into the aging process, emphasizing menopause. The measure also gave permanent status to the NIH Office of Research on Women's Health. Among its mandates were to identify research projects on women's health and to insure inclusion of women in appropriate clinical trials. The Office was also given the task of monitoring and promoting the status of women physicians and scientists at the NIH and at NIH-funded institutions. Other health-related measures passed in 1993 authorized construction of a National Women's Health Resource Center in the District of Columbia, and provided for primary and preventive health care services for women at military hospitals and clinics.

The 103rd Congress also passed sweeping legislation in the area of domestic violence and sexual assault. A 1994 anti-crime act established penalties for spouses or partners who crossed state lines to continue their abuse; provided funds for rape crisis shelters and for training police, probation officers, judges and other officials who come in contact with rape victims and offenders; increased penalties for hate crimes against women and children; and strengthened federal "rape shield" laws regarding evidence of a victim's past sexual history. Childhood immunization legislation, more frequent and safer mammography testing for poor women, and child support enforcement measures designed to increase collection rates were among the dozens of Caucus-supported measures enacted. Late in 1993, Patricia Schroeder remarked:

"Issues of concern to women and families truly came of age during the first session of the 103rd Congress. We have never come so far so quickly. If we follow our present pace, the 103rd Congress will go down in history as the most productive ever for women." (*Update*, Nov. 30, 1993)

Among the congresswomen interviewed in 1993, few disputed this prospect. On matters of health equity, particularly, there was broad agreement on the pivotal role the Caucus played in placing women's health needs on the national agenda. According to one Caucus member:

The General Accounting Office's 1990 finding that females were excluded from NIH clinical trials was to women's health concerns what the Senate Judiciary Committee's treatment of Anita Hill was to the issue of sexual harassment. It may not have made as dramatic an impact publicly, but in Congress it sounded an alarm bell like you wouldn't believe. Even some men who never before supported health equity bills fell into line.

Caucus success fostering women's health needs and the eventual passage of the Family and Medical Leave Act should not be construed to mean that CCWI influence has become either ubiquitous or controlling. As has been noted, House caucuses are normally as effective as the ability and commitment of those who lead them and as strong as the convictions of those who join them. With these reservations in mind, mid-1993 interviews with thirty-five female and twelve male Representatives revealed a wide range of assessments about the scope and amount of Caucus influence. Most said the Caucus was more influential in the 103rd Congress than it had been in the past, if for no other reason than its increased female membership. Caucus members and the feminist policies they articulate were no longer readily marginalized, as was once the case, and their membership on so many key subcommittees provided a presence that could not be ignored. "Caucus influence was negligible before this year," said one veteran Republican congressman. "Now it can be described as moderate."

Still, its ability to shape policy was limited mainly to issues in which women have a direct stake. Unlike the Congressional Black Caucus, it could not trade a solid bloc of votes for acceptable compromises on a diverse range of policies. Most African-American members of the Congressional Black Caucus have constituent interests as well as their race in common. Women members of the CCWI, on the other hand, represented disparate constituencies and they understandably avoid speaking with a single voice on a broad spectrum of issues. Moreover, some male Representatives in the 103rd Congress denigrated or were oblivious to Caucus activities. One senior Democrat said the organization was irrelevant, and a senior Republican saw it as little more than a consciousness-raising group. A third congressman acknowledged he was unaware the CCWI admitted men.

Passage of Women's Health Equity bills was possible primarily because Caucus sponsors undeniably spoke for these measures' immediate beneficiaries. The same can be said about the anti-crime act's provisions addressing violence against women. These are social policies on which constituency differences and niggling partisanship are unlikely to undermine group consensus. And party leaders, particularly Democrats—perhaps because thirty-four of the thirty-five female Democrats were members in 1994—had come to rely on and respect the Caucus. One veteran Democratic congresswoman reported that she was regularly asked by the Speaker or the Majority Leader "what the Caucus thinks about an issue or if there is a Caucus position on an issue." Others said that the increasing number of Caucus members who would soon serve as chairs and ranking members of subcommittees could be expected to give the Caucus agenda a future viability greater still than was enjoyed in the 103rd Congress.

Some Caucus members suggested that while the CCWI continued to be an effective catalyst and advocate for feminist goals, it had "graduated" to the role of "agenda setter" in selected policy domains. They pointed out that affiliation allows congresswomen to initiate egalitarian and affirmational measures long before they were ripe for national debate. They also noted that the Caucus was the crucible in which ideas are allowed to germinate and in which they take on universal as well as practical relevance. And it was the Caucus leadership that capitalized on a "focusing event"—such as the Clarence Thomas confirmation hearings or the murder of a woman who had been battered when she was the wife of O.J. Simpson—to force an issue on to the national agenda.[10]

The larger size and increased potential influence of the Caucus were two of the reasons it decided to reconsider its bylaws during the 103rd Congress. In June 1994 the Executive Committee approved a draft produced by Maxine Waters' task force on the bylaws. Among the changes made was an imposition of term limits on all officers—no member could serve in the same office for more than one consecutive term—and creation of Democratic and Republican vice chairs. The bylaws also gave formal sanction to creation of task forces, defining their composition and powers, as well the procedures they were required to follow. A justification for the changes was offered by Nita Lowey, who said: "The Caucus is becoming a power, a power that is evolving. As our numbers increase, it is important to share that power."

The Caucus's future became uncertain when, in January 1995, the House eliminated Legislative Service Organizations. The new Republican majority prohibited LSOs from using clerk-hire funds to pay their staff, and LSOs were stripped of House office space and equipment allowances. Caucus members could continue to meet as they had in the past, but Caucus-supported Capitol Hill staffs were barred from promoting, coordinating and overseeing Caucus-sanctioned actions. Newsletters like *Update* would have to be published privately using non-public space if they were to be published at all.

The CCWI immediately designated itself a Congressional Membership Organization, as did most other now-defunct LSOs, and it began to consider ways of maintaining itself as a catalyst and as a source of ideas and strategic information. In a matter of weeks, its staff incorporated under the title "Women's Policy, Inc." By the end of January, it had moved out of the Rayburn Building and into temporary, private space. In the meantime, the new co-chairs, Democrat Nita Lowey and Republican Connie Morella, made it clear they were committed to CCWI's continued viability. The two shared professional and policy interests, and their close working relationship augured well for CCWI's future.

Although the Caucus had lost ten women members to election defeat, a retirement, and a bid for another office, some of their places were expected to be filled by at least a half-dozen first- and second-term congresswomen.[11] Another positive sign was the willingness of many male Caucus members to retain their affiliation, and to use their subscription allowances to pay for whatever package of weekly, monthly, quarterly and intermittent publications and reports Women's Policy, Inc. would be producing. The privatization of CCWI's information and communication arm made it possible for WPI to accept subscription fees from corporations, universities, non-profit agencies, women's groups and other private organizations, an option closed to CCWI while it was funded by public money and housed in public space. Funds raised through these subscriptions were expected to help sustain the CCWI's organizational integrity.

What remains to be addressed is how the Caucus has served its members and how it has served the House.

PERSONAL AND POLITICAL USES OF THE CAUCUS

Women active in the Caucus have enjoyed valuable personal and political advantages traceable directly to group affiliation. Although some of these benefits could have been obtained in other ways, such avenues would probably have required a larger expenditure of members' resources.

First, Caucus participation has permitted congresswomen to exchange specialized information economically. Second, it has allowed each to articulate her priorities to a sympathetic audience of legislative peers and administrative officials. Third, affiliation has made it possible for members efficiently to distribute the "women's issues" workload among themselves and among their staffs. Unlike their female predecessors—congresswomen who were usually viewed by public, press, and colleagues as experts on all matters affecting women—most Executive Committee members carved out a relatively narrow range of matters over which they could claim mastery and, perhaps, influence. They shared this knowledge with other group members and felt comfortable referring more challenging queries on matters outside of their expertise to other female House members, without feeling guilty about letting other women down.

Fourth, members' legislative aides specializing in women's problems have been integrated into the group's network and educated to the range of issues preoccupying the Caucus. Fifth, Caucus membership has tended to improve the representative image congresswomen have cultivated within their districts. Finally, congresswomen have gained a measure of personal satisfaction from meeting regularly with other women. The social support derived from this association has been one of the more important consequences of affiliation.

Information Generation, Retrieval, and Exchange

Meetings among themselves and with Cabinet officials have generated information about proposed legislation and administrative practices Caucus members would not otherwise so readily obtain. Sessions with leaders in the executive branch produce information which is either unknown or unavailable in a form useful to the Caucus. During the earliest such meetings, for example, Commerce Secretary Juanita Kreps was asked what proportion of Small Business Administration loans had been secured by women entrepreneurs; whether it was feasible to collect data on alimony and child-support payments in the 1980 census; and how more business-women could become regular participants in Commerce Department seminars. Kreps' staff looked into each of these matters and addressed them in a subsequent report to the Caucus. In 1991, Health and Human Services Secretary Louis Sullivan provided, at the Caucus's request, an action plan for addressing women's health issues within the Public Health Service. Shortly thereafter, NIH Director Bernadine Healy advised the Caucus about the steps her organization planned to take to compensate for previous exclusion of women from clinical trials.

Efforts to generate more data have grown out of the group's concern over gender discrimination in the Social Security system and in federal hiring and promotion. Over the years, the Caucus has been supplied with comprehensive, detailed information about how the language and implementation of social security laws have affected women. Among the questions raised were how often women move in and out of the labor force; the number of women who are "poor"; and the number not covered by Social Security Disability Insurance. Caucus members have been interested in the statistical techniques employed by the Social Security Administration to estimate the answers to these and other questions. They have also co-sponsored dozens of Capitol Hill briefings on such subjects as "Older Women's Issues" and "Women and Health," and the Caucus periodically publishes "Fact Sheets" and "Briefing Papers" on topical issues. From time to time, more comprehensive information was provided to members in the form of special reports on, for example, "Displaced Homemakers," and "Women, Children and Housing."

Perhaps the most useful information disseminated was that which the members communicated to one another. Meetings among themselves have been devoted to the intricacies and expected consequences of bills being considered by committees on which they served. Discussed were the legislative stage bills had reached, and levels of congressional and administration support. One first-termer in the 103rd Congress said the chief benefit of membership was the ready access she had " to large pools of information about issues affecting women and children." Another remarked that the Caucus is an "early warning system," providing members with usable information about late-breaking developments or about proposals in the pipeline. A veteran Republican woman welcomed the opportunity to share information within a constructive, bipartisan setting, a rare experience in a chamber so often divided along party lines.

In sum, Caucus activities permitted undiluted concentration on matters affecting women. The information developed and exchanged provided members with knowledge they would not have obtained at so little cost and promoted a familiarity with issues their feminist constituencies expected them to have. Caucus activities also helped participants estimate more accurately a legislative measure's implications for women. The insights they gain permitted them to adopt informed positions on matters to which they were expected to react publicly.

Articulation of Political and Personal Priorities

Caucus membership also provided participants with opportunities to express feminist policy preferences in an audience that was both sympathetic and capable of doing something about them. Congresswomen acted as a sounding board for their colleagues and made constructive suggestions. Members used Caucus meetings to fashion a consensus for pet projects and, together with the Caucus staff, to alert one another to developments that dovetailed with individual interests.

Congresswomen interviewed in 1993 said they benefitted from the "networking" they were able to set in motion during and after Caucus meetings. Several recalled finding co-sponsors for bills they had introduced. They were helped, they said, by Caucus discussions unexpectedly revealing the presence of like-minded colleagues. Others valued the ability to work collectively to identify problems women face and to create legislative remedies for these problems.

Members' concerns were often expressed to better purpose when offered in a meeting with a Cabinet member. Soon after the Caucus was formed Commerce Secretary Juanita Kreps was asked whether the Census Bureau was collecting enough information about elderly and single women. And Attorney General Griffin Bell was queried about progress being made by the Justice Department's Task Force on Sex Discrimination, and about his Department's role in a case involving alleged sex discrimination against a House staff member. During the Bush administration, the Caucus presented HHS Secretary Sullivan with a copy of its Women's Health Equity omnibus bill on the day it was introduced and asked him to support it. In 1993, Caucus members shared their views on health care with Hillary Clinton.

Thus, the Caucus facilitated interaction between congresswomen and administrative decision-makers and provided the former with frequent opportunities to influence both pending legislation and implementation of measures already enacted. Caucus sessions also permitted members to vent their frustrations before an audience whose members often held a common view but who, in any case, were usually polite enough to listen.

Division and Specialization of Labor

Members of most overwhelmingly male political and social groups expect the few women in their midst to make informed, "representative" observations whenever a women's issue arises. Male House members are no exception, and for years prior to Caucus formation, virtually all congresswomen were called upon to provide definitive answers whenever questions requiring a "woman's point of view" materialized. Consequently, female Representatives were expected to have more information at their disposal on a wider range of congressional concerns than their male counterparts, and, given the diverseness and complexity of national issues, they were unlikely to satisfy most expectations—including their own. Moreover, the usefulness of whatever response they gave was likely to be limited, even though those who requested the intelligence were prepared to act on it.

Formation of the Caucus made female Representatives more conversant with the intricacies of women's issues and facilitated among them a process that has been institutionalized in the House for decades—namely a division and specialization of labor. With each Caucus member specializing in two or three women's issues, perhaps because they were within the jurisdiction of standing committees upon which each serves, and with at least one member developing expertise on every issue, women Representatives relied on one another far more than they did in the past. Questions on women's issues about which a member knew relatively little were passed on to a Caucus member (or her staff) who had already invested the resources sufficient to acquire the anticipated expertise. Formation of Task Forces within the Caucus institutionalized this process.

Regular interaction among Caucus members also allowed them to determine on which women's issues they should concentrate. One first-term Democrat in the 103rd Congress said:

By being part of the Caucus, I have learned what other women's interests are and I have once or twice abandoned an issue because several other women were focusing on it. My involvement with it would have simply duplicated the efforts of others, and I picked something else that interested me that no other Caucus member was working on.

This division of labor among women members relieved them of the obligation of trying to know everything about all women's issues, and permitted them to make better use of resources that would otherwise be expended in an impossible task. Caucus membership made them better informed about a wider range of issues while, at the same time, relieving them of the responsibility of claiming a range of expertise beyond the grasp of any House member.

Educating Members' Staffs

Caucus members are not the only ones whose understanding was enriched by virtue of their affiliation with CCWI. At least one aide for each member acted as a liaison to the Caucus staff. These aides became important links between congresswomen and the Caucus's Executive Director. They were generally familiar with the entire range of issues with which the Caucus came to grips, as well as with the issues important to their employers. They met together monthly with the Executive Director to discuss pending organizational, policy, and legislative issues. The ideas and information generated at these sessions were shared with the congresswomen for whom they worked, and recently appointed liaisons were brought up to date about Caucus priorities and activities. Through 1994 *Update* and the Weekly Report served as the principal communication links among members' offices, and, although some congresswomen chose not to read them regularly, staff aides almost always did. Transformation of the Caucus into a CMO and the privatization of the CCWI staff may alter these practices.

In the past, office liaisons were allowed to represent congresswomen at Caucus meetings. Given the "members only" policy governing Executive Committee meetings, this is no longer possible.[12]

Improving Their Representative Image

Affiliation with the Caucus permitted members to be (or appear to be) more responsive to a specialized constituency within their districts. To gain the trust of voters, Representatives must find ways of identifying with them, of showing they have the same values, needs, and frustrations shared by constituents. For many legislators, service on a standing committee provides opportunities to demonstrate these qualities. A seat on the Veterans' Affairs Committee, for example, gives members a chance to personify ideas and symbols that resonate with meaning for people who once served in the armed forces. Congresswomen wishing to demonstrate a generalized concern for women's needs have no comparable standing committee to which to aspire, and the Caucus was a convenient instrument for refining their constituency appeal. The Caucus staff provided members with information, recent findings, and other materials they wished to share with female constituents and women's organizations. While CCWI was an LSO, each member, male, as well as female, received one hundred copies of *Update* to distribute to interested district residents and groups. Women's Policy, Inc. is likely to try to expand distribution of its publications, with private subscribers, as well as members, paying for the service.

Social and Emotional Support

Congress is a social as well as a political institution, and many of its members derive satisfaction from the emotional ties they establish among themselves. As has been noted, male Representatives often use the "gym fellowship" and collective ties to interest groups to fulfill social needs. Congresswomen, on the other hand, historically have had few opportunities to establish close personal relations with female colleagues. The Caucus filled this void.

It provided a vehicle for conviviality, affection, and good feelings. Members were generally friendly and considerate of one another, even when they disagreed on substantive issues, and the atmosphere in the Lindy Boggs Reading Room was cordial and occasionally ebullient. For many, meetings were a respite from the heavy pressures under which they labored. In 1978, one member described Caucus ambience in this way:

The Reading Room is like a men's smoking room. We stop in and get together in there and we are concerned about reaching a consensus. . . . We share our thoughts with one another and support each other as much as we can. We have developed an affection for each other.

In the same year, a staff aide described the feelings of the congresswoman for whom she worked as follows:

She spends a good deal of time on Caucus matters and she enjoys it a great deal. She finds it interesting and has great camaraderie with several of the other women. Some of them have running gags going on all the time. When they all met last week for a picture-taking session, with Muriel Humphrey, the atmosphere was almost electric. All those women together, filled with energy, and vitality, generating all sorts of good feelings. They are all supportive of one another, with very little competition among them.

Some of the good feelings referred to had their roots in the early days of the Caucus, when congresswomen traveled to China together. The occasion was both a personal and collective success, and a forty-five minute film of their sojourn won three television documentary awards and nearly captured an Emmy.

Since then the Executive Committee has more than doubled and competition among congresswomen has surfaced more often. A sub-group of African-American Caucus members has formed, and the unyielding united front of this tightly-knit coterie sometimes presented on selected issues occasionally irritated other members. But, for the most part, the warmth and comity of the earlier years have been preserved. Caucus camaraderie continues to lift members' morale. In 1993, one first-termer said:

Caucus members delight in one another's company. When I talk to other women, whether it's one-on-one or when we meet as a group, I get inoculated with vitality. I experience an excitement, a real high when sharing concerns with these kindred spirits.

Another new member remarked: "When I leave a Caucus meeting, I feel invigorated, revitalized."

The personal satisfaction to which these members referred is linked to the sense of community other Caucus members said they derived from their affiliation. One Democrat stated:

Life on the Hill is isolating. You do so much in the course of a day, working under intense pressure and unable to establish or savor personal relationships with the people you're dealing with. The Caucus milieu, on the other hand, offers a truly communal experience, and the frantic pace and pressures seem less restricting, even if they do not go away entirely.

Another member said:

The major benefits of the Caucus are cultural in nature. Women meet with other women in an all female setting, and you don't have to explain what you mean when you say something. Everyone present "gets it" the first time.

Not all Caucus members were able or willing to derive personal satisfaction from their association with one another. But most extracted pleasure from membership in the all-female group, and the social and personal support they gained from it were not the least important benefits derived from affiliation.

THE CAUCUS AND THE HOUSE

Informal groups in Congress have "assumed a leading role in performing functions historically associated with the party and committee systems" (Stevens et al. 1981, p. 428). They help identify national problems, develop possible responses to these problems, and build coalitions large enough to deal with them. Accordingly, group projects and activities assist the committee and party systems in dealing with issues inherently difficult for them. When, for example, neither party nor committee leaders take the initiative on issues deemed important by rank-and-file members, or when these leaders fail to provide for comprehensive consideration of pressing problems, informal groups often fill the void. In the process, they temporarily usurp the traditional roles of these leaders. In the long run, however, they serve to support rather than supplant those structures which are "primarily responsible for congressional policy output" by responding to pressures which would otherwise get little or no institutional response (Stevens et al. 1981, p. 435).

Thus, informal groups help to identify and deal with problems that fall between the cracks of standing committees, and they oversee the administration of programs in which these panels have little interest. At the same time, they may help party leaders establish a legislative agenda, build winning coalitions, or devise legislative strategies. The CCWI has tried to do most of these things, but its attempts to supplement the activities of party leaders have rarely gotten very far. Only during the fight for ERA-extension in 1978 did the Caucus effectively carry out the coalition-building, strategy-planning responsibilities customarily overseen by House leaders. Some have argued the CCWI played a leadership role on women's health issues as well. But the Caucus's successful efforts to carry out tasks normally reserved to committees are more readily documented.

The Caucus as "Committee"

Unlike committees, informal groups lack the authority to hold hearings, compel the testimony of witnesses, or rely on large appropriations for a skilled staff. Furthermore, they are unable either to act as custodians of bills considered for enactment or report measures for floor consideration. In some respects, however, they are the functional equivalents of standing committees, and the CCWI has carried out responsibilities normally undertaken by committees.

First, it has identified and dramatized problems which other congressional instrumentalities have ignored. It supported efforts to look into the plight of displaced homemakers and to respond legislatively to the startlingly pervasive tendency of husbands to beat their wives. It induced federal agencies to produce more information about such matters as the number of single and older women who were "heads of households," the proportion of guaranteed loans distributed to women by the Small Business Administration, and the percentage of women occupying responsible positions within the federal bureaucracy. Moreover, it helped amplify agency findings about the high frequency of unnecessary mastectomies, the abnormally high percentage of women addicted to Librium, Valium, and other drugs, and the problems produced by sexism in the armed forces. Issuance of the Caucus-requested GAO report on NIH-sponsored clinical trials was a defining moment for the future of women's health care.

Second, the Caucus has established a documented record of actions taken by government and the private sector to deal with issues directly affecting women. Relying upon reports from federal agencies, studies by the Congressional Research Service, testimony of cabinet officials, the research of staff members, and the efforts of private organizations, the Caucus has generated a body of information on part-time and flextime job opportunities in the bureaucracy, the treatment of women under the Social Security system, the accessibility women have to pension and retirement funds, and the changing status of women in the military.

Activities associated with this second function are not easily isolated from a third committee-like task performed by the Caucus—overseeing bureaucratic implementation of the law—since the former is normally a prerequisite for the latter. Among the matters examined by the Caucus have been the Commerce Department's implementation of equal employment opportunity and affirmative action programs; the extent to which the Federal Reserve Board was encouraging financial institutions to abide by the Equal Credit Opportunity Act; the application of bias-free admission standards by the service academies; and the inclusion of women in clinical studies of heart disease and lung cancer.

Fourth, Caucus activities have helped call attention to neglected and "invisible" issues affecting women, and they have altered the frame of reference within which these issues have been understood. Meetings of Caucus members among themselves and with representatives of women's groups, labor and business organizations, and federal administrators have permitted an exchange of ideas which stretch the awareness participants have about problems facing women. These sessions institutionalized public-private sector collaboration, inasmuch as conferees were able to relate to, and build on, one another's experiences and insights. A meeting with labor union leaders in 1977, for example, revealed that women were affected more adversely than men by hard times in the retail industry because, as sales personnel and cashiers, the former made up a majority of industry employees. Moreover, many were close to retirement when dismissed and, after years of low wages, they were often left with no nest egg, no health insurance, and no retirement benefits. Unemployment, then, is as much of a "women's issue" as equal pay for equal work.

Practices which are inegalitarian on their face are simple enough to recognize as such. But patterns of behavior resulting in discrimination not immediately identifiable as gender-based sometimes have to be teased out of empirical observations initially gathered with little thought to their implications for women. Sources of the discrimination are similarly obscure. As a result, legislative remedies that speak to problems most citizens believe have nothing to do with gender have to be couched in terms they can understand, accept, and support. The Caucus has been an important instrument for defining and generating responses to these public needs, and the years between 1977 and 1994 saw a sharp increase in affirmative legislative proposals.

Finally, the Caucus has established mutually beneficial links with an interest group clientele. Feminist organizations have had readier access to Congress than they had before 1977, and congresswomen have been better able to take advantage of the systematic support and reinforcement of groups such as NOW, AAUW, and the Older Women's League—in much the same way as Agriculture Committee members, for example, have relied on leaders of the country's farm organizations. This rapport was important for extension of the time limit for approval of the Equal Rights Amendment, for promoting economic and health equity legislation and for passing the Family and Medical Leave Act. The nexus between the Caucus and women's groups provided a clearer voice for a female public unwilling to mimic traditional images of women. It has also made Congress a more representative institution than it would have been had there been no Congressional Caucus for Women's Issues.

NOTES

1. In 1978, the FCC began granting preferences to female applicants for television and radio licenses, although regulations governing the practice were never formally adopted. The woman in question was awarded a radio license under the preference system, but the action was challenged and ultimately overturned by a federal court. The woman, joined by the FCC, appealed the decision. However, by 1986, the FCC was controlled by Reagan appointees and it reversed its policy. The agency argued the guidelines were unconstitutional because there was no evidence of past discrimination by the Commission. That 3 percent of television stations and 9 percent of radio stations were owned by women had little impact on the administration.

2. The most notable of their triumphs was adoption of the Civil Rights Restoration Act, a measure nullifying the Supreme Court's narrow interpretation of Title IX. Final passage required two-thirds vote in each chamber to override President Reagan's veto.

3. Six of the Committee's first twenty-five members were congresswomen.

4. The Caucus sent at least four letters requesting meetings with President Bush. Each received a negative response. His inaccessibility became a sore point with Schroeder and she appeared on the House floor with copies of the letters glued to a poster board. She then addressed the House for one minute about the President's contempt for the Caucus and later missed few opportunities to criticize him for it.

5. Caucus members urged that the NIH Office of Women's Health Research be permanent. They feared that a temporary office would have difficulty obtaining funding. However, they could not get their colleagues to agree, and the Office's permanence was not vouchsafed until June, 1993, when President Clinton signed the NIH Revitalization Act.

6. Two first-term Republicans, Jennifer Dunn and Deborah Pryce, declined to join the Caucus during the 103rd Congress. When all other new congresswomen affiliated with the group, the Executive Committee increased from twenty-five to forty-two. This number includes veteran Republican Marge Roukema, who began serving in the House in 1981, but did not join the Caucus until 1994. The figure excludes District of Columbia Delegate Eleanor Holmes Norton, who is a Caucus member. The number fell to forty-one in mid-1994 when first-term Missouri Democrat Pat Danner resigned from the Caucus.

7. First-termers Carrie Meek and Lynn Woolsey were assigned to the Appropriations and Budget committees respectively. The intense interest in the Appropriations Committee exhibited by a half-dozen new women members could only have helped similar, successful efforts of the more senior Nita Lowey, Rosa DeLauro, and Helen Bentley. Their appointments brought to a record seven the number of women serving on that Committee.

8. Two additional Task Forces were established later in the session—one on Children, Youth and Families, the other on Older Women. Both were created after Select Committees on these subjects had been abolished.

9. About a dozen males who were members of the Caucus in the 102nd Congress did not affiliate in the 103rd, but it is difficult to know whether their actions were affected by the Caucus's decision to adopt a pro-choice position. A few members drop out in every Congress and some return in subsequent Congresses. Those who leave often explain their departures as efforts to save money. Most males departing in 1993 offered this reason. Kaptur's public position is that she is neither pro-life nor pro-choice. Like many other House members, she may not object to a woman's right to choose but believes that federal funds should not be used to pay for an abortion. In 1994, she was one of thirty-five Democrats to sign a letter to the Speaker stating she would vote against the health care reform bill if it included abortion coverage. Danner's resignation from the Caucus may have been rooted in a pro-life orientation, although she waited more than a year after the CCWI adopted its pro-choice stance before leaving the organization.

10. Kingdon (1984, p. 99) points out that problems often "need a push to get the attention" of policy makers. The push is sometimes provided by a "focusing event," such as a crisis or a scandal that serves as a powerful symbol that "catches on."

11. Eight Democratic incumbents, six of whom were first-termers, were defeated. Marilyn Lloyd retired and Olympia Snowe won a seat in the U.S. Senate. Soon after the new Congress convened, all four new Democratic congresswomen—Sheila Jackson-Lee, Zoe Lofgren, Karen McCarthy, and Lynn Rivers—expressed an interest in joining the Caucus, as did Republican Sue Kelly. At the same time, second-term Republican Deborah Pryce affiliated with the group and Democrat Pat Danner rejoined the Caucus after having left it six months earlier. The only congresswoman to resign from the organization was Democrat Elizabeth Furse. Furse had been elected to a second term by the narrowest of margins and was angered by Congresswoman Susan Molinari's campaign appearance in her Oregon district. The New York Republican, a CCWI member and a feminist, called for Furse's defeat and the election of a Republican male who was supported by Oregon's formidable conservative coalition. Furse believed that the potential Caucus membership of a half-dozen new, pro-life Republican women would dilute the organization's pro-choice stance.

12. The "members only" policy was adopted because congresswomen were regularly sending staff to represent them at Caucus meetings. Sometimes as many as fifteen staffers and three members showed up for these sessions. Little was accomplished and subsequent meetings would attract even fewer members.

Part V

Past, Present, and Future

12

Changing Gender and Legislative Roles

The patterns of recruitment, integration, and behavior traced in the preceding chapters are closely linked. Pathways congresswomen followed en route to the House affected the pace of integration, as well as the activities in which they engaged once they arrived in Washington. Of course, their congressional experiences were colored by additional factors, most notably the prior attitudes male members held about women in general and congresswomen in particular. But male attitudes and behavior have not been immune to the influence of female aspirations and achievement. They, too, are linked to changes in the recruitment and behavioral patterns described here.

LINKAGES

Although a large majority of widows of congressmen who died in office did not succeed their husbands, those who reached the House in this way constituted 50 percent of the women who served from 1917 through World War II. They and many other congresswomen of their era did not have the political or occupational experience possessed by most of their male colleagues, having secured their seats through family connections and substantial wealth. By and large, they were recruited and elected because of characteristics ascribed to them rather than because they had exhibited either political skill or public achievement.

Women who entered the House with no political experience were usually accorded gentlemanly deference but little professional respect by male House members. Their access to important committee and party leadership positions was either denied or delayed. They invested their energies in subjects deemed peculiar to the interests and capacities of members of their gender, and only infrequently identified with issues directly affecting women. Their limited political experience served to reinforce an existing male bias against women in politics, and their activities in the House were sharply curtailed. Thus, recruitment through ascription contributed to unequal treatment and circumscribed behavior.

Women elected after World War II and through the mid-1960s brought considerably more political and vocational experience with them, and, while they were by no means fully integrated into the workings of the House, they were given a greater measure of responsibility and respect than that accorded their female predecessors. Past achievements made more credible their search for policy-making opportunities on committees once routinely closed to women. And party leaders began to distribute secondary leadership positions among them. They tended to be younger than earlier congresswomen, better prepared to serve in Washington for an extended period, and willing (and able) to join the increasing number of informal House groups. During this period, Congress continued to be a male institution. Nevertheless, women began to provide the House with leadership on legislation dealing with equal-rights issues, sharing with congressmen the credit for securing approval of these measures.

Most of the congresswomen elected since the mid-1960s have brought with them even more politically relevant experience than their immediate predecessors, and they have been more interested in pursuing careers in Congress. Political achievements and increased seniority have made requests for assignment to valued House committees more difficult to refuse, and these women became more conspicuous among members holding middle-level strategic and integrative party posts. They were also less apt to accept "token" party positions.

As obstacles to informal group membership dissolved, an increasing number of women gained access to important internal communications channels. Fuller participation in House activities brought increased respect from male colleagues. And precongressional achievements, along with the confidence and purposiveness such success fosters, induced congressmen to take more seriously the feminist orientations most of these women brought with them or acquired once in Washington. In 1977, they established a Congresswomen's Caucus to help them represent American women and "feminize" the legislative agenda. In 1981, the Caucus gave limited membership to male Representatives, men who expected affiliation with what was once an exclusively women's group to reap legislative and political rewards. The newly titled Congressional Caucus for Women's Issues grew incrementally in succeeding years, with the sudden burst of new women members in the 103rd Congress giving it unprecedented opportunities to shape policies affecting women.

The implications of these developments are significant. They suggest that the electorate has become sufficiently impressed with the political skills and experiences of female candidates to choose women whose qualifications address the job responsibilities House members normally undertake. They also indicate that palpable achievements, rather than ascriptive attributes (so important in the years before World War II) contribute to the victories of most contemporary congresswomen. Changes in the criteria the electorate has been applying to evaluate successful women candidates have expanded the limits of the political opportunity structure and established new role models for women aspiring to House seats. They have also produced a more democratic political recruitment process.

Democratization of the process had a demonstrable impact on public policy because the newly recruited women were willing to become champions of a population component long denied a direct voice in the House. These women also formulated legislative and administrative remedies addressing women's needs, and they converted electoral success into legislative effectiveness. As has been argued in preceding chapters, congresswomen have come to be accepted as equals by a majority of the men with whom they serve, and male chauvinism has become an institutional as well as a political liability. Congresswomen have also begun to acquire influence within their political parties, in the committees on which they serve, and in the informal groups with which they identify. Thus, an expanded political opportunity structure and fuller integration into the House have led to a more egalitarian system of mutual obligations.

Congresswomen have also contributed to the adoption of programs designed explicitly to help women—to promote their economic well-being, to augment their social options, and to nourish their physical and mental health. Female House members today represent not only the roughly 600,000 people who live in their districts. They also serve the tens of millions of other women who make up more than 50 percent of the country's population. The benefits they provide are fashioned by perspectives and values which, although currently shared by many male Representatives, were absent from the range of views held by virtually all former members of Congress.

It is possible that some institutional responses (formation of the Caucus for Women's Issues, for example), some policy initiatives (the Women's Health Equity package, for instance), and, particularly, the increased saliency of selected women's issues (sexual harassment and women's health, for example) would have materialized even if the recruitment and integration patterns described here had not evolved as they did. But it is more reasonable to believe that these responses, initiatives, and emerging issues would have been retarded at the very least if the democratizing impulses resonating through the body politic had not been fostered by congressional women.

Moreover, changes in recruitment and integration patterns of congresswomen produced and accompanied alterations in gender role orientations. These shifts in the way male and female House members interact with one another constitute developments even more fundamental than the policy reorientations reflected in Congress's handling of women's issues. Policy reorientations are vulnerable to manipulation by Presidents and lawmakers who are in a position to redefine both national priorities and the frameworks within which these priorities are understood. Role orientations, on the other hand, are apt to be more durable, and they are likely to have significant policy consequences, as well.

Consequently, the last major task of this study will be to explore changes in the way House members have come to identify themselves as men and women and as lawmakers. A broader perspective within which to view changes in gender and legislative role orientations—a perspective that takes into account the source of gender roles and the stages through which these roles undergo alteration—helps illuminate not only where the House has been with respect to the relationship between male and female members, but also where it may be going.

MYTH AND GENDER ROLES

In 1923, when the newly elected Idaho state legislature convened in Boise, the handful of women legislators present were told how they might avoid tarnishing their image as lawmakers. "Never carry a pocketbook or bag," they were advised, and "never point to an audience with a lorgnette or pencil." They were warned not to wear skirts so short that colleagues would look at their ankles instead of listening to what was being said, and they were instructed, above all, to avoid wearing flapper earrings (Swank 1978).

If male lawmakers were given a similar set of guidelines, the strictures were certainly of a different sort. Furthermore, we can be reasonably confident that sartorial pointers were not the only ones communicated to either group. Legislative leaders must have surely reinforced the already learned differences in the expected comportment of men and women, driving home to their apprentices more comprehensive behavioral norms for each.

The principal source of these norms, then as now, are the myths underlying cultural discourses, social institutions, and individual psyches (Bem 1993, p. 2)—those that shape and reinforce values and provide a framework for understanding the world around us. These myths define and enforce morality, express and codify beliefs, and generate and legitimize the rituals and practices that constitute behavior. Myths serve human needs by reinforcing convictions, by justifying resentments, and by providing bonds of common feeling (Janeway 1971, p. 42). They also promote roles for people to play, and we come to understand who we are and what we do in terms of mythically inspired role delineations. Moreover, our behavior is perceived and evaluated by others within the perspectives of these role prescriptions: "what people are can only be understood in terms of [what we believe] . . . they ought to be" (Parsons 1953, p. 18. Emphasis in original).

The social order in the United States, like that in virtually all other countries, prescribes different patterns of behavior for men and women (Epstein 1988, p. 6). As a result, the expectations we have for each vary considerably, and gender roles, unlike, say, occupational roles, are ascribed to men and women. These assignments are distributed among members of each group according to physical characteristics. Elizabeth Janeway maintains that gender roles are of some use in that "we find in them definitions for living which we feel to be deeply needed" (1971, p. 74). But she is far more concerned about the negative consequences of calculating and inferring behavior on the basis of ascribed roles, and she takes pains to distinguish between them and roles which are "based upon activities and the relationships that grow out of these activities" (p. 83). Being a woman is not the same thing as being a teacher or a lawmaker. The role of the first is assigned and its occupants have virtually no say in accepting or rejecting it. The expectations others share about their behavior emerge from a stereotype, and those to whom it is ascribed are judged by criteria having no necessary relationship to their full range of skills and talents.[1] Adoption of occupational roles, on the other hand, involves some discretion for those who fill them, and these roles are defined by what these people *do* rather than who they *are*.

Holders of ascribed roles are often pigeonholed not only with respect to the behavior in which they are expected to engage, but also with regard to the psychological orientations they hold. Thus, expected predispositional differences between men and women are a part of our mythology. According to this mythology, men are purported to be confident, self-reliant, and serious; women are expected to be insecure, dependent, and frivolous. The former are viewed as assertive, rational, and objective, the latter as tentative, emotional, and subjective. Men are perceived as deliberate and original, women as impulsive and reactive. From the constraints of the mythology flow important consequences. Men are customarily evaluated in terms of instrumental success; women are measured by expressive standards. Thus, the former are supposed to be task-oriented, employing their managerial skills, competitive proclivities, physical aggressiveness, and thirst for power to achieve material, economic goals—goals pegged to survival. Women, on the other hand, are perceived as people-oriented. They manifest a sensitivity to those around them, a kindliness toward the deprived, a desire to please others, and an inclination to reduce tensions and establish bonds of affiliation. Their goals are social.[2] Descriptions of the two are prescriptive, as well, and men and women are channeled into "different and unequal life situations" (Bem 1993, p. 154).[3]

Based upon these mythically inspired variations between men and women, observers are inclined to place different values on typically male and typically female behavior, and there is little doubt that they see the former as preferable to the latter. "Masculine initiative and activity are valued more highly than feminine decorum and passivity," says Janeway (1971, p. 97). Women are regarded as the "second sex," and they are experienced by men as "other" rather than as equals (de Beauvoir 1953). They are identified in terms of their biology while men are regarded as social beings (Bem 1993, p. 2; and Epstein 1988, p. 6). Moreover, they are likely to be more conscious of their subordinate role and its restrictions than men are aware of the advantages they enjoy by being perceived as possessing the preferred attributes. Epstein notes "Because men . . . have held greater resources than have women, it is their version of human nature that has been most evident. Furthermore, their version has been adopted by most women as well as men" (1988, p. 8). Once women recognize their subordinate state, they construct an identity consistent with it (Bem 1993, p. 3). Characteristics consistent with that identity are patience, endurance, and, above all, the ability to please (Janeway 1971, p. 114).

To the extent that women live up to expectations linked to their ascribed role, they are considered "normal" females, even if subordinate human beings. If they adopt behavior patterns perceived as male, they are considered "aberrant women." They cannot be both normal women and admirable people, however, and, as a result, they find themselves in what some have called the "double bind" (Janeway 1971, p. 104; and O'Leary 1974, p. 812.)

Historically, distinctions in gender roles have been the most important impediment to women's full participation in the American political system (Kirkpatrick 1974, p. 239). And, despite the relative success of contemporary women aspirants to elective office, few hold important public positions. Even when they overcome deterrents to public life, they still must hurdle gender-related obstacles within the political settings in which they find themselves.

ASCRIBED AND ASSUMED ROLES

When women Representatives come to Washington, they are perceived by others as fulfilling two very different types of roles. One is "assumed" and is linked to legislative politics, with all of the representational, political, and constitutional obligations this occupation implies. The other is "ascribed" and emerges out of those anticipated differences between male and female behavior which are nourished by stereotypes and embodied in our cultural mythology. Male Representatives have little difficulty performing the two simultaneously. The qualities, orientations, and goals they are expected to possess as men are the very same attributes which are most valued in the House, an institution which is defined as "male" by both men and women lawmakers. (See Chapter 4.) The confident, assertive demeanor of unselfconscious and rational males—congressmen who are determined to solve the fundamental problems affecting the economy and national security and who work in an arena in which male hegemony is the norm—is precisely the behavioral mode that has been most admired by House members generally.

Congresswomen, on the other hand, have, until recently, managed their behavior differently. Like most women, they were taught to be sensitive to the feelings of others, to demonstrate kindliness, concern and affection, and to please others—qualities useful for producing social amelioration. They are, moreover, mindful of the stereotypical traits ascribed to them. While determined to exhibit characteristics which will convince colleagues and constituents that they are capable lawmakers, they are aware (sometimes painfully so) that there is a repertoire of gender-role items which most people accept as appropriate to the identities of women. Many of these items are believed to be incompatible with the legislative role. Thus, they confront the double bind, a reluctance on the part of others to define them as both normal women and successful legislators.

One of the earliest evocations of the problem in the House was provided by a male Representative, former Congressman Jerry Voorhis of California. In 1947 he observed:

In recent years an increasing number of women have been elected to Congress, particularly the House. As I watched their work I could see how difficult is the problem they face, for they must steer a course midway between two fatal mistakes. The woman member must take care that she does not base her appeal for the cause in which she is interested on the fact of her womanhood. She cannot expect chivalry from the male members when it comes to casting their votes. Neither, on the other hand, can she hope to gain a strong position for herself if she attempts the role of hail fellow well met and tries to be like a man. What she has to do is to be simply a member of the House who quite incidentally happens to belong to the female sex. (p. 35)

The tactic proposed by Voorhis, then, was to steer a middle course between legislative role demands, on the one hand, and behavior that was expected of a woman by virtue of her gender, on the other. Some congresswomen followed that course, others did not. Even though no two of them responded to the challenge in precisely the same way, it is possible to distill a few common patterns of adaptation that emerged over time. As will be made clear, some ignored or were unable to fulfill their legislative responsibilities. Others tried to mask their identities as women, while, at the same time, adopting a professional orientation toward lawmaking. And recently many women have worked to change conventional role orientations and expectations.

STAGES OF ROLE CHANGE

To describe and analyze the adaptive responses of these women, it is useful to conceive of role change as occurring in four stages, stages defined by the repertoire of role items a role occupant is prepared to exhibit.[4] In the beginning stage, role behavior is *undifferentiated*. Persons holding a position in the social structure are but dimly aware of the role requirements or the expectations of others, and they proceed either to neglect their responsibilities or fulfill them in a diffuse and unspecialized fashion. They may organize components of the role (components which include orientations, activities, and expectations) in the most general of ways and offer inconsistent or superficial responses to demands made upon them. At stage two, role behavior becomes *differentiated*. It reflects an awareness of the demarcation between appropriate and inappropriate action, and an inclination to abide by the constraints normally imposed upon the role occupant. The nature of the responsibilities undertaken, the limitations observed, the privileges claimed, and the rewards accepted conform to expectations about what constitutes appropriate behavior for persons holding such a position.

The third stage of role development, role *de-differentiation*, occurs when some items of one or more role components are abandoned, or when items heretofore found exclusively in the component or components of another role, become part of the first role's repertoire. Both may occur at the same time. Stage four of the transformation process is the *reconfiguration* period. During role reconfiguration, the "major role elements of a given role, redefined under the process of de-differentiation, may become stabilized or rigidified." Thus, the cycle is returned to stage two (or stage one if persons unfamiliar with the role requirements are suddenly asked to live up to them), and the groundwork is laid for future circumstances and events to bring about another role de-differentiation (Lipman-Blumen 1973, p. 116).

GENDER AND LEGISLATIVE ROLE TYPES

This conceptualization of role change is useful for explaining shifts that have taken place in the way congresswomen have identified themselves— as both women and lawmakers—while trying to reconcile these identities with one another and with the expectations they knew others held about them. Moreover, our understanding of these shifts is substantially improved when distinctions are made among types of gender and legislative role orientations.

Over the years, female Representatives' identities as women have been reflected in three types of gender role orientations. At the same time, their behavior as elected officials has been exhibited in three types of legislative role orientations. Variations in the orientations of both roles are summarized in Table 12.1. One gender role orientation is associated with a woman's precongressional career as wife, mother, and homemaker, and is defined largely by a status most recognize as subordinate to that of men. This type is referred to here as *Gentlewoman*.[5] A second type linked to gender is revealed in a congresswoman's efforts to minimize the impact of her identity as a woman by avoiding those items of her ascribed role which are too easily interpreted as typically female. This woman is labeled *Neutral*. Role behavior which exhibits pride in being a woman and which openly challenges the mythic superiority of males is referred to as *Feminist*.[6]

The legislative role type defined as *Amateur* applies to congresswomen whose grasp of the lawmaking role is undifferentiated, whose career aspirations are virtually nonexistent, and whose policy concerns are superficial. A congresswoman who fulfills lawmaking responsibilities normally carried out by a House member, who contemplates and often realizes an extended House career, and whose policy interests are broad, but exclude those which

Table 12.1
Types of Gender and Legislative Role Orientations

Gender Role Orientations		*Legislative Role Orientations*	
Type	*Brief Description*	*Type*	*Brief Description*
Gentlewoman	Accustomed to performing subordinate, traditionally female responsibilities	Amateur	Lawmaking orientation: undifferentiated Career aspiration: negligible Policy concerns: superficial
Neutral	Inhibited about exhibiting behavior calling attention to her identity as a woman	Professional	Lawmaking orientation: differentiated Career aspiration: developed Policy concerns: truncated
Feminist	Unselfconsciously proud of her identity as a woman and insistent on equality with men	Colleague	Lawmaking orientation: de-differentiated Career aspiration: integrative Policy concerns: comprehensive

threaten to place her in a position of representing women's interests, is referred to as a *Professional*. And a congresswoman whose behavior promises to alter the traditional legislative role, whose career aspirations include not only extensive House service, but full integration into the life of the House, and whose range of policy interests knows no necessary limits is defined as a *Colleague*.

Accordingly, most of the widows who succeeded their husbands in the years before World War II, along with some who came to Washington later, constitute one of the three combined gender and legislative role types. Their relationships with male Representatives were significantly influenced by their previous identities as congressional wives, and they were treated by male House members as *Gentlewomen* with all the deference and condescension the term implies. Furthermore, they possessed an "undifferentiated" understanding of their legislative role and were either unable or disinclined to take their lawmaking responsibilities seriously. Thus the term *Gentlewoman Amateurs* is an appropriate one to describe their combined gender and legislative role orientations.

Many of the women who came to the House after World War II and through the early 1970s had previously served in public office and they adapted to their responsibilities differently than did most widows. Unlike the *Gentlewomen*, these women had carved out independent lives and careers. Their political identities were distinct from those of their husbands or other relevant males, and they sought the acceptance of congressmen as equals. Moreover, their experience in public life had given them the opportunity to become familiar with the lawmaking role and to "differentiate" between appropriate and inappropriate behavior associated with that role. They harbored behavioral and career orientations that were "professional," and this professionalism added to their effectiveness as legislators. As will be demonstrated, however, these *Neutral Professionals* were inclined to hedge their behavior in the House so as to avoid threatening the men with whom they served.

Most congresswomen belonging to the third combined types of gender and legislative role orientations began to arrive in the House in the 1970s, although a few who came to Washington before that period also qualify. One difficulty in defining this combination is that its contours are still being shaped in the 1990s. Unlike the women *Neutrals*, members of this group often go out of their way to accentuate their identities as women. They are not nearly as concerned as most of their female predecessors about "rocking the boat," nor do they take extraordinary pains to please the men with whom they work. Rather they have been inclined to adopt a "feminist" perspective, even if it means that their behavior is unacceptable to some Representatives.

This ongoing "de-differentiation" is reflected in the increased tendency of both male and female House members to represent women as a discrete constituency, to promote and organize groups in and out of Congress to serve that end, and to evaluate legislative proposals, no matter how gender-free they may seem on their face, in terms of their impact on women. It has also had the effect of increasing the frequency with which women seek and secure secondary leadership positions and valued committee assignments. Thus, female Representatives in this category are referred to as *Feminist Colleagues*.

Further elaboration of the three combined role types makes possible a fuller account of changes in the contributions women have made to the legislative process, as well as a more comprehensive description of how women elected to the House have changed over time.

Gentlewoman Amateurs

Not all women elected to succeed their husbands were objects of exaggerated deference, and a number were serious about their legislative responsibilities. Edith Nourse Rogers, Frances Bolton, and Margaret Chase Smith are three who were among the exceptions. But most who reached the House through the matrimonial connection were *Gentlewoman Amateurs*, and, according to some Representatives interviewed during the 97th Congress, at least one congresswoman fitted comfortably into that category as recently as the early 1980s.

For many of these widows, the responsibilities of congressional office were understandably inconsistent with their identities as women. They had neither held public office nor, indeed, had they even contemplated the prospect. They were wives, social secretaries, and mothers. Their brief congressional tours filling vacancies entitled them to the remainder of their husbands' wages, and the sympathy and support of male Representatives. It is difficult to imagine House members and their spouses treating the new congresswomen differently than they had when the latter were wives of living Representatives. Politicos in Washington and in home districts were likely to offer these fledgling House members little more than the respect due a grieving widow.

At the same time, most of these women were disinclined seriously to adopt well-developed legislative role orientations. They either neglected or rarely exhibited role items associated with lawmaking. They introduced few legislative proposals, and only infrequently participated in committee and floor deliberations. Constituency service was a task with which they were probably more familiar, but even this function was likely to be performed in a relatively desultory, diffuse fashion inasmuch as abbreviated House service provides little incentive for promoting constituency satisfaction. Congresswomen who succeeded husbands with whom they had worked closely were likely to be better able and more willing to carry out requisite responsibilities. Their grasp of legislative role behavior was almost certain to be more fully developed than those of widows whose familiarity with their husbands' vocations was minimal. But even the former depended heavily upon their deceased husbands' staffs and the *Gentlewoman Amateurs* left Congress at the first opportunity.[7]

Neutral Professionals

Most of the women elected to the House who did not succeed their husbands were experienced politicians. Many brought mature political and legislative role orientations to Washington, and a few had compiled outstanding records as public servants. They were independent, career officeholders who had managed to overcome community prejudice against politically ambitious women. And they had developed a self-confidence and sense of purpose to which the heady experience of election victory contributes so materially.

But these women knew that as members of a small, conspicuous minority, they would be operating within a goldfish bowl. Behavior that would be overlooked or quickly forgotten if engaged in by a male Representative would trigger derision or worse if enacted by a congresswoman. There were simply too many House members and constituents who did not need much of an excuse to interpret their activities within the framework of a female stereotype. *Gentlewoman Amateurs* faced no such threat. They had never claimed expertise as politicians and they had retained their reputations as normal women. But the *Professionals* had no intention of relinquishing a rare opportunity to be effective lawmakers and they were determined to persuade colleagues, constituents, and themselves that they were both successful women and able House members, characterizations which for many observers represented a contradiction in terms.

Individual responses to the challenge varied, but most reflected a dominant pattern—that of stripping their public images of features which could be interpreted by others as typically female. Some of these *Neutral Professionals* resolved the identity problem by limiting their House careers to a few terms, thereby reducing the period during which they would be compelled to cope with the contradiction. These women served long enough to leave a small imprint on the House and on American political history, but not long enough to suggest pretensions to a career in Congress or to gain sufficient seniority to warrant consideration for leadership positions.

Jessie Sumner, for example, left the House after four terms at the age of forty-eight even though she probably could have been reelected in the same district for as long as she cared to serve. Iris Blitch also settled for early retirement, relinquishing her seat during a period when most Representatives left the House only because of advanced age or because the voters insisted upon their departure. And Clare Boothe Luce declined to run again after serving only two terms, a decision influenced in part by personal tragedy.

But Luce was unusually sensitive to the burden of the female stereotype, and she and Representative Helen Gahagan Douglas, although adversaries on many substantive issues, agreed to avoid public confrontations, or even the semblance of a rivalry, lest the press interpret the dispute as a "hair-pulling, fingernail-scratching catfight" (Shadegg 1970, pp. 122–123). Differences in their foreign policy views led the press to feature prospective legislative performances of the two as a "battle of the glamour queens," and reporters found it useful to suggest that Luce and Douglas would "claw one another," once the 80th Congress convened. "The implication was that we were frivolous, vacuous women rather than serious, committed politicians," Douglas observed, and she decided "to clear the air of such insulting innuendo" as soon as possible (Douglas 1982, p. 198).

Efforts to deal with ascribed and assumed roles were also reflected in the objections some congresswomen raised to their being called "Gentlelady," or "Congresswoman." Both Mary Norton and Frances Bolton preferred to be referred to as "Congressman," and they chastised male House members who did otherwise. Bolton, who spent twenty-nine years in Congress, also became the unofficial guardian of female deportment, cautioning other female House members about chewing gum and wearing curlers on the House floor (Lamson 1968, p. 44). Certainly there were times when women tried to use feminine charm to achieve their ends, but they were more likely to mask their sexuality. A young woman serving in the 95th Congress described the precautions she took to retain a professional demeanor. "I work hard, and I don't run around with the men here. I don't flirt with anyone," she added, "and I have gained the admiration and respect of all my colleagues."

Attempts to improve their reputations as lawmakers took other forms. Several actively sought influence in policy areas traditionally viewed as beyond the competence of women, while systematically avoiding association with feminist issues. Positions on the Armed Services and Science Committees, among others, were aggressively pursued, even if not always secured. Margaret Chase Smith, for example, fashioned an image as a frugal, defense-minded member of the Naval Affairs and (later) Armed Services Committees. At the same time, she scrupulously avoided being identified as a feminist. Many *Neutrals* shunned the ERA until massive support for the resolution weakened claims it was exclusively a woman's issue. Exceptions to this practice in the late 1940s and early 1950s included a handful of mostly conservative female Representatives who had established reputations of indifference to most women's issues and who had stockpiled credit as *Neutral Professionals* among male Representatives by rejecting radical, "bleeding-heart" causes.

Many of these *Professionals* also aspired to party leadership positions, vacancies on the more prestigious standing House committees, and membership in selected informal groupings. Marjorie Holt's bid for a Republican leadership post was rebuffed, but Katharine St. George was assigned to the Rules Committee, even though she had to wait fourteen years before receiving the appointment. And the highly respected Julia Butler Hansen did not allow the uneasiness she perceived among Appropriations Committee members to affect her leadership as chair of one of that panel's subcommittees (*Congressional Quarterly Weekly Report*, July 10, 1970, p. 1748). To be sure, some of these women wrote off informal groups as unimportant and as having little impact on their influence as House members. On the other hand, many *Professionals* found affiliation with the more structured groups useful for fulfilling lawmaking responsibilities.

A common tactic employed by some *Neutrals* was to maintain a low profile, remaining as inconspicuous among their colleagues as legislative goals and continuation in office would permit. They thereby reduced the frequency with which they would have to choose publicly between risking, on the one hand, the disapprobation of male members by appearing too "womanly," and, on the other hand, denying their integrity and spontaneity as people by masking their identities. When taking the initiative or when forced to react, they sought to steer the path recommended by Congressman Jerry Voorhis in 1947, that is, to "be a member of the House who quite incidentally happens to belong to the female sex" (p. 35).

Thus, many tried to avoid appearing emotional, tentative, or impulsive on the one hand, while, on the other, dispelling suspicions that they were in competition with male House members. After her 1962 interviews with male and female House members, Gehlen (1969, p. 39) noted that the women most accepted by men were those who were "rational rather than emotional, articulate, intelligent, and not too prudish; that is, the men did not have to modify their own behavior greatly to accommodate them." The most competent women, she added, had "moved the most toward changing their ascribed role behavior from women to a pattern much more nearly like that of men."

Sometimes they were caricatures of congressmen, never more than when they resorted to cliché-ridden House rhetoric, the language used ad nauseam to impose a dispassionate, impersonal cloak over fundamental disagreements. At the same time, they emphasized constituency service at the expense of lawmaking activities because the former, exercised outside the ken of other members, did not entail the risk of rubbing male Representatives the wrong way. Moreover, it gave congresswomen more opportunities to reflect a sensitive, caring image without appearing "soft" (and therefore vulnerable) in the eyes of other Washingtonians.

But, by maintaining a low profile, by masking their identities as women, and by trying to balance assigned and achieved roles, most *Neutrals* were, in effect, opting for the subordinate status that females have traditionally held in their relationships with males. For underlying these efforts carefully to manage their behavior and avoid calling attention to their gender was the more fundamental objective of not upsetting men. They wanted to be effective legislators, and they could not gain that reputation by "rocking the boat." They did not want to sacrifice the interests of their constituents, but neither did they challenge institutional norms and leadership prejudices which defined them as "other."

Most *Neutrals* suffered the inequitable distribution of House rewards in silence and patiently waited for the seniority rule to elevate them to subcommittee chairs on less-sought-after standing committees. They took credit for successful policy initiatives, many of which were important, but they eschewed the dramatic claims and grandstanding of some male colleagues. And they were inclined to be more flexible, more willing to compromise, and less insistent about imposing their own vision of "the good, the true, and the beautiful," on legislation. One exception to this pattern was Oregon's Edith Green, whose strong views on education policy contributed ultimately to her leaving the Education and Labor Committee and relinquishing her subcommittee chair after eighteen years in the House. Some informants serving in the 95th Congress believed she was hounded off.

Feminist Colleagues

Green's assertive style foreshadowed that of other women who began to come to the House in the early 1970s, about the time she left. They were just as sensitive to the potential contradictions implicit in their roles as women and lawmakers, but, unlike *Neutrals*, they felt little obligation to make concessions in order to adjust to these conflicts.

The new type of congresswoman saw herself as a representative of both her constituents and American womanhood. She adopted feminist causes and she did not necessarily abjure or dilute behavior which could be defined as typically female by those who were of a mind to do so. Neither did she go out of her way to placate men with whom she worked—expecting rather than seeking equal treatment, and objecting when she did not get it. Thus, the latest group of congresswomen has begun to alter expectations males have about their behavior while at the same time modifying role orientations that all House members, male as well as female, possess as lawmakers. The process defies precise description, however, because role de-differentiation has not yet run its course. As a result, the new gender and legislative roles that will emerge are impossible to depict with certainty. Their origins and some of their manifestations are worth exploring, however.

Women who qualify as *Feminist Colleagues* began to come to the House before the 1970s, but the woman who, more than any other, heralded and facilitated the role change was Bella Abzug. The Manhattan Democrat conceived of women as having a policy orientation unique to their gender and more humane, more civilized, more liberated, and more desirable than any combination of public policy visions men could possibly conjure up. Her feminism and her belief in the superiority of women's policy orientations were articulated often and unambiguously. She was, in fact, Congress's first female chauvinist, and in the journal she kept during her first year in the House, she envisioned the United States and the world as better places because women were represented in Congress in proportion to their numbers in the population. Such a Congress, she said, would not stand for laws that discriminate against women. Neither would it countenance the absence of national health care and child care legislation. She asked rhetorically, would Congress

consent to the perverted sense of priorities that has dominated our government for decades, where billions have been appropriated for war while our human needs . . . have been neglected? Does anyone think that a Congress with large numbers of women would ever have allowed the war in Vietnam to go on for so long, slaughtering and maiming our children . . .? (Abzug 1972, pp. 30–31)

Many House members first viewed Abzug's behavior with surprise and amusement. Her like had never been seen in the House chamber, and male Representatives exchanged knowing winks and nods whenever she was recognized in committee or on the House floor. Before long, congressmen who found her behavior objectionable turned to ridicule, and her detractors said that when she rose to speak, she cost her side twenty-five votes. For some, there seemed to be no limit to the lengths to which she would go to persuade the House to accept her views. Her criticism of other Representatives and of Congress as an institution seemed unrelenting, and it was difficult to predict what she would do next. She thus became an object of hostility among congressmen who were accustomed to a reasonably predictable network of professional interactions. Now they had to work with a woman whose behavior made them uneasy about their own identity and about what responses they were expected to make. Inasmuch as she saw herself as representing a national constituency of women, the poor, and opponents of the Vietnam War, Abzug was unconcerned about her colleagues' discomfiture.

Ironically, one consequence of Abzug's behavior was legitimation of the *Feminist* gender orientation of other congresswomen—those whose personal styles were not quite so threatening. Male Representatives who agreed with Abzug's goals, but found her tactless, were now more willing to support the objectives of women who were as feminist in their orientations, but less controversial. Unlike some *Neutral Professionals* who preceded them, many of these women did not ask other Representatives to call them "Congressman," but insisted, instead, that they be referred to as "Ms." They were not interested in making male House members forget they were women. Rather, they tried to reinforce their image as politicians and legislators in order to gain acceptance as women colleagues.

Some who did not arrive in Washington as feminists soon defined themselves as such when they realized that men came to Congress with "a presumption of competence," but that women came with "a burden of proof" (Plattner 1983, p. 784). And if the new generation of congresswomen was not as outspoken as Abzug had been, the difference was not a substantial one. Millicent Fenwick maintained that women should not go into politics unless they were "prepared to take a perfectly firm stand like anybody else—just the way men do and the way all successful women do . . . without being afraid of being called aggressive" (Lamson 1979, p. 32).

While they did not go out of their way to bait male Representatives, they were not overly anxious to please them, either. Whereas *Neutrals* were flexible, willing to compromise, prepared to settle for less rather than more, *Feminists* were more insistent upon achieving their goals. They were sometimes openly critical of the House and its members and less willing to "go along" if it meant only that they would "get along." During a legislative session that was particularly unproductive and rancorous, Patricia Schroeder suggested that the Congress hire "nannies for the boys," aides who would serve warm milk and cookies—nourishment which would contribute to better House decorum and more attention to business. Hiring nannies would improve the employment situation, as well, she argued, while encouraging "this body to deal with substance once again" (*Congressional Record*, March 14, 1978, p. 6,845).

Younger and more active feminists harbored fewer inhibitions about being women. The romantic relationship between a widowed congresswoman and a divorced first-term Representative became an open secret soon after the latter took his seat in the 97th Congress. A few years earlier, Martha Keys had married Indiana's Andy Jacobs after her first year in Washington. They met while serving together on the Ways and Means Committee. She had been divorced for less than a year and was cautioned to postpone marriage until after the 1976 election lest it affect the contest's outcome. But she refused to "apply a political test to her personal life," and she went ahead just as male Representatives in similar circumstances might have (Kronholz 1976, p. 1). A second marriage between House members occurred in 1994, when New Yorkers Susan Molinari and William Paxon tied the knot.

Meanwhile, social and professional relationships between male and female House members became less strained, more natural, with congressmen prepared to accept women as equals and with congresswomen convinced that, no more than any male colleague, they were under no obligation to do and say things simply to gain the approbation of men. And if the strains, anxieties, and frustrations of legislative life prompted them to utter expletives, people began not to notice.

Changes in gender orientation were accompanied by changes in legislative role behavior. In the House, women increasingly began to stake out leadership positions on feminist issues, insisting, unlike some predecessors, that their identities as women made them better qualified to write laws addressing the needs of women. Several devoted large shares of time to mobilizing support for the Equal Rights Amendment and, later, for extension of the time period during which states could approve the measure. Most of these same women joined House caucuses to help them frame and pursue issues important to them. At the same time, they began to evaluate legislative measures within a feminist perspective. They asked how proposed bills might affect poor women, pregnant women, married women, widowed women, handicapped women, military women, bureaucratic women, and women in general. Few measures were immune from this kind of scrutiny, and congresswomen began to redefine what was customarily referred to as "women's issues."

Acquaintance with the details of a broad range of legislation alerted them to the fact that bills most important to women were not necessarily those which mentioned women's rights directly. Proposals dealing with pensions, jobs, taxes, savings, insurance, health, and welfare were critically important. They proceeded to exploit the rationalizations that *Neutrals* and antifeminists had used to justify their contempt for feminist issues. For years, the latter had maintained that legislation which singles out women as beneficiaries either ignored the fact that all bills ultimately affect all people, or that women were not the only ones deserving special treatment. Now feminists were saying that bills which did not single out women for benefits had a profound effect on women as a class and that a feminist perspective was indispensable to any lawmaker worth his or her salt. In the process, they raised the consciousness of male colleagues, politicized issues which had until then been considered private rather than public in character, and began to alter the national agenda.

Increased activity, greater visibility, and readier male acceptance led to more appointments to valued House and party leadership positions. Not all who benefitted were *Feminist Colleagues*, but all capitalized on the drive for broader representation of women on important House instrumentalities. After a while, congresswomen invited males to join their Caucus, perhaps as much to preserve the organization's financial viability as to foster a spirit of colleagueship. Over one hundred accepted the offer and began contributing annual dues. Mixed membership helped awaken and reinforce dormant feminist sympathies of congressmen who had not been sensitive to the breadth of issues affecting women as a constituency. In the meantime, the Democratic House leadership began regularly to consult with Caucus leaders, increasing their influence and agreeing in 1983 to assign the number "one" to the reintroduced ERA Resolution.

Recent accessibility to the Chowder and Marching Society and its functional equivalents constitutes erosion of one of the few remaining obstacles to the colleagueship women are currently trying to establish. Admission of women to these once all-male social and political organizations is a signal of further role de-differentiation.

Change in the legislative role orientation of *Feminist Colleagues* has been no small achievement. Some male Representatives continue to define virtually all congresswomen as aberrations. For them, female refusal to accept a subordinate status or to shape behavior to please men is puzzling, at best. They are troubled as much by the fact that women are doing something new and different, as they are by the fact that women are not doing something old, something expected. Moreover, de-differentiation of gender and legislative roles has not been made easier by decisions of some congresswomen to reject the *Feminist Colleague* role orientation. Beverly Byron, who served in the House until 1992, attributed her more traditional view to the fact that she had never run into inequity in her own experience and, therefore, "It's hard for me to understand people who have doors closed on them" (Plattner 1983, p. 785).

But, for many male Representatives, female members have found a way to change the ascribed identity of women by engaging in behavior that is both new and familiar. Most congressmen had difficulty accepting the style of an Abzug, but many find the gender role orientation of women House members in the 1990s not terribly different from those of women with whom they went to college and graduate and professional school. Moreover, it is identical to that of the women who lead feminist groups within their own districts. Thus, just as contemporary congresswomen are reflecting the values of a growing number of such groups, their own legitimacy is being validated in the expectations of male colleagues by the activities and the ubiquity of these same organizations.

In the meantime, the legislative role orientations of many contemporary congresswomen are having an effect on the substance of measures lawmakers are considering. Private, social relationships once considered beyond the authority or jurisdiction of Congress—issues such as domestic violence and sexual harassment—are increasingly being introduced into its deliberations. More and more male, as well as female, lawmakers are acting on the belief that power relationships in private, domestic arenas have significant public consequences. Subject matter once deemed inappropriate for congressional consideration has become part of the public discourse.

Male members' understanding of their representative responsibilities has also been undergoing change. Congressmen have become less likely to ignore or treat cursorily the women's constituency and they are much less diffident today about identifying with and even dramatizing their support for feminist causes. As Republican William Gradison has said: "It's a new ballgame. Anyone who fails to consider the impact of legislation on women does so at his or her peril" (*New York Times*, March 3, 1983).

Congressmen who once treated the women's movement as a source of humor and its goals as insignificant are now less likely to exchange wise cracks and locker room jokes about matters which women have always taken seriously. Although the term "legislator" may not conjure up images of male and female lawmakers for some House members, these holdouts are a shrinking minority. Congresswomen have begun to shed their subordinate status in the eyes of most male Representatives. If "colleagueship" has not quite been established among male and female members, the groundwork has been laid for them to begin to ignore gender differences when dealing with one another professionally.

THE FUTURE OF CONGRESSIONAL WOMEN

Predicting the future of women in the House is tempting, but difficult. It assumes that the factors affecting patterns of recruitment and behavior are fully understood, and that their impact is grasped well enough to forecast future developments. But all these factors are not well known, and the manner in which many of them influence one another is more uncertain still. Nevertheless, what happened in the past and what is happening today permit formulation of a few contingent generalizations.

First, the number of women who enter public life is likely to increase if young women continue to aspire to and train for vocations heretofore dominated by men. That the precongressional career convergence of female and male Representatives has narrowed significantly is worth noting in this connection (Whicker et al. 1993, p. 149).

Second, the increase is especially likely to occur if women pursue those vocations whose skills and orientations are valued in a political setting. The legal profession comes to mind, but it is by no means the only one. Business administration, the communications and education fields, and sales are also useful. In the meantime, military service, an experience on which so many male candidates have been able to capitalize, is no longer as common an advantage, and, barring another protracted war, women aspirants to the House are less likely to be required to find ways of matching male opponents' claims of patriotic self-sacrifice.

Third, the number of prospective female candidates having palpable qualifications for national office will increase if the number of women elected to state, county, and local offices continue to grow. Recent findings indicate women in public offices are just as likely as men in similar offices to seek another term, "to aspire to some other elective or appointive position and to desire ultimately to be a governor or to hold national office" (Carroll 1993, p. 204). They are, in short, "strategic politicians."

Fourth, increasing numbers of women strategic politicians make more likely their presence in those congressional districts featuring elections to "open" House seats. Therefore, more women with political experience and an established constituency will be in a position to seek party nominations for an office they have a reasonable chance of winning.

Fifth, women elected to Congress are more likely to possess the legislative and political virtuosity valued in that body if voters, would-be candidates, and those who recruit them place a higher priority on achievement in public life than they do on contestants' ascribed characteristics.

Sixth, inasmuch as a significant proportion of women officeholders support feminist positions and work on legislation benefitting women (Carroll 1993, p. 205), the larger the number of women elected to the House, the greater the likelihood that the feminist agenda will be addressed by Congress (Mezey 1993, p. 266).

Seventh, as its female membership grows, the Congressional Caucus for Women's Issues will strengthen its roles as a catalyst and as an advocate for egalitarian and affirmational public policy. If its male membership grows and more of these men take CCWI's objectives seriously, the Caucus will be in a position to shape the national agenda, especially if the President is sympathetic to its goals. Much will depend on the commitment and political skills of its leaders. Among CCWI's stiffest challenges will be retaining its bipartisan orientation in the face of continued, fractious party and ideological divisions within the House, and accommodating the needs of the growing number of African-American women. Much will also depend on whether the Caucus can be as effective as a CMO, as it was in the 103rd Congress as an LSO.

Eighth, greater numbers of congresswomen will also lead to their improved positioning within the committee structure, with gains likely on Ways and Means, Appropriations and Budget Committees, as well as on those panels already possessing prominent female representation. Legislative and spending measures considered by these committees are likely to be examined in terms of whether they promote feminist goals. This does not mean that party, ideology and constituent interests will exert less influence on female members' roll call votes than has customarily been the case. What it does mean is that feminist initiatives taken by congresswomen at the introductory and intermediate stages of the deliberative process will be fully integrated into the language of a bill well before partisan or ideological concerns are brought to bear in a public vote. Under these circumstances such provisions are likely to be less vulnerable to excision or dilution.

Ninth, the highly developed political ambitions and skills that contribute to congresswomen's elections and to their institutional effectiveness are likely to result in their selection for top House leadership positions in the foreseeable future.

Tenth, all of these developments are likely to promote fuller integration of women into the workings of the House and to blur differences in the legislative and gender role orientations of female and male Representatives.

Generalizations of this sort cannot be exhaustive. Social changes contributing to role de-differentiation are still at work, and the nature and implications of female colleagueship will not be fully understood until it has been acted out and accepted by both men and women inside and outside of Congress. Consequently, no one can say when or in what form "role reconfiguration" will emerge. Furthermore, the full integration of women into congressional life will not take place until myths about women's subordinate social role are rejected. Only then will it be possible for ascribed qualities to be peeled away from the identities of men and women, for women's identities as "other" to be discarded, and for gender distinctions to become irrelevant while men and women are undertaking the public's business together.

NOTES

1. This is not the place to explore the nature *v.* nurture controversy, but recent literature on the subject suggests that there are relatively few characteristics that are inherently female or inherently male, and that even with respect to most of these traits, differences between men and women are more matters of degree than of kind. Furthermore, men and women often possess in significant measure characteristics attributed to the other gender. As a result, we can make few if any reliable predictions about the political orientations and behavior of individual men and individual women solely on the basis of their physical characteristics (Hubbard 1990, p. 69).

2. Attributes purported to be peculiar to members of each gender (and which they are often expected to learn because of their gender) are defined by Bardwick (1976, p. 31); Iglitzin (1974, p. 26); Janeway (1971, p. 8); and Kelly and Boutilier (1978, p. 31), among others.

3. But Bem points out that the gendered personality is more than a collection of masculine and feminine traits. "It is also a way of looking at reality that produces and reproduces those traits during a lifetime of self-construction." Thus, the concept of the "gendered personality" embraces a process, as well as a product (1993, p. 154).

4. Lipman-Blumen (1973) defines these stages while discussing role change during crisis. They lend themselves to gradual, or evolutionary change, as well, however, and to variations in the role behavior that congresswomen have exhibited over time.

5. The term is an awkward one, but it was adopted because it was commonly used in floor debate by congressmen when referring to congresswomen. See Chapter 4.

6. The term "feminist" has been defined differently both among those who call themselves by that name and among those for whom the word produces revulsion. It is employed here in much the way most dictionaries define it: One who supports "the doctrine advocating social, political and all other rights of women equal to those of men" (*The Random House Dictionary of the English Language*, Second Edition, 1987).

7. These women did not always leave willingly. A few were forced to alter their intentions to run for reelection by party leaders at home.

Appendixes

Appendixes

Appendix A
Women Elected to the House of Representatives, 1916–1995
(in order of election)

Congresswoman	Date of First Election	Term Expired	Political Party	State
Jeannette Rankin	11/ 7/1916	3/ 4/1919[a]	R	MT
	11/ 5/1940[b]	1/ 3/1943		
Alice M. Robertson	11/ 2/1920	3/ 4/1923	R	OK
Winnifred S.M. Huck	11/ 7/1922	3/ 4/1923	R	IL
Mae Ella Nolan	1/23/1923	3/ 4/1925	R	CA
Mary Teresa Norton	11/ 4/1924	1/ 3/1951	D	NJ
Florence P. Kahn	2/17/1925	1/ 3/1937	R	CA
Edith Nourse Rogers	6/30/1925	9/10/1960[c]	R	MA
Katherine G. Langley	11/ 2/1926	3/ 4/1931	R	KY
Ruth Hanna McCormick	11/ 6/1928	3/ 4/1931[d]	R	IL
Ruth B. Owen	11/ 6/1928	3/ 4/1933	D	FL
Ruth B.S. Pratt	11/ 6/1928	3/ 4/1933	R	NY
Pearl P. Oldfield	1/ 9/1929	3/ 4/1931	D	AR
Effiegene L. Wingo	11/30/1930	3/ 4/1933	D	AR
Willa McCord Eslick	8/ 4/1932	3/ 4/1933	D	TN
Virginia E. Jenckes	11/ 8/1932	1/ 3/1939	D	IN
Kathryn O'Loughlin McCarthy	11/ 8/1932	1/ 3/1935	D	KS
Isabella S. Greenway	10/ 3/1933	1/ 3/1937	D	AZ
Marian W. Clarke	12/28/1933	1/ 3/1935	R	NY
Caroline L.G. O'Day	11/ 6/1934	1/ 3/1943	D	NY
Nan W. Honeyman	11/ 3/1936	1/ 3/1939	D	OR
Elizabeth H. Gasque	9/13/1938	1/ 3/1939[e]	D	SC
Jessie Sumner	11/ 8/1938	1/ 3/1947	R	IL
Clara G. McMillan	11/ 7/1939	1/ 3/1941	D	SC
Margaret Chase Smith	1/ 3/1940	1/ 3/1949[f]	R	ME
Frances P. Bolton	2/27/1940	1/ 3/1969	R	OH
Florence R. Gibbs	10/ 1/1940	1/ 3/1941	D	GA
Katharine E. Byron	5/27/1941	1/ 3/1943	D	MD
Veronica G. Boland	11/ 3/1942	1/ 3/1943	D	PA
Clare Booth Luce	11/ 3/1942	1/ 3/1947	R	CT
Winifred C. Stanley	11/ 3/1942	1/ 3/1945	R	NY
Willa L. Fulmer	11/ 7/1944	1/ 3/1945	D	SC
Emily Taft Douglas	11/ 7/1944	1/ 3/1947	D	IL
Helen Gahagan Douglas	11/ 7/1944	1/ 3/1951[d]	D	CA
Chase Going Woodhouse	11/ 7/1944	1/ 3/1947	D	CT
	11/ 2/1948[b]	1/ 3/1951		
Helen D. Mankin	2/ 2/1946	1/ 3/1947	D	GA
Eliza Jane Pratt	5/25/1946	1/ 3/1947	D	NC
Georgia L. Lusk	11/ 5/1946	1/ 3/1949	D	NM
Katharine P.L. St. George	11/ 5/1946	1/ 3/1965	R	NY
Reva Beck Bosone	11/ 2/1948	1/ 3/1953	D	UT

Appendix A (continued)

Cecil M. Harden	11/ 2/1948	1/ 3/1959	R	IN
Edna F. Kelly	11/ 8/1949	1/ 3/1969	D	NY
Marguerite S. Church	11/ 8/1950	1/ 3/1963	R	IL
Ruth Thompson	11/ 8/1950	1/ 3/1957	R	MI
Maude Elizabeth Kee	7/16/1951	1/ 3/1965	D	WV
Vera D. Buchanan	7/24/1951	11/26/1955[c]	D	PA
Gracie B. Pfost	11/ 4/1952	1/ 3/1963[d]	D	ID
Leonor K. Sullivan	11/ 4/1952	1/ 3/1975	D	MO
Iris F. Blitch	11/ 2/1954	1/ 3/1963	D	GA
Edith Green	11/ 2/1954	1/ 3/1975	D	OR
Martha W. Griffiths	11/ 2/1954	1/ 3/1975	D	MI
Coya G. Knutson	11/ 2/1954	1/ 3/1959	D	MN
Kathryn E. Granahan	11/ 6/1956	1/ 3/1963	D	PA
Florence P. Dwyer	11/ 6/1956	1/ 3/1973	R	NJ
Catherine D. May	11/ 4/1958	1/ 3/1971	R	WA
Edna O. Simpson	11/ 4/1958	1/ 3/1961	R	IL
Jessica McCullough Weis	11/ 4/1958	1/ 3/1963	R	NY
Julia Butler Hansen	11/ 8/1960	1/ 3/1975	D	WA
Catherine D. Norrell	4/18/1961	1/ 3/1963	D	AR
Louise G. Reece	5/16/1961	1/ 3/1963	R	TN
Corrine B. Riley	4/10/1962	1/ 3/1963	D	SC
Charlotte T. Reid	11/ 6/1962	10/ 1/1971[g]	R	IL
Irene B. Baker	3/10/1964	1/ 3/1965	R	TN
Patsy T. Mink	11/ 3/1964	1/ 3/1977[a]	D	HI
	9/22/1990[b]	j		
Lera M. Thomas	3/26/1966	1/ 3/1967	D	TX
Margaret M. Heckler	11/ 8/1966	1/ 3/1983	R	MA
Shirley A. Chisholm	11/ 5/1968	1/ 3/1983	D	NY
Bella S. Abzug	11/ 3/1970	1/ 3/1977[a]	D	NY
Ella T. Grasso	11/ 3/1970	1/ 3/1975[h]	D	CT
Louise Day Hicks	11/ 3/1970	1/ 3/1973	D	MA
Elizabeth B. Andrews	4/ 4/1972	1/ 3/1973	D	AL
Yvonne Brathwaite Burke	11/ 7/1972	1/ 3/1979[i]	D	CA
Marjorie S. Holt	11/ 7/1972	1/ 3/1987	R	MD
Elizabeth Holtzman	11/ 7/1972	1/ 5/1981[d]	D	NY
Barbara Jordan	11/ 7/1972	1/ 3/1979	D	TX
Patricia Schroeder	11/ 7/1972	j	D	CO
Corinne (Lindy) Boggs	3/20/1973	1/ 3/1991	D	LA
Cardiss Collins	6/ 7/1973	j	D	IL
Millicent Fenwick	11/ 5/1974	1/ 3/1983[d]	R	NJ
Martha Keys	11/ 5/1974	1/ 3/1979	D	KS
Marilyn Lloyd	11/ 5/1974	1/ 4/1995	D	TN
Helen Meyner	11/ 5/1974	1/ 3/1979	D	NJ
Virginia Smith	11/ 5/1974	1/ 3/1991	R	NE
Gladys N. Spellman	11/ 5/1974	2/24/1981[k]	D	MD
Shirley N. Pettis	4/29/1975	1/ 3/1979	R	CA

Barbara Mikulski	11/ 2/1976	1/ 3/1987[f]	D	MD
Mary Rose Oakar	11/ 2/1976	1/ 3/1993	D	OH
Beverly Byron	11/ 7/1978	1/ 3/1993[l]	D	MD
Geraldine Anne Ferraro	11/ 7/1978	1/ 3/1985[m]	D	NY
Olympia J. Snowe	11/ 7/1978	1/ 4/1995[f]	R	ME
Bobbi Fiedler	11/ 4/1980	1/ 3/1987[a]	R	CA
Lynn M Martin	11/ 4/1980	1/ 3/1991[d]	R	IL
Margaret S. Roukema	11/ 4/1980	j	R	NJ
Claudine C. Schneider	11/ 4/1980	1/ 3/1991[d]	R	RI
Barbara Bailey Kennelly	1/12/1982	j	D	CT
Jean Ashbrook	6/29/1982	1/ 3/1983	R	OH
Katie Hall	11/ 2/1982	1/ 3/1985	D	IN
Barbara Boxer	11/ 2/1982	1/ 3/1993[f]	D	CA
Nancy L. Johnson	11/ 2/1982	j	R	CT
Marcy Kaptur	11/ 2/1982	j	D	OH
Barbara Vucanovich	11/ 2/1982	j	R	NV
Sala Burton	6/21/1983	2/ 1/1987[c]	D	CA
Helen Delich Bentley	11/ 6/1984	1/ 4/1995[n]	R	MD
Jan Meyers	11/ 6/1984	j	R	KS
Catherine Small Long	3/30/1985	1/ 3/1987	D	LA
Constance A. Morella	11/ 4/1986	j	R	MD
Elizabeth J. Patterson	11/ 4/1986	1/ 3/1993	D	SC
Patricia Fukida Saiki	11/ 4/1986	1/ 3/1991[d]	R	HI
Louise M. Slaughter	11/ 4/1986	j	D	NY
Nancy Pelosi	6/ 2/1987	j	D	CA
Nita M. Lowey	11/ 8/1988	j	D	NY
Jolene Unsoeld	11/ 8/1988	1/ 4/1995	D	WA
Jill Lynnette Long	3/28/1989	1/ 4/1995	D	IN
Ileana Ros-Lehtinen	8/29/1989	j	R	FL
Susan Molinari	3/20/1990	j	R	NY
Barbara-Rose Collins	11/ 6/1990	j	D	MI
Rosa DeLauro	11/ 6/1990	j	D	CT
Joan Kelly Horn	11/ 6/1990	1/ 3/1993	D	MO
Maxine Waters	11/ 6/1990	j	D	CA
Karan English	11/ 3/1992	1/ 4/1995	D	AZ
Blanche Lambert	11/ 3/1992	j	D	AK
Lynn Woolsey	11/ 3/1992	j	D	CA
Anna G. Eshoo	11/ 3/1992	j	D	CA
Lucille Roybal-Allard	11/ 3/1992	j	D	CA
Jane Harman	11/ 3/1992	j	D	CA
Lynn Schenk	11/ 3/1992	1/ 4/1995	D	CA
Corrine Brown	11/ 3/1992	j	D	CA
Tillie Fowler	11/ 3/1992	j	R	FL
Karen L. Thurman	11/ 3/1992	j	D	FL
Carrie Meek	11/ 3/1992	j	D	FL
Cynthia McKinney	11/ 3/1992	j	D	GA
Pat Danner	11/ 3/1992	j	D	MO
Nydia M. Velazquez	11/ 3/1992	j	D	NY
Carolyn B. Maloney	11/ 3/1992	j	D	NY
Eva Clayton	11/ 3/1992	j	D	NC

Deborah Pryce	11/ 3/1992	j	R	OH
Elizabeth Furse	11/ 3/1992	j	D	OR
Marjorie Margolies- Mezvinsky	11/ 3/1992	1/ 4/1995	D	PA
Eddie Bernice Johnson	11/ 3/1992	j	D	TX
Karen Shepherd	11/ 3/1992	1/ 4/1995	D	UT
Leslie L. Byrne	11/ 3/1992	1/ 4/1995	D	VA
Maria Cantwell	11/ 3/1992	1/ 4/1995	D	WA
Jennifer Dunn	11/ 3/1992	j	R	WA
Zoe Lofgren	11/ 8/1994	j	D	CA
Andrea Seastrand	11/ 8/1994	j	R	CA
Helen Chenoweth	11/ 8/1994	j	R	ID
Lynn Rivers	11/ 8/1994	j	D	MI
Karen McCarthy	11/ 8/1994	j	D	MO
Sue W. Kelly	11/ 8/1994	j	R	NY
Sue Myrick	11/ 8/1994	j	R	NC
Sheila Jackson-Lee	11/ 8/1994	j	D	TX
Enid Greene Waldholtz	11/ 8/1994	j	R	UT
Linda Smith	11/ 8/1994	j	R	WA
Barbara Cubin	11/ 8/1994	j	R	WY

a. Unsuccessfully sought party's nomination for the Senate.
b. Served nonconsecutive terms.
c. Died in office.
d. Secured party's nomination for Senate, but lost the general election.
e. Never sworn in to the House.
f. Secured party's nomination for Senate and won the general election.
g. Resigned to accept appointment to an independent regulatory agency.
h. Ran successfully for Governor.
i. Ran unsuccessfully for state Attorney General.
j. Serving in the 104th Congress.
k. Seat declared vacant following a disabling heart attack.
l. Defeated in Primary.
m. Secured party's nomination for Vice President, but lost general election.
n. Unsuccessfully sought party's nomination for Governor.

Sources: Women in Congress, 1917-1976. U.S. Congress Joint Committee on Arrangements for the Commemoration of the Bicentennial, 1976; Office of the Historian, U.S. House of Representatives, *Women in Congress, 1917-1990,* 1991; *Congressional Directory,* 1917-1993; *Congressional Quarterly Special Report,* Nov. 12, 1994.

Appendix B
Southern and Non-Southern Widows Receiving Major Party Nominations, 1916–1993

Southern Widows

Widow	Year of First Nomination	Husband's Seniority Status	Husband's Leadership Status	Competitiveness of District	Primary or General Election Opposition	Renominated	Age	Worked Closely with Husband
Langley	1926	High	Leader	Competitive	Yes	Yes	38	Yes
Oldfield	1929	High	Leader	Safe	No	No	52	No
Wingo	1930	High	Leader	Safe	No	No	47	Yes
Eslick	1932	Moderate	Nonleader	Safe	No	No	53	No
Kemp	1933	Moderate	Leader	Safe	No	*	N.A.	N.A.
Gasque	1938	High	Leader	Safe	No	No	42	N.A.
McMillan	1939	High	Leader	Safe	No	No	45	N.A.
Gibbs	1940	Low	Nonleader	Safe	No	No	50	No
Fulmer	1944	High	Leader	Safe	No	No	60	No
Norrell	1961	High	Leader	Safe	No	No	60	Yes
Reece	1961	High	Leader	Competitive	Yes	No	62	Yes
Riley	1962	High	Nonleader	Safe	Yes	No	68	No
Baker	1964	Moderate	Nonleader	Safe	No	No	62	Yes
Thomas	1966	High	Leader	Safe	No	No	65	Yes
Pool	1968	Low	Nonleader	Competitive	Yes	*	51	N.A.
Andrews	1972	High	Leader	Safe	No	No	61	Yes
Boggs	1973	High	Leader	Safe	Yes	Yes	57	Yes
Lloyd	1974	**	**	**	Yes	Yes	45	Yes
Long, C.	1985	High	Leader	Safe	Yes	No	61	Yes
McDonald	1983	Moderate	Nonleader	Competitive	Yes	*	34	No
Smith, S.	1990	Low	Nonleader	Competitive	Yes	*	45	Yes

Nonsouthern Widows

Widow	Year of First Nomination	Husband's Seniority Status	Husband's Leadership Status	Competitiveness of District	Primary or General Election Opposition	Renominated	Age	Worked Closely with Husband
Huck	1922	Moderate	Nonleader	Competitive	Yes	No	40	Yes
Nolan	1923	Moderate	Leader	Safe	Yes	No	36	Yes
Kahn	1925	High	Leader	Safe	Yes	Yes	56	Yes
Rogers	1925	Moderate	Leader	Safe	Yes	Yes	44	Yes
Clarke	1933	Moderate	Leader	Competitive	Yes	No	53	Yes

Appendix B (continued)

Bolton	1940	Moderate	Nonleader	Competitive	Yes	Yes	54	Yes
Smith, M.C.	1940	Low	Nonleader	Competitive	Yes	Yes	42	Yes
Schwert	1941	Low	Nonleader	Competitive	Yes	*	50	N.A.
Byron, K.	1941	Low	Nonleader	Competitive	Yes	No	37	Yes
Boland	1942	Moderate	Leader	Competitive	No	No	43	N.A.
Barry	1946	Moderate	Nonleader	Competitive	Yes	*	37	Yes
Church	1950	Moderate	Nonleader	Competitive	Yes	Yes	58	Yes
Kee	1951	High	Leader	Competitive	Yes	Yes	57	Yes
Buchanan	1951	Moderate	Leader	Competitive	Yes	Yes	49	Yes
Sullivan	1952	Moderate	Nonleader	Competitive	Yes	Yes	49	Yes
Granahan	1956	Moderate	Nonleader	Competitive	Yes	Yes	60	Yes
Smith, E.J.	1958	High	Nonleader	Competitive	Yes	*	62	Yes
Simpson	1958	High	Leader	Competitive	Yes	No	67	Yes
Reid	1962	**	**	**	Yes	Yes	49	N.A.
Collins	1973	Low	Nonleader	Safe	Yes	Yes	41	Yes
Pettis	1975	Moderate	Nonleader	Safe	Yes	Yes	50	Yes
Byron, B.	1978	Moderate	Nonleader	Safe	Yes	Yes	46	Yes
Ashbrook	1982	High	Leader	Competitive	Yes	No	47	Yes
Burton	1983	High	Leader	Competitive	Yes	Yes	58	Yes

Note: "N.A." indicates information not currently available.

* indicates woman was never elected.

** indicates inapplicable because husband never served.

Appendix C
Questionnaire Administered to Twenty-four Representatives in the 95th
Congress and Forty-seven in the 103rd Congress

First I would like to ask you some questions about the character of the House as an institution, and about the personal and professional relationships between the men and women who serve in it.

1. One political scientist has said that state legislatures have strongly "masculine" traditions, that these masculine traditions affect the relationships of their members, and that the legislatures share a macho culture—the same macho culture one finds in a locker room, a smoker, and a barracks. Would you characterize the House in the same way?

2. Why do you think the House is similar to (or dissimilar from) state legislatures in these ways?

3. Can you give me some concrete examples of what you're talking about?

4. Back in the mid-1940s, a congressman made a speech on the House floor, part of which went like this:

I have my anxieties about the present Congress and the future and, as an older member, I am anxious to know what the new members will bring to us in abilities and opinion. As I look to my left, I see the face of a new lady member. I wish that all other lady members were present. May I say to her, one of the great worries I have in Congress itself is lest we have too many of you. Although I say this in a somewhat jocular way, still I am a little serious about it. The lady members are extremely satisfactory to us. But they, like all women, can talk to us with their eyes and their lips, and when they present us an apple it is most difficult to refuse. Even old Adam could not resist. Women have a language all their own. . . . They are dangerous in that they may influence us too much. Suppose we had fifty of them. Seemingly I note flirtations enough now, but what would there be with fifty of them?

Are there members of the House today who might express these same sentiments?

5. Are there members who think that way even though they may not say this sort of thing publicly or in mixed company?

6. What sort of reactions, if any, do you think other members would have if a congressman said something like that today?

7. State legislators say that they often witness discrimination against women and that it takes four general forms. First, routine conversation, legislative debate, and language in bills refer to "men" and "male" legislators, with women thought of as part of neither the legislature nor the public affected by legislation. Second, women lawmakers are subjects of excessive deference, they are patronized or condescended to. Third, women are expected to concentrate on a limited range of subjects, like welfare and

education, but are routinely prevented from dealing with things like banking and tax regulations. And, fourth, women are victims of snide or insulting remarks and are put down by men. Have you witnessed or heard about instances of these kinds of behaviors?

8. (If "yes") Do they occur often?

9. (If answer to question 7 was "yes") Can you give me some examples?

10. (If answer to question 7 was "yes") How have the people present responded when these things occurred?

Next, I would like to ask you some questions about the extent to which women are members of House caucuses and other informal groups, some of which do not have a formal title.

11. Do you belong to any informal groups or caucuses in the House?

12. (Asked of males only) Do women belong to the groups of which you are a member?

13. Do you find membership in these groups valuable?

14. (If "yes") How?

15. As far as you know, are there groups from which women are excluded?

16. (If "yes") Why is this so?

17. Have you ever heard of Sam Rayburn's Board of Education?

18. As far as you know are there groups like that in the House today?

19. Have you ever heard of the Chowder and Marching Society?

20. Do you believe that exclusion from one or more of these groups affects a person's ability to be an effective House member?

Now I would like to ask you some questions about the extent to which women have access to top leadership positions.

21. Do you think that it is likely that a woman will be selected for a top leadership position, say, Speaker, floor leader, or chief whip, in the foreseeable future?

22. What makes you think that?

23. Can you visualize the circumstances or conditions under which a woman would be selected for such a position?

24. What obstacles, if any, do you think limit a woman's access to a top leadership position?

25. (Asked of males only) Would any of these factors affect your thinking about the matter?

26. (Asked of females only) Are you interested in sometime securing a top leadership post?

Now I would like to ask you about your decision to run for Congress.

27. (Asked of females only) What factor or factors prompted you to seek a House seat?

28. (Asked only of first-term females in the 103rd Congress) Did the Clarence Thomas Senate confirmation hearings affect that decision in any way?

Note

Every effort was made to conduct the interviews in a relaxed, conversational manner. They usually lasted between twenty and forty-five minutes, but some took one hour, and one, with a congresswoman, continued for three hours. Representatives were informed at the outset that their observations would not be attributed to them and that, if they wished, I would withhold the fact that they had discussed these subjects with me. Not all questions were asked of all interviewees. If an answer to one or more of them had been provided in responses to preceding questions, they were omitted. Many queries were raised that were not part of the questionnaire. They were prompted by responses to questionnaire items.

Respondents included thirteen female and eleven House members in the 95th Congress, and thirty-five female and twelve male Representatives in the 103rd Congress.

Congresses (years)	Caucus Officers	Whip Officials	Democratic Agencies				
			Steering Committee	Campaign Committee	Committee on Committees	Rules Committee	Patronage Committee
80th(1947-48)	NA	NA	NA	NA	None	None	NA
81st(1949-50)	Woodhouse[1]	NA	Woodhouse[2]	None	None	None	None
82nd(1951-52)	NA	NA	NA	NA	None	None	NA
83rd(1953-54)	Kelly[1] Sullivan[3]	NA	None	NA	None	None	NA
84th(1955-56)	Kelly[1] Sullivan[3]	NA	None	NA	None	None	NA
85th(1957-58)	NA	NA	-	Green	None	None	NA
86th(1959-60)	Sullivan[1]	NA	-	Green Pfost	None	None	None
87th(1961-62)	Sullivan[1] Kee[3]	None	Sullivan[2]	Green Griffiths[4]	None	None	None
88th(1963-64)	Sullivan(1st)[1] Kee(2nd)[1]	None	NA	Green Griffiths[4] Hansen	Griffiths	None	None

Republican Agencies

Congresses (years)	Conference Officers	WHIP Officials	Policy[5] Committee	Campaign Committee	Comm. on Committees	Rules Committee	Patronage Committee
80th(1947–48)	None	NA	None	None	May	None	NA
81st(1949-50)	None	None	Bolton	None	None	None	None
82nd(1951-52)	None	St.George[6]	NA	None	None	None	NA
83rd(1953-54)	None	NA	NA	None	None	None	NA
84th(1955-56)	None	NA	None	None	None	None	NA
85th(1957-58)	None	NA	None	None	None	None	NA
86th(1959-60)	None	NA	Bolton	None	St.George[4]	None	None
87th(1961-62)	None	May[6] St.George[6]	Bolton Church St.George[2] Weis[7]	None	St.George[4]	St.George	None
88th(1963-64)	None	May[6] St.George[6]	Bolton St.George[2]	None	St.George[4]	St.George	None

"NA": Information Not Available
1. Caucus Secretary
2. Member *Ex Officio*
3. Caucus Assistant Secretary
4. Executive Subcommittee Member
5. Known as "Steering" Committee from 1947 to 1949
6. Regional Whip
7. Nonvoting Member

Sources: Congressional Record, Congressional Quarterly Almanac, Congressional Staff Directory, "Minutes of the Republican Conference of the Members of the U.S. House of Representatives".

Appendix D.2
Congresswomen in Secondary Leadership Positions, 1965–1984

Congresses (years)		Democratic Agencies					
	Caucus[1] Officers	Whip Officials	Steering and[2] Policy Committee	Campaign Committee	Comm. on Committees	Rules Committee	Personnel[3] Committee
89th(1965-66)	Sullivan	NA	Sullivan[4]	Green Griffiths[5] Hansen	Griffiths	None	None
90th(1967-68)	Sullivan	None	Sullivan[4]	Green Griffiths[5] Hansen	Griffiths	None	None
91st(1969-70)	Sullivan	Green Sullivan	Hansen Sullivan[4]	Green Griffiths[5] Hansen	Griffiths	None	None
92nd(1971-72)	Sullivan	Green Sullivan	Hansen Sullivan[4]	Green Griffiths[5] Hansen	Griffiths	None	None
93rd(1973-74)	Sullivan	Green	Hansen[6]	Green Griffiths[5] Hansen	Griffiths	None	None
94th(1975-76)	Mink	Abzug[7] Collins[7]	Jordan[6]	Keys	-	None	None
95th(1977-78)	Chisholm	Collins[7] Schroeder Spellman	Jordan[6]	Burke[5] Keys	-	Chisholm	None

Congresses (years)	Conference Officers	Whip Officials	Policy Committee	Campaign Committee	Comm. on Committees	Rules Committee	Personnel Committee	Research Committee
96th(1979-80)	Chisholm	None	Spellman[6]	Boggs[5]	-		Chisholm	None
97th(1981-82)	Ferraro	Oakar[7] Schroeder[7]	Ferraro[4] Schroeder[6]	Boggs[5]	-		Chisholm	None
98th(1983-84)	Ferraro	Oakar[7] Schroeder[7]	Ferraro[4] Schroeder[6]	NA	-		None	None

Republican Agencies

Congresses (years)	Conference Officers	Whip Officials	Policy Committee	Campaign Committee	Comm. on Committees	Rules Committee	Personnel Committee	Research Committee
89th(1965-66)	None	NA	Reid	None	May	None	None	May
90th(1967-68)	None	None	None	None	May	None	None	May
91st(1969-70)	None	None	None	None	May	None	None	May
92nd(1971-72)	None	None	None	None	None	None	None	None
93rd(1973-74)	None	None	None	None	Heckler	None	None	None
94th(1975-76)	None	None	None	Holt	Heckler	None	None	Fenwick
95th(1977-78)	None	None	Holt	Heckler	Holt	None	None	None
96th(1979-80)	None	None	Smith	Heckler Holt	Smith Snowe	None	None	None
97th(1981-82)	None	None	None	Heckler Holt[8] Schneider	Holt Schneider Snowe	None	Fiedler	None

Appendix D.2 (continued)

98th(1983-84)	None	Martin	Johnson	Holt	Fiedler[10]	None	Vucanovich	Roukema
		Snowe[9]	Martin	Johnson[8]	Holt			
				Schneider	Schneider			
				Vucanovich[8]	Smith			
					Snowe			
					Vucanovich			

"NA": Information not Available

1. All were Caucus Secretary
2. Known as "Steering" Committee until 1973
3. Known as "Patronage" Committee until 1977
4. Member *Ex Officio*
5. Executive Subcommittee member
6. Selected by Speaker
7. Selected by leadership as "at large" whip
8. Committee Vice Chairwoman
9. Deputy Whip
10. Appointed late in 1st session as representative of the 97th Class

Sources: Congressional Record, Congressional Quarterly Almanac, Congressional Directory, Congressional Staff Directory, "Minutes of the Republican Conference of the Members of the U.S. House of Representatives".

Appendix D.3

Congresswomen in Secondary Leadership Positions, 1985–1994

		Democratic Agencies				
Congresses (years)	Caucus Officers	Whip Officials	Steering Committee	Campaign Committee	Rules Committee	Personnel Committee
99th(1985-86)	Oakar[1]	Boxer[2] Oakar[2] Schroeder[2]	Collins[6] Kennelly[6] Oakar[5]	Oakar[6] Schroeder	Burton	NA
100th(1987-88)	Oakar[1]	Boxer[2] Kennelly[2] Schroeder[3] Slaughter[2]	Kaptur[6] Oakar[5]	Byron Oakar[6] Schroeder	None	NA
101st(1989-90)	None	Boxer[2] Kennelly[2] Oakar[2] Pelosi[4] Schroeder[3] Slaughter[2]	Kaptur[6]	Byron Oakar Schroeder	Slaughter	NA
102nd(1991-92)	None	Schroeder[3] Pelosi[4] Boxer[2] Kennelly[2] Oakar[2] Slaughter[2] Patterson[4]	Kennelly[6]	Pelosi[7] Kennelly[7] Schroeder Oakar Lowey Waters	Slaughter	NA

281

Appendix D.3 (continued)

Congresses (years)	Conference Officers	Whip Officials	Policy Committee	Campaign Committee	Comm. on Committees	Rules Committee	Research Committee
103rd(1993-94)	None	Schroeder[3] Unsoeld[4] Byrne[2] B.R.Collins[2] DeLauro[2] E.B.Johnson[2] Lowey[4] Slaughter[2] Waters[2] Eschoo[4]	Cantwell[6] Kennelly[5] Mink	Kennelly[5] Pelosi[7] DeLauro[6] Schenk[6] Waters[6]		Slaughter	NA
Republican Agencies							
99th(1985-86)	Martin	Snowe[3]	Martin[5] Vucanovich Meyers	Bentley[7] Holt Johnson[7] Martin[5] Schneider Vucanovich[7]	Holt Schneider Smith Snowe Vucanovich	None	Martin[5]

100th(1987-88)	Martin	Snowe[3]	Martin[5] Vucanovich	Martin[5] Morella Saiki Schneider[7] Snowe Vucanovich[7] Bentley[7]	Johnson Bentley Saiki Smith Snowe Schneider Vucanovich Meyers	None	Meyers Snowe Vucanovich Johnson
101st(1989-90)	None	Johnson[3] Snowe[8]	Snowe Johnson	Morella[7] Saiki[7] Schneider Smith Snowe Vucanovich[7] Bentley[7]	None	Martin	None
102nd(1991-92)	None	Johnson[3] Snowe[8]	Ros-Lehtinen Meyers	Morella[7] Roukema Snowe Vucanovich[7]	None	None	Snowe Molinari Bentley
103rd(1993-94)	None	N.Johnson[3] Snowe[8] Ros-Lehtinen[9] Vucanovich[9]	Fowler N.Johnson Meyers Ros-Lehtinen Vucanovich	Molinari[7] N.Johnson[7] Pryce[7] Bentley Dunn Ros-Lehtinen Snowe Vucanovich	Dunn	None	Molinari Snowe Vucanovich

Appendix D.3 (continued)

"NA": Not Available
1. Secretary of the Caucus
2. At Large Whip
3. Deputy Whip
4. Assistant Whip
5. Ex Officio
6. Appointed by Speaker
7. Excutive Committee
8. Assistant Deputy Whip
9. Regional Whip

Bibliography

BOOKS

Abzug, B. 1972. *Bella: Ms. Abzug goes to Washington*. New York: Saturday Review Press.

Almond, G. A., and Coleman, J. S., eds. 1960. *The politics of developing areas*. Princeton, N.J.: Princeton University Press.

Amundsen, K. 1971. *The silenced majority: Women and American democracy*. Englewood Cliffs, N.J.: Prentice-Hall.

de Beauvoir, S. 1953. *The second sex*. New York: Knopf.

Baum, L. 1994. *American courts*. Boston: Houghton Mifflin.

Becker, S. D. 1981. *The origins of the Equal Rights Amendment: American feminism between the wars*. Westport, Conn.: Greenwood Press.

Bem, S. L. 1993. *The lenses of gender: Transforming the debate on sexual inequality*. New Haven: Yale University Press.

Bibby, J. F., Mann, T. E., and Ornstein, N. J. 1980. *Vital statistics on Congress*. Washington, D.C.: American Enterprise Institute.

Breckinridge, S. P. 1933. *Women in the twentieth century: A study of their political, social and economic activities*. New York: McGraw-Hill.

Brookes, P. 1967. *Women at Westminster: An account of women in the British Parliament, 1918–1966*. London: Peter Davies.

Brownson, C. B., ed. 1983. *Congressional staff directory*. Mount Vernon, Va.: Congressional Staff Directory, Ltd.

Chamberlin, H. 1973. *A minority of members: Women in the U.S. Congress*. New York: New American Library.

Clarke, I. C. 1925. *Uncle Sam needs a wife*. Philadelphia: The John C. Winston Co.

Congressional Quarterly Inc. 1985. *Guide to U.S. elections*. Washington, D.C.: C. Q. Press.

Cook, E. A. et al. 1994. *The year of the woman: Myths and realities*. Boulder, Colo.: Westview Press.

Currell, M. 1974. *Political woman*. London: Croom Helm.

Darcy, R., et al. 1987. *Women elections and representation*. White Plains, N.Y.: Longman.

Diamond, I. 1977. *Sex roles in the State House*. New Haven: Yale University Press.

Dodd, L. C., and Oppenheimer, B., eds. *Congress reconsidered*. 4th ed. Washington, D.C.: Congressional Quarterly Press.

Dodson, D., ed. 1991. *Gender and policy making: Studies of women in office*. New Brunswick, N.J.: Center for the American Woman and Politics.

Douglas, H. G. 1982. *A full life*. Garden City, N.Y.: Doubleday.

Duke, L. L., ed. 1993. *Women in politics: Outsiders or insiders?* Englewood Cliffs, N.J.: Prentice-Hall.

Duverger, M. 1955. *The political role of women*. Paris: United Nations Educational, Scientific and Cultural Organization.

Engelbarts, R. 1974. *Women in the United States Congress, 1917–1972: Their accomplishments; with bibliographies*. Littleton, Colo.: Libraries Unlimited.

Epstein, C. F. 1981. *Women in law*, New York; Basic Books.

———. 1988. *Deceptive Distinctions: Sex, gender and the social order*. New Haven: Yale University Press.

Epstein, L. 1958. *Politics in Wisconsin*. Madison: University of Wisconsin Press.

Fenno, R. 1966. *The power of the purse: Appropriations politics in Congress*. Boston: Little, Brown.

Ferraro, G. A., and Francke, W. L. B.. 1985. *Ferraro: My Story*. New York: Bantam Books.

Galloway, G. B. 1953. *The legislative process in Congress*. New York: Crowell.

Gelb, J., and Palley, M. L. 1987. *Women and public policies*. rev. ed. Princeton, N.J.: Princeton University Press.

Gladieux, L. E., and Wolanin, T. R. 1976. *Congress and the colleges: The national politics of higher education*. Lexington, Mass.: Lexington Books.

Greenstein, F. I., and Polsby, N. W., eds. 1975. *Handbook of political science*, vol. II. Reading: Addison-Wesley.

Gruberg, M. 1968. *Women in politics*. Oshkosh: Academia Press.

Hernnson, Paul S. 1988. *Party campaigning in the 1980s*. Cambridge, Mass.: Harvard University Press.

Hess, S. 1966. *America's political dynasties: From Adams to Kennedy*. Garden City, N.J.: Doubleday.

Jacobson, G. C. 1992. *The politics of Congressional elections*. 3rd ed. New York: Harper Collins.

Janeway, E. 1971. *Man's world, woman's place: A study in social mythology*. New York: William Morrow.

Jones, C. O. 1964. *Party and policy-making: The House Republican Policy Committee*. New Brunswick, N.J.: Rutgers University Press.

———. 1965. *The Republican Party in American politics*. New York: Macmillan.

Kelly, R. M., and Boutilier, M. 1978. *The making of political women: A study of socialization and role conflict*. Chicago: Nelson-Hall.

Kingdon, J. W. 1984. *Agendas, alternatives and public policies*. Boston: Little, Brown.

Kirkpatrick, J. J. 1974. *Political woman*. New York: Basic Books.

Lamson, P. 1968. *Few are chosen: American women in political life today*. Boston: Houghton Mifflin.

———. 1979. *In the vanguard: Six American women in public life*. Boston: Houghton Mifflin.

Lemons, J. S. 1973. *The woman citizen: Social feminism in the 1920s.* Urbana: University of Illinois Press.

Lewis, W. C., ed. 1972. *Declaration of conscience: Margaret Chase Smith.* New York: Doubleday.

Loomis, B. A. 1988. *The new American politician: Ambition, entrepreneurship and the changing face of political life.* New York: Basic Books.

McNeil, N. 1963. *Forge of democracy: The House of Representatives.* New York: David McKay.

Mandel, R. B. 1981. *In the running: The new woman candidate.* New York: Ticknor and Fields.

Manley, J. F. 1970. *The politics of finance: The House Committee on Ways and Means.* Boston: Little, Brown.

Mann, J. 1962. *Women in Parliament.* London: Odhams Press.

Mansbridge, Jane J. 1986. *Why we lost the ERA.* Chicago: University of Chicago Press.

Margolies-Mezvinsky, M. 1994. *A woman's place: The freshmen women who changed the face of Congress.* New York: Crown Publishers.

Margolis, D. R., and Stanwick, K. 1979. *Women's organizations in the public service.* New Brunswick: Center for the American Woman and Politics, Eagleton Institute.

Martin, J. 1960. *My first fifty years in politics.* New York: McGraw-Hill.

Matthews, D. R. 1960. *U.S. Senators and their world.* Chapel Hill: University of North Carolina Press.

Mooney, B. 1964. *Mr. Speaker: Four men who shaped the United States House of Representatives.* Chicago: Follett.

Paxton, A. 1945. *Women in Congress.* Richmond: The Dietz Press.

Peabody, R. L. 1976. *Leadership in Congress: Stability, succession and change.* Boston: Little, Brown.

Prewitt, K. 1970. *The recruitment of political leaders: A study of citizen-politicians.* Indianapolis: Bobbs-Merrill.

Putnam, R. D. 1976. *The comparative study of political elites.* Englewood Cliffs, N.J.: Prentice-Hall.

Rhoodie, E. M. 1989. *Discrimination against women: A global survey of the economic, educational, social and political status of women.* Jefferson, N.C.: McFarland.

Ripley, Randall B. 1983. *Congress: Process and policy.* 3rd ed. New York: W. W. Norton.

Rix, S. E., and Stone, A. J. 1981. *Impact on women of the administration's proposed budget.* Washington: Women's Research and Education Institute.

Rohde, D. W. 1991. *Parties and Leaders in the post-reform house.* Chicago: University of Chicago Press.

Rule, W., and Zimmerman, J. P., eds. 1992. *Electoral systems: Their impact on women and minorities.* New York: Praeger, 1992.

Seligman, L. G., King, M. R., Kim, C. L., and Smith, R. E. 1974. *Patterns of recruitment: A state chooses its lawmakers.* Chicago: Rand McNally.

Shadegg, S. 1970. *Clare Boothe Luce: A biography.* New York: Simon and Schuster.

Sorauf, F. J. 1963. *Party and representation: Legislative politics in Pennsylvania.* New York: Atherton Press.

Swank, G. R. 1978. *Ladies of the House (and Senate), Idaho 1899–1978.* Boise: author.
Tolchin, S., and Tolchin, M. 1974. *Clout: Womanpower and politics.* New York: Coward, McCann and Geoghegan.
Vallance, E. M. 1979. *Women in the House: A study of women members of Parliament.* London: Athlone Press.
Voorhis, J. 1947. *Confessions of a congressman.* Garden City, N.Y.: Doubleday.
Wiley, A. 1947. *Laughing with Congress.* New York: Crown Publishers.
Williams, S. and Lascher, E., Jr., eds. 1993. *Ambition and beyond: Career paths of American politicians.* Berkeley, Calif.: Institute of Government Studies Press.
Witt, L., et al. 1994. *Running as a woman: Gender and power in American politics.* New York: The Free Press.

CHAPTERS IN EDITED WORKS AND ARTICLES IN PROFESSIONAL JOURNALS

Andersen, K., and Thorson, S. 1984. Congressional turnover and the election of women. *Western Political Quarterly* 37: 143–156.
Bardwick, J. M. 1976. The great revolution. In D. G. McGuigan, ed., *New research on women and sex roles,* 25–34. Ann Arbor: University of Michigan Center for Continuing Education of Women.
Benze, J., and Declerq, E. 1985. The importance of gender in congressional and statewide elections. *Social Science Quarterly* 66: 954–963.
Bernstein, R. A. 1986. Why are there so few women in the House? *Western Political Quarterly* 39: 155–164.
Biersack, R., and Herrnson, P. S. 1994. Political parties and the year of the woman. In Cook, et al., eds. *The year of the woman: Myths and realities,* 161–180. Boulder, Colo.: Westview Press.
Bone, H. A. 1956. Some notes on the Congressional Campaign Committee. *Western Political Quarterly* 9: 116–137.
Buchanan, C. 1978. Why aren't there more women in Congress? *Congressional Quarterly Weekly Report* 36: 2108–2110.
Bullock, III, C. S., and Heys, P. L. F. 1972. Recruitment of women for Congress: A research note. *Western Politics Quarterly* 25: 416–423.
Burrell, B. 1985. Women's and men's campaigns for the U.S. House of Representatives, 1972–1982: A finance gap? *American Political Quarterly* 13: 251–272.
————. 1988. The political opportunity of women candidates for the U.S. House of Representatives in 1984. *Women and Politics* 8: 51–68.
————. 1992. Women candidates in open-seat primaries for the U.S. House: 1968–1990. *Legislative Studies Quarterly* 17: 493–508.
Carroll, S. 1985. Political elites and sex differences in ambition: A reconsideration. *Journal of Politics* 47: 1231–1243.
————. 1993. The political careers of women elected officials. In *Ambition and beyond: Career paths of American politicians,* Shirley Williams and Edward Lascher, Jr., eds. 197–230. Berkeley, Calif.: Institute of Government Studies Press.

Chaney, C. and Sinclair, B. 1994. Women and the 1992 House elections. In *The year of the woman: Myths and realities,* Cook, et al., eds., 124–139. Boulder, Colo.: Westview Press.

Clubok, A. B., Wilensky, N., and Berghorn, F. J. 1969. Family relationships, congressional recruitment, and political modernization. *Journal of Politics* 31: 1035–1062.

Comstock, A. 1926. Women members of European parliaments. *American Political Science Review* 20: 379–384.

Czudnowski, M. M. 1975. Political recruitment. In *Handbook of political science,* vol. II, Greenstein, F. I., and Polsby, N. W., eds., 155–242. Reading, Pa.: Addison-Wesley.

Deber, R. B. 1982. The fault dear Brutus: Women as congressional candidates in Pennsylvania. *Journal of Politics* 44: 463–479.

Dodd, L. C. 1979. The expanding role of the House Democratic whip system: The 93rd and 94th Congresses. *Congressional Studies* 7: 27–56.

Dreifus, C. 1972. Women in politics: An interview with Edith Green. *Social Policy* 2: 16–22.

Ferraro, G. 1979. Women as candidates. *Harvard Political Review* 7: 21–24.

Fiellin, A. 1962. Functions of informal groups in legislative institutions. *Journal of Politics* 24: 72–91.

Fowler, L. L. 1993. Candidate recruitment and the study of Congress. In *Ambition and beyond: Career paths of American politicians,* Shirley Williams and Edward Lascher, Jr., eds. 71–107. Berkeley, Calif.: Institute of Government Studies Press.

Gehlen, F. L. 1969. Women in Congress. *Transaction* 6: 36–40.

Gelb, J., and Palley, M. L. 1979. Women and interest group politics: A comparative analysis of federal decision making. *Journal of Politics* 41: 362–393.

Gertzog, I. N., and Simand, M. M. 1981. Women and "hopeless" congressional candidacies: Nomination frequency, 1916–1978. *American Politics Quarterly* 9: 449–466.

Githens, M., and Prestage, J. 1978. Women state legislators: Styles and priorities. *Policy Studies Journal* no. 2 (Winter): 264–270.

Hammond, Susan Webb. 1989. Congressional caucuses in the policy process in Dodd, Lawrence C., and Oppenheimer, Bruce, eds., *Congress reconsidered,* 4th ed., Washington, D.C.: CQ Press.

Hubbard, R. 1990. The political nature of "human nature" in D. H. Rhode, ed., *Theoretical perspectives on sexual differences,* New Haven: Yale University Press.

Iglitzin, L. B. 1974. The making of the apolitical woman: Femininity and sex stereotyping in girls. In J. Jaquette, ed., *Women in Politics,* 25–35. New York: John Wiley.

Jaquette, J. S. 1974. Introduction. In J. Jaquette, ed., *Women in Politics,* XIII–XXXVII. New York: John Wiley.

Kincaid, D. D. 1978. Over his dead body: A positive perspective on widows in the U.S. Congress. *Western Political Quarterly* 31: 96–104.

Lasswell, H. D. 1954. The selective effect of personality on political participation. In R. Christie, and M. Jahoda, eds., *Studies in the scope and method of the authoritarian personality,* 197–225. Glencoe, Ill.: The Free Press.

Lee, M. M. 1977. Toward understanding why so few women hold public office: Factors affecting the participation of women in local politics. In M. Githens, and J. Prestage, eds., *A portrait of marginality*, 118–138. New York: David McKay.

Lipman-Blumen, J. 1973. Role de-differentiation as a system response to crisis. *Sociological Inquiry* 43: 105–129.

Loomis, B. A. 1981. Congressional caucuses and politics of representation. In L. C. Dodd, and B. I. Oppenheimer, eds., *Congress reconsidered* (2nd edition), 204–220. Washington, D.C.: Congressional Quarterly Press.

Lynn, N. 1975. Women in American politics: An overview. In J. Freeman, ed., *Women: A feminist perspective*, 264–285. Palo Alto, Calif.: Mayfield.

Matthews, D. R. 1985. Legislative recruitment and legislative careers. In G. Lowenberg, et al., eds. *Handbook of legislative research.* Cambridge, Mass.: Harvard University Press.

Mezey, S. G. 1994. Increasing the number of women in office: Does it matter? In Elizabeth Cook, et al., eds., *The year of the woman: Myths and realities*, 255–270. Boulder, Colo.: Westview Press.

Nelson, C. J. 1994. Women's PACs in the Year of the Woman. In Elizabeth Cook, et al., eds., *The year of the woman: Myths and realities*, 181–196. Boulder, Colo.: Westview Press.

Norris, P. 1986. Women in Congress: A policy difference. *Politics* 6: 34–40.

O'Leary, V. 1974. Some attitudinal barriers to occupational aspirations in women. *Psychological Bulletin* 11: 809–826.

Oleszek, W. 1969. Age and political careers. *Public Opinion Quarterly* 33: 100–102.

Parsons, T. 1953. The superego and the theory of social systems. In R. F. Bales, E. Shils, and T. Parsons, eds., *Working papers in the theory of action*, 13–29. New York: The Free Press.

Plattner, A. 1983. Various legislative styles, philosophies . . . found among Congress' 23 Women. *Congressional Quarterly Weekly Report* 41: 784–785.

Polsby, N. W. 1968. Institutionalization of the U.S. House of Representatives. *American Political Science Review* 62: 144–168.

———. 1969. The growth of the seniority system in the U.S. House of Representatives. *American Political Science Review* 3: 787–807.

Rule, W. 1981. Why women don't run: The critical contextual factors in women's legislative recruitment. *Western Political Quarterly* 34: 60–77.

Rule, W., and Norris, P. 1992. Anglo and minority women's underrepresentation in Congress: Is the electoral system the culprit? In W. Rule and J. P. Zimmerman, eds., *Electoral systems: Their impact on women and minorities*, 41–54. New York: Praeger.

Stevens, A. G., Jr., Mulhollan, D. P., and Rundquist, P. 1981. U.S. Congressional structure and representation: The role of informal groups. *Legislative Studies Quarterly* 6: 415–437.

Sullivan, W. E. 1975. Criteria for selecting party leadership in Congress: An empirical test. *American Politics Quarterly* 3: 25–44.

Thompson, J. H. 1985. Career convergence: Election of women and men to the House of Representatives, 1916–1975. *Women and Politics* 5: 69–90.

Van Hightower, N. R. 1977. The recruitment of women for public office. *American Politics Quarterly* 5: 301–314.

Welch, S. 1985. Are women more liberal than men in the U.S. Congress? *Legislative Studies Quarterly* 10: 125–134.

Werner, E. E. 1966. Women in Congress, 1917–1964. *Western Political Quarterly* 19: 16–30.

_____. 1968. Women in the state legislatures. *Western Political Quarterly* 21: 40–50.

Whicker, M. L., et al. 1993. Women in Congress. In L. L. Duke, ed., *Women in politics: Outsiders or insiders?* 136–151. Englewood Cliffs, N.J.: Prentice-Hall.

Wilcox, C., 1994. Why was 1992 the "year of the woman"? Explaining women's gains in 1992. In Cook, et al., eds., *The year of the woman: Myths and realities,* 1–24. Boulder, Colo.: Westview Press.

ARTICLES IN POPULAR MAGAZINES AND NEWSPAPERS

Anderson, G. E. 1929. Women in Congress. *The Commonweal* (March 13): 532–534.

Anderson, J., and Cappaccio, T. 1980. Jack Anderson rates the Congress. *The Washingtonian* (October) 166–171.

Auletta, K. 1975. "Senator" Bella–seriously. *New York Magazine* (August 11): 27–34.

Blair, E. N. 1925. Are women a failure in politics? *Harper's* (October): 513–522.

_____. 1927. Are women really in politics? *The Independent* (December 3): 541–544.

_____. 1931. Why I am discouraged about women in politics. *The Woman's Journal* (January) 20 ff.

Brenner, M. 1977. What makes Bella run? *New York Magazine* (June 20): 54–64.

Davis, F. 1943. Beauty and the East. *Saturday Evening Post* (July 17): 216.

Dudar, H. 1967. Women in the news—Representative Leonor Sullivan: If I want something bad enough. *New York Post Weekend Magazine* (September 2): 3.

Geist, W. E. 1982. Millicent Fenwick: Marching to her own drum. *New York Times Magazine* (June 27): 21 ff.

Gilfond, D. 1929. Gentlewomen of the House. *The American Mercury* (October): 151–160.

Glaser, V., and Elliott, L. 1983. Woman power. *The Washingtonian* (May): 156–164.

Huck, W. M. 1923. What happened to me in Congress. *Woman's Home Companion* (July): 4.

Kronholz, J. 1976. For congresswoman, issue in Kansas is a "messy" divorce. *Wall Street Journal* (October 7): 1.

Lockett, E. P. 1950. FDR's Republican cousin in Congress. *Colliers* (August 19): 26 ff.

Owen, R. B. 1933. My daughter and politics. *Woman's Home Companion,* October: 27–30.

Payne, L. 1982. Mrs. Chisholm calls it quits: A conversation with Shirley Chisholm. *Essence* (August): 72 ff.

Porter, A. 1943. Ladies of Congress. *Colliers* (August 28): 22.

Pratt, R. S. (Baker). 1926. Plea for party partisanship. *Woman Citizen* (March): 23.

Winfrey, C. 1977. In search of Bella Abzug. *New York Times Magazine* (August 21): 15 ff.

GOVERNMENT DOCUMENTS

Rundquist, P. S. 1978. Formal and informal congressional groups. *Congressional Research Service*, Report No. 78–83 GOV, March 25.

Schwemle, B. L. 1982. Women in the U.S. Congress. *Congressional Research Service*, Report No. 82–37 GOV, March 9.

U.S. Congress. 1976. Joint Committee on Arrangements for the Commemoration of the Bicentennial. Women in Congress, 1917–1976, prepared by Tolchin, S. J. Washington, D.C.: U.S.G.P.O.

UNPUBLISHED SOURCES

Smith, K. S. 1976. The characteristics of American women who seek positions of political leadership. Dissertation submitted to the Graduate Faculty of Political and Social Science of the New School for Social Research, New York.

Stevens, A. G., Jr., Mulhollan, D. P., and Rundquist, P. S. 1980. Congressional structure and representation: The role of informal groups. Paper delivered at the 76th Annual Meeting of the American Political Science Association, the Washington Hilton Hotel, August 28–31.

Thompson, Joan Hulse. 1993. The Congressional Caucus for Women's Issues: A study in organizational change. Paper delivered at the 89th Annual Meeting of the American Political Science Association, Washington, D.C.

Index

About the Author

IRWIN N. GERTZOG is the Arthur Braun Professor of Political Science at Allegheny College in Pennsylvania.